Indian Traffic

Indian Traffic

Identities in Question in Colonial and Postcolonial India

Parama Roy

UNIVERSITY OF CALIFORNIA PRESS

Berkeley   Los Angeles   London

University of California Press
Berkeley and Los Angeles, California

University of California Press, Ltd.
London, England

Versions of chapters 1 and 2 appeared in *boundary 2* ("Oriental Exhibits: Englishmen and Natives in Burton's *Personal Narrative of a Pilgrimage to Al-Madinah and Meccah*," *boundary 2* 22, no. 1 [1995]: 185–210) and the *Yale Journal of Criticism* ("Discovering India, Imagining *Thuggee*," *Yale Journal of Criticism* 9, no. 1 [1996]: 121–45), respectively. I thank both journals for their permission to reprint this material. A shorter version of chapter 4 appeared as "As the Master Saw Her," in *Cruising the Performative: Interventions into the Representation of Ethnicity, Nationality, and Sexuality*, edited by Sue-Ellen Case, Philip Brett, and Susan Leigh Foster, 112–29 (Bloomington: Indiana University Press, 1995).

Photographs reprinted courtesy of the Vedanta Society of Northern California.

Library of Congress Cataloging-in-Publication Data

Roy, Parama.
    Indian traffic: identities in question in colonial and postcolonial India / Parama Roy.
        p.   cm.
    Includes bibliographical references and index.
    ISBN 0-520-20486-7 (alk. paper).—ISBN 0-520-20487-5 (alk. paper)
        1. Indic literature (English)—History and criticism.   2. National characteristics, East Indian, in literature.   3. Literature and society—India—History—20th century.   4. Anglo-Indian literature—History and criticism.   5. Group identity in literature.   6. Decolonization in literature.   7. Nationalism—India—History.   8. Imperialism in literature.   9. British—India—History.   10. Colonies in literature.   11. Group identity—India.   12. India—Civilization.   I. Title.
PR9485.2.R69   1998
820.9'954—dc20   96–42104

Printed in the United States of America
9   8   7   6   5   4   3   2   1

The paper used in this publication meets the minimum requirements of American National Standards for Information Sciences—Permanence of Paper for Printed Library Materials, ANSI Z39.48–1984.

CONTENTS

ILLUSTRATIONS

ACKNOWLEDGMENTS

This book owes a great deal to the critical perspicacity and generosity of friends, colleagues, mentors, and institutions, whom I am grateful to be able to name and thank. These pages would have been impossible to bring to fruition without the encouragement and intellectual support of Sandhya Shetty and Carole-Anne Tyler, who consistently asked the difficult questions and who taught me through the inspiration of their own scholarship. I am also grateful to Lalitha Gopalan, who so often told me what I was thinking before I knew it myself. I am grateful too to the many other friends and colleagues who read the manuscript, either in full or in part, or who responded to my work at conferences: Katherine Kinney, Joe Childers, R. Radhakrishnan, Inderpal Grewal, Vincent Cheng, Daniel Boyarin, Kim Devlin, Kalpana Seshadri-Crooks, Bette London, Ron Inden, Robert Goldman, Aditya Behl, Gayatri Spivak, Jennifer Brody, George Haggerty, Lawrence Cohen, Sue-Ellen Case, Philip Brett, and Susan Foster. I am indebted to the readers for the University of California Press, especially Caren Kaplan and Sangeeta Ray, for their meticulous, constructive, and sympathetic evaluation of the project. My editor, Doris Kretschmer, has been unfailingly helpful and patient. I am also grateful to Dore Brown and Diane Jagusiak of the University of California Press, and to Sarah Myers, for their scrupulous editing. I am indebted above all to my parents, Amalendu and Ramola Roy, as well as to Bharat Trehan for (among other things) his recall of a youth productively spent watching Bombay films.

This project has been funded by a University of California President's Research Fellowship in the Humanities in 1991–1992, a fellowship in the University of California, Riverside's Center for Ideas and Society in the spring of 1994, and by two pretenure faculty-development awards from the University of California, Riverside. I am grateful for this support.

Introduction

Identities and Negotiations in Colonial and Postcolonial India

IMAGINARY ORIGINS, IMAGINARY CROSSINGS

The specter of originality and its lack seems to haunt much of the work on colonialism and the postcolonial condition at the current conjuncture. This preoccupation with originality and secondariness has, of course, a history, one that is frequently rehearsed. Its imaginary origin can be traced back to Macaulay's notorious "Minute on English Education" of 1835, which defined what Gayatri Spivak has termed the "subject-constituting project" of colonialism as the production of secondariness: westernized (male) subjects, "a class of persons, Indian in blood and colour, but English in taste, in opinions, in morals, and in intellect."[1] The melancholy success of such an interpellation was confirmed more than a century later by Frantz Fanon, writing (in the resonantly titled *Black Skin, White Masks*) on the conflictual economies of colonialism and racism: "For the black man there is only one destiny. And it is white."[2] That the access to such a destiny was racially barred while remaining the only imaginative possibility for the (westernized) black male could not but be productive of profound pathologies. What was even worse, as Diana Fuss astutely suggests, was that "the black man under colonial rule finds himself relegated to a position other than the Other. . . . Black may be a protean imaginary other for white, but for itself it is a stationary 'object'; objecthood, substituting for true alterity, blocks the migration through the Other necessary for subjectivity to take place."[3]

More recently, Homi Bhabha, whose work bears the unmistakable imprint of Fanon's thought, has sought an entry into questions of originality and repetition through Lacanian psychoanalysis and Derridean deconstruction.[4] But where Fanon sees the command to mimic as a subjective death sentence, Bhabha plays with the deconstructive possibilities of that colonial stereotype. He theorizes colonial mimicry as the representation of a partial presence that disrupts the colonizer's narcissistic aspirations and subjects Englishness to profound strain, whereby "the familiar, transported to distant parts, becomes uncannily transformed, the imitation subverts the identity of that which is being represented, and the relation of power, if not altogether reversed, certainly begins to vacillate."[5] The ambivalence that undergirds the procedure of colonial mimicry produces simultaneous and incommensurable effects, destabilizing English and Indian identities as part of the same operation. This insight has proved enormously useful for scholars of colonial discourse, and indeed has found significant purchase among a large number of feminist, African Americanist, and queer scholars, who have long had a marked sense of the import of the concept of mimicry—and its cognates, masquerade, passing, and drag—for the theorization of a variety of identity politics. As is well known, feminists from Simone de Beauvoir to Luce Irigaray to a range of film theorists have pondered questions of identity, identification, and resistance through the lens of that ensemble of positions, affects, and activities to which one can assign the portmanteau term *mimicry*. Queer theorists have devoted considerable critical attention to the political-semiotic possibilities, radical and otherwise, of camp. For African Americanists, the subject of passing has a tremendously long and textured history in the overlapping domains of performance, theory, and literary production.[6]

I would argue that even postcolonial scholars whose work is ostensibly remote from debates on identity politics have been engaged with the problematic of originality and mimicry; they have been engaged with the problematic that—for want of a better term—one might call "philosophical or epistemic secondariness." Many of the debates about these issues have cohered not so much around individual subjects or identities as around the question of the nation, but in terms that resonate quite powerfully with debates on identity formation, whether in the metropolis or elsewhere. Specifically, the debates on nation formation have focused on the nation's failure to "come into its own" in decolonization; "it is the study of this failure," says Ranajit Guha, "which constitutes the central problematic of the historiography of colonial India."[7] The classic articulation of this problematic is to be found in Partha Chatterjee's splendid *Nationalist Thought and the Colonial World: A Derivative Discourse* (1986). In this book, Chatterjee takes to task Benedict Anderson and several other (western) theorists of the nation for the universalizing logic of their conceptualization of the nation. For Chatterjee, Anderson, for instance, conceives of the national idea almost entirely in terms of the contours of its Enlightenment and western European genealogy. Conceived and refined in Europe (despite its first verifiable appearance in the Americas), the idea of the nation proves to be one of the Continent's most lasting and successful exports, reproducing itself

globally and bearing an irresistible appeal (for a variety of reasons, including colonial ones) in places very distinct from its point of origin.[8] Chatterjee reproaches Anderson and others for their refusal to see that repetition
must engender disparities and for taking as a given the "modularity" of
twentieth-century nationalisms, "without noticing the twists and turns, the
suppressed possibilities, the contradictions still unresolved";[9] he taxes them,
in other words, with effecting an erasure of (post)colonial difference. Using the case of India and of three prominent Indian nationalist males,
Chatterjee demonstrates the *difference* of Indian nationalisms (from a western European blueprint) in their critical and equivocal negotiation of post-
Enlightenment reason and modernity even as he establishes their dependence on the very conceptual categories they sought to disavow or
overturn.[10] The "failure" of the nation that Guha had identified as key to an
understanding of Indian postcoloniality is thus the effect of an aporia,
transfixed as the nation (or its representative) is between an insufficient
originality and an insufficient imitativeness. In his more recent book, *The
Nation and Its Fragments: Colonial and Postcolonial Histories*, Chatterjee provides an analysis of the modes through which (primarily male) nationalist
elites undertook to establish their own spheres of sovereignty and originality and sought to reject a colonially scripted secondariness.[11]

Much other recent work on colonial and postcolonial South Asia has
turned on these poles of identity and difference, engaging these questions
at a broad epistemic level as well as through specific tropes, figures, and
texts.[12] Dipesh Chakrabarty, in his important essay, "Postcoloniality and the
Artifice of History," has mournfully pondered the fact of a European uni-
versality that allows European historians to theorize without any particular
attention to the "Third World"; this obliviousness nonetheless is productive
of insights that postcolonial scholars find indispensable for their own work:
"The everyday paradox of third-world social science is that *we* find these
theories, in spite of their inherent ignorance of 'us,' eminently useful in
understanding our societies. What allowed the modern European sages to
develop such clairvoyance with regard to societies of which they were em-
pirically ignorant? Why cannot we, once again, return the gaze?"[13]

The question of originality and its Other has thus been an irreducible if
sometimes camouflaged component of our models of colonial and postcolonial elite identity formation as well as of nation formation; one of the
aims of this book is to foreground it as such. And in aiming to reconstellate
and extend some of the debates on originality, repetition, and negotiation,
this book hopes to open up the field of identity formation and nation formation to a more heterogeneous model than that of anglicization. The
model of identity formation proffered by the trope of the mimic man has
been, it should be noted, subject to some friendly criticism. Feminists, while
sympathetic to theorizations of colonial mimicry, have pointed to the gen-

dered provenance of this figure and have noted Bhabha's silence about crucial feminist theorizations of mimicry.[14] (Fanon's explicit marginalization of, if not hostility toward, the black woman in the raced and gendered psychopathologies he excavates in *Black Skin, White Masks* is, on the other hand, almost ostentatiously scandalous.) Besides, Jenny Sharpe notes, in a meticulous and indispensable critique of Benita Parry, "the tropes of 'mimicry,' 'sly civility,' and 'hybridity' that Bhabha deploys to stage what he identifies as the ambivalence of colonial discourse are all derived from the colonial production of *an educated class* of natives [whom Parry mistakenly describes as subaltern]."[15] None of this, of course, is meant to suggest that the work currently available on colonial mimicry and identification *disallows* any engagement with questions of sexuality, gender, religion, and class. My project, then, is to stage precisely such an encounter and, in the process, to imagine another scene of impersonation and doubling, since it seems to me that the representational functions in other contexts of this trope have not yet been significantly extended and complicated by postcolonial theory in its South Asian incarnation. This trope is, as I have already noted, central to the ways in which nationalism imagines itself: hence the production of the nation is almost invariably mediated—as we shall see—through such practices as Gandhi's impersonation of femininity, an Irishwoman's assumption of Hindu feminine celibacy, or a Muslim actress's emulation of a Hindu/ Indian mother goddess. Several of the chapters will seek to understand why such impersonation functions as a governing trope in nation formation and identity formation.

If questions of originality and simulation function, as one must assume they do, not just for and among "western" (a category that includes "westernized" Indian elites) subjects, how do they "translate" across or intersect with (relatively) heterogeneous cultural and discursive formations, some of which may be designated premodern or nonmodern and/or subaltern? With what traditions or conventions of (nonmodern or premodern) doubling, possession, and identification might the colonial sense of the term interact? What productive catachreses might emerge from such translations?[16] What are the ways in which models of identity, difference, and imitation might have been prized from their occasions of (original) enunciation and indigenized, made "original," for a variety of ends? We need to be vigilant, in considering these questions, about the specific ways in which impersonation/mimicry functions as a (cultural) relation rather than an essence, within specific conditions of enunciation and a specific address. The Vaishnava religious tradition in Bengal, for instance, has a long history of (male) female impersonation: male devotees have routinely assumed feminine garb and feminine modes of behavior in deference to a deity who is conceived of as masculine. What are the ramifications of such a staging in the face of a colonial disdain of "feminized" Indian males? The fourth chapter takes up this question in some detail. Another chapter (the sixth) studies a more "modern," though provisionally Indian, mode of understanding impersonation and its affects through juxtaposing Bombay cinema's protocols of (religious and gendered) representation and the production and policing of gendered religious identities. One of the ways in which to examine how authenticity and impersonation themselves are translated and become defamiliarized in alien territory is to track some notable moments in the indigenization of this trope; I do this not by way of providing an etiology or a grand narrative but in order to provide a heuristic model of the ways in which the trope can signify or translate *differently*.

Indian Traffic, then, hopes to chart a trajectory of a long century, encompassing colonial and post-Independence India, in order to explore the consequences and transmutation of the trope of originality and impersonation in the subject-constituting project of a range of subjects from Englishmen to Indian women nationalists. It seeks to demonstrate the irreducible significance of this trope to questions of colonial subject effect, indigenous subject constitution, and nation formation. Such a focus inevitably raises a host of articulated questions. What kinds of representation serve to establish the colonial or postcolonial (elite) subject as "different" or "the same"? What identifications and desires are transformed and negotiated for both Indian *and* British subjects in the (uneven) field of colonial encounter? Within what symbolic orders or discursive formations does one account for the colonizer's desire to "go native"? In what ways do Indian subjects themselves understand, deploy, and reinflect the mandate to impersonate? How does this resonate with the equally powerful imperative (proceeding with equivalent force from colonizer and nationalist) to "be oneself"? How is the terrain of the familiar on which impersonation depends imagined or imaginable? What losses and gains, pleasures and unpleasures are produced through this traffic? What kinds of displacements, repressions, and rearticulations can be said to occur when the place of the normatively male and normatively elite mimic is gendered and/or classed differently, occupied either by women, whether Indian or western, Hindu or Muslim, elite or otherwise, or by males not necessarily heterosexual and perhaps subaltern?

What I would also wish, importantly, to draw attention to is the multivalence of the trope, which we are sometimes in danger of forgetting. The effects of colonial mimicry are all too often read off exultingly as (almost unequivocally) menacing, without sufficient attention to the double and contradictory charge of the operation; despite Bhabha's careful delineation of the dual charge of the operation, too many critics have been willing to read mimicry as another name for subversion. Without disregarding the uncovenanted and unsettling effects that are a by-product of mimicry, we would do well to remind ourselves at the same time of the enormous profitability to the colonial enterprise of the mimic man; mimicry can be harnessed to retrogressive ends and produce retrogressive consummations in addition to progressive ones. Certainly the instance of *Kim* illustrates powerfully for us the ways in which the very locutions and operations of impurity, dislocation, and hybridity that attach to this trope can be invoked as the ground of possibility for the consolidation of a colonial (rather than an anticolonial) legitimacy.[17] Professions of hybridity and liminality—which are sometimes claimed as the badge of disenfranchised and oppositional groups—can be marshaled quite easily and persuasively for the self-aggrandizing (because self-marginalizing) cause of colonialism.[18]

What I propose to consider here are not so much the volatile effects of the mimicry that generates the "not quite/not white" subject of colonialism (on which much work has been done) but the range of *other*, relatively untheorized prospects and identity formations beyond the bounds of male anglicization that emerge in colonial and postcolonial South Asia in the nineteenth and twentieth centuries around the problematic of repetition and difference: the English (male) fascination with "going native," the subaltern or indigenous (male) playing at indigenous subject positions, the Anglo-Indian homosocial assumption of both whiteness and Indian national(ist) status, the Irishwoman's simulation of Hindu womanhood, (elite) Hindu and Muslim women's negotiations of models of femininity and national identity (both colonial and nationalist), and the English mimicry of Englishness. The book is thus orchestrated around readings of some symptomatic moments and significant instantiations of the questions of originality and impersonation. I should add, if it is not already clear, that I read these questions less as governed by an intentionality or by a "habit of mind" than as a cluster of effects that are always required to be read. I should declare, moreover, that the book does not aim so much at being *exhaustive* (a clear impossibility, given the breadth of its object of investigation) as at opening up some (new) questions that must inform our understanding of how colonial originality and repetition are processed or negotiated.

I am interested in situating work on the organization of identities in colonial and postcolonial India within the immense and heterogeneous terrain of sociopolitical, ethicoreligious, legal, and popular-mythic discourses that have mediated Indian and British experience in the last century and a half. An irreducible horizon, then, for the analyses is the modern (colonial and postcolonial) history of the region, with its porous, intersecting, and mutually constitutive formations like colonialism, bourgeois nationalism, and modernity/modernization (later called "development"). My readings are addressed to the semiotic and discursive dimensions of such configurations; to this end I draw upon a variety of disciplines, media, and texts, colonial and postcolonial, literary, filmic, archival, journalistic, religious/mythic, and popular cultural. The regional and historical coherence of the material is not simply a way to rein in the endlessly proliferating possibilities of a topic that by its very nature seems to invite multiplication but a way also of examining the historical production of colonial ideas of originality and mimicry. Nonetheless, it is my hope that these readings may prove serviceable in other colonial and postcolonial contexts. Finally, in seeking to inaugurate a complex and context-specific understanding of the historicity of identity formation and the idioms of originality and secondariness, this book seeks to respond (albeit tentatively and fitfully, and often not in the same terms) to the theoretical challenge posed by Spivak's 1989 essay, "The Political Economy of Women." Here Spivak articulates one of the fundamental problems underlying the theorization of colonial and postcolonial subject formation:

> The theories of subject-formation that we know are either psychoanalytic or counter-psychoanalytic. . . . *We* ["western" subjects, a category that includes elite postcolonials] are used to working with variations on, critiques of, and substitutions for, the narratives of Oedipus and Adam. What narratives produce the signifiers of the subject for other traditions? Always in a confrontation and complicity with the epistemic re-constitution of the subject-in-imperialism, traces of this psycho-biography can be found in the indigenous legal tradition, in the scriptures, and of course, in myth.[19]

Given its emergence in the late-twentieth-century U.S. academy, this book is ineluctably situated in the terrain of the identity politics that continues to engross critical energies in the contemporary moment. Femininity has long been theorized as a nonidentity that masquerades as the real thing, fetishistically securing the illusion of male phallic plenitude. In more recent years, mimicry, drag, and passing—which form the terrain on which claims of difference and identity are contested—have become the practices/affects through which complicity and opposition have been investigated in the western academy. Although analyses of these practices have often tended to emphasize their destabilization of dominant identity formations through modes of irony, burlesque, or the affirmation of positive differences, scholars have also pointed to the fact that identities can never be fully self-sufficient even as they assert their difference from a compulsory sameness.[20] My own investigation is informed by such a deconstructive sense of the discursive construction of dominance/originality *and* resistance/difference. It has been enriched by, and exists in a critical conversation with, the work in feminist, queer, and African American studies on the problematic of originality and difference for identity formation. My own interest in these questions, which are somewhat differently inflected in colonial and postcolonial situations, is less in the lack of coevality that marks the colonial or neocolonial terrain (though that is irreducible) than in the internally differentiated and negotiated terrain of such secondariness or impersonation, and its varied effects, pleasures, and costs.[21]

The book hopes to demonstrate, then, that the representational and performative economies of colonial and nationalist discourses need to be resignified in relation to questions of originality and impersonation. The relations that *Indian Traffic* traces between symbolic orders, psychic processes, and colonial/national institutions in India will, I hope, offer a historically attentive, varied, and continually negotiated sense of how national and other identities have been perceived and performed. And it bears repeating that these questions need to be thought of not only in terms of the always already secondary status of that which comes "*after* the Empire of Reason"[22] but in terms of their vastly different, incommensurable, and incalculable modalities and effects. I have no wish to imply that such traffic was a form of free trade or that exchanges were voluntaristic, coeval, or unmarked by violence and distress. Instead, I wish to insist on the productiveness (in the sense of invariably producing effects, shocks, and transmutations, though often of unequal degrees) of such commerce for all concerned.[23]

If the prototypical comic actor in such an exchange is the babu whose anglicization guarantees his distance from Englishness, the first chapter, "Oriental Exhibits: The Englishman as Native," takes up that figure who seems to be his converse (and his superior); it seeks to account for the peculiarly *colonial* (English) drive to occupy the place of Indianness. It focuses on the career of Richard Burton, colonial adventurer, linguist, and disguise artist par excellence. It examines the ways in which Burton assumes the identities of "your genuine Oriental," considering the personae assumed both in Sind (India) and, more notoriously, in the *Personal Narrative of a Pilgrimage to Al-Madinah and Meccah* (1855). I argue that the pilgrimage involves something more complex than passing for an Indian/Afghan/Muslim/native. Burton seeks to resignify—rather than imitate—native identity, so that the native, in order to have access to a subject position as a native, can only do so by modeling himself after Burton. And yet, despite Burton's drive to name nativeness as his own creation rather than as a category that might be at least contingently autochthonous, he can only do so from a position of marginality, from a place that is a nonplace and an identity that is not one. As a "half-Arab, half-Persian" merchant in Sind, or as a Rangoon-bred Afghan in Arabia, he is an outsider who can pass as an "Oriental" because of his unknowability rather than his familiarity or, more properly, an unknowable familiarity; wherever he goes, he signifies not so much indigeneity as a ubiquitous and uncanny liminality.

Chapter 2, "Discovering India, Imagining *Thuggee*," investigates the perils (and pleasures) engendered for colonial authority by a mimicry that is—

like Burton's—outside the familiar ambit of anglicization but—unlike Burton's—engineered by Indian actors. What happens when Indians rather than Englishmen "go native"? And what happens when mimicry, which is meant to a guarantor of difference, becomes indistinguishable from mimesis? Such a narrative of an unsanctioned indigenous mimicry is to be found in the discourse of *thuggee*, a discourse that takes its most substantial form in the archives of the Thuggee and Dacoity Department as well as in some fictionalized accounts of thug life. The thugs were—according to this colonial archive—a professional cult of religious killers who, disguised as ordinary (Indian) citizens, lured unwary travelers to their death on the highways of the colonial state. The instance of *thuggee* intimates that far from being an easily recognizable and faintly ludic figure, the mimic man (in his incarnation as a thug) is a figure who "passes" in law-abiding society with unsettling ease; he embodies the *failure* of the difference supposedly guaranteed by such an interpellation. The thug's conformity, not to a particular and exceptional Indian identity but to an infinite range of everyday Indian ones, opens up the unspeakable possibility that *all* Indian identities might be a matter of impersonation. Hence, for the colonial state, the problem of *thuggee* can only be resolved through the criminalization of the thug's capacity for impersonation and through the production and sequestration of a distinct identity designated as thug.

Chapter 3, "Anglo/Indians and Others: The Ins and Outs of the Nation," on Kipling's *Kim*, examines the bar, or hyphen, that simultaneously couples and uncouples the Anglo and the Indian and that establishes both as hyperreal identities. It probes the ways in which a colony, rather than a nation, is figured as an "imagined community," so that the Anglo-Indian male (who is carefully distinguished from the "foreign" Englishman) can perform as founding father and first citizen of India, displacing or placing under erasure the Indian (male) nationalist, the English (male) colonialist, and the symbolic figure of Mother India. Neither Angloness nor Indianness (the two components of this hybrid identity) is incontrovertible for Kim but must be unceasingly secured through an elaborate relay of identifications, desires, and impersonations enacted in the Great Game of colonial espionage. Kim is Irish, a poor boy of the Indian bazaars and more than once (mis)recognized as a "half-caste." The nature of his (interstitial) whiteness or Angloness and its relation to an Indianness that is traversed at almost all points by anticolonial intimations are the focus of this chapter, which argues that the relationship is negotiated through Anglo-India's attempt to make the subject of Indian nationalism its own.

Chapter 4, "As the Master Saw Her: Western Women and Hindu Nationalism," addresses the gendered Indian subject of Indian nationalism—that which *Kim* must remember to forget. It investigates how the problematic of originality and impersonation might signify for Indian (male) nationalists and for the western women associated with them, or how it might signify differently from the paradigmatic model of anglicization. I focus on the relationship of three late-nineteenth-century figures—Ramakrishna, Vivekananda, and Sister Nivedita (Margaret Noble)—who were tied to each other through relations of religious mentorship and discipleship. Each was notable, in the capacity of mentor or disciple, for "putting on" a gendered (and/or raced) identity: Ramakrishna became a Hindu woman; Vivekananda, a hypermasculine Indian/western male; and Nivedita, a Hindu/ Indian woman. I examine the gendered politics of these transactions of early Hindu nationalism, reading them as a significant constitutive moment in the gendering of national identity. Through what forms of impersonation, displacement, and surrogacy do Indian/Hindu nationalist males assume a position of mastery, in relation to Indian women and to western women and men? And why might such a project conceive of western woman as central to its imagination of itself? What is the functionality of the subordinate white woman turned Indian within a Hindu nationalism in pursuit of hegemony?[24] Such a reading of the white female mimic in Hindu nationalism will, I hope, pose some new questions about globality and (western) feminism, especially in reopening a consideration of the role of western women (usually described as privileged, rather than masochistic or subordinate, in relation to Indian women and men) in colonial and postcolonial economies of power and desire.[25]

Chapter 5, "Becoming Women: The Genders of Nationalism," in turn takes up the women displaced by the white woman's inscription as Indian woman, examining the identifications and identities made available for (elite) *Indian* (and implicitly caste Hindu) women in the high nationalist period. What is the trajectory of an Indian woman's assumption or mediation of Englishness and/or Indianness? What are the implications for Indian women (and men) of the feminizing of male nationalisms or nationalists? As in the case of the previous chapters, I approach the questions of authenticity, impersonation, and delegation through the prism of an intersubjective dynamic. I read the poetry and biography/politics of an outstanding female poet and nationalist of the twentieth century, Sarojini Naidu (whose entry into Indian nationalism was facilitated by her exemplary triumph as a "feminine" anglicized poet) in relation to the biography/ politics of Gandhi, whose cultivation of a "feminine" style of politics (in marked contrast to the muscular Hinduism of Vivekananda) is well known. I do this in order to thematize Indian nationalism's difficulties with competing notions of "becoming Indian woman"; I speak, therefore, to the ways in which it must solicit and disavow Sarojini's putatively frivolous (female) identity as a travesty of Gandhi's more seemly and serviceable Indian femininity.

The sixth and concluding chapter, "Figuring Mother India: The Case of Nargis" examines how considerations of originality and impersonation structure questions of identity in the popular-cultural imaginary of the postcolonial Indian (Hindu) nation. It examines the career of Nargis, a female Muslim star of the Bombay cinema who achieved lasting fame for her representation of Radha, an idealized Hindu peasant woman in what may be the best-known popular Indian film, *Mother India* (1957). The chapter examines the transformation of Nargis into an icon of Indian (Hindu) womanhood, on screen and in domestic life, and the tense yet intimate relationship of such iconicity with the residual and repressed Muslimness of the star. The tension between Bombay cinema's protocols of iconicity (where a Muslim actress repeats, offscreen, the [Hindu] role she plays onscreen) and the monitoring of Muslim identity (in which the Muslim's Hinduness—coded as Indianness—is always wanting) must be read as a partial allegory of the place of the "good/assimilated Muslim" in the Indian/Hindu polity and psyche. In the Hindu fantasy of assimilation, this figure is simultaneously a locus of fantasy and desire *and* a problem that continually erupts into the self-possession of Indian/Hindu identity.

DISCIPLINE AND NEGOTIATION: AUDIENCES, CONSTITUENCIES, AND RESPONSIBILITIES

This book, like others of its kind, does more than thematize negotiation; it is perforce made to rehearse a series of disciplinary and theoretical negotiations in the very process of mapping it. Such a process is, I think, clarified and contextualized by routing it through in some of the debates and engagements currently under way in what is called "postcolonial (cultural) studies"; these debates, like those on identity formation and nation formation, are also suffused—in ways that are perhaps not surprising but still worth attending to—with the idioms of originality and simulation, purity and pollution, legitimacy and usurpation.

Among the most prominent of these engagements is the critique of the some of the governing assumptions of postcolonial studies that has been proffered by historians from a particular kind of marxist perspective; some of the best-known contributions are the ones by Rosalind O'Hanlon and David Washbrook, Arif Dirlik, and Aijaz Ahmad.[26] For O'Hanlon and Washbrook the most immediate target of criticism is Gyan Prakash's "Writing Post-Orientalist Histories of the Third World: Perspectives from Indian Historiography," an important essay that offers a sustained critique of foundational historiographies—Orientalist, nationalist, and conventionally marxist—of India.[27] Their response to this specific essay, though, becomes the occasion for a severely critical and wide-ranging analysis of the allegedly

pernicious dependence of postcolonial studies on theories of radical inde-
terminacy supposedly derived from poststructuralism and postmodernism.
For them postfoundational approaches, such as the ones favored by Prakash,
cannot come to terms with the necessity of explanatory categories or explanatory fictions (however one designates these) and are inadequate for
historical understanding or for theorizing any kind of change or contesta-
tion of a progressive kind; they can only be productive of intellectual and
political paralysis. Poststructuralism is, in this analysis, indicted as unoriginal (we always knew that the grounds of our knowledge were uncertain and
fictive) and unimaginative in its deployment of this (unoriginal) insight (its
literal-mindedness disallows any work that is not repetitive and complacent
and functions as mimicry without menace). As Prakash (in his response) rec-
ognizes, such a representation of postfoundational epistemologies (which
are quite indiscriminately rendered as identical with each other, in addition
to being imperfectly understood) may itself be embroiled in a certain impulse to mastery in its purist disavowal of "the productive tension that the
combination of Marxist and deconstructive approaches generates."[28]

The same repudiation of a hyphenated marxism with its concomitant
pollutions that marks O'Hanlon and Washbrook's essay informs Dirlik's essay as well as Ahmad's book, though the latter are concerned—in somewhat
different ways—with the formation of that figure who has come to be
known as the "postcolonial intellectual." Both locate the emergence and institutional consolidation of such a figure within a late-capitalist formation
and speak to the decisive coimplication of the "rise" of postcolonial studies
in the academy with the increasing prominence of this relatively privileged
diasporic/immigrant figure. I would not necessarily argue with such an ap-
praisal, but where for a deconstructive reader this complicity would constitute the irreducible starting point for an analysis, for Dirlik and Ahmad it
constitutes in the last instance forceful evidence of the corrupt and camouflaged careerism of diasporic postcolonial intellectuals. Such complicity, for
them, is a powerful indictment of the subfield itself as opportunistic and politically retrogressive in its inescapable entanglement with the structures of
late capitalism.

Outside the discipline of history, the debates over the ontological and
political character of postcolonial studies have assumed a somewhat different hue, though—as we shall see—they, too, invoke in many instances a
rhetoric of lawful limits and unlawful appropriation. Postcolonial (cultural)
studies as it has evolved in the literary studies branch of the Anglo-U.S.
academy has in some notable instances taken as its category of analysis the
scrutiny of colonialism and its aftermath, or more broadly, North-South
relations and their modern genealogy. It is a category not easily accommodable within the conventional periodizations and national formations

favored by English and comparative literature departments or within the rubrics of the disciplines themselves; this categorically and disciplinarily anomalous condition is something it shares with—for instance—feminist studies, queer studies, and African American studies. It is a subfield that has, almost from the moment of its emergence in the metropolitan academy, been beset by profound doubts and apprehensions about its own institutional, political, and intellectual/disciplinary status; one scholar has wittily likened the anxieties surrounding it to those that traditionally have attended "the birth of a female child."[29] The very term has aroused—both among the scholars situated within postcolonial studies so called and those "outside"—a large and often immoderate measure of hostility. Among the most celebrated and cited of these are the essays in *Social Text* of Anne McClintock and Ella Shohat, who have decried the term's lack of iconicity and its ostensible abdication of a political charge; both accuse it of a prematurely celebratory character.[30] McClintock and Shohat are surely in the right to insist that the question of decolonization must never be allowed to detach itself from the question of postcoloniality. Nonetheless, the call for an ideographic term that will perfectly mirror the discontinuities and heterogeneities of the field seems to me to be posing the wrong kind of demand, structured as it is by a logic of authenticity/fullness and masking/lack. In such a reading, the term *postcolonial* functions as a form of (failed) camouflage, the theoretical analogue to the mimic man of colonial discourse, whose difference from the genuine article invariably undermines his claims to legitimacy. Besides, as Stuart Hall observes in his learned and meticulously thorough response to the criticisms of Dirlik, Shohat, and McClintock, the term/description *postcolonial* endeavors to "construct . . . a notion of a shift or a transition conceptualised as the reconfiguration of a field, rather than as a movement of linear transcendence between two mutually exclusive states. Such transformations are not only not completed but they may not be best captured within a paradigm which assumes that all major historical shifts are driven by a necessitarian logic towards a teleological end."[31]

Somewhat different from the interrogations of the term *postcolonial* within literary/cultural studies by Shohat and McClintock[32] is Spivak's reproach about the majority of literary critical attempts at work that is commonly called interdisciplinary: "the history of the institutional study of literature is one of great permissiveness. . . . When a literary critic makes like a political economist or a psychoanalyst she is speaking as an insider of her discipline in terms of her fantasy about what kinds of social value those other disciplines carry . . . If she does not attend to the generalizations I have laid out before you . . . [she] . . . acts out the pretentious self-marginalization of the sanctioned ignorance of so-called interdisciplinary

talk."[33] More urgently than perhaps any other scholar in the field, Spivak
has warned us against becoming too comfortable in our (new) critical practices, insisting that we "do our homework," that we "*earn* the right to criticize," and that we remember never to forget the compelling character of
our disciplinary formation, interests, and responsibilities. It is a caution
against disciplinary impersonation, or piracy, that we ignore at our peril. It
is, moreover, a caution that has been repeated for literary critics directly
and indirectly by historians, who have pointed out that though literary studies and, more recently, cultural studies, needs history, "historicizing" is not
and should not be easy. And yet there is much to be said, too, for Ellen
Rooney's rejoinder that "disciplines posit objects of inquiry that cannot be
useful to oppositional critics without being fundamentally revised,"[34] as well
as for Spivak's own assertion in innumerable instances that "knowledge is
made possible and is sustained by irreducible difference, not identity."[35]
Neither do I understand Spivak's caveats about interdisciplinary work to
function as a prohibition. To her credit, she herself, despite the often stern
quality, even purism, of her "disciplinary talk," has not desisted from rang-
ing far afield from literary criticism, claiming the terrain of philosophy, eco-
nomics, history, and psychoanalysis (among others) as her own, violently re-
fashioning them to other ends. In an argument about her critical (not
disciplinary) practice, she has claimed that her undertaking is "the irreducible but impossible task" of letting (nonintersecting) philosophical formations like marxism, feminism, and deconstruction critically "interrupt"
one another.[36] This, it seems to me, is an intellectual move that could anal-
ogously be made across the discontinuities of the disciplines.

This question of (an always inadequate) dissembling and expropriation
is a particularly live issue for those of us who are trained as literary scholars
and situated in postcolonial studies, especially since we solicit multiple and
sometimes reciprocally uneasy if not contentious constituencies of readers,
whose demands or expectations are often incommensurable. It is conceivable that literary and other scholars in feminist and (British and American)
cultural studies, whom I would wish to solicit as readers, might find the
South Asian scholarship unfamiliar and therefore uninviting. It is also possible that some (though by no means all) South Asianist historians and social scientists might find in such an enterprise (which borrows materials
from a number of disciplines and media) an instance of poaching or, more
simply, of lack. Yet such risks must be taken if one is to address more than a
very slender constituency of scholars exactly like oneself, trained in (English) literary studies, committed to an interdisciplinary cultural studies,
and working on South Asian materials. I can only respond to such a situation by multiplying the questions that must be asked, rather than providing
solutions or resolutions. How do intellectuals trained as English literary critics approach, prepare for, or lay a claim to the terrain of South Asian stud-

ies, where so much of the current work on colonialism and postcoloniality is taking shape? What indeed can—or should—the domain of postcolonial studies claim as its own, in ways that are different from the traditional claims of the disciplines? Given that postcolonial studies has its greatest visibility (under this banner) in departments of English and comparative literature (which do not necessarily teach or promote modern or classical Asian and African languages) but is in many ways parasitic upon the materials traditionally claimed by history, anthropology, political science, and philosophy, what are the ways in which it must move between and through disciplines? What are the forms of verifiability in each discipline, and how does postcolonial studies negotiate these discontinuities? What is its projected audience, its constituency, for its research and its teaching? What methods and what knowledge must it learn and unlearn? How does it understand its own limits, if these limits can ever be known in advance?

It is obvious that what these queries speak to, in many ways, is the institution of cultural studies, which has gained a large measure of respectability in (English) literary studies though not necessarily in postcolonial studies outside English departments. Predicated upon a notion of culture that is understood in terms of institutions, languages, and ideas as well as a large gamut of products and practices like books, films, fashion, and architecture, cultural studies is necessarily interdisciplinary and often antidisciplinary. It is, of course, not without its considerable risks. One of these is its instant metaphorizability, so that it can function as all things to all people. But, more seriously, in undertaking cultural studies one takes the risk of never being erudite enough to satisfy the demands of all the disciplines that one is using, addressing, and inhabiting; what one *should* know is quite literally incalculable. One's work is always in peril of being construed as an instance of the mimicry that betrays its distance from the "real thing" (Spivak's caricature of the interdisciplinary scholar). The risk of this insufficiency is, I would argue, fundamentally different from the "sanctioned ignorance" against which Spivak so often and so correctly inveighs. I believe I do not overstate the case when I say that cultural studies can only be undertaken with considerable fear and trembling. Nevertheless, it must be undertaken if certain kinds of questions are to be asked or reinflected, and in the face of the knowledge that (what one sees as) the *difference* of one's questions may register as the wrong kind of question.

I pose this situation as a challenge and as a site of ongoing negotiation; I do it not in order to reconcile the differences in the divergent audiences that one is necessarily addressing or to argue for any kind of pluralism ("Can't we all just get along?") but in order to highlight the philosophical and disciplinary impasses and questions of methodology and accountability that confront many of us who are situated in that liminal and contested zone between and outside traditional literary studies, cultural studies, history, and area studies. I would like to adapt for my purposes Stuart Hall's description of the "theoretical" and "political" questions in the cultural studies project as existing in an "ever irresolvable but permanent tension. It constantly allows the one to irritate, bother, and disturb the other, without insisting on some final closure."[37] Perhaps such a tension between the cultural studies contingent and the disciplinarians is just what one must hope to sustain, explore, and dispute; it may be another name for negotiation.

ONE

Oriental Exhibits

The Englishman as Native

In "The Adventure of the Empty House" Sherlock Holmes recounts for Watson his ascent from the abyss of Reichenbach Falls after his struggle with Moriarty and proceeds to fill in the blanks of his own history. The Reichenbach Falls episode, we learn, opens up an interesting gap in Holmes's professional life, mandating a condition of perpetual secrecy and disguise that replicates—with interesting variations—his professional activity as consulting detective. During his absence from London, he tells Watson, he has been concealing his identity and safeguarding himself by becoming an explorer and disguise artist manqué:

> I travelled for two years in Tibet, therefore, and amused myself by visiting Lhassa, and spending some days with the head lama. You may have read of the remarkable explorations of a Norwegian named Sigerson, but I am sure that it never occurred to you that you were receiving news of your friend. I then passed through Persia, looked in at Mecca, and paid a short but interesting visit to the Khalifa at Khartoum, the results of which I have communicated to the Foreign Office.[1]

The offhand reference to Mecca as an appropriate site for Orientalist scrutiny and information retrieval seems calculatedly to invoke Sir Richard Burton and that extraordinary two-volume travel book, the *Personal Narrative of a Pilgrimage to Al-Madinah and Meccah* (1855), which made its author a byword for romantic adventuring and cross-cultural impersonation among his contemporaries in England. Obviously there are several layers of mimicry at work in the account of the detective's travels—Holmes mimicking Burton mimicking eastern / Muslim ontology. It seems to me a suitable point of departure for a consideration of the questions embedded in the categories of colonial identify formation, performance, and cross-cultural exchange.

I propose to examine these through the ways in which Burton performs and hyperbolizes "your genuine Oriental" in his accounts of Sind and in the *Personal Narrative*. What I probe is not so much Homi Bhabha's theoretical construction of the constitution of the colonial subject through the process he calls mimicry but a specular version of that subject. I consider not the hybrid reformulations of the colonized native, the mimic man who is "not quite/not white" but instead the colonial observer who assumes the postures of authenticity and seeks to displace the native informant.[2] My interest here lies in establishing what the appropriation of such a subject position does for the field of colonial encounter. A consideration of the semiotic of disguise within the economy of cultural and racial exchange that operates in this text, together with its manipulations of bodies, frontiers, and identities, allows us to read the *Personal Narrative* as an engagement with, and response to, the unsettling and sometimes even counterhegemonic possibilities of native inaccessibility and native insurgency. It also illuminates in fascinating ways the discursive reach in the colonial context of a concept of identity grounded in mimicry, as well as the epistemic contradictions and contestations that provided the (uncertain) conditions of possibility for colonialism.

By 1852, when he conceived of his pilgrimage to Mecca, Burton had already made a minor reputation for himself in India as a polyglot Orientalist and an expert in manipulating the complexities of cultural exchange. He had "attacked Arabic" at Oxford and been tutored in Hindustani in preparation for his Indian service. He made such rapid progress in London and on his voyage to Bombay that he was, as he claimed, able upon reaching India in 1842 "to land with *eclat* as a raw griff and to astonish the throng of palanquin bearers that jostled, pushed and pulled me in the pier head, with the vivacity and nervousness of my phraseology."[3] In Bombay he resumed his language lessons, learning Gujarati, Hindustani, and some Persian from a Parsi *munshi* (teacher), eventually finishing first out of twelve candidates in the Hindustani examination given by the government of the East India Company; later he was to achieve similar honors in the Gujarati examination.[4] During his seven-year Indian sojourn he also learned, with differing degrees of expertise, Sanskrit, Marathi, Sindhi, Punjabi, Telugu, Arabic, Persian, and Toda.[5] His schooling in Indian languages and the Indian social text appears to have been further supplemented by a liaison, or a series of liaisons, with Indian women, which were not at all uncommon at the time: "The Bibi (white woman) was at this time rare in India; the result was the triumph of the Bubu (coloured sister). I found every officer in the corps [at Baroda, where he was stationed initially] more or less provided with one of these helpmates. We boys naturally followed suit."[6] These were liaisons whose pedagogical usefulness he underlines: "The 'walking dictionary' is all but indispensable to the Student, and she teaches him not only Hindostani grammar, but the syntaxes of native life."[7] And, further, "It connected the white stranger with the country and its people, gave him an interest in their manners and customs, and taught him thoroughly well their language."[8] To him the *bubu* system was configured as the arena of mutual exchange and diplomacy. He was to regret as politically damaging the onset of Victorian morality, and the arrival in India of Victorian women, that disallowed such interracial sexual arrangements: "The greatest danger in British India is the ever-growing gulf that yawns between the governors and the governed; they lose touch of one another, and such racial estrangement leads directly to racial hostility."[9] But he also noted the occasional perils of such individual-ized instruction and of any unthinking and inappropriately gendered mim-icry of what is presumed to be nativeness: "It was a standing joke in my regiment that one of the officers always spoke of himself in the feminine gender."[10]

In 1843 Burton was appointed regimental interpreter and was ordered, with the 18th Bombay Native Infantry, to Sind, which had recently been conquered, with considerable brutality and in contravention of treaties with local rulers, by Sir Charles Napier. Since he had by this time already quali-fied as an interpreter in Hindustani and Gujarati, he soon hired a Persian *munshi* teach him Persian, Arabic, and Sindhi.[11] At this time he also adopted the clothing of the region and—to a substantial degree—the company of Sindis and other "natives" of many nationalities (including Persia), a move that allegedly made him unpopular with his fellow officers: "My life became much mixed up with these gentlemen, and my brother officers [again] fell to calling me the 'White Nigger.'"[12]

Despite the enormous reputation as a heroic figure that Burton seems to have acquired in our own century (witness the number and popularity of Burton biographies, including the latest one, by Edward Rice, and the film version of *Mountains of the Moon* [1989]), Burton does not seem in his own day to have been particularly well thought of or greatly liked by his peers. Notwithstanding his extraordinary linguistic skills, his undoubted bravery, and his host of other talents, he was something of an outcast both in the In-dian Army and in the Foreign Office, and he spent most of his life in unim-portant, unprestigious diplomatic missions and outposts of the empire. Whether this was the cause or the effect of his fascination with the liminal character of masquerade is impossible to establish. It should be noted that Burton was fond of promoting himself as a free and unorthodox spirit who was bound to shock the intellectual and sexual sensibilities of his Victorian contemporaries. Even the notorious Latin footnotes on clitori-dectomy and infibulation in the *Personal Narrative*, presented in rather os-tentatious and loudly protested defiance of sanctimonious editors and pub-lishers, are grounded quite unambiguously in the discursive practices of a(n) (increasingly respectable) discipline (anthropology) that often took a

delight in outraging sexual decorum and religious pieties. In the same spirit
that had prompted the Latin footnotes, he made the following acerbic comment about contemporary Christianity: "A visit after Arab Mecca to Angle-
Indian Aden, with its 'priests after the order of Melchisedeck,' suggested to
me that the Moslem may be more tolerant, more enlightened, more charitable, than many societies of self-styled Christians."[13]

Burton was to stay in Sind and serve under Napier, who had been appointed governor of the province, until 1849. A number of important ethno-
graphical works resulted from this sojourn—*Scinde; or, The Unhappy Valley*
(1851); *Sindh, and the Races That Inhabit the Valley of the Indus* (1852); and
Falconry in the Valley of the Indus (1852). But what was perhaps most interesting about the years in Sind was that Burton began for the first time to impersonate "natives" or "Orientals" (though never locals) on a fairly regular
basis in the service of the colonial state. In a departure from the practice of
other British intelligence officers, who bought their information from native agents, Burton decided to absorb the office of the native informant in
himself. The great difficulty, and yet the absolute necessity, of passing as a
native was continually underlined by Burton: "The first difficulty was to pass
for an Oriental, and this was as necessary as it was difficult. The European
official in India seldom, if ever, sees anything in its real light, so dense is the
veil which the fearfulness, the duplicity, the prejudice and the superstitions
of the natives hang before his eyes."[14] He decided to pose as Mirza Abdullah, a "half Arab, half Iranian" merchant from Bushire in the Persian Gulf,
and in this guise he enjoyed—so he tells us—considerable social and
amorous success, including—according to his niece Georgiana Stisted—an
unfortunate affair with "a beautiful Persian girl of high descent";[15] he also
brought back for Napier lurid details of infanticide, wife killing, and wrong-
ful executions among the Sindi population. His charm, especially with
women, and his status as a cloth merchant apparently gave him access to
private homes, even to harems, and brought him matrimonial proposals
from the fathers of marriageable women. He played no ordinary merchant
but a man of expansive interests:

> Sometimes the Mirza passed the evening at a mosque listening to the ragged
> students who, . . . mumbled out Arabic from the thumbed, soiled and tattered
> pages of theology upon which a dim oil light shed its scanty ray, or he sat de-
> bating the niceties of faith with the long-bearded, shaven-pated blear-eyed
> and stolid-faced *genius loci*, the Mullah. At other times, when in a merrier
> mood, he entered uninvited the first door, whence issued the sounds of mu-
> sic and the dance;—a clean turban and a polite bow are the best "tickets for
> soup" the East knows. Or he played chess with some native friends, or he con-
> sorted with the hemp-drinkers and opium eaters in the estaminets, or he vis-
> ited the Mrs. Gadabouts and Go-betweens who make matches amongst the

Faithful and gathered from them a precious budget of private histories and domestic scandal.[16]

Nonetheless, his mastery of native identity was as yet incomplete. His accent would not allow him to impersonate a Sindi, and there were gaps in his knowledge of Shia practice that had to be plugged by his *munshi* (though he claimed to have fooled his teacher on one occasion with the perfection of his disguise).[17]

Burton was rarely content simply to pass as a native of this variety. His fondness for multiplying identities, as well as his penchant for coming off as wilier than the natives, led him to impersonate an English official as well as the official's factotum and confidant, Mirza Abdullah. Thus by day he played Burton the English officer, surrounded in his tent by *munshis*, scribes, servants, telescopes, and the other appurtenances of English power and given to "a sort of Oriental dress." In the evening, the Mirza circulated among the hangers-on in the Englishman's camp, gathering information and dispensing details about his English patron. Frequently, he says, "had he to answer the question how much his perquisites and illicit gains amounted to in the course of the year."[18]

Burton seems to have affected on occasion the exulting self-confidence in his own knowledge and cunning that is manifest in the passage above. It is certainly not difficult to imagine that his description (through the words of a Goan man) in the book on Goa of "Lieut.———, of the———Rgt." may have been a wish-fulfilling self-portrait, though it is important to note that a satirical note is by no means absent: "[He] was a very clever gentleman, who knew everything. He could talk to each man of a multitude in his own language, and all of them would appear equally surprised by, and delighted with him. Besides, his faith was every man's faith."[19] This must be juxtaposed with what he wrote elsewhere at about the same time:

> Thus you see how it is that many of our eminent politicals—men great at Sanscrit and Arabic, who spoke Persian like Shirazis, and had the circle of Oriental science at their fingers' ends; . . . turned out to be diplomatic little children in the end, which tries all things. They had read too much; they had written too much; they were a trifle too clever, and much too confident. Their vanity tempted them to shift their nationality; from Briton to become Greek, in order to meet Greek on the roguery field; and lamentably they always failed.
>
> So much for active dealings with natives.[20]

While these comments can usefully be read as expressions of scholarly and professional competitiveness directed at other, armchair Orientalists, they cannot but be seen also as a commentary on Burton's own ambitions; they do speak to his sense that only superior force could prevail against eastern peoples, who were invariably more practiced than Englishmen in craftiness. His invocation of the political officer (and spy), Alexander Burnes, and of the British commander in Kabul, Sir William Macnaghten (both of whom had been assassinated by Afghans in Kabul in 1841), doubly underscored the futility and the danger of engaging in deceit with such enemies. Such oscillations between a sense of infallibility and a sense of helplessness were to persist, as we shall see, in his Meccan sojourn.

Burton was involved in some diplomatic missions while in Sind. And it appears that Napier sought Burton's linguistic and shape-changing skills for another important project in 1845. The source for information on this project is Burton himself; the following is his account of the production and effects of the "scandalous report" that he claimed brought his Indian career to a close. It seems that Napier was told

> that Karachi supported no less than three lupanars or bordels, in which not women, but boys and eunuchs, the former demanding nearly a double price, lay for hire. . . . Being then the only British officer who could speak Sindi, I was asked indirectly to make enquiries and to report upon the subjects; and I undertook the task on express condition that my report should not be forwarded to the Bombay Government, from whom supporters of the Governor's policy could expect scant favor, justice, or mercy.[21]

This was a serious problem for Napier, as the brothels were supposedly catering to British troops, both white and brown. Burton accordingly visited the brothels as Mirza Abdullah, accompanied by his *munshi*; just how his information was obtained is never specified, though there has been a great deal of speculation on the question of Burton's participation in the activities he describes. In any event, he apparently produced a report on the Karachi brothels that was full of details so candid that his superior put the report away in his secret file, where it was to remain for two years, until it was brought to light by one of Burton's opponents and used to punish its unorthodox author. Burton was to allude briefly but pointedly to this report in the famous "Terminal Essay"—which includes a section on pederasty—that is positioned at the conclusion of his translation of the *Alf Laylah wa Laylah* (rendered by Burton as *The Book of the Thousand Nights and a Night*),[22] but the "original" has apparently disappeared. Fawn Brodie speculates that it was burned by Isabel Burton or her sister.[23] Edward Rice, like at least one other Burton scholar, suggests that the report, if there was one, was an oral report that never existed as a written document.[24]

Burton was usually careful to maintain—no matter how much he might occasionally attempt to titillate or outrage his metropolitan audience with hints of his own participation in "abominable rites"—that none of this cross-cultural traffic could be allowed to dislodge the semiotic of racial and cultural difference in which colonial epistemology was grounded; and in *Goa, and the Blue Mountains* (1851), he speaks with a profound revulsion of the Eurasian body that resulted from Portuguese-Indian miscegenation in Goa: "It would be, we believe, difficult to find in Asia an uglier or more degraded looking race."[25] Miming the native, especially for the purpose of decentering native identity, retained, however, a powerful hold on his imagination. Gail Ching-Liang Low usefully points to the pleasures and disavowals that mark such impersonation: "Constantly aware of the whiteness underneath the disguise, he derives great pleasure from his warding off of the native threat (the fear of castration); his clothes as fetish permit both the acknowledgement of difference (on which his identity as master is based) and the simultaneous disavowal of that castrating difference."[26] In the book on Goa Burton describes, not without admiration, Portuguese methods of conversion in that territory: "The Portuguese sent out in all directions crowds of missionaries, who, as Tavernier informs us, assumed the native dress, and taught under the guise of Jogees and other Hindoo religious characters, a strange, and yet artful mixture of the two faiths. That these individuals sacrificed the most vital points of their religion to forward the end they proposed to themselves, we have ample proof; at the same time that they were eminently successful, is equally well known."[27]

After a few years in Europe following the unsatisfactory cessation of his Indian service,[28] Burton applied to the Royal Geographical Society for funding that would enable him to undertake a trip to the holy cities of Islam and thereby remove a "huge white blot" from the European cartographic construction of the Near East. It is instructive at this point to read Burton through the Conrad of "Geography and Some Explorers" and of *Heart of Darkness*. Conrad speaks of looking at the map of Africa as a boy and seeing satisfyingly numerous blank spaces that left room for the enactment of imperial fantasies.

> At that time there were many blank spaces on the earth, and when I saw one that looked particularly inviting on a map . . . I would put my finger on it and say, When I grow up I will go there. . . . I have been in some of them. . . . But there was one yet—the biggest, the most blank so to speak—that I had a hankering after. . . . True, by this time it wasn't a blank space any more. It had got filled since my boyhood with rivers and lakes and names. It had ceased to be a blank space of delightful mystery—a white patch for a boy to dream gloriously over. It had become a place of darkness.[29]

As a boy Conrad dreams of visiting these blank spaces, conscious, even as he fetishizes the blankness of Africa, that his arrival signals the erasure of that blankness. When he is a man, however, the blank spaces have been "filled up" by the twin inscriptions of geographical knowledge and colonial possession. Likewise, in the *Personal Narrative*, the white blot that is Arabia (or Sind) in the British imagination provides the perfectly constructed theater for the authorized script of colonial impersonation, inscription, and occupation.

Burton was not by any means the first white man to make a successful pilgrimage to Mecca, but his predecessors (among them Giovanni Finati, Joseph Pitts, and Ludovicus Vertomannus) had compromised their standing either by embracing Islam or by failing to provide full and accurate details of the city and the shrine. In other words, some had dispensed with the necessity of disguise by converting; others had failed to complete the purpose of the pilgrimage, which for them as Europeans and non-Muslims extended beyond the experiential domain and embraced the discursive; it entailed not just the successful completion of the physical act of pilgrimage but also its appropriate (and exhaustive) narrativization. It was possible, as Burton himself concedes, to make the pilgrimage to Mecca after a formal declaration of conversion to Islam. As Thomas Assad notes, such an option would have relieved Burton of the unremitting pressures of miming native identities and orthodoxies of various kinds.[30] But such a move would have been counterproductive to the project as Burton conceived it. As a new convert (and a European), he would, he felt, run the risk of being unpopular with the locals; certainly he would be the object of native scrutiny: "My spirit could not bend to own myself a *Burmá*, a renegade—to be pointed at and shunned and catechised, an object of suspicion to the many and of contempt for all" (*Personal Narrative*, 1: 23). He had therefore to be a "real" Muslim, which also meant being a "real" native; this was a paradoxical position that allowed him to be free of obvious scrutiny (and therefore free to observe and document and categorize all that came his way) while enforcing on him an unrelenting vigilance in order to stave off that very scrutiny.

Burton's journey was, he tells us, successfully undertaken in 1853 in the guise of Shaykh Abdullah, a Pathan (Afghan from India) *darwaysh* (dervish), and doctor of colorful reputation who had been born in Bombay and educated in Rangoon. This identity was built up and modified—often by fits and starts and often in response to suggestions from friends and well-wishers as well as in response to the difficulties his disguise of the moment created—during his passage through several Muslim lands. In Alexandria he was Mirza Abdullah; there, he tells us, "the better to shield the inquisitive eyes of servants and visitors, my friend, Larking, lodged me in an outhouse, where I could revel in the utmost freedom of life and manners. And although some Armenian Dragoman, a restless spy like all his race, occasionally remarked *voilà un Persan diablement dégagé*, none, except those entrusted with the secret, had any idea of the part I was playing" (*Personal Narrative*, 1: 11). Later he became Shaykh Abdullah rather than Mirza Abdullah (thus effecting the transition from Shia to Sunni in nomenclature). The initial mistake of assuming Persian and therefore Shia identity could not be as easily forgotten by those around him, who it seems looked upon him as a Shia posing as a Sunni: "Although I found out the mistake and worked hard to correct it, the bad name [of Ajami, Persian] stuck to me:

bazar reports fly quicker and harder than newspaper paragraphs" (*Personal Narrative*, 1: 14).

In Cairo, where Burton spent a considerable amount of time and began publicly to appear as a Pathan educated in Rangoon (the better, he said, to rationalize his linguistic and other errors), he also assumed the professional status of a hakim (doctor) and a *darwaysh*. This procured him entry—as his status as purveyor of fashions had in Sind—into private homes, including women's quarters, though his reputation for sanctity and wisdom was severely compromised on the eve of his departure by an act of public drunkenness and boisterous conduct.

The figure of the pilgrim or the religious mendicant was, or was to become, a favored disguise for other fictional and real colonial characters. Kim O'Hara, as the lama's disciple in Rudyard Kipling's novel, is an obvious instance. And, as Thomas Richards reveals to us, the secret mapping of Tibet by the British India Survey involved the deployment of Hindu pandits garbed as pilgrims, whose beads and staves served as instruments of reading and measurement. What he says about the mode of production of such knowledge is not without its applicability to the situation of someone like Burton:

> [N]ot only did [Captain] Montgomerie's [of the British India Survey] monastic technology integrate topological surveillance into the rhythm of everyday Tibetan life (thus making it also imperceptible), but it also introduced a paradigm of surveillance as a migratory phenomenon (thus rendering obsolete the fixed fortifications of blockhouse, conning tower, escarpment, and frontier). At one and the same time the Tibetan project combined an extended form of measuring extended space using body-based units of measure (as with the span and the fathom), a medieval form of clocking time by dividing the day into units of prayer (as called for by St. Benedict's *Rule*), and a modern form of vehicular surveillance by projectile (as compiled by stealth flights and satellite reconnaissance).[31]

For Burton, the assumption of *darwaysh* status was carefully thought out. As he saw it, the *darwaysh* was a figure of total subjective license in the Islamic world, bound by no orthodoxies or regulations:

> No character in the Moslem world is so proper for disguise as that of the Darwaysh. It is assumed by all ranks, ages, and creeds; . . . Further, the Darwaysh is allowed to ignore ceremony and politeness, as one who ceases to appear upon the stage of life; he may pray or not, marry or remain single as he pleases, be respectable in cloth of frieze as in cloth of gold, and no one asks him—the chartered vagabond—Why he comes here? or Wherefore he goes there?. . . . In the hour of imminent danger, he has only to become a maniac, and he is safe; a madman in the East, like a notably eccentric character in the West, is allowed to say or do whatever the spirit directs. Add to this character a little knowledge of medicine, a "moderate skill in magic, and a reputation

for caring for nothing but study and books," together with capital sufficient to save you from the chance of starving, and you appear in the East to peculiar advantage. (*Personal Narrative*, 1: 14–15)

This already available prototype allowed him an unscripted, subjective space in which he could establish his own identity as adventurer and disguise artist as well as an identity as a model—if idiosyncratic—Muslim. Edward Rice advances the thesis that Burton's pilgrimage was not, in the strictest theological sense, a transgressive act. He claims that Burton actually embraced Islam, albeit an unorthodox variety of it (he apparently became a Sufi-influenced Ismaili), and that the pilgrimage to Mecca was no more than his right as a Muslim. Rice bases the evidence of Burton's so-called conversion on his descriptions of his initiation into the Sufi brotherhood in *Sindh, and the Races That Inhabit the Valley of the Indus*. He points, too, to the fact that Burton's comments on Islam and Islamic culture were almost invariably sympathetic and respectful.[32] Such an attempt to investigate Burton's "sincerity" or to clarify his position in positivist terms seems to me not just dubious but beside the point. (I will point out, however, that no other evidence—however broadly defined—of such a conversion exists: Burton himself claims only to have been initiated into a number of exotic socioreligious fraternities, including those of the Sikhs and the Nagar Brahmans.) Certainly the speaker in all of Burton's writings—travelogues, letters, journals—positions himself always as an unassimilable subject: in relation to his metropolitan audience, he is the knowing insider who has penetrated and participated in every exotic and forbidden mystery. In relation to Islam or the Orient, he is a "Frank" who must ceaselessly and vigilantly encode his behavior within a cultural system and must keep establishing his credentials, which are, however, much more impeccable than those of the Muslims or Orientals by whom he is surrounded. It also seems to me that Burton's regard for Islam can most suggestively be read in the light not of his religious loyalties but of the opportunities it provided him to dramatize his heterogeneous affiliations in unorthodox and provocative ways.

These manipulations of subject positions need to be foregrounded in a reading of Burton's work, and Homi Bhabha's work on the unstable economies of identity production in colonial discourse allows us a way of reading Burton's impersonations. Bhabha locates in mimicry the site of an ambivalence and uncertainty that can throw into question the grounds of the entire imperial enterprise. He draws our attention to the subversive or at least the destabilizing potential of the move that reproduces asymmetrical difference under the sign of assimilation/sameness; the mimic man, the subject-in-process, functions as a supplementary instance that, far from (only) stabilizing the imperialist self, (also) interrupts its coherence through defamiliarization.[33] Thus "colonial mimicry is the desire for a reformed, recognizable Other, as *a subject of difference that is almost the same, but not quite.* Which is to say, that the discourse of mimicry is constructed around an *ambivalence;* in order to be effective, mimicry must continually produce its slippage, its excess, its difference."[34] Yet this necessary difference—which cannot be uncoupled from repetition—is itself the source of anxieties about the ontological stability of the original. Thus the mimic man, rather than simply capitulating to the colonizer's narcissistic desire to reproduce himself, articulates through an imperfect doubling, through repetition and difference, a challenge to the notion of the normative, authoritative, and reproducible colonial self even as he acquiesces to and upholds colonial authority.[35]

What happens when Bhabha's formulation of the inherent ambivalence of colonial discourse and its hybridized effects is traversed by related preoccupations and anxieties—the necessity for impersonating the native or the fear of going native? The last is of course one of the defining tropes of colonial discourse, which plays in innumerable ways with that ominous and ever-present possibility; and it meshes rather neatly with Bhabha's analysis of the colonizer's paranoid anxiety about the integrity and stability of his identity. But the project of native impersonation seems to point not to the ambivalence but to the self-possession and single-mindedness of colonial discourse; it seems to open up a different set of ontological and positional possibilities in texts like those of Burton or Kipling, reformulating the tropes of mimesis, mimicry, fluidity, and exchange. When figures like Burton or Kim O'Hara assume their disguises, they seem to do so with the fullest faith in their own unfragmented subjectivity and in their ability to disguise and conquer. Their miming of native identity is part of a successful rearguard action that not only renders the native transparent but also undoes the effects of the "sly civility" of the native (the "sly civility" that, through the process of prescriptive mimicry, re-presents or reconstructs the colonizing subject).[36]

This miming of nativeness is an imperative in several colonial texts. In speaking of the staging of cultural identity in nineteenth-century British India, Satya Mohanty points to the endeavor in Kipling to render "the white man as simultaneously invisible, or at least capable of invisibility in a context that renders him eminently spectacular."[37] This staging of the white man as invisible and inscrutable is obviously and intimately tied to the production of the native as a scrutable object. In Burton, this is typically accomplished by portraying native identity as a literal narrative of the body. For him, training as a Muslim in preparation for his pilgrimage involves making an inventory of certain elaborately ritualized behaviors and "unnatural acts":

> Look, for instance, at the Indian Moslem drinking a glass of water. With us the operation is simple enough, but his performance includes no fewer than five

novelties. In the first place he clutches his tumbler as though it were the throat of a foe; secondly, he ejaculates, "In the name of Allah the Compassionate, the Merciful!" before wetting his lips; thirdly, he imbibes the contents, swallowing them, not sipping them as he ought to do, and ending with a satisfied grunt; fourthly, before setting down the cup, he sighs forth, "Praise be to Allah!"—of which you will understand the full meaning in the Desert; and, fifthly, he replies, "May Allah make it pleasant to thee!" in answer to his friend's polite "Pleasurably and health!" Also he is careful to avoid the irreligious action of drinking the pure element in a standing position. (*Personal Narrative*, 1: 6)

Elsewhere, too, the *Personal Narrative* avers that the eastern body must be read literally, and the lower the subject on the racial-social-moral hierarchy, the more literally must the body be read. Phrenology and "physiognomy" are, for Burton, the ideal critical practice in the face of the native body; and the sacred name of Gall, the founder of the pseudoscience, is invoked as an aid in reading the features of the Badawin (*Personal Narrative*, 2: 81). While the civilized (European) body is rendered either impenetrable or at least metaphorical by the influences of civilization, the native body that is un-marked by anglicizing influences (Burton abhors the "denatured" native, and in this he is typical of many colonial officials) is available in a natural and unmediated state for scrutiny.

What are the implications of the native's seeming imitability? How do we read the multiple and contradictory valences of disguise, mimicry, and/or impersonation in the field of colonial discourse? On the one hand Burton's easy transition between varied identities underwrites imperialism's avowal of faith in a stable and coherent colonial self that can resist the potential pollutions of this trafficking in native identity. If the colonial self is stable and unassailable, then it might be expected to follow by the logic of impe-rialism that the native self is, like all the blank or dark spots on the map, a void, an uninscribed and infinitely malleable space. The native can thus be made over in the image of the colonizer. Not only this, the colonizer can in turn simulate the native in a movement that Kaja Silverman designates, in the instance of the T. E. Lawrence of *Seven Pillars of Wisdom*, a "double mimesis."[38]

It is important at this point to specify the manifold implications of double mimesis, to note the disjunctions between Burton's miming and Lawrence's. In Silverman's reading of *Seven Pillars*, Lawrence offers himself up as a para-gon of essentially Arab heroism to his Arab followers: "Lawrence suggests in that text [*Twenty-Seven Articles*] that the best way to lead is to constitute one-self as an ideal within the terms of the native culture—to outdo the Arabs in representing 'Arabness,' becoming in the process a standard to follow."[39] Burton's objectives in the other-producing strategy called double mimesis are in effect similar, though he does not spell them out as seemingly self-

consciously as Lawrence does. But both the conditions of his impersonation and the epistemic parameters of his "identities" are very differently
constituted from the way they are in Lawrence; he deploys a radically different technology of representation. Lawrence was very obviously and
openly an Englishman in Arabia; despite his putative popularity among the
rebel soldiers or his assumption of Arab clothing, it would have been, from
the evidence of his writing, extremely difficult (for Englishmen or Arabs) to
(mis)recognize him as an Arab. His erotic and masochistic investment in
Arab masculinity also may have created a dynamic of masquerade that, one
imagines, must have been conspicuously different from the conditions that
obtained for his nineteenth-century predecessor.

Burton, unlike Lawrence, has an ethnographer's curiosity about the
"mysteries" of Islam; his public identity as Englishman has to be methodi-
cally and thoroughly erased in order to guarantee the authenticity of all that
he observes. At the same time, the *Personal Narrative* is even more the story
of "Shaykh Abdullah" than it is the story of Muslim pilgrimage; the narrator
has to be both voyeur and exhibitionist at the same time, enacting a more
embellished and legitimate Muslim identity than those "real" Muslims
around him even as he takes great pains to observe their behaviors without
exposing himself. Thus Burton, hoping to pass for a Muslim making a pilgrimage to Mecca, is never content to blend in, to be inconspicuous, to be
one of the crowd. In a situation that would appear to call for self-effacement
more than anything else, he stages his identity in the most flamboyant of
ways, constantly drawing the attention of his Muslim companions to his
learning, his linguistic facility, his skill with medicine, his sexual charm, and
his unusual courage. He corrects Muslim divines on points of Koranic law,
performs "miracles" when the ship to Mecca is mired in mud, calls ostentatiously for food in the midst of an attack by the Badawin, and flirts conspicuously with the wives of patients, noting with delight his companions' comments about "the Afghan Haji's obstinacy and recklessness." He has, as Said
points out, a percipient understanding of the fact that identity is the result
of one's mastery over particular systems of signification: "All of his vast information about the Orient, which dots every page he wrote, reveals that he
knew the Orient in general and Islam in particular were systems of information, behavior, and belief, that to be an Oriental or a Muslim was to know
certain things in a certain way, and that these were of course subject to history, geography, and the development of society in circumstances specific
to it."[40] His moment of greatest tension—and triumph—occurs when he
meets a "real" Pathan, who he fears might unmask him. Instead, the Pathan,
asked to guess Burton's nationality, identifies him as a fellow Pathan. He is
also triumphant—though less so—at those moments when other Englishmen take him for a native; Burton desired not simply to pass for a native in

the east but also to have it suspected in England that he had actually gone native and that he had put a dangerous distance between himself and the cultural appurtenances of the west, particularly "civilization" and Christianity.

There is more at work here than just a sensational display of Burton's manipulation of identity through his proficiency in eastern languages and vast knowledge of Muslim culture. The point is not only to blend in but to stand out, not only to see but also to be seen—and to be seen as one *wishes* to be seen. Burton seeks to create in the process of display a model of native behavior for natives to admire and imitate; hence the acts of representation that will establish him as both actor and creator of native identity. Thus, while anglicized natives (who are always presumed to be male) are capable only of imperfect acts of mimesis that point to their condition of perpetual lack, they themselves are entirely imitable by the colonizer. The colonizer in fact can enact the natives better than the natives can simply be themselves; double mimesis allows the natives to be interpellated as natives, not just as mimic men. It is no coincidence that this process conforms in many ways (though without the important mediating process of mimicry) to the anthropological/ethnographic mode, in which a native informant reproduces for the benefit of the ethnographer the information about indigenous societies that was generated by the discipline in the first place.[41] Burton was, we might remember, one of the pioneers of the discipline of anthropology, helping to found, along with James Hunt, the Anthropological Society of London in 1863 and delivering several papers before its members in his capacity as one of the society's "lions."[42]

It should be clear by now that this double mimesis differs at important points from Lawrence's. In Silverman's reading, there is a distinct and an external racial Other whom Lawrence essentializes and in whom he can misrecognize himself, an Other who is substantialized in figures like Feisal and Ali ibn el Hussein.[43] This Arabness or otherness is separate from and anterior to his arrival on the Arab scene. Burton, on the other hand, resemanticizes—instead of simply imitating—native or, more properly, Muslim (these categories often function as one in Burton) identity; it is not possible for the native to be properly a native, to have access to a subject position as native, without imitating Burton. Part of this drive to call Muslimness into being must have derived from Burton's own powerful (if equivocal) identification with Arab culture and with Islam; Patrick Brantlinger comments that "Burton's ideal Arab is an idealized self-portrait."[44] However, there is, for Burton, no essential—that is to say, unique, unchanging, and ahistorical—native identity since it can be reconfigured, revised, and re-presented by him. (British identity is not an issue in the same way, though, as we shall see, it is by no means unproblematic.) What is designated native identity, then, is an act, an impersonation—but with important qualifications. Manipulation, play, and impersonation are only available to those on the *right* side of the colonial divide. So for the native, identity, while not essential in the usual sense of the word—since it can be and is subject to colonial dislocation and manipulation—is not an act; natives are denied irony or distance with respect to their identity. Each new identity created for them by the colonizer or the colonial situation becomes in turn essential for them; theoretically they could occupy a series of essential identities in response to the models offered by the colonial state or its emissaries (like Burton).

Somewhat uneasily linked to this notion of native permeability, malleability, and lack of essence is the notion that the native is an opaque entity who must be known, categorized, and fixed in the most complete way possible. But while natives have a capacity (an imperfect one) for mimicry, they have no capacity for self-examination or self-representation or for offering up their subjectivity in any way that will usefully mesh with the colonizer's various information systems. So, while "[c]olonial power produces the colonized as a social reality which is at once an 'other' and yet entirely knowable and visible,"[45] it is nonetheless a system of representation that simultaneously entertains a profound anxiety about the native's slipperiness and inscrutability. It is in order to constitute the native, then, as a *knowable* entity that impersonation, surveillance, and interpellation by a colonial observer are necessary; the last procedure would in fact banish the necessity for surveillance altogether. Even the native informant is not to be trusted (not in Burton's narrative, at least) in this enterprise of making the racial Other transparent, not the least because the native informant is often the anglicized, upper-class native who is most conversant with the codes constituting colonial selfhood and thus supremely in a position to order and control the flow of colonial knowledge. In Kipling, the collaborationist native of Macaulay's fantasy has been transformed into the Bengali babu. It is almost always the babu—the subject who, because of his education, class position, and racial identity, is the most appropriate candidate for the position of native informant—who is the most sinister of all anticolonial forces. The impersonation of the native by the colonizer is thus deployed as the most appropriate heuristic device in a context that relies on the contradictory—and unstable—tropes of native permeability and native resistance to definition.

What emerges is the following equivocatory notion: the native is without history and identity (that is, without any significant subjective autonomy and without any of the psychosocial components that might complicate the work of colonial interpellation) and capable of radical reconstitution by the colonizer; since the native does not possess a stable and coherent self, s/he can be easily imitated by the colonizer; the native is also opaque and secretive and resistant to rendering her/himself accountable to western modes of reportage. Hence individuals like Burton must insinuate themselves into eastern life in order to render it accountable.

The assumption of such a subject position has, however, some decentering implications for the hegemony of the colonial self, as it becomes evident
that Englishness and nativeness are part of a single signifying chain and that
each forms the other's horizon. In Burton the schoolboy glee at being able
to hoodwink the natives is generally paramount, though at various points
the process of endless impersonation and exchange is problematized and
made inseparable from a profound sense of ontological incompleteness. In
later years Burton was to speak of this desire to splurge in a constant flux of
identities as constituting for him a somewhat embarrassing psychic need:

> I can scarcely persuade myself that great events are brought about by mere im-
> posture, whose very nature is feebleness: zeal, enthusiasm, fanaticism, which
> are of their nature strong and aggressive, better explain the abnormal action
> of man on man. On the other hand it is impossible to ignore the dear delights
> of fraud and deception, the hourly pleasure taken by some minds in finessing
> through life, and in playing a part till by habit it becomes nature.[46]

We see here, quite clearly, I think, Burton's sense of the contradictions of his
position—not just his sense, for instance, of the discrepancy between the
heroic male action of imperial conquest and the feminizing pursuit of deception and indirection that is supposed to assist and even authorize the imperial project but also his sense of a somewhat disconcerting confusion of
selves and roles. Englishness here is nothing other than the capacity for the
impersonation of non-Englishness, even as native identity has proved to be
only that which is not English.

What is also worthy of note is the fact that despite Burton's drive to name
Muslimness and nativeness as his own creation rather than a category that
might be at least provisionally indigenous and despite his insistence on out-
doing natives at being natives, he must always occupy a space on the margins
of the discourse he wishes to recast.[47] As a "half-Arab, half-Persian" merchant in Sind, he is an outsider who can pass as an Oriental because little
is known about the national/ethnic, linguistic, and other categories he supposedly inhabits. He must depend to some degree on local ignorance of
"the real thing." Similarly, in Hejaz and Arabia he can be an outsider once
more, this time a Pathan; wherever he goes, he signifies a pervasive liminality, if not a pervasive alterity. As a native, he is both familiar and alien;
and all imperfections in knowledge, language, and other behaviors can be
the function of his always being from "somewhere else." Note, too, that the
fantasy of the (English) man who can be all things to all people, as well as
the liminal figure who is neither outside nor inside, must borrow its model
from Sufism. The figure of the *darwaysh* is a peculiarly privileged one in the
Islamic world, a figure representing scholarly curiosity, mobility, and freedom from all provincial constraints.

What also needs to be stressed is the way in which these manipulations and self-dramatizations are subtended by, or in dialectical relationship with, a keen sense of anxiety—anxiety about native inscrutability, insurgency, and threats to personal safety. The sense, however temporary, of mastery achieved by Lawrence through reflexive masochism and double mimesis is never fully achieved for Burton; colonial mastery is never fully or convincingly stabilized. There is the profound insecurity and uncertainty that authorizes the miming of native identity in the first place; if natives were transparent they would not require scrutiny and interpellation. Besides, there is always the fear, in the *Personal Narrative*, that the natives might be observing Burton, rather than he them. His attendant Mohammed al-Basyuni ("the boy Mohammed") identifies him unerringly as a white man upon the chance discovery of his instruments and has to be argued out of this belief by the other pilgrims. On the road to Medina Burton feels himself watched during his (ritual) ablutions and prayers (*Personal Narrative*, 1: 168); at other moments he has to evade inquisitive and observant companions. Moreover, while Burton (and his companions) may be convinced of the effectuality of his performance as native, there is always the fear that he may be the wrong kind of native, and he often needs advice from friendly natives before and during his pilgrimage about the ethnic and professional roles he should assume. His initial and ill-conceived assumption of Persian (Shia, that is, and therefore heretical in Sunni Hejaz and Arabia) identity dogs him all the way from Egypt to Mecca, reminding him of the limits of his enterprise, just as he is identified as a detested Turk in East Africa, where he wishes to pass for an Arab.[48] In Mecca he is drawn into conversation with some Meccans, who concur in their conviction of his being Persian. And at the conclusion of the pilgrimage, Mohammed once again, and most categorically, names him as a sahib, an incident that raises interesting questions about what passes for success in Burton's account of his pilgrimage. By the time he boards a ship to return to Suez, he is marked as "an Englishman rumoured to have gone to the Holy City" (*Personal Narrative*, 2: 276) and is bemused by the failure of the Turkish pilgrims on board to respond in an appropriately hostile fashion to this report.

Burton himself seems fairly self-conscious about his anxieties, which are repeatedly invoked and displaced. These anxieties are often mediated, unsurprisingly enough, by memories of India. In an early footnote he says of the British presence there:

> As regards Indian opinion concerning our government, my belief is, that in and immediately about the three presidencies, where the people owe everything to and hold everything by our rule, it is most popular. At the same time I am convinced that in other places the people would most willingly hail any change. And how can we hope it to be otherwise,—we, a nation of strangers, aliens to the country's customs and creed, who, even while resident in India, act the part which absentees do in other lands? Where, in the history of the

world, do we read that such foreign dominion ever made itself loved? (*Personal Narrative*, 1: 37–38, n. 1)

Not coincidentally, this is followed by a footnote (added to the second edition of *Personal Narrative* in 1879) about the Indian Mutiny of 1857. Clearly, India must have been very much on Burton's mind as he made this pilgrimage; he had spent a good part of his adult life there, and, once in West Asia, he decided that he could most safely and convincingly assume the role of a Pathan apothecary raised in India. The matter of India thus becomes an important subtext to the account of Burton's presence in the Muslim holy land. His skills as a disguise artist, undercover agent, and ethnographer are corroborated by repeated invocations of his ethnography of Sind, undertaken at Napier's behest in the interest of surveying and pacifying a turbulent—and recently colonized—population. Hejaz and Arabia reminded him at every turn of his years in Sind (as Sind—so named after its conquest as "Young Egypt" on account of its putative fertility—was to evoke a land he had never seen). The memory of India, which on this pilgrimage became the memory of the familiar, the memory of a colonial home as it were, must also be seen at the same time as a psychic device for territorializing the unfamiliar.

In speaking of the Indians, Burton makes an interesting point about staging the colonial identity for the benefit of the natives:

> I am convinced that the natives of India cannot respect a European who mixes with them familiarly, or especially who imitates their customs, manners, and dress. The tight pantaloons, the authoritative voice, the pococurante manner, and the broken Hindustani imposes upon them—have a weight which learning and honesty, which wit and courage, have not. This is to them the master's attitude: they bend to it like those Scythian slaves that faced the sword but fled from the horsewhip. (*Personal Narrative*, 1: 40)

The man who would be king must constitute himself as a spectacle for an adoring native audience. The civilizing mission demands the careful maintenance of nonpermeable boundaries. Difference and discipline are thus maintained as part of the same process. Imitating the native as, presumably, East India Company officials in the eighteenth century were in the habit of doing,[49] is inadvisable because the Indian does not acknowledge innate superiority: s/he reads the colonizer's body absolutely literally. It is possible to read in this an anxiety about what it is that constitutes British superiority, since it must be so zealously guarded and embedded in precise systems of signification. Can this superiority inhere in nothing more than appearances? And if imitation is not the proper role for the Englishman in the tropics, then what can be said about Burton's own subject position? Burton of course is careful to distinguish himself from the great body of colonial administrators—"what might be perilous to other [European] travellers was safe to me," he boasts at the start of his narrative. Thus his tale presents itself to us as the story of one man's unduplicable encounter with the inscrutability of Islam and the Orient. He feels that he alone can *be* a native as successfully as he is a sahib. He is capable of a fungibility of identity that can deceive the natives as well as preserve the prestige of the empire.

In Egypt and in Arabia, though, Burton is reminded continually of the double-edged implications of this fungibility through his evocations of his Indian experience. The subject of India arouses a fairly acute anxiety, an anxiety that is generally displaced onto Indian subjects. The Indian (for the British imagination in the nineteenth century, the quintessential colonial subject) is identified as "the most antipathetical companion to an Englishman"; s/he is the practitioner of a "sly civility," wily, slippery, discontented, outwardly subservient but always in anticipation of "a general Bartholomew's Day in the East, . . . look[ing] forward to the hour when enlightened Young India will arise and drive the 'foul invader' from the land" (*Personal Narrative*, 1: 38). Even the reported Anglomania of a British ally like Ranjit Singh is simply a cover for the most treacherous designs. In a later, related footnote, Burton remarks: "This was written three years before the Indian Mutiny. I also sent into the Court of Directors a much stronger report—for which I duly suffered" (*Personal Narrative*, 1: 38, n. 1). Burton loved to embellish his narratives with proofs of his own prescience and complaints of ill-usage from Philistine superiors. The question of whether or not Burton was a good prophet is not, however, relevant here, nor do I think the question a particularly compelling one. The fact is that, no matter where Burton traveled in Asia or Africa, he always found proofs of various kinds testifying to the rebellious and hostile spirit of the native population. In his account of Goa he had voiced his certainty about impending Indian violence against their English rulers; and toward the end of the *Personal Narrative* there is a footnote that claims to have anticipated the 1858 "Jeddah massacre" of Europeans and Christians. In *The Lake Regions of Central Africa* (1860), that account of the journey to the source of the White Nile, the murder of a European provides the impetus to narrative, and reminders of this murder resurface periodically over the course of the work. This testifies less to oracular or prognosticative abilities than to a profound, indeed almost a paranoid, anxiety about the British presence in the colonies, a presence which is indissociable from an ur-text of native violence and insurgency that threatens to repeat itself endlessly in colonial history. Besides, this construction of the native as an always potentially murderous subject nudges the reader toward reading the protagonist's actions in a particular register, translating espionage into besieged heroism. An encounter with the east that is traversed by fear and threat may establish the power of the east and its capacity to deflate grandiloquent imperial pretensions. What it also does is name the east as aggressor, opposing itself to what is constructed, as Mary Louise Pratt reminds us, as "a non-interventionist European presence."[50]

But the specter of a reversal of the balance of power in colonial relations is no sooner raised than it is framed, distanced, and rendered absurd. Burton thus fixes the "bombastic Babu" with his nationalist pretensions within a moral-racial hierarchy that forecloses on the possibility of the babu's success. He turns for support—as he will continually during his pilgrimage—to the textual evidences of Orientalism, invoking a talismanic name that immediately guarantees its truth value and reinforces Said's point that the accuracy of Orientalist textual representations was validated above all by ascertaining their correspondence with the works of other Orientalists:[51]

> As my support against the possible, or rather the probable, imputation of "extreme opinions," I hold up the honoured name of the late Sir Henry Elliot. . . . "These idle vapourers (bombastic Babus, and other such political ranters), should learn that the sacred spark of patriotism is exotic here, and can never fall on a mine that can explode; for history will show them that certain peculiarities of physical, as well as moral organisation, neither to be strengthened by diet nor improved by education, have hitherto prevented their ever attempting a national independence; which will continue to exist to them but as a name, and as an offscouring of college declamations." (*Personal Narrative*, 1: 40–41, n. 2)

Nonetheless, in spite of the dexterous textual management of the babu's anticolonial and nationalist pretensions, the text continues to register a very precise sense of the writer's vulnerability. The delight in disguise, in playacting, and in deceiving others is inevitably bound up with reminders that this is more than a game; if it is a game it is the kind of Great Game that is played in *Kim*, where the penalties for failure may be fatal. The anxieties Burton expresses about the British presence in India must have been multiplied enormously in Mecca and Medina. He was, as he conceived it, engaging in an act of explicit territorial and psychic aggression by which he sought to force the Muslim world to submit to a series of hermeneutic violations. The narrative predictably oscillates between a gusto at the success of various maneuverings and stratagems by which its author bested the entire east and an extreme and anguished sense of vulnerability. Throughout there is close attention to the details of disguise, to all the manipulations of the body (including circumcision), to all those ceremonies that permit European man to offer himself up as a simulacrum of the Muslim without actually surrendering identificatory autonomy.

The various extended descriptions of the stratagems Burton had to employ in order to make notes and sketches also register this equivocal sense of mastery and threat. Arabs are represented as innately suspicious of activities like note taking, measurement, mapmaking, and surveying, an attitude Burton attributes to ignorance and superstition:

> Pilgrims, . . . carry, I have said, a "Hamail," to denote their holy errand. This is a pocket Koran, in a handsome gold-embroidered crimson velvet or red morocco case, slung by red silk cords over the left shoulder. . . . For this I substituted a most useful article. To all appearance a "Hamail," it had inside three compartments; one for my watch and compass, the second for ready money, and the third contained penknife, pencils, and slips of paper, which I could hold concealed in the hollow of my hand. These were for writing and drawing: opportunities of making a "fair copy" into the diary-book, are never wanting to the acute traveller. He must, however, beware of sketching before the Badawin, who would certainly proceed to extreme measures, suspecting him to be a spy or a sorcerer. Nothing so effectually puzzles these people as the Frankish habit of putting everything on paper; their imaginations are set to work, and then the worst may be expected from them. The only safe way of writing in the presence of a Badawi would be when drawing out a horoscope or preparing a charm; he also objects not, if you can warm his heart upon the subject, to seeing you take notes in a book of genealogies. (*Personal Narrative*, 1: 239–40)

Not all suspicion can be so ingeniously circumvented. Note the following observation, one among many that testifies rather querulously to the Arab/Muslim dislike of being observed and catalogued: "A stranger must be careful how he appears at a minaret window, unless he would have a bullet whizzing past his head. Arabs are especially jealous of being overlooked, and have no fellow-feeling for votaries of 'beautiful views.' For this reason here, as in Egypt, a blind Mu'ezzin is preferred, and many ridiculous stories are told about men who for years have counterfeited cecity to live in idleness" (*Personal Narrative*, 2: 318). The connections that are gestured at here, between colonial sight and oversight, are a not uncommon feature of colonial travel literature. Pratt describes a characteristic placement of the observer in such writing, a placement she reads as central to "the monarch-of-all-I-survey scene."[52] In such a scene, and in such a position, the observer can subject the circumambient landscape to an endless and all-encompassing gaze. Moreover, such a posture can without any obvious strain be absorbed into the discourse of aesthetics and Romantic conceptualizations of landscape. Thus, Burton implies, it is not simply the western traveler ("a stranger") who is denied access to a panoptical vision; access is denied as well to easterners, who have then to resort to trickery to obtain their ends.

Yet Burton seems fully capable of eluding the putative paranoia of the Arabs. When he actually gains entrance, through the intercession of his attendant, the boy Mohammed, to the Kaaba itself (not a routine part by any means of the ordinary Muslim's pilgrimage, as he is careful to inform his readers) he acknowledges fear openly—"my feelings were of the trapped-rat description" (*Personal Narrative*, 2: 207)—but is still collected enough to continue on his mission: "This did not, however, prevent my carefully observing the scene during our long prayers, and making a rough plan with a pencil upon my white Ihram [pilgrim's robe]" (*Personal Narrative*, 2: 207).

What, moreover, we are never allowed to forget is Burton's own separation from the collective cultural experience of pilgrimage.[53] This experience, however persistently coded as authentic, is always also raw material to be organized into a narrative for Orientalists, ethnographers, and the reading public in England. Indeed, when Burton is face to face with the Kaaba, he is not overcome as the other pilgrims apparently are by a sense of religious awe (though he does hint, significantly, that his emotional response to the sight of the shrine is deeper and richer than theirs); he is filled instead with a sense of mastery and of his difference from all his companions:

> There at last it lay, the bourn of my long and weary pilgrimage, realising the plans and hopes of many and many a year. . . . and how few have looked upon the celebrated shrine! I may truly say that, of all the worshippers who clung weeping to the curtains, or who pressed their beating hearts to the stone, none felt for the moment a deeper emotion than did the Haji from the far-north. It was as if the poetical legends of the Arab spoke truth, and that the waving wings of angels, not the sweet breeze of morning, were agitating and swelling the black covering of the shrine. But, to confess humbling truth, theirs was the high feeling of religious enthusiasm, mine was the ecstasy of gratified pride. (*Personal Narrative*, 2: 179)

The trope of dual cultural and racial citizenship is staged and restaged by Burton, only to unravel at moments like these. Thus, when he enters Medina, he is momentarily moved, like his companions, at the sight of the city, but soon the traveler's duties of observing, measuring, and recording reassert their preeminence. At the sight/site of the Kaaba, this breakdown is complete. He can only view the shrine in the light of the discoverer's prize; Mecca becomes, like the European maps of Arabia, a blank space emptied of history and human presence (except his own). All his fellow pilgrims and friends are swallowed up by the margins, and all that is left is the romantic colonial *tableau vivant* in which the explorer sees, names, and claims the east for the first time. Even as he penetrates the Forbidden City, he proleptically envisages the enactment of the British imperial design—"It requires not the ken of a prophet to foresee the day when political necessity . . . will compel us to occupy in force the fountain-head of Al-Islam" (*Personal Narrative*, 2: 231). Later he contemplates the extinction of the slave trade in Mecca— to Burton always a synecdoche for imperial intervention and the deployment of the civilizing mission—and delights in the fact that none of his companions suspects him of such subversive thoughts.

Burton, though, is rarely as explicit as he is here about the appropriation of the holy places of Islam for the British Empire. What we are given instead is a variety of legends about the impending desecration or takeover of Mecca by infidel forces: "almost every Meccan knows the prophecy of Mohammed, that the birthplace of his faith will be destroyed by an army from Abyssinia. Such things bring their own fulfilment" (*Personal Narrative*, 2: 323, n. 2). Muslim legend writes itself here as congruent with British imperial ambitions. It is worth noting that all these prophecies of defeat are located in the body of the text, whereas the statement of imperial aims is written almost as a footnote, *in* the footnotes, and in a manner which preempts British intentionality and makes the British simply the agents of world-historical processes: "till the day shall come when the tide of events forces us to occupy the mother-city of Al-Islam" (*Personal Narrative*, 2: 268, n. 2).

This vision of the overthrow of the Arabs is positioned, appropriately, at the conclusion of the *Personal Narrative*, and it provides the most apposite of codas for the profoundly self-referential narrative of the double mimesis. Earlier in his account Burton had mentioned Egypt's special qualities as the "most tempting prize which the East holds out to the ambition of Europe" (*Personal Narrative*, 1: 114), though with characteristic ambivalence he had noted the inhabitants' "contradictory" loathing of the Europeans (especially the English) and their "long[ing]" for European rule. Here Burton's (re)production of an idealized eastern subject position becomes even more comprehensive and ambitious in its reach at this moment of projected closure, as he recasts himself as more than just an agent of British imperial destiny. Hitherto he has exhibited himself as both the originator and the model of nativeness; here he positions himself as the interpreter par excellence of the texts of the Arabs, texts that encouragingly mirror imperial fantasies of aggrandizement and prefigure a colonial history that can only have one trajectory. In such a scenario, neither natives nor their futurity can hold any mysteries: they can but inhabit identities and destinies constituted elsewhere, but they must nonetheless claim that destiny as their own. The ultimate aim of colonial mimicry is not simply to constitute natives as objects to be studied; it must also produce natives as self-reflexive subjects, who know themselves as others (the colonizers) know them. What Gayatri Spivak terms the "territorial and subject-constituting project"[54] of colonialism is authorized in this Whiggish invocation of Arab prophecies and the Arab collective memory, which demand nothing less than the imperial yoke. What Burton envisions, in other words, is the mapping of British India onto the to-be-British territories of Egypt and Arabia. What had occasionally proved for him an uncomfortable fit between the psychic and territorial space called India and the territory of Al-Islam (including Egypt, Aden, Hejaz, and Arabia), the former inviting disidentification, if not outright revulsion, while the latter was not without a powerful appeal to his sense of an intensely masculist honor, is, temporarily at least, held in abeyance at this moment.

The use of the Arab prophecies as the figuring of the legitimacy of colonialism is an arresting exercise, one that surely calls for a gloss, however brief. For this I turn to Dipesh Chakrabarty, whose compelling discussion of the "failure" of modernity in postcolonial India, albeit about a later and quite different moment in colonial history, resonates with the one under consideration in this chapter. In "Postcoloniality and the Artifice of History," he speaks persuasively of the differences between a bourgeois and a colonial (in his case, Indian) modernity. Among other things, he calls our attention to the "antihistorical and antimodern" elements in the latter; he takes note for instance of the "devices of collective memory," including subaltern and elite constructions of "'mythical' pasts/futures," which were deployed by (colonial) Indians in the process of claiming subjecthood.[55] What the instance of the *Personal Narrative* would suggest is that such modes of remembering/foretelling are also, (perhaps) paradoxically, a staple of the teleology of a bourgeois (and colonizing) modernity, which demands the "premodern" and "mythic" as a condition of the narrative of history and universal reason. Burton must remember an Arab past in order to imagine a British imperial futurity.

TWO

Discovering India, Imagining *Thuggee*

I am a Thug, my father and grandfather were Thugs, and I have thugged with
many. Let the government employ me and I will do its work.
CONFESSION OF THE THUG BUKHTAWAR IN JAMES SLEEMAN,
THUG, OR A MILLION MURDERS

He had met hundreds of other Deceivers, and the notes were a complete tale of all
he had seen and heard and done; of all the Deceivers who had engaged in any
action, with their descriptions, habits, and homes; of each murder, and how it had
gone, and how it might have been prevented—or improved upon. The words could
be read for either purpose, according to the spirit of the reader.
JOHN MASTERS, *THE DECEIVERS*

At the time that Burton was impersonating Mirza Abdullah in the bazaars of
Sind, another important narrative of disguise, surveillance, and racial crossing was being written in the subcontinent, this one under the auspices of the
Thuggee and Dacoity Department of the East India Company's government.
This was the narrative of the exposure and extirpation of a form of hereditary criminality called *thuggee;* it was to form a significant constitutive component of the authoritarian and interventionary reform of the 1830s and
1840s and to contribute to the still-emerging project of "discovering India."
"It was with the flourish of mystery unveiled and mastered," writes a contemporary historian, "that a group of officers of the Political Department
had lobbied for special operations against [a] 'murderous fraternity' and
for special laws to deal with it."[1] It is that tale of *thuggee* that this chapter will
take up, at least in part as a counterpoint to the Burtonian record of the Englishman as native. It examines the phenomenon designated *thuggee* by colonial authority in nineteenth-century India, a phenomenon whose emergence, codification, and overthrow was to become perhaps *the* founding
moment for the study of indigenous criminality, as a problem of impersonation, visibility, and the transactions of reading. I use the example of *thuggee*
to explore one of the various and often mutually discontinuous kinds of
identities that were created, fixed, or rendered ambivalent for Indian colonial subjects. In approaching the problematic of *thuggee* in the colonial context through the optic of identity formation and subjection, I broach a
nexus of concerns that cohere around the epistemes of representation and

knowledge: the problematic of the formation of colonial knowledge, the contested, changing, and uneven definitions of law, order, criminality, and reform in early-nineteenth-century India, the theorization of colonial identities (Indian and British), and the discursive problems associated with generating the moral subject of the civilizing mission of British colonialism.

This chapter has three sections, with significant amounts of overlap. The first examines the official records of the Thuggee and Dacoity Department (first established in the 1830s), a cluster of documents that I have perhaps rather arbitrarily designated the *thuggee* archive. This includes first and foremost the files on *thuggee* and dacoity in the India Office Library and the National Archives of India. Also incorporated in this *thuggee* archive are the works (*Ramaseeana, or a Vocabulary of the Peculiar Language Used by the Thugs* [1836]; *Report on Budhuk Alias Bagree Dacoits and Other Gang Robbers by Hereditary Profession* [1849]; *Report on the Depredations Committed by the Thug Gangs* [1840]) of William Henry Sleeman of *thuggee* fame, as well as of other officials associated directly or indirectly with the antithug campaign: James Sleeman, *Thug, or A Million Murders* (1920); Charles Hervey, *Some Records of Crime* (1892); Edward Thornton, *Illustrations of the History and Practices of the Thugs* (1837); and the anonymously authored *The Thugs or Phansigars of India* (1839), an abridged version of the *Ramaseeana* for an American audience. This inventory of *thuggee* materials also includes a number of biographies, fictionalizations, and nonofficial accounts of the "discovery" of the phenomenon and its eradication: James Hutton, *A Popular Account of the Thugs and Dacoits, the Hereditary Garroters and Gang-Robbers of India* (1857); A. J. Wightman, *No Friend for Travellers* (1959); George Bruce, *The Stranglers: The Cult of Thuggee and Its Overthrow in British India* (1968); Francis Tuker, *The Yellow Scarf* (1961); and Philip Meadows Taylor, *Confessions of a Thug* (1839). These are collectively designated the archive in this chapter, despite the incommensurability in their generic status; this has been done because there appears to be very little significant difference between one text and another in this collection. Each seems to repeat the others in an uncanny fashion; each narrates the same incidents in almost exactly the same rhetorical mode; and each looks to W. H. Sleeman's productions as the founding texts of the *thuggee* narrative. (Meadows Taylor's novel differs from these only in its focus on a single thug and its accumulation of additional [fictional] detail.)

The second section focuses on the special juridical procedures that had to be instituted in order to deal with some of the most intractable problems associated with a bizarre and enigmatic variety of criminality. The final section provides a reading of the 1952 work on the thugs by John Masters, *The Deceivers*, a novel that was popularized in the 1980s in a film of that name by Merchant Ivory. What sets this novel apart from the rest of the archive is the turn it gives to the always already familiar narrative of *thuggee* through its focus on the tensions of the investigating subject and its interest in the *English* impersonation of Indianness and Englishness. It allows us a way of (re)visiting and (re)inflecting the *thuggee* archive through its stress on the colonizing male's desires and identifications, and thus forms an apposite corollary to the accent on Indian impersonation that informs the discourse of criminal law.

At this point I should add a note about the limits of the enterprise undertaken in this chapter. In the first place, I do not wish to furnish another account of *thuggee* or to enter the traffic in competing narratives of what might have constituted a material thug organization or practice. Nor am I interested in reinscribing the practices of the thugs in the register of subaltern insurgency, though, given that subalternity is most properly construed as a *relational* rather than an essential category,[2] I am not unwilling to grant the thugs' subaltern status. I am certainly sympathetic to Ranajit Guha's model of reading subaltern insurgency (as a "turning things upside down") through the texts of counterinsurgency.[3] But, given the exclusions listed earlier in this paragraph, for me to read *thuggee* as resistive, anticolonial, protonationalist, or even antistate may be philosophically not discontinuous with the reading practices that produced the thug as a demonized and completely irrational entity. My object here is not to recuperate a subaltern consciousness, even one that is acknowledged to be ineluctably discursive, "a theoretical fiction to entitle the project of reading,"[4] though I concede that the question of "subaltern consciousness" cannot be completely bypassed.

I shall confine myself instead to examining the performative subjectivity of the thug, as it is constructed in the discourse of *thuggee*, as a way of teasing out, extending, and transforming some of the implications of representation, mimicry, and visibility in the colonial context. What I will engage are the models of reading that are provided by the *thuggee* archives—how they are formed, consolidated, or (partially) interrupted. And what I do argue is that the reading of the uncovering of *thuggee* as an enabling moment for the colonial state in its quest for the consolidation of judicial power needs to be, if not displaced, at least complicated, by the acknowledgment that *thuggee* forms an especially intransigent moment within the colonial construction of criminality; it is a moment that confounds and unsettles the received wisdom about identity formation, truth production, and meliorative possibilities in early-nineteenth-century India. What I also argue is that the discourse on and around *thuggee* can be instrumental in opening up our present understanding of the theorization of colonial identity, especially as it engages questions of familiarity, visibility, and reproducibility. The text of *thuggee* provides, for instance, a point of entry into a wider range of mimic desires, identifications, and positions than someone like Bhabha explicitly engages[5]—for instance, the colonizer's fascination with going native, the

English miming of Englishness, or the indigenous miming of indigenous subject positions—as well as foregrounding questions of class, gender, and sexuality.

THE THUG

The first thugs were not arrested by the British until 1799, after the defeat at Seringapatam of Tipu Sultan, one of the most potent threats to the expansionist ambitions of the East India Company; it was not evident to the British at the time, though, that the stranglers were thugs or hereditary killers. The first mention of the law-and-order problem posed by thugs occurs in 1810, in the commander-in-chief's instructions to sepoys proceeding on leave about the dangers of traveling at night and carrying large sums of cash instead of bills of exchange;[6] but *thuggee* as a significant social arrangement or discursive formation does not feature in this caution to the sepoys. Thornton reproduces some correspondence between British magistrates and police officials of the Western Provinces in the years 1814–1816 on the subject of thugs; at this point knowledge about them appears very fragmentary, with no reference to shared religious rituals or language or an idiosyncratic form of murder. It appears that the notion of *thuggee* as a system rather than a disarticulated set of violent acts was first broached in 1816 by Dr. Richard Sherwood, who wrote an essay detailing its genealogy, organization, and argot for the *Madras Literary Gazette*.[7] It proved, however, enormously difficult to compel belief in the existence of such a fraternity (this was to remain a problem in the decades to come), even among British political officers, magistrates, and law-enforcement officials. Meadows Taylor describes the capture of large numbers of thugs in Bundelkhand and Malwa in the 1820s, an event that failed to "[excite] more than a passing share of public attention."[8] It was not until Captain W. H. Sleeman undertook the exercise of decoding and exposing *thuggee* in 1830, after the unexpected confession of the captured bandit Feringheea, that a grand narrative of *thuggee* began to emerge.

Despite this relatively recent discovery, however, *thuggee* as praxis and as identity was always represented as being of almost inconceivable antiquity, conceived in the precolonial past and sanctioned by long duration and popular Hindu mythology, if not textual doctrine. A. J. Wightman, echoing his nineteenth-century predecessors, asserts that though evidence of the existence of *thuggee* is first found in records of the late thirteenth century, "it is obvious that they must have been well-established at a much earlier date."[9] Some writers, like Sherwood, traced its origins to the Arab, Afghan, and Mughal conquests of India of several centuries earlier; James Sleeman and others traced the thugs back to the times of Herodotus. The thug Feringheea is said to have claimed that the sculptures at Ellora, which included representations of all the professions on earth, featured a depiction of a thug ply-ing his deadly trade.[10] All the reports without exception demonstrate a tena-cious need to generate a creation myth, to locate not just a point of discov-ery but a point of origin, and to establish a precolonial genealogy. But at the beginning, as Geoff Bennington has said about national histories, is also the myth of a beginning; and the origins of *thuggee* keep receding into a more and more distant historical/mythological point of inauguration.[11] In fact, several of the accounts end up locating its beginning in a Hindu myth of creation.

The thugs, as they are represented in nineteenth- and twentieth-century colonial representations, were a cult of professional stranglers who preyed on travelers—though never on Englishmen—as an act of worship to the popular Hindu goddess Kali. They were represented as hereditary killers drawn from all regions, religions, classes, and castes, united by their devo-tion to Kali and the act of strangulation, which was, in this reading, quite literally sacralized. The thugs were bound to their calling—and to each other—by shared signifying systems: a language, a belief in the divine ori-gin of the practice, and a dizzying array of minutely observed rituals, prohi-bitions, and superstitions. The *thuggee* system functioned as a quasi-religious fraternity that, paradoxically, would accommodate just about every Indian. It was defined as a compelling and characteristically Indian form of social (ir)rationality, and the practice was represented as resting upon an inter-locking network of constitutive contradictions.

Though the thugs robbed their victims and the confessions usually dem-onstrate a very lucid recall of the division of the plunder, *thuggee* was not conceived as having any economic base, particularly because those involved in it appeared to have fixed abodes, peaceful occupations, and a respectable place in the social and caste hierarchies during those times when they were not engaged in killing and plunder. While Sherwood does speculate, albeit briefly and unevenly, on the proximate material causes of *thuggee*, the ques-tion becomes progressively leached out of subsequent, and more hege-monic, exegeses of *thuggee*. All the writers on the subject are insistent, to greater or lesser degrees, that the thugs must not be regarded as exigent, dispossessed, or rebellious subjects; they are unlike the bandits of folk myth in being devious, unmartial ("cowardly" is the adjective most often used), and almost obscenely respectable.[12] They are characterized instead as hereditary killers whose "joyous occupation" was, paradoxically, not only a matter of caste duty and therefore ontological necessity but also a prime instance of unalienated labor. By the time we come to James Sleeman's hagiographic account of his grandfather's exploits, the act of strangulation has not only been uncoupled from the usual motives for murder but has ac-quired a quasi-libidinal charge: "The taking of human life for the sheer lust of killing was the Thugs' main object: the plunder, however pleasant, being a secondary consideration. . . . Here was no body of amateur assassins, driven to crime by force of circumstance, but men of seeming respectability and high intelligence, often occupying positions of importance and responsibility in their normal lives, secretly trained from boyhood to the highest degree of skill in strangulation."[13] Sleeman is not alone in this reading of the combined erotic and religious investment in murder. Taylor, in *Confessions of a Thug*, hints at the homoerotic subtext of a thug's murder of a handsome lad; and George MacMunn explicitly couples the left-hand Tantrism (including exorbitant and unauthorized sexual acts) of Kali worshipers with behaviors like *thuggee* and nationalist violence:

> The murder trials that have followed on the sedition and secret murder cult in Bengal, and indeed throughout India, show in their records how the Hindu student depraved and often injured by too early eroticism, turns to the suggestiveness of the murder-monger, and worships the nitro-glycerine bomb as the apotheosis of his goddess [Kali]. . . . The student and the assistant editor of the rag, that but exists to inflame students and pays its way by advertising the potent aphrodisiacs among them, are the nidus of the bomb-cult.[14]

Katherine Mayo also locates the worship of Kali, premature and excessive sexual activity, and acts of anticolonial terrorism within a single perceptual grid.[15] This confluence of violence, illegitimacy, and homoerotic desire is to resurface in *The Deceivers*.

Some twentieth-century scholars of colonial history have sought to posit alternative, materialist histories of the phenomenon called *thuggee*. Hiralal Gupta traces the development of *thuggee* or banditry in the early nineteenth century to the success of the East India Company's expansionist policy, speculating that a significant number of people captured as thugs by the Thuggee and Dacoity Department in the 1830s and 1840s were erstwhile soldiers or officials in the employ of rulers whose states had recently come under British control. These people were among those who had lost their employment or fallen from favor as a result of the annexation or reconfiguration of the Indian princely states.[16] Sandria Freitag on the other hand points to the displacement of peripatetic groups as a result of the ousting of local settled rulers who had traditionally provided some protection to such groups and to the establishment of the land-revenue-based state as a possible explanation for the instances of collective acts of violence. She also glosses the violence of dacoits—as of similar groups—as bids for power and upward social mobility that would have been acknowledged as such and accommodated by precolonial Indian state formations.[17] Stewart Gordon argues that the large number of marauding groups that were jockeying for political power in Malwa (where most of the thugs seemed to be based) in the late eighteenth century posed a threat to the stable sources of revenue in the region and necessitated the creation of external sources of revenue.

Those designated thugs were "locally recruited, locally based" marauders hired to plunder outside the neighborhood, as it were, in order to make up for revenue that might have been lost to larger marauding groups.[18]

As I have already mentioned, Englishmen were never targeted by the thugs; a few of the written accounts attribute the unsolved murder of a Lieutenant Maunsell (or Monsell) in 1812 to thugs (as does the film version of *The Deceivers* [1987], which opens with that killing), but most of the *thuggee* texts point to the fact that the British had no personal investment in the problem. Almost unfailingly these accounts point to the antithug campaigns as exemplary instances of the active benevolence of British rule, so often unjustly maligned or compared unfavorably with indigenous rule. James Sleeman, who is particularly apoplectic on this issue, argues that twentieth-century Indian demands for independence were in effect a call for a return to the days of *thuggee*: "Had this small handful of British officials, scattered like poppies in a corn-field, shown the slightest timidity in grappling with this gigantic task, they would surely have fallen victims to the Thugs at the outset, in which case millions of Indians alive to-day would never have been born, including possibly those who now agitate for a restoration of the conditions under which Thuggee thrived and battened."[19]

Colonial accounts thus represent *thuggee* as outside a realm of political and economic rationality (since it is religiously sanctioned, grounded in caste, and linked to exorbitant pleasures). Nonetheless, as the obsessive invocations of the Mutiny of 1857 and of the Bengal revolutionaries of the twentieth century indicate, *thuggee* was simultaneously addressed (even if not overtly acknowledged) as a peculiarly potent threat to the authority and benevolence of the empire in India. "To the colonial regime," writes David Arnold, "crime and politics were almost inseparable: serious crime was an implicit defiance of state authority and a possible prelude to rebellion; political resistance was either a 'crime' or the likely occasion for it."[20] Freitag points to the departures of British police action from those of their Mughal predecessors; while the Mughals delegated responsibility for containing collective crime to local functionaries, the British felt such corporate criminal behaviors were nothing other than a defiance of the state itself.[21] She points to the fundamental distinctions, in terms of both the allocation of resources and the formulation of legal procedures, that the Raj made between crimes committed by individuals ("ordinary crime") and those committed by collectivities ("extraordinary crime"):

> Elaboration of legal codes and police establishments to deal with individual crime conveyed the impression that "the rule of law" had been introduced into British India; yet the annual compilation of crime and police statistics makes clear the minimal state resources committed to policing individual crime. Unless such crime grew alarmingly in a short period, or its policing fell

significantly short of what came to be seen as the norms of efficiency (for an inefficient force), the state did not reckon individual crime to be of great importance. By contrast, however, the British perceived collectively criminal actions to be either directed against, or weakening, the authority of the state. As a consequence, the British repeatedly felt the need to launch centralized police forces against "extraordinary" crime and viewed their inefficacy as a measure of the Raj's impotence.[22]

The *thuggee* records (including the confessions of thug approvers) endeavor to provide—through the dominant tropes of ritualized, religiously ratified, and libidinally charged slaughter—a tightly knit, seamless, and self-validating account of an exceptional Indian criminal practice. Yet, even as the record invokes the unvarying trademarks of thug practice, it inescapably registers the provisionality of its own categorization. The thug's signature—murder by strangulation, using a (silk) handkerchief—does not appear in every act labeled *thuggee;* swords and poison feature as agents of destruction quite as much as the talismanic *rumal* (handkerchief). Such wide variations along a continuum of criminal activity were to lead, after the 1830s, to an expansion of the provenance of *thuggee*: the term came to include all kinds of organized and corporate criminal activity (including poisoning and the kidnapping of children) that was understood to be hereditary and/or itinerant. The confessions also seem to demonstrate that at least some thugs were initiated into professional practice not in adolescence or early manhood by older male family members but later in life, most typically in response to a situation of financial exigency.

Not only was it difficult to isolate certain crimes as the acts of thugs, it was never easy either to establish the exceptional and profoundly aberrant character of *thuggee*. The common complaint in all the *thuggee* accounts without exception is that the activity of the thugs seemed to mesh with exasperating ease into existing indigenous networks of wealth and power, since they were supported by zamindars (landowners), Indian princes, law-enforcement officials, merchants, and even ordinary people. As Freitag suggests, "among organized criminals the thags may have been the group most thoroughly embedded in local society."[23] The worship of Kali (also called Devi, or Bhawani) could not easily be coded as an eccentric religious practice either. Though some narratives do interpret the thugs' invocation of the goddess on the scaffold as proof positive of guilt ("Their invocation of Bhawani at the drop was a confession of their guilt, for no one in such a situation invokes Bhawani but a Thug, and he invokes no other deity in any situation, whatever may be his religion or sect")[24], they also point to the widespread adoration of Kali across regions and religions, among those identified as law-abiding as well as those constituted as criminal.[25] Finally, while Thug beliefs and rituals, especially those enacted at the start of an expedition, were elaborately detailed, it was also asserted that in India expeditions in quest of plunder were qualitatively no different from expeditions undertaken for territorial aggrandizement; rulers and robbers alike took the auspices after the Dasehra festival, before setting out on their *badshashi kam* (kingly work).

Hence at least two contesting readings emerge: one defines the thugs as a community apart, existing in enmity against law-abiding, scrutable, and locally anchored subjects; the other identifies them as natural to indigenous society, aided and abetted by all, and mirroring and reproducing that society's values. The uneasy fit between the contextualizing move and the essentializing one was productive of an aporia, which could only be resolved by invoking that most powerful of all Indological epistemes—that of caste.[26] All the contradictions and the seemingly endless heterogeneity of the subject category of the thug are subsumed within that category, which is reified as coherent and inflexible and emptied of any possibility of subjective freedom. Once *thuggee* as social alliance was taxonomized as homologous to, if not identical with (and the slippage from homology to identity occurs without any apparent discursive strain), a caste, the thug could simultaneously inhabit what had earlier been discrepant subject positions: he could simultaneously be an exceptional criminal *and* a representative Hindu, or Indian, since in the colonial imaginary the territory of Hinduism is often coextensive with that of India.[27] Even this reconciliation was not without its tensions, of course, since *thuggee* as a philosophical system and a social formation seemed to work strongly against the grain of the received colonial view of India as irrevocably fractured along the fault lines of caste and religion.

Nor was the caste explanation completely adequate to the great and, as it seemed, illogical hybridity of *thuggee*. As a socioreligious formation *thuggee* seemed to colonial investigators to be aligned with popular, indeed demotic, forms of Hinduism in its reverence for Kali, except that it attracted a large number of Muslim adherents, who seemed to pay homage quite unproblematically both to the goddess and to the strictures of the Koran. Here it is important to point to the varied, contingent, and often irreconcilable constructions of Hindu tradition in colonial discourse; the representation of Hinduism in the discourse of *thuggee* is, for instance, quite discontinuous with that which is operative in the discourse on sati, which was formulated in a roughly contemporaneous moment. In the case of sati, as Lata Mani has argued, colonial officials made energetic and systematic attempts to establish Hinduism as a religion of the book; and Brahmanical readings and textual authorities were privileged over custom and local religious and social practice.[28] But in the instance of *thuggee*, Hinduism is defined entirely as and by custom. Moreover, at the popular or subaltern level, Hindu and Muslim forms of worship and systems of belief may well have been less distinct than they were to become (especially for more elevated castes and classes) later in the century. The whole question in fact of Hindu doctrine and praxis and its relation to thug identity is notoriously murky and ill defined.

Further complicating this discursive construction of *thuggee* was the fact that professional thugs cultivated the appearance of the most civic-minded of citizens and were conscientious about the discharge of familial, social, and religious obligations. The very characteristics that made them success-ful con men—their polish, their social and rhetorical skills, their extraor-dinary capacity for duplicating identities—also ensured their immense re-spectability in civil society. But what rendered *thuggee* particularly elusive and frustrating to British observers was its relative invisibility, its skill at camouflage, and the difficulty of establishing it as a pervasive yet eccentric form of lawlessness. Thug murders were typically performed without shed-ding blood and without using identifiable offensive weapons of any kind: they were performed far from the victims' homes, and the bodies were care-fully buried. Because of the care exercised in the killing and the disposal of the corpses (victims were buried with great dispatch, and their graves were filled with rocks to keep out any marauding animals) and the hazards attendant upon travel in nineteenth-century India, these murders gener-ally failed to register as murders. Local landowners, rulers, and policemen connived at these murders for their own benefit, or because they were prompted, it was argued, by the heavy demands of superstition; and the peasantry, we are told, simply ignored the bodies that occasionally appeared in fields and wells. This raised the question of how far the circuit of crimi-nality actually extended: if local officials and the police tolerated and even encouraged *thuggee* and ordinary folk made no complaint about it, who could be said to remain unimplicated in it? Under the circumstances, every-thing and everyone was liable to suspicion, since the system of *thuggee* was both remarkably inclusive and remarkably discreet in its operations. Hence British *thuggee* inspectors were in the discomfiting position of focusing on crimes that no one else acknowledged, certainly not (from the evidence of these writers) most Indian princes or zamindars or even common folk and generally not even the majority of the British magistracy or the civil service. British scholars of *thuggee* were thus involved in a detective project hobbled by an almost-fatal lack of empirical detail. All natives were potentially thugs, since the system of *thuggee* was remarkably inclusive; and the most seemingly innocent objects, like handkerchiefs or *gur* (unrefined sugar, ritually con-sumed at the commencement of an expedition), could participate in a diabolical signifying system. And while British ignorance of *thuggee* (at least until the 1830s) might contrast favorably with Indian knowledge—and therefore complicity—it was susceptible of more objectionable interpreta-tions; in Masters's novel, there is the danger that British "ignorance" of *thuggee* can be read by the natives in a particularly unflattering light: "In the nine years of the English Company's rule nothing had been done against the Deceivers. But William realized now that most Indians knew at least of the existence of the Deceivers; and, knowing, they could not believe the English did not also know; therefore the English officials too were sharing in the spoils; so what was the use of informing?"[29] (In the film version, the Indians have good reason to be suspicious: George Angelsmith, the exemplary servant of the East India Company, has full knowledge of the activities of the thugs and profits from it.) Here it is not simply the natives who are the object of investigation, codification, and supervision; an alternative modality of interpretation is imaginable, in which colonial authority is itself open to variant readings, including those it has not authorized.

All these factors made the retrieval of information and the policing of *thuggee* particularly vexing. And creating an archive and standardizing reader response was not easy either. Though each *thuggee* expedition and each act of *thuggee* was performed by the book, attended by minutely detailed rituals and scrupulously observed omens, and was immediately identifiable as such to those who could read the signs, it was not immediately *visible* as such to those who could not or did not see *thuggee* as a semiosis. Even in the 1860s, when knowledge about *thuggee* had been codified, circulated, and reproduced and was underwritten by wide-ranging institutional and legal support, Charles Hervey complained that his subordinates were yet imperfect readers of the complex and mysterious text of *thuggee*,

> some correctly recognizing Thuggee in instances which were palpably the deed of experts, although death should not have taken place; others only doing so where death had resulted; some classing certain murders as cases of "Thuggee" without reference to the means resorted to in the perpetration thereof; others who wholly pass by cases of poisoning whether followed by death or not, although they bore evidence of being the acts of class criminals; some who restrict their notice to selected cases only of its occurrence, passing by other similar instances; some who endeavour to distinguish between different degrees of poisoning, some calling "murder by poison" *Thugee* [sic], others not doing so[;] . . . others who lump all such kindred offences under round numbers without any narration of the attendant circumstances, contented only with quoting against them the sections of the Penal Code under which they were triable or were tried.[30]

With all the discrepant valences of this discourse, one factor remained crucial in the determination of *thuggee*: the idea of hereditary criminality. This was not a particularly novel reading of corporate criminal activity in colonial India; as far back as 1772, the dacoits of Bengal were strenuously and repeatedly characterized not as individual or collective subjects responding to socioeconomic transformations engendered by the sudden ascendancy of the East India Company or indeed to any other material circumstance, or even to chance, but as fulfilling a hereditary calling, if not a genetic predisposition.[31] And, as Sanjay Nigam has convincingly demonstrated, the colonial reification of caste as coherent and inflexible, combined with the received notion of hereditary criminality (most fully exemplified in the instance of *thuggee*), was to have a long and ominous history in colonial and postcolonial India; the Criminal Tribes and Castes Act of 1872 was to designate (without any possibility of appeal) a number of vagrant and impoverished "communities" as "criminal by birth" and thus subject to surveillance, control, and attempted rehabilitation.[32] I am struck here by the considerable (though not complete) overlap of this discourse with Michel Foucault's description of the emergence of the homosexual as a distinct ontological category in the nineteenth century:

> The nineteenth-century homosexual became a personage, a past, a case history, and a childhood, in addition to being a type of life, a life form, and a morphology, with an indiscreet anatomy and a mysterious physiology. Nothing that went into his total composition was unaffected by his sexuality. It was everywhere present in him: at the root of all his actions because it was their insidious and indefinitely active principle; written immodestly on his face and body because it was a secret that always gave itself away. It was cosubstantial with him, less as a habitual sin than as a singular nature. . . . The sodomite had been a temporary aberration; the homosexual was now a species.[33]

Because *thuggee* was such a slippery issue, a kind of legal, disciplinary, and discursive apparatus was brought to bear on it that did not occur in the case for instance of sati, another retrograde and horrific practice apparently authorized by Hinduism. This is not of course to assert that sati as a discursive formation was unproblematic for colonial administrators and reformers; Lata Mani has pointed that the abolition of sati in colonial India was preceded by its legalization and has drawn attention to the valorization of the "voluntary" sati in colonial and nationalist discourses. But *thuggee* was not so much spectacular—as sati was (at least until 1829)—as invisible. As a result it was much more difficult to discursively track its trajectory and to determine the success of the pacification. Sati was abolished in 1829, and there are no official records after that date of the practice; it was presumed that it had simply been legislated out of existence. But in the instance of *thuggee*, such faith in the efficacy of legislative sanction is much more uncertain.

In the juridical domain, *thuggee* was defined as an "exceptional case" in the name of a colonial contingency, since *thuggee* by definition was exorbitant to standard law-and-order discourse and marked at all points by immoderation.[34] This enabled the establishment of a discursive and juridical system that was entirely self-referential and self-validating, in which it was sufficient to be identified as a thug or "hereditary criminal" through an approver's testimony, without actually being convicted of a specific crime, to be liable to arrest, trial, and, almost inevitably, conviction. I will return to this shortly.

Knowledge of *thuggee* as an essence then had to be constructed, crucially, around an absence; and all the confessions, all the subject effects produced by the testimony of approvers, were a strenuous effort to recover a "consciousness," a consciousness that would provide the foundation for the revelations that ratified the antithug campaign. But if *thuggee* was as far-reaching and as subtle as W. H. Sleeman and his associates insisted, and if thug ontology and practice was determined by birth, how could an Englishman ever hope to know the whole truth and nothing but the truth? How could one verify the confessions of the approvers and establish checks over their control of the official record? Thornton registers exasperation at the contaminated nature of the confessions: "Few things are more difficult to a native of India than to tell the truth, under any circumstances; and the confessions of criminals, in all countries, may be expected to contain a mixture of truth and falsehood. The deposition of Moklal is not consistent with the rest; nor even with another statement made by himself, made in conversation with Captain Sleeman."[35] He also cites (as do other accounts of *thuggee*) the instance of an approver who functioned as a double agent, beguiling his English employer into believing him committed to the capture of thugs while providing information and English passes [documents authorizing unimpeded travel within, and between, designated territories] to his criminal comrades.[36]

While James Sleeman claims that W. H. Sleeman and his colleagues, in the 1830s, "resolved that this trade of Thuggee should no longer be any more a mystery than tailoring or carpentering, began to initiate themselves into all the secrets of the craft, and were soon, in their knowledge of the theory of the profession, little behind the professors themselves,"[37] the "secrecy" of *thuggee* never disappeared as a threat. W. H. Sleeman—speaking of course with the superior wisdom of his newfound knowledge—records a state preceding revelation with combined horror and incredulity:

> While I was in the Civil charge of the district of Nursingpore . . . no ordinary robbery or theft could be committed without my being acquainted with it; nor was there a robber or a thief of the ordinary kind in the district, with whose character I had not become acquainted in the discharge of my duty as magistrate; and if any man had then told me, that a gang of assassins by profession resided in the village of Kandelee, not four hundred yards from my court, and that [in the] extensive groves of the village of Mandesur, only one stage from me . . . was one of the largest Beles, or places of murder in all India; and that large gangs from Hindustan and the Deccan used to rendezvous in these groves, remain in them for many days altogether every year, and carry their dreadful trade along all the lines of road that pass by and branch off them,

with the knowledge and connivance of the two landholders by whose ances-
tors these groves had been planted, I should have thought him a fool or a mad
man; and yet nothing could have been more true.[38]

Indeed, the entire discourse of *thuggee* is troped by figures of darkness,
mystery, inscrutability, unpredictability, and unexpected menace, even as
W. H. Sleeman and his assistants are inserted into a heroic narrative of battle against evil. "Secrecy is indispensable" for thug ceremonies, and "[a]n
impenetrable veil of darkness is thrown over their atrocities";[39] "danger was
everywhere, unseen and unexpected"[40] for the Englishmen involved in the
anti-*thuggee* enterprise (even though Englishmen were known never to be
attacked by thugs); they were like "men isolated in the midst of a dangerous, trackless and gloomy jungle, without map or compass";[41] and "[the]
old Thug Associations, which have been now effectually put down in all
parts of India, . . . would assuredly rise up again, and flourish under the as-
surance of religious sanction, . . . were the strength of the special police, em-
ployed in the suppression, hastily reduced, or its vigilance relaxed."[42] Once
again, Foucault on the discourse of sex and sexuality is apropos: "What
is peculiar to modern societies, in fact, is not that they consigned sex to a
shadow existence, but that they dedicated themselves to speaking of it *ad
infinitum*, while exploiting it as *the* secret."[43]

This very obscurity, this elusiveness that characterizes the thug as discursive object, could and did function as an enabling moment for the colonial
law-and-order machine. Since it could never be decisively established—
given the terms of the discourse—that *thuggee* had been extirpated, the
need for endless vigilance was ratified. The moral viability of the civilizing
mission, indeed the very ground of its possibility, is the never-satisfied, endlessly proliferating need for reform. In the case of *thuggee*, colonial officials
were confirmed in their belief that the work of civilizing is never done. Thus
many writers warn repeatedly of the dangers of celebrating the demise of
thuggee prematurely; in 1893, Charles Hervey, successor to Colonel W. H.
Sleeman of *thuggee* fame, was still chasing after thugs. These officers point
not only to the hypnotic lure of *thuggee* for its practitioners but also to the
fact that native policemen and landlords are only too anxious to conceal
evidence of thug crimes from credulous British officials overeager to con-
gratulate themselves on the cessation of this practice and overoptimistic
about the all-encompassing vigilance of colonial power. *Thuggee* never really
goes away as a *present* problem as sati might be said to do; it may almost be
said to function as a trope for all that is uncontrollable in the law-and-order
situation. In fact, the construction of hereditary, pervasive, and socially or
religiously sanctioned criminality inaugurated in the discourse on *thuggee*
reappears throughout the nineteenth century in the discourse on dacoits,

buddhuks, dhatoora poisoners (all of whom came to occupy the same criminal category as the thug), and specifically designated criminal tribes and castes.

How else might we understand this absence or unknowability that tropes the discourse of *thuggee?* Certainly this simultaneous fear of and pleasure in the duplicity and omnipresence of the thug deserves some consideration, especially in light of the questions it raises about the status of knowledge, subject positions, and representation in the colonial state. Bhabha's model of the emergence of shifty civil subject of the colonial polity through mimicry can be extended here, it seems to me, to some of the other possibilities of mimicry in the colonial theater.[44] The situation of the thug is analogous to but certainly not identical to that of the not quite/not white native—the thug after all is not mimicking colonial ontology—though his capacity for traffic in identities and positions is staggering. The instance of *thuggee* intimates, I think, that the colonized subject's mimicry need not necessarily have the colonizer as its focus in order to function as menace; mimicry, even if it is mimicry of indigenous subject positions, frustrates the colonial desire for homogenized, duplicable, and knowable native subjects in whom subalternity is sought to be reproduced through the authorized version of mimicry. If there is one thing that characterizes the thug of the archives, it is the multiplicity and unpredictability of his manifestations. As we have seen, it was what was perceived as this faculty for disguise and invisibility that had to be criminalized by the laws designed to convict thugs; theoretically there was no such entity as an honest thug, and many so-called thugs were convicted who were, according to the official records, engaged in "honest labour." There is an ongoing and strenuous endeavor in the discourse of *thuggee* to interpellate the thug as an essence, a move which attests to the anxiety of rupture that subtends the totalizing epistemologies of colonialism. Yet the thug as discursive object is strikingly resistant to such fixity; he is all things to all people. If native identity can be staged, can be plural, then what are the implications for colonial authority and colonialism's project of information retrieval? *Thuggee,* I would suggest, introduces a disturbance in the paradigm of information retrieval that often seems dominant in texts like *Kim* and *A Personal Narrative of a Pilgrimage to Al-Madinah and Meccah,* as well as the notion of native authenticity and ontological purity that is a governing trope of colonial discourse. The thug, through his capacity for disguise and impersonation and his skill at negotiating multiple and competing identities, usurps the colonizer's privilege of complex subjectivity and of movement between subject positions and thus can be read to assume some control over both the construction and flow of colonial knowledge. So he never becomes fully naturalized as the disciplinary subject or, in other words, the knowable subject, of the colonial polity. And *thuggee,* later rewritten as dacoity, continues to function within the law-and-order context in the colonial and postcolonial state formations as a trope for the unruly and unreformable energies that cannot easily be accommodated to the needs of the civilizing mission.[45]

THE LAW

The writings and reports of W. H. Sleeman, which form the core texts around which the tale of *thuggee* is orchestrated, represent a concerted and monumental effort to illuminate and classify the obscurity of *thuggee*. Sleeman emerges, in both nineteenth- and twentieth-century accounts of *thuggee*, as the hero of his own story. Even those works, like George Bruce's *The Stranglers* and James Sleeman's *Thug, or A Million Murders*, that purport to be histories of the thugs rather than biographies, present the account of *thuggee* as coextensive with the life of Sleeman. Sleeman emerges from these texts (and his own, of course) as an exemplary figure in nineteenth-century criminal and judicial procedures, who undertakes a self-appointed messianic task of uncovering and reading. Nothing in his story happens by chance. The discovery of the scope of *thuggee* as a result of Feringheea's confession is (re)written as an inevitability in the task of reconstructing *thuggee*, and Sleeman's anti-*thuggee* efforts traced back to the moment of his arrival in India in 1809. All of Sleeman's life and work before 1830 is thus written as a prelude to the climactic scenes of thug hunting and as a preparation for reading the mysteries of this esoteric Indian cult. Sleeman above all is transformed in this telling into an almost Saidean figure of knowledge; he is the *shikari* (hunter) who, with his gift of languages, long residence in India without being "Orientalized," and experience in war and in settling newly conquered territories, can present an ideal model of the exegete. Though a crime like *thuggee* is quite literally inconceivable to those "living under an efficient government," Sleeman is no Inspector Clouseau, no naive Englishman who stumbles unaware upon a vast organized conspiracy. He knows what he is looking for; indeed, Tuker's biography imagines Sleeman becoming the butt of his colleagues' jokes during his early years in India because of his eagerness to "discover" *thuggee*.[46] In this telling, *thuggee* predates Sleeman; indeed, it is as old as India itself. Yet the text of *thuggee* remains unread until Sleeman, the reader-as-savior, provides the hermeneutic key to the mystery. He establishes the exceptional quality of *thuggee*, distinguishing it from outlawry, banditry, and other illegalities necessitated by privation; he establishes the story of *thuggee* as a moral narrative and embeds it in the culture of an Orientalist India.

The man whose ideal was, like that of a Sherlock Holmes, "to be everywhere, and to see everything,"[47] proved phenomenally successful—in his own terms—at cracking the code of *thuggee*. He showed a remarkable capacity—far greater than that of Sherwood or even that of the few officers who had harassed the thugs in the early decades of the century—to global-ize and codify discrete accounts of crimes in different times and places into a metanarrative of hereditary crime. On the evidence of approvers, he cre-ated gigantic and detailed "family trees" of captured and uncaptured thugs that provided copious details of each man's crimes, place of origin, place in the caste hierarchy, and personal and professional antecedents; he also mapped out all the *bhils* (places of slaughter and burial) in central India. Every thug could then be located on Sleeman's gigantic grid, and informa-tion and operations were centralized. The local knowledge of the approvers now became part of a giant signifying chain. For the thug, there was no es-cape: his history and his nature were always already known to the all-seeing eyes of the colonial bureaucracy and criminal-justice system; his experience formed a narrative even before he made his confession and was in no way dependent on it. As Ameer Ali says in *Confessions of a Thug*, "The man un-folded a roll of paper written in Persian, and read a catalogue of crime, of murders, every one of which I knew to be true; a faithful record it was of my past life, with but few omissions."[48] Sleeman also prepared a dictionary of Ramasee, the secret language of the criminal fraternity, with a vocabulary made up entirely of descriptions of criminal actions. This linguistic, geo-graphic, and genealogical grid left out little that was germane to the needs of criminal justice in colonial India:

> I have, I believe, entered in this vocabulary every thing to which Thugs in any part of India have thought it necessary to assign a peculiar term; and every term peculiar to their associations with which I have yet become acquainted. I am satisfied that there is no term, no rite, no ceremony, no opinion, no omen or usage that they have intentionally concealed from me; and if any have been accidentally omitted after the numerous narratives that I have had to record, and cases to investigate, they can be but comparatively very few and unimportant.[49]

The doctrine of *thuggee* was not simply a novel yet apposite way of read-ing Indian criminality at a moment when the pressures to reform the East India Company by reforming India were particularly marked. The conse-quences of the discovery of *thuggee* were, in other words, not simply a philo-sophical reconstellation of Indian criminality. *Thuggee* also gave rise to a ver-itable cottage industry of policing and surveillance techniques, as well as ethnographic documentation. Like the system it purported to study, the dis-course on *thuggee* was totalizing in its scope. In the juridical domain, *thuggee* was defined as an "exceptional case"; this enabled the establishment of a radically new machinery of arrest, conviction, and punishment in thug tri-als. The production of penal truth in thug trials proved, as we have seen, no-toriously difficult. Since thugs were peripatetic operatives, who always committed their crimes far from home and disposed of their plunder quickly, evidence was not only destroyed but questions were raised about jurisdictional authority. Local functionaries were not just uncooperative; many were allegedly bound by a utilitarian calculus to thug gangs. In addition, the relatives of the putative victims displayed no zeal in the punishment of crime or the redress of wrongs; the vast majority refused to identify those missing as murdered at all. This uncooperative behavior was attributed to their fatalistic acceptance of all disasters (including, apparently, cholera, poisonous snakes, and sudden death). Even when thugs were captured, convicting them was rendered even more troublesome by the fact that Muslim criminal law disallowed the testimony of approvers.

The lack of independent witnesses, the unavailability in many cases of both bodies and booty—the sheer paucity of positivist evidence, in other words—could only be resolved in one way. The most important criminal conspiracy of the century (of all time, some of the authors claimed) could be adequately engaged only by a new conception of law. Many of the tactics adopted by those spearheading the antithug drive were not novel but had been pioneered earlier in Bengal; however, it was the Thuggee and Dacoity Department's use of these tactics that proved not only successful but replicable.[50] Since the law as currently defined made the complicity of individuals in particular crimes almost impossible to establish, specific criminal acts were no longer punishable as such. Instead, it was a subject position, or rather, an ontology, that was criminalized. It was enough to be a thug, without actually being convicted of a specific act of *thuggee*, to be liable to the exorbitant measures of the Thuggee and Dacoity Department. As Radhika Singha wrote, "The strangest feature of this enactment was the use of a cant term 'Thugs' without explaining what precisely the offence of 'Thuggee' was. That such a term was acceptable at a time when a penal code upholding precision and exactness was on the agenda is an indication of the success of a publicist campaign in official circles."[51] Act XXX of 1836 directed that any person who was convicted of "having belonged to a gang of Thugs, [was] liable to the penalty of imprisonment for life; and [that] any person, accused of the offence, made punishable by the Act, [was] liable to be tried by any Court, which would have been competent to try him, if his offence had been committed within the district where that Court sits."[52] (Act XXIV of 1843 extended the punitive sanctions of the *thuggee* laws to those found guilty of belonging to dacoit gangs.) Act XXX also dispensed with the last vestiges of Muslim criminal law (which is said to have provided greater protections for the accused and greater clemency for the convicted than the Thuggee and Dacoity Department thought advisable for those standing trial as thugs) by doing away with the necessity for the *fatwa* (formal legal opinion) of the Muslim law officer. It applied with retrospective effect, and it established special courts for the trial of thugs—including those captured outside company territory, within the kingdoms of the Indian princes—often with special magistrates appointed by the governor-general. It permitted the arrest of entire families, including women and children, as legitimate means of entrapping active (male) thugs; since *thuggee* was supposed to be a family affair anyway, transmitted in the genes and passed on from father to son, wives and children were also fit targets for the colonial state's punitive and corrective measures. The act admitted the testimony of approvers in lieu of the testimony of independent witnesses (which had been disallowed under Islamic law), a move which created a remarkable mechanics of truth production and conviction. (Act XIX of 1837, under the direction of Macaulay, did away with this "dual standard of evidence" in criminal law by making the testimony of approvers admissible in all courts of law, not just those prosecuting cases of *thuggee*.) [53] Yet it is by no means to be assumed that empiricism and observation were peripheral to the process, though it was observation of a very carefully demarcated kind; there is in the colonial archive an overwhelming weight given to the experiential dimension of the knowledge of such canonical figures as Sleeman. All disagreements encountered on the British side are attributed to inexperience, to the lack of a proper interpretive framework within which to place certain kinds of discoveries, or to a willful ingenuousness about the success of British rule.

The definition of *thuggee* as a form of hereditary, corporate, and religiously sanctioned identity allowed for no appeal by a thug convicted under its special decrees; in theory—and in practice—there was no such entity as an innocent thug. All those identified as thugs by approvers' testimony were automatically guilty, even if no specific crimes could be proved against them and even if there was no (other) evidence of their ever having associated with other thugs. Once the thug hunts began, criminal activity was not always necessary for arrest and conviction; even those "thugs" engaged in "honest labour" (a theoretical impossibility, given the terms of the discourse) were rounded up, tried, convicted, and imprisoned since the compelling, hereditary lure of *thuggee* was always latent in the thug. An overwhelmingly high proportion of those arrested were convicted, a fact which validated, the Thuggee and Dacoity Department believed, the thoroughness of its efforts and the justice of its cause.

Confessions were key to the discursive constitution of *thuggee;* not so much at the actual thug trials as in the manifold accounts of *thuggee* that were produced in the nineteenth and twentieth centuries. Meadows Taylor's novel, as far as structural organization is concerned, reads not very differently from the nonfictional official accounts of *thuggee*: a brief introduction followed by hundreds of pages of confession, interspersed more and more intermittently by the narrator's moral commentary. The confessional mode lent itself nicely to the narrative conventions and imperatives of the nineteenth-century English novel, which encompassed both the Newgate novel and the spiritual autobiography.

One of the best approvers, Bukhtawar, provided a confession (which I quoted at the beginning of this chapter) that was a model for all thug confessions: "I am a Thug, my father and grandfather were Thugs, and I have thugged with many. Let the government employ me and I will do its work."[54] The confessions serve not to elicit what is not already known but to authenticate and authorize official knowledge of *thuggee* in general and specific crimes in particular, as well as to produce the thug as (colonial) criminal subject. For Foucault, the confession "transcend[s] all other evidence; an element in the calculation of the truth, it [is] also the act by which the accused accept[s] the charge and recognize[s] its truth; it transform[s] an investigation carried out without him into a voluntary affirmation. Through the confession, the accused himself [takes] part in the ritual of producing penal truth."[55] In the eyes of the Thuggee and Dacoity Department, a failure to confess was evidence less of innocence than of hardihood and an acquaintance with the byzantine ramifications of Indian criminal law.

And yet these confessions that dominate and drive all accounts of *thuggee* are not confessions as such, but approver's testimonies; the two, as Shahid Amin so appositely reminds us, are not identical. For while the confession proper seeks to dilute the guilt of the confessing subject, the approver's testimony, to be fully credible in the eyes of the law, must implicate its speaker as fully as possible in the illegality being described.[56]

The fact that approvers' testimony was "tainted" and that they might either wittingly or unwittingly implicate the innocent was undeniably an issue, though anxiety on the score was aired only to be promptly shown up as unfounded. The *thuggee* records continually stress the ways in which the truth of each approver's testimony was tested against all the others. But even in these official accounts, it does not escape remark that the approvers' testimony regarding dates and other details do not always match,[57] though all discursive contradictions are always sought to be smoothed away. Bruce, who is the only one to raise overtly the possibility of the conviction of the innocent, blames not the system but its most visible instruments, the approvers: "Were innocent men convicted upon the evidence of revengeful informers?. . . . Those Thugs who were no longer free to strangle on the roads may have conspired together to send victims to the gallows instead, for by killing in this way they could at once show Kali their continued devotion and save their own lives."[58] These testimonies were not required, under Act XXX, to be matched against the reports of independent witnesses or against the weight of circumstantial evidence; and none of the accused had the benefit of counsel, so the approvers were never cross-examined by anyone other than the officers of the Thuggee and Dacoity Department.

Even though the approvers were indispensable for forming the text of *thuggee* and for prosecuting thugs, their own status remained somewhat nebulous. On making "a full and ingenuous confession," an approver would be eligible to have his sentence of hanging or transportation commuted. But an approver could never be released, since the lure of the *rumal* made him irreclaimable for honest society. It was also necessary that all approvers be convicted (not just arrested) thugs, since it was contrary to the nature of British justice to hold its subjects indefinitely without trial. How, though, could the government convict approvers when it had no evidence except for what they provided? The solution was to advise approvers to plead guilty to the general charge of being thugs, under the provisions of Act XXX, rather than to plead guilty to the charge of committing specific capital crimes (which could result in the death penalty); this would ensure their conviction, and then they could be held for life without questioning the authority that held them.[59] It was easier and more useful to hold approvers than to hang them; and they needed to be held forever in order to ensure the uninterrupted production of truths about *thuggee*. The above proceeding did away with the necessity of a regular trial (that is to say, one conducted under the special courts established by Act XXX) by having one whose outcome was known in advance; and it guaranteed that there would be no escape from the government's mercy.

Truth production and conviction was only part of the job of the Thuggee and Dacoity Department. Rehabilitation was also part of the program, though the official wisdom on rehabilitation was marked by considerable ambivalence. To be a part of a moral narrative, the antithug campaign could not be purely punitive in nature, especially in the instance of those prisoners who had not been convicted of particular capital crimes. At the same time, if thugs were hereditary murderers who found the call to blood irresistible, they were not reformable subjects. The government's response to the problem of identity and rehabilitation was, even in its own terms, a markedly uneven and patently hierarchized one. Some of the most distinguished among the thugs were recruited into the police force. Some others were rewarded by W. H. Sleeman by being allowed to live near him with their families and followers in his compound, an arrangement about which Freitag observes: "The similarity between the spatial and psychological configurations of his compound and those of thag-landlord relations in a village is not coincidental."[60] Other thug approvers and prisoners and their families were settled in colonies and put to manual labor; from being dishonest and itinerant, they were compelled to be poor and settled. The focus of reform was the children of the thugs: they were taught various skills, though not taught to read and write (because it would make them dissatisfied with their condition). The sexuality of the sons of the thugs was

strictly regulated; they were not allowed to marry and breed a new genera-
tion of thugs. (A female thug was a rarity and was, presumably, a less potent
conduit of the genetic material of hereditary criminality than was a male.)

Mature thugs, however, were less easily assimilable into a regime of morality and normalcy. Even captured thugs and informers emerge in the reports as notoriously impervious to all efforts at moral transformation. They
repudiate repentance and reform, ascribing their cooperation entirely to
pragmatic motives and describing their activities in professional terms, without the obligatory change of heart normally central to the confessional narrative. Not only that, they understand their present circumstances in terms
of their failure to observe omens and follow proscriptions and to be fully
professional about their work; the official success against themselves is simply the result of the East India Company's *iqbal* (good fortune), not its moral
or religious superiority or even its greater strategic skill. They seem to refuse
in other words to be drawn into the moral narrative of the civilizing mission
(though it must always be remembered that the production of the thug
as unreformable subject was not necessarily contrary to the aims of the discourse on *thuggee*). The following is a typical exchange; the questioner is
presumably W. H. Sleeman, the respondents thug informers:

> *Q:* If Davey's displeasure visits all who punish Thugs, how is it that you all es-
> cape so well?
>
> *Moradun:* Davey's anger visited us when we were seized. That was the effect of
> her resentment; she cast us off then and takes no notice of us now.
>
> *Q:* And if you were to return to Thuggee, she would still guide and protect
> you?
>
> *Moradun:* Yes, but what gang would now receive us?
>
> *Q:* And are you not afraid to assist in suppressing Thuggee?
>
> *Moradun:* No; we see God is assisting you, and that Davey has withdrawn her
> protection on account of our transgressions. We have sadly neglected her
> worship. God knows in what it will all end.
>
> *Q:* True, God only knows; but we hope it will end in the entire suppression of
> this wicked and foolish system; and in the conviction on your part that
> Davey has really nothing to do with it.
>
> *Nasir:* That Davey instituted Thuggee, and supported it as long as we at-
> tended to her omens, and observed the rules framed by the wisdom of our
> ancestors, nothing in the world can ever make us doubt.[61]

THE ENGLISHMAN

This section, on *The Deceivers*, John Masters's novel about *thuggee*, serves as a
(deconstructive) supplement to the official narrative of the thug, in taking
up some of the questions and figures that occupy a recessive status in that
account. Here we see that if the thug of the archive provides one (admittedly slippery and fixed at the same time) model of staging identities, there

is another model that is crucial for a comprehension of the thug-English engagement. This model is the obverse of the process that generates the mimic man of colonial discourse; it is the lure of going native. The term here both resonates with and fails to correspond to the mimetic model provided by Burton in the last chapter.[62] The will to mimicry governs (Indian) thug and Englishman alike, as we shall see in *The Deceivers*, where the plot is driven—as is the thug archive—by a fascination with the absent and never fully recuperable thug. In engaging this scenario, the novel also recasts the paradigmatic narrative of mimicry, in which the native may mimic the colonizer but without any access to essential Englishness, while the colonizer can trade identities freely, with no strings attached, without actually being interpellated as a colonized subject. *The Deceivers* makes manifest the precariousness of such self-possession.

The dialectical dependence of the fantasy of complete knowledge on the paranoid fear of native inscrutability is staged in this novel, where there is a suturing of the ostensibly antithetical figures of the English policeman and the thug approver. This novel allows for an examination of the tension between the received wisdom about *thuggee* and some of the marginal issues located at the pressure points of the official discourse. This novel tells the story of William Savage, a mediocre and distinctly unheroic English magistrate. Wracked by sexual and professional anxieties, an alienated subject of the British colonial machine in India, and sneakingly sympathetic to such Indian customs as sati, he transforms himself into the exemplary colonial officer by taking on—albeit temporarily—the calling of the thug. At the urging of his young wife, Mary, he initially takes on the persona of the absent Gopal the weaver in order to save Gopal's wife from sati; he, however, meets the renegade thug Hussein and decides to continue as Gopal in order to track down the thugs. Once he assumes the role, he finds himself powerfully drawn to the practice and goes on to become a noted thug leader. He does not continue as a thug, of course—even though at one point Hussein suggests to Savage that the East India Company become a sponsor of thugs, like the other rulers of the land; with a little help from his newly (re)constructed Englishness and his friends, he returns to propriety at the end. (The Merchant Ivory film production is even more skeptical than the novel is of the progressivist teleology of the civilizing mission, as well as of its "success": in the film, George Angelsmith is led off in chains, but Savage, estranged from his wife and his Christian god and unable to prevent the sati that he has actually made possible, is destined to be perpetually haunted by Kali.)

The Deceivers considers the unspoken and unspeakable possibility that subtends so much of colonial discourse: what if identity can be unhinged from race and national origin? And if (racial/national) identity is unstable and subject to negotiation with each crossing of a frontier, then in the name of what telos or destiny does Englishness speak? What if, as R. Radhakrishnan so compellingly asks, on the subject of diasporic, transnational culture, "identities and ethnicities are not a matter of fixed and stable selves but rather the results and products of fortuitous travels and recontextualizations? . . . Is ethnicity nothing but, to use the familiar formula, what ethnicity does?"[63] In the more lurid enactments of this alternative history, a Kurtz, representing the loftiest intellectual and ethical possibilities of the Enlightenment, can "go native" in the Dark Continent. But, closer to "home," there were, as Arnold has revealed, more troubling English subjects—those poor white orphans and vagrants (who were to have their own moment of glory in *Kim*) who lived lives not often distinguishable from those of lower-class Indians.[64] William Savage, the protagonist of *The Deceivers*, is located somewhere between these two subject positions.

Despite the putative restoration to wholeness, Englishness, and legality of William Savage at the close of the story, the narrative nonetheless opens up a space for investigating the "double and split subject" of the colonial enunciation, for what Bhabha calls—in the context of the nation's fissured enunciation—"dissemi-nation": "a space that is *internally* marked by cultural difference and the heterogeneous histories of contending peoples, antagonistic authorities, and tense cultural locations."[65] As in the case of so many other Englishmen, Savage will have to turn to Indianness in order to return to or consolidate or improve his English self; in doing so, he will come back as a new and more English Englishman, but he will also, temporarily at least, be transformed into a border subject, changed by his experience of Indianness, surrendering illusions of full autonomy and Englishness in the crossing of boundaries. Here I invoke Burton again as a point of reference. Burton had an occasionally vexed relationship with national identity: his ancestry was partly Irish and Welsh, and he grew up on the Continent, only coming to live in England in his late teens. Yet for him identity, whatever guises it might assume and however far it might roam, is usually more persuasively anchored than is that of Masters's protagonist in an imperial Englishness. Burton can be, at different times, a West Asian merchant or a Muslim hajji, but his identities are clearly hierarchized and more manipulable than Savage's. While the success of his passing is always, in a sense, conditional upon his being a man from elsewhere/nowhere, he can also claim nativeness as his own production, wrenching an (imaginary) autonomy from the dominion of necessity. Savage passes through Indianness en route to Englishness, but, unlike Burton, he cannot pass in and out without constraint. Indianness, while indispensable to Englishness, must also be violently cast out if Englishness is to be secure(d). In *The Deceivers*, identity is the locus of strain and contradiction. For Savage, identity cannot be expansive, assimilationist, and pluralist; each new identity competes with and displaces the last. That is why Savage can at the end afford to take no prisoners or recruit any approvers from among his erstwhile comrades; the thugs whom he has led and who are now pursuing him must be wiped out in an act of punitive and frenzied brutality that not only precludes the need for approvers but also does away with any witnesses against, and rem(a)inders of, his own thug self.

The Deceivers stages, indeed foregrounds, the positionality and politics of that ordinarily self-effacing hero of thug narration, the investigator, and the plurality of determinations that produces him. In this context, Gayatri Spivak's cautionary reminders about the urgent necessity of disallowing the neutrality of the intellectual or investigator should be borne in mind. In "Can the Subaltern Speak?" she proffers a critique of the sanctioned myopia of the Foucault and Deleuze of "Intellectuals and Power," who are unable or unwilling to acknowledge the complicity of the intellectual in the mechanisms that produce representations of subaltern subjects and groups and who fail to recognize that subaltern subjects are constrained to fashion themselves in terms of already scripted epistemologies.[66] Her introduction to Mahasweta Devi's "Draupadi" resonates with, and provides another useful point of entry into, this problematic of reading and engagement; the usefulness of deconstruction, she tells us, lies in "the recognition, . . . of provisional and intractable starting points in any investigative effort; its disclosure of complicities where a will to knowledge would create oppositions; its insistence that in disclosing complicities the critic-as-subject is herself complicit with the object of her critique; its emphasis upon 'history' and upon the ethico-political as the 'trace' of that complicity—the proof that we do not inhabit a clearly defined critical space free of such traces."[67] Where in the archives the English scribe was progressively effaced from the scene of the crime as well as the scene of writing, no such modesty is permitted the protagonist of Masters's novel. The novel accents above all his position of enunciation. He cannot be, as in the normative thug account, the neutral conduit of something clearly identified as a thug consciousness: the thug's voice cannot but inscribe Savage as both subject and object of his own discourse.

The central aspect of Savage's mission is not merely to bear witness; he must above all produce a record, transform that irreducible obscurity, that absence that is Indian corporate criminal activity, into what Spivak terms an "interpretable text." This of course was the primary gift of Sleeman and his associates to the criminal justice system in colonial India—to synthesize various and discrepant occurrences as a semiosis under centralized control; against *thuggee*—conceived of as a vast, well-articulated, and centralized conspiracy—could be opposed the concentrated power/knowledge of the state. What is required is a text and a model of reading that is reproducible in the different temporalities and contexts of the colonial polity in India. However, the novel intimates the limitations and complexities of authorial intention. Savage produces his account in a condition of profound subjective instability, opening his text up to multiple and mutually contentious readings: "He had met hundreds of other Deceivers, and the notes were a complete tale of all he had seen and heard and done; of all the Deceivers who had engaged in any action, with their descriptions, habits, and homes; of each murder, and how it had gone, and how it might have been prevented—or improved upon. The words could be read for either purpose, according to the spirit of the reader" (p. 223). Above all, Savage's account draws attention to the transactional nature of reading. What ought to be a classic of information retrieval and a master text on *thuggee* for colonial authority is also a text *for* other thugs, a manual for reproducing thug practice. Savage's text (within the text of the Masters novel), even though cast in the model of strict representational realism, is susceptible of an Other reading; its meanings are ambushed, deflected, and augmented en route to a destination it can never reach. The Thuggee and Dacoity Department strove to produce, in its extensive records on thug affiliation and activity, a text without nuances or fissures, something that was not susceptible of any misreadings or contesting interpretations. It sought, in its meticulous record keeping and its attempts to square all the approvers' testimonies with each other and make them speak with one voice, to produce a record that would have what was presumed to be the authority of material fact. But for Savage, at least, it is impossible to engage in such an enterprise without also inscribing his own complicity in his testimonial. In this respect, he does approximate the classic approver of the Thuggee and Dacoity Department, who cannot bear witness against others without simultaneously bearing witness against himself.

While the novel insists that only impersonation can yield the truth, it also illuminates the heterodox desires that underlie the exercise of going native. Moreover, this impersonation is quite detached from any agency on the part of William Savage and from any sense of originary identity. Forced into the disguise of the Indian weaver Gopal (by the *patel* [village headman] Chandra Sen) in an unwilling and ultimately fruitless attempt to save a would-be sati, he is recognized as an impostor by Hussein. Hussein is ideal material for an approver: he has brains, courage, and resourcefulness, and he is remarkably eager to undo the institution of *thuggee*, but his testimony alone is not enough to compel belief in the practice. So he recruits an Englishman to the anti-*thuggee* cause, knowing that only he can be fully convincing as a figure of knowledge. And this knowledge can only be acquired experientially, and by going outside the law as currently constituted, as Savage learns when he follows the more conventional methods of information retrieval. As Hussein says,

> Several times some English official or other has got hold of information about us. Then he has chased us out of his district, and reported, I suppose. But

they've never worked together, and it always blew over. They'll never destroy us until one of them finds out everything, and forces the Lat Sahib [the governor-general] to believe everything, and plans a campaign to cover all India. And that one who finds out must fear Kali, or he will not understand her. But he must not love her. (p. 208)

Unable to ignore the thugs as the other English functionaries are ready to do, eager to discard the Englishness he so uncomfortably inhabits, and pressured by Hussein and Mary, Savage decides to continue as Gopal the weaver, who, as it turns out, is also Gopal the thug. For an unsuccessful and insecure man like Savage, wracked by anxieties about (heterosexual) masculinity and Englishness, it is the very abdication of authority involved in playing a thug that is peculiarly attractive; inhabiting the subject position of the most criminalized and most scrutinized indigenous subject holds out the promise of psychic satisfactions not ordinarily available to colonial authority.

The novel dallies with the idea (as many crime fictions often do, though less explicitly) of the fragility of the barriers that separate the custodian of law and morality from the criminal. It actually makes available the proposition (though it has to drop it at the end) that Savage is at heart a thug and that his initiation into *thuggee* by Hussein is no accident. He takes naturally to the trade, is attended by good omens, and enjoys a facility of thought, speech, and action that is alien to his English self. The idea of mimicry itself is transformed in his performance of it and begins to assume to assume the contours of possession, if not those of originary identity. There is no difference for him between the mimicry of an identity and the identity itself.

In order to pass for an Indian or a thug (ultimately these two categories are collapsed, as we have seen in the other narratives of *thuggee*) Savage must slough off certain normative aspects of Englishness in the tropics—the militant Christianity, the revulsion against disease and cruelty, the reforming impulse. He must instead embrace what is described as the nondualistic moral economy of Hinduism that sees both creation and destruction as suffused with the divine. Needless to say, the psychic territory of "India" is always coextensive with Hinduism, despite the fact that Muslims as well as other religious groups are shown to practice *thuggee* as much as do Hindus; and this Hinduism is consistently and exclusively fetishized as blood lust and hyperbolic sexuality. As an Indian, and Hindu, and thug, Savage must participate in a series of paradoxes. He must be Indian, and thug, to return more securely to Englishness, and legitimacy; he must allow evil to be done in order to do good; and, since the contexts of legality are always shifting and are particularly in need of redefinition in India, he must go outside the law in order to uphold the law. Always relatively indifferent to the finer points of legal procedure and defendants' rights (here written as an inaptitude for "paperwork"), the antithug drive allows him to rethink the concepts of justice and legality in the colonial context, where it is notoriously difficult to punish crime anyway:

> "What does justice mean?" ... "Fair trial, the rules of evidence, no double hazard, no hearsay, and so on and so on? Or protection against injustice, against violence? The means, or the end?. . . . Oh, I know we have no *evidence* about them yet. That's just what I mean. I tell you, sir, they cannot be run down within our rule of law. Indians aren't English. "No man dies by the hand of man," they think, so they won't give evidence because they are not angry with the murderers. They think men who kill are driven by God to kill. And there are too many jurisdictions, too far to go to give evidence, too long to wait. We've got to go outside the law to catch them, to prevent more murders."
> (pp. 128–29)

Caught between a colonial government and an Indian populace unwilling, for different reasons, to do what is necessary to end *thuggee* and pressured, moreover, by Hussein, Savage becomes Gopal again, only more completely in earnest this time. In his new role Savage discovers that passing for a thug involves a radical (re)contextualization of his once and future Englishness. Moreover, as Gopal he has to inhabit a role and a history that is already in place. Impersonation involves not freedom but strict adherence to a scripted identity; he cannot start afresh, or make himself up as he goes along. He discovers that as Gopal, he is already an expert strangler and strategist, destined to be "the greatest the Deceivers have ever known" (p. 218). And once he participates in the sacramental ritual of *gur*-sharing and tastes the transubstantiated body of the goddess, his allegiance and destiny are fixed. Savage is born to *thuggee*, as his comfort in his role of thug demonstrates; indeed, his story undoes the usual weighting of "self" and "role" in the Englishman's subjectivity, since he is more convincing (to himself, and apparently to Indians and Englishmen alike) and comfortable as Indian and thug than as Englishman and Christian. Hussein, who is more percipient than he about the complexities of subject formation, reminds him that "free will" is an adjunct (or an illusion) of Englishness alone. Savage must find out that intentions guarantee nothing; not even the Englishman, once he has decided to play the Indian, can escape the formulaic constraints of Indian/thug ontology: "You are a Deceiver, from this dawn on for ever. A strangler. Only stranglers may stand on the blanket: you stood on it. Only stranglers may take the consecrated sugar of communion: you took it. It doesn't matter what a man *thinks* he is. When he eats consecrated sugar, on the blanket, in front of the pick-axe, he is a strangler, because Kali enters into him." (p. 182)

Such a script also demands of course that he confront his double, the original Gopal. In order to protect himself and in order to wrest some autonomy for himself, Savage strangles Gopal and thus becomes Gopal himself. But strangling the "real Gopal" only makes him more fully Gopal, for he can now develop into his predestined role. From this point on, all paradoxes are held in abeyance. From being complicit in murder through inaction Savage proceeds to strangulation himself and becomes, in an extraordinary take on the man-who-would-be-king vision that tropes so much colonial discourse, a noted leader of thugs. Like Burton the Muslim, Savage the thug is characterized not simply by mastery but by an extraordinary surplus of subject effects. (Unlike Burton, though, he is tempted, and he is corrupted—although not irredeemably.)

The desire for Gopal, which is closely articulated with the desire to *be* Gopal, is mediated, interestingly enough, through the figure of the sati who frames the novel and who foregrounds the question of gender that has been bypassed or placed under erasure in the *thuggee* archives. I find the entry into *thuggee* through sati to be a particularly productive conjuncture for the problematic of mimicry, identity, and the colonizer's desire. The sati, most obviously, provides an occasion for access to Gopal. The sati has to be set up in the beginning so that Savage can play Gopal; and then it has to be deferred so that he can continue to play Gopal *and* go in search of Gopal. Her presence in the novel displaces homoerotic desire and returns Savage to heterosexuality. It also ensures his successful miming of Indianness and Englishness. But the consolidation of heterosexuality, masculinity, and Englishness demands not simply her presence but her death. She is insistently narrativized as a *voluntary* sati; she is a romanticized figure, whose sacrifice Savage has no desire to thwart. He desires her, and his desire for her takes the form of wanting her to die for him, which he ensures by killing Gopal. In this way, he can enjoy the satisfactions of Indian as well as English masculinity. As an Indian, he can have the woman die for him (and deliver him of his sexual anxieties); but being fully Indian also means that he himself must die, for the sati requires a dead husband. As an Englishman, therefore, he can distance himself from the violent implications of Indianness. The sati's death releases him from the exigent identity of the Indianness into which he had temporarily descended and frees him to enact the rituals of Englishness with greater plausibility. The most convincing Englishman—as indeed the most expert thug—turns out to be the mimic man after all.

AFTERWORD

Masters's novel serves in many ways as the most apt of epilogues to the colonial accounts of *thuggee*, given its excavation of the erotic/affective and metaphysical seductions of that institution—and of the thug—for English masculinity in the tropics and given its suggestion that the lure of the thug for the Englishman may be as compelling as that of *thuggee* for the (Indian) thug. It charges the project of unveiling and chastisement with a profusion of guilty, even delirious, appetites and obsessions that call for continual incitement and consummation. It does not, of course, fail to play upon the received colonial narrative of *thuggee* as timeless Indian duplicity; but it also reconfigures it as an erotic tale of the fraternal, closeted, and homicidal desire that drives Indian and English impersonation. Perhaps most remarkably, it showcases the seamless self-referentiality of the discourse on *thuggee* (as evidenced in an archive composed of biographies, histories, novels, legal records, and rumors) by collapsing the thug and the thug hunter into a single figure; with a literalism quite unprecedented in any of the other texts it confirms that wherever there is an Englishman there is a thug.

THREE

Anglo/Indians and Others
The Ins and Outs of the Nation

The subject of identities and traffic in *Kim* is best approached through indirection. One approach is through Policeman Strickland (who makes his initial appearance in "Miss Youghal's *Sais*"), Kipling's first experiment in casting the impersonator par excellence. Strickland, though, is a curious figure, a not quite/not right disguise artist who exists in an oblique and complex relationship, not just to official wisdom but also to the extraofficial masters of impersonation. He recalls Sherlock Holmes's extraordinary capacity for being all things to all people; like that preeminent detective, he operates in the implicit belief that all knowledge is knowledge of criminality. He recalls Burton, too, in his often contentious relationship with official power and in the psychosexual nature of his investment in "going Fantee." Like these illustrious fictional kin, he "[holds] the extraordinary theory that a Policeman in India should try to know as much about the natives as the natives themselves,"[1] though, curiously, his own simulation of nativeness appears to be itself a simulation of a simulation of nativeness: "Now, in the whole of Upper India, there is only one man who can pass for Hindu or Mahommedan, hide-dresser or priest, as he pleases. He is feared and respected by the natives from the Ghor Kathri to the Jamma Masjid. . . . Strickland was foolish enough to take that man for his model" ("Miss Youghal's *Sais*," 51).

What kind of Englishman is Strickland, and what is the nature of the knowledge that he relentlessly seeks and obsessively embodies? How, indeed, is he himself known? Consider, for instance, the lines that introduce him:

He was perpetually "going Fantee" among natives, which, of course, no man with any sense believes in. He was initiated into the *Sat Bhai* at Allahabad once, when he was on leave. He knew the Lizard-Song of the Sansis, and the *Halli-Hukk* dance, which is a religious can-can of a startling kind. When a man

71

knows who dance the *Halli-Hukk*, and how, and when, and where, he knows something to be proud of. He has gone deeper than the skin. But Strickland was not proud, though he had helped once, at Jagadhri, at the painting of the Death Bull, which no Englishman must even look upon; had mastered the thieves'-patter of the *changars;* had taken a Yusufzai horse-thief alone near Attock; and had stood under the sounding-board of a Border mosque and conducted service in the manner of a Sunni Mullah. ("Miss Youghal's *Sais*," 51–52)

The knowing tone of the narrator of *Plain Tales from the Hills* seems to be of a piece with Strickland's own knowingness. But what effects might be generated by this catalogue of Strickland's accomplishments? It is not always easy, in these early tales, to gauge the kinds of irony (or the contrary) that might be at work in such representation. One can read the cognitive surfeit elaborated in the sketch above as the sort of Orientalist construction (by a metropolitan "globetrotter") that Kipling (along with other, like-minded Anglo-Indians) was fond of caricaturing.[2] The stories in this volume were in fact produced for the largely Anglo-Indian readership of the *Civil and Military Gazette* in Lahore and later revised for a metropolitan audience at "home." On the other hand, the list of Strickland's esoteric accomplishments may be no more than a characteristic gesture designed to conserve the mysteriousness of India.[3]

In any event, in this story Strickland is a curiously vacant figure, with little autonomy or effectivity, and the narrative details not so much the triumph as the undoing of the policeman. He falls in love with a Miss Youghal—who, we are told, "could not understand him"—but is forbidden her company by her disapproving parents. Thereupon he assumes the disguise of a *sais* (coachman) and takes employment with her parents, thus partially circumventing their prohibition. He is not so much a representative *sais* as a "paragon among *saises*," performing his duties more like a London coachman than his shiftless Indian counterpart. In this capacity, he pays court to Miss Youghal, but he is driven to abandon his disguise one day when he overhears an elderly general flirting with her. This betrayal of himself, however, wins him the respect of the general, who then proceeds to intercede for him with the senior Youghals. He is accepted as a son-in-law, but only on the condition that he repudiate decisively all identities but his English one. This he concedes, though at considerable emotional and intellectual cost to himself: "It was a sore trial to him; for the streets and the bazars, and the sounds in them, were full of meaning to Strickland, and these called to him to come back and take up his wanderings and his discoveries" ("Miss Youghal's *Sais*," 56).

But the story seems deliberately to fudge the question of why he assumes this disguise, or any disguise, in the first place, except to be with and learn about *saises;* his assumption of a native persona in this case at least seems insistently gratuitous in an erotic plot, which seems to resolve itself without his assistance. What the story may illustrate instead are the ways in which cross-racial traffic provides a range of erotic excitements unknown to the respectable and domesticated English self (as a *sais* he becomes a fully eroticized figure for the first time, an object of desire for an Indian woman, even though he dutifully ignores her overtures). The story also demonstrates that the (hetero)sexual satisfactions of Anglo-India are not only impossible without the homosocial bonds generated by "going native" but that the marriage plot may itself have been engineered to allow Strickland an excuse to play the *sais*. Here as elsewhere, the policeman's fungibility seems to represent the always incomplete and profoundly narcissistic character of impersonation.

In later stories, particularly the gothic ones, Strickland's status as the figure of (extra)legal rationality becomes even more inflected with ambivalence. As Gail Low reminds us, "Gothic narratives cultivate uncertainty and offer a 'double-take' on a realist and mimetic enumeration of names and things."[4] In "The Return of Imray" (in *Life's Handicap*) he belongs very uneasily in the terrain of realism, accompanied as he is by a clairvoyant dog. In this as in other narratives, impersonation is coded quite explicitly as a deeply anxious activity, an activity that generates and multiplies anxiety even as it seeks ostensibly to relieve it.[5] A tale like "The Mark of the Beast" (also in *Life's Handicap*) confirms not only that the depths of the Indian psyche are unspeakably horrific but also that India always defers a full accounting of itself, holding its worst horrors in reserve: "Strickland hates being mystified by natives, because his business in life is to overmatch them with their own weapons. He has not yet succeeded in doing this, but in fifteen or twenty years he will have made some small progress" (*LH*, 198).

A refusal of such abominable knowledge, however, is a refusal of the cunning that is necessary to colonial existence; the ingenuous and kindly Imray ("The Return of Imray") is murdered by his servant of four years for having casually remarked on the beauty of the latter's little son, who dies soon after; this apparently perfunctory remark identifies him in the servant's regard as the bearer of the evil eye. In India, good intentions guarantee nothing. What counts is knowledge of natives; and not knowing natives can kill you. And yet knowledge, for the narrator, cannot dispel fear. The tragedy of Imray becomes not a mystery solved but a warning about the peculiar proliferation and reproducibility of Indian crime, especially against the British. He discovers, too, that what has been mysterious to Strickland and himself until the end has always been transparent to the Indian servants who understand the communications of Imray's ghost but who repeat the obfuscatory fictions of Imray's voyage to Europe for their masters' benefit. And while it is the narrator who registers confusion, and shock, and nervousness, this could be seen as a displacement of the uneasiness about the limits of

Strickland's power and knowledge. Certainly the misgivings of this story resonate in some of the other fiction as well as with a letter that Kipling wrote
to his cousin Margaret Burne-Jones when he was nineteen: "Immediately
outside of our own English life, is the dark and crooked and fantastic, and
wicked: and awe-inspiring life of the 'native.' Our rule, so long as no one
steals too flagrantly or murders too openly, affects it in no way whatever—
only fences it around and prevents it from being disturbed."[6]

If the all-seeing and all-knowing Englishman is diminished in "The Return of Imray," "To Be Filed for Reference" (*Plain Tales from the Hills*) further complicates the will to knowledge that is also the will to power. This
story takes the form of a prelude to McIntosh Jellaludin's Great Indian
Novel, and is orchestrated at least partially as a contest between two (English) native informants. The protagonist is a figure both like and unlike
Strickland. Unlike Strickland, Jellaludin is an Englishman gone native rather
than the impersonator who crosses cultural formations at will, and one of
the most important indices of his distance from Englishness is miscegenation, an option always available, but always disavowed by Strickland as
Indian. Sexual and emotional involvement of English men with Indian
women usually carries a price, as is evident from "Lispeth," "Beyond the
Pale" (both in *Plain Tales from the Hills*), "Without Benefit of Clergy" (*Life's
Handicap*), and "The Man Who Would Be King" (*The Man Who Would Be
King and Other Stories*), though it is by no means the case that the chief suf-
ferer in such encounters is invariably the Englishman. Like the policeman,
though, Jellaludin does lay claim—despite his marriage to an Indian woman
and his descent into a rather sordid Indian life—to Englishness, and Englishness of a particularly class-marked sort, which is undergirded by memories of a classical education at Oxford. Like him, too, Jellaludin is pos-
sessed of an archival ambition: "What Mirza Murad Ali Beg's book is to all
other books on native life, will my work be to Mirza Murad Ali Beg's!" (*PTH*,
276). However, he dismisses Strickland as "an ignorant man—'ignorant
West and East'" (*PTH*, 275). But Jellaludin is not quite permitted to replace
Strickland as the colonial figure of omniscience; for Strickland in his turn
dismisses Jellaludin's account of the an Indian underworld (though he does
not find it easy to claim certitude): "[Strickland] said that the writer was either an extreme liar or a most wonderful person. He thought the former.
One of these days you may be able to judge for yourselves" (*PTH*, 277).
Moreover, Zohreh Sullivan adumbrates, Jellaludin is a figure who, even if he
can believed to be speaking the truth, has been damaged by that excess of
knowledge which always has the potential to injure the knower: "The price
of such knowledge is complete alienation from colonial society, marriage to
a native woman, and alcoholism. . . . Too much knowledge about India tests
the boundaries of the social system, victimizes both the knower and the

known, the fictional and the real author, and ironically looks ahead to the powerlessness of Kipling himself to author his ultimate epic about India."[7]

IMAGINED COMMUNITIES AND RESIDENT ALIENS

Jellaludin's magnum opus remains unpublished in "To Be Filed for Reference," as did *Mother Maturin*, Kipling's own Great Indian Novel about the dark underbelly of Anglo-Indian sexual traffic in the subcontinent (apparently on the advice of his parents).[8] The Great Indian Novel that Kipling actually published turned out to be a radically different narrative from the one projected in the earlier tales, even as it redeployed the familiar tropes of disguise and racial-cultural exchange.[9] It has been remarked of *Kim* by Irving Howe that it "is unsubdued by the malignity at the heart of things";[10] Mark Kinkead-Weekes even goes so far as to say that "the Game is given less than justice because there is no powerful enough experience of evil."[11] Similarly, J. M. S. Tompkins says of Kim and his world that he is "a casteless waif, curious, flexible, resilient, accustomed to blows, but quite free from tyranny, and fed by the charitable gifts of the people who are always called gentle and kindly. Intrigue and murder are part of his world, but, since he is wary and spirited, they excite without oppressing his imagination."[12] The novel has also been credited with having re-created the "light and colour and golden and purple fruits" that for the adult Kipling made up his early life in Bombay,[13] as well as the sense of intuitive intimacy (uncomplicatedly combined with a sense of one's own superiority) with Indians that the young English child is said to have enjoyed.[14] (As James Harrison puts it, "a child of four or five whose merest whim is law to the adult servants around him is already a fully-fledged Anglo-Indian.")[15] While Howe's and Tompkins's assertions seem to me to be a simplification of the novel's psychic investments, it is nonetheless true that the anxiety, aggression, and general grotesquerie that attend the earlier narratives of mimicry seem to assume less obviously somber and more *ambivalent* inflections in *Kim*.[16] Nonetheless, Strickland has a place in the world of this novel, even if a marginal one. It is, however, Strickland in a gentler incarnation; the Strickland who had willingly tortured a leper with white-hot irons in "The Mark of the Beast" has assumed the guise of a genial Anglo-Indian who can flirt lightheartedly with the Sahiba and who is less anxious to terrify natives into submission through the reports of his superior—indeed, preternatural—shrewdness and knowledge than to be persuasive in the role of the inept and vacuous colonial official. In other words, he has graduated from the performance of nativeness to the performance of Englishness. *Kim*, which is regarded as unique in Kipling's corpus and perhaps in colonial discourse as a whole, must, like Strickland, detach itself from all the narratives of mimicry that have preceded it in order to name India and to (un)name Britain's relationship to it. As Homi Bhabha says, paraphrasing Ernest Renan on the problematic of the nation, nationness can only be generated and reproduced by "forgetting to remember" or, perhaps even more strongly, remembering to forget.[17] This willful forgetting that induces a sense of nationness is, as I hope to demonstrate, central to Kipling's novel.

What, however, must the novel remember to remember, and what must it remind itself to forget? In a novel about the everyday vigilance necessary to sustain India as British,[18] how must it remember the dismemberment of the (Sepoy) Mutiny, for instance? For one thing, it must remember by invoking the proper name India as a totalizable phenomenon; in no other novel about the subcontinent does the name have such talismanic value. What *Kim* offers is a world governed less by oppositions (as most of Kipling's other fictions are) than by paradoxes and differences that are nonetheless articulated within a system that is loosely congruent with "national space." The Indian theater offers—within this totality—an infinite multiplication of possibilities and positionalities. And India—in this novel about the putative threat to empire—remains on the whole an unproblematic landscape. It is a luminous and salubrious terrain that encouragingly mirrors self-aggrandizing aspirations. Despite its size and apparent variety of languages, religions, castes, and other differences, it remains transparent and knowable; its knowability, moreover, is not here of the kind described (however ironically) in "The Phantom Rickshaw," in which knowing India is knowing Anglo-India:

> One of the great advantages that India has over England is a great Knowability. After five years' service a man is directly or indirectly acquainted with the two or three hundred Civilians in his Province, all the messes of ten or twelve Regiments and Batteries, and some fifteen hundred other people of the non-official caste. In ten years his knowledge should be doubled, and at the end of twenty he knows, or knows something about, every Englishman in the Empire, and may travel anywhere and everywhere without paying hotel-bills.[19]

Kim's India encompasses the natives as well, but this by no means compounds the problem of knowability. In India, everyone who is not part of the Great Game can be assigned an unchanging identity, and everyone's mark of identity is visible, even conspicuous. Not unsurprisingly, caste becomes the trope for knowability in the novel; indeed, it becomes one of the tropes for—to use Ronald Inden's evocative phrase—"imagining India."[20]

In the midst of all this, Kim is (even before his formal induction into the Great Game) a figure who embodies some of the paradoxes of identity that the novel seeks to stage. He is the only one who cannot be pinned down, who is always addressed in ecumenical, nonsectarian terms as "Little Friend of all the World" or "Friend of the Stars," while he is also always attended by a prophecy of his sahib's patrimony: "'There will come for you a great Red Bull on a green field, and the Colonel riding on his tall horse, . . . and . . . nine hundred devils.'"[21] It comes as no surprise to learn that Kim, even as a boy on the streets of Lahore, is acutely conscious of his difference from and superiority to the Hindu and Muslim lads who are his daily companions: especially in his games on the Zam-zammah cannon ("first of the conqueror's loot") with the other boys, he registers a very precise sense of being the representative of an imperial race:

> "Off! Off! Let me up!" cried Abdullah, climbing up Zam-Zammah's wheel.
> "Thy father was a pastry-cook, Thy mother stole the *ghi*," sang Kim. "All Mussulmans fell off Zam-Zammah long ago!"
> "Let me up!" shrilled little Chota Lal in his gilt-embroidered cap. His father was worth perhaps half a million sterling, but India is the only democratic land in the world.
> "The Hindus fell off Zam-Zammah too. The Mussulmans pushed them off." (*Kim*, 52)

Furthermore, he alone can read the scene around himself properly and make discriminations, even as he delights in its heterogeneity; no one else shares either his discriminating eye or his pleasure in the spectacle by which he is surrounded. He alone seems to be self-conscious about the fact that the social world is structured by categories of knowledge that are complex but eminently manageable. The teeming life of the Grand Trunk Road is also, in Kim's classifying imagination, a highly ordered world:[22]

> The lama, as usual, was deep in meditation, but Kim's bright eyes were open wide. This broad, smiling river of life, he considered, was a vast improvement on the cramped and crowded Lahore streets. There were new people and new sights at every stride—castes he knew and castes that were altogether out of his experience.
> They met a troop of long-haired, strong-scented Sansis with baskets of lizards and other unclean food on their backs, their lean dogs sniffing at their heels. These people kept their own side of the road, moving at a quick, furtive jog-trot, and all other castes gave them ample room; for the Sansi is deep pollution. Behind them, walking wide and stiffly across the strong shadows, the memory of his leg-irons still on him, strode one newly released from the jail; . . . Kim knew that walk well. . . .
> The lama never raised his eyes. He did not note the money-lender on his goose-rumped pony, hastening along to collect the cruel interest; or the long-shouting, deep-voiced little mob—still in military formation—of native soldiers on leave, rejoicing to be rid of their breeches and puttees, and saying the most outrageous things to the most respectable women in sight. . . . But Kim was in the seventh heaven of joy. (*Kim*, 109–11)

One of the necessary paradoxes of this multiplicity is that only the English, or their agents, can fully understand, delight in, and indulge in the variety of roles and subject positions (the two are the same thing in many respects here) that are offered. As Patrick Williams points out, this is the very reverse of what might be expected to be the colonial norm. Where the white man in the colonial theater was often conspicuous because of his racial and linguistic difference and cultural ignorance,[23] here it is the Indian who stands out, who has nowhere to hide. And while Indians remain, in good Orientalist tradition, ontological liars, in contrast to the British, who always tell the truth except when it is necessary to lie, it is Englishmen who are more wily than the Indians and who are involved in spying on Indians. It is of such a scenario that Spivak remarks with considerable perspicacity (though she is speaking not so much the discourse of colonialism as that of a benevolent radicalism which is eager to hear the subaltern speak), that "the person who *knows* has all the problems of selfhood. The person who is *known*, somehow seems not to have a problematic self."[24]

In a world where understanding identity—which is the same as fixing it—apparently involves little more than using a semiotic key to clothing, identities for players in the Great Game are continually in flux. Kim can apparently pass as anything, from a Muslim boy of the streets to a *chela* (religious novice) of a Tibetan Buddhist lama to a scullion boy to a young sahib, and so on ad infinitum. But Kim is not the only one to possess such a gift—though he alone can mimic across a racial divide. Hurree Babu is another, particularly complex, instance of identity formation through mimicry. He is the classic mimic man interpellated by an English literary education, a process superbly analyzed by Gauri Viswanathan;[25] it is a process that Spivak describes (speaking of postcolonial India, but with an obvious glance backward at its colonial incarnation), as effecting "the subtlest kind of cultural and epistemic transformation, a kind of upward race-mobility, an entry, however remote, into a geopolitical rather than merely national 'Indian'-ness."[26]

> [Hurree], an MA of Calcutta University, would explain the advantages of education. There were marks to be gained by due attention to Latin and Words-worth's *Excursion* . . . French, too, was vital, . . . Also, a man might go far, as he himself had done, by strict attention to plays called *Lear* and *Julius Caesar;* . . . Still more important than Wordsworth, or the eminent authors, Burke and Hare, was the art and science of mensuration. A boy who had passed his examination in these branches—for which, by the way, there were no cram-books—could, by merely marching over a country with a compass and a level and a straight eye, carry away a picture of that country which might be sold for large sums in coined silver. (*Kim*, 210–11)

But Hurree Chunder Mookerjee is also an extraordinarily able student of another kind of text. He is the mimic man, but he can also mimic the mimic man: he can assume the persona of the "fearful" Bengali, the Bengali babu showing off his learning, or the Bengali nationalist fulminating against the inequities of colonial rule, though it is not always clear in his case where Bengali identity begins and its mimicry ends. He is, nonetheless, an able man; he can even take in Kim and can advise him on the consistency of a role. But he, of course cannot be the Englishman. Much of what he does is admirable and arouses the profound respect of Kim, who even, at one point, acknowledges him as a superior. But few things that he does are completely right. His ambition to be a Fellow of the Royal Society, while shared by Creighton, can only produce the repetition of a knowledge that Englishmen have already; what Hurree seeks to learn from the lama, for instance, is familiar and not very exciting knowledge to Lurgan.

Like Kim and Hurree Babu, E23, who exists only as a number and only in disguise, produces and discards identities in his flight from his pursuers; the point, and the pleasure, of disguise is its ceaseless repetition—though it should be noted that E23 keeps being unmasked until his disguise is stabilized for him by Kim and Strickland. Strickland himself plays at Englishness far more convincingly than he has been able to do in the other tales; Colonel Creighton, too, delights in playing the bumbling English fool, speaking a *koi hai* variety of the Urdu he knows in all its idiomatic complexity and affecting an inane and uninformed, because typically colonial, passion for horseflesh.

This mimicry underwrites the primary discursive object of the novel, which it seems to me is to produce the idea of the nation and of the citizen. This may seem like an extraordinary claim to make for a novel of which it has been said that "no one is seen who challenges British rule, and no one articulates any of the local Indian challenges that must have been greatly in evidence—even for someone as obdurate as Kipling—in the late nineteenth century."[27] It is undoubtedly true that the novel ostensibly speaks the absence of conflict rather than conflict and that the figure of the anticolonial insurgent or the nationalist is unrepresented—or, rather, unrepresentable—in the novel.[28] Opposition to British rule must be expressed through the comic pathos of the two Russians, abandoned by their attendants and led by the resourceful Hurree Babu from village to village in order to be mocked; anticolonial activity, in other words, must be represented through the most unlikely and liminal figures, figures, moreover, in whom there is the least psychic investment.

This absence cannot but invoke its opposite, and nationalism returns through the interstices of the text—through the figures of the Mutiny and of the Bengali babu (who represents bourgeois nationalism), to cite two of the most obvious instances. The Indian Mutiny, so called, of 1857 was a defining moment in British imperial history, and its hold on the public imagination in both England and India was to remain powerful for decades. Patrick Brantlinger states that at least fifty novels about the mutiny were written before 1900; at least another thirty were written before 1939.[29] There were also innumerable eyewitness accounts, journal articles, histories, poems, and plays (including George Trevelyan's famous *Cawnpore*) [1865]) that dealt with the events of 1857–1858. The Mutiny offered, to colonial officials through the nineteenth and twentieth centuries, the classic paradigm of Indian ingratitude and brutality; it served as an ur-text of insurgency and miscegenation that threatened to repeat itself endlessly in colonial history. Jenny Sharpe writes that, in the 1890s, a reviewer for *Blackwood's* anticipated—despite the countless representations of the events of 1857—that Kipling would be the one to write the as-yet-unwritten "great Mutiny novel."[30]

Kim is everything that a Mutiny novel cannot be. Yet in the novel memories of the event serve as a lurid subtext to the boy hero's indomitable cheerfulness in playing the Great Game; it serves as a reminder that policing can never be too radically isolated from playfulness. Here the Mutiny, which demands a disavowal of the possibility of nationalism or insurgency (it can only be narrated as dementia) also demands a debt of remembrance—the old Rissaldar must ceaselessly repeat his tale to his neighbors and, more importantly, to English officials: "A madness ate into all the Army, and they turned against their officers. That was the first evil, but not past remedy if they had then held their hands. But they chose to kill the Sahibs' wives and children. Then came the Sahibs from over the sea and called them to most strict account" (*Kim*, 100).

By the time of the writing of Kipling's great novel, though, there was a pluralization of anticolonial initiatives in India. The formation of the Indian National Congress in 1885 marked an important reconfiguration in the energies of nationalism; it signaled the beginning of bourgeois dominance in nationalist politics and the corresponding elision (both in colonialist and bourgeois nationalist narratives) of armed insurgency (which often took the form of peasant uprisings) in favor of demands for constitutional reforms.[31] This context is made available to us, though in a decidedly oblique fashion, through the figure of the Bengali Hurree Babu. The Bengali babu has a particularly suggestive colonial history; he is the quintessential mimic man of colonial discourse, the English-educated, confused, epicene, and pathetically mutinous figure who can achieve neither the rationality and poise of the Englishman nor the simplicity and purity of the unanglicized, unhyphenated native.[32] Bengal was, it should be remembered, the site in the nineteenth and early twentieth centuries of a broad spectrum of anticolonial and nationalist activities. Terrorist acts (committed by women and men) aimed against colonial officials emanated from here; in the judicial discourse of the place and time, this violence was located within a nexus of religious and sexual "abominations."[33] Bengal was also notable for its involvement in the politics of bourgeois nationalism; the Indian National Congress convened in Calcutta for its first meeting. The Bengali babu, then, was a figure who existed in a profoundly conflictual relationship with the colonial polity. In many of Kipling's stories, of which "The Head of the District" is symptomatic, the Bengali is despised by Englishmen and other Indians alike, as "a *kala admi*—a black man—unfit to run at the tail of a potter's donkey."[34]

The novel, then, both invokes and rejects two apparently indigenous modes—the violence of the Mutiny and the civility of Congress demands—of conceiving nationalism and nationness. But what *Kim* does, above and beyond this uneasy and furtively represented engagement with available nationalisms, is to make the subject of nationalism its own; it seeks to generate a myth of the nation and of the national subject.

Let us consider for a moment the paradoxes that constitute the idea of nationness. In the classic essay, "What Is a Nation?" (1882), Renan identifies the nation as the most compelling and pervasive formation of modern western politics while systematically eliminating any "rational" or "natural" basis for national identity. Language, religion, race, geography, dynastic continuity, even a commonality of material interests—none of these can generate nationness or account for the sentimental charge of national identity. Renan delights, in fact, in the contradictions that not only inhere in the national idea but provide its very grounds of possibility. Thus nations originate in violence, conquest, and oppression, and a national memory and national unity in the nation's present can only be achieved if the citizen makes it a point to forget much of the past: "Forgetting, I would even go so far as to say historical error, is a crucial factor in the creation of a nation."[35] A nation nonetheless transcends its immanent contradictions in a collective will-to-nationness which is also a will-to-homogenization; it exists on a democratic, voluntaristic basis, being the result of a "daily plebiscite." Benedict Anderson's *Imagined Communities* (1991) plays upon some of the ambivalences in the idea of the nation, but his objective is explicitly *not* to supply or invent a principle of nationness. For him, the nation is not a principle of transcendence or reconciliation but the supreme fiction of modern politics.[36] There can be no objective definition of a nation, no authentic and inauthentic nations; a nation is an "imagined community" that can mean whatever its members want it to mean. The word *imagined* is key, because Anderson argues that the nation as political principle was conceived, historically, through certain forms of representation, most notably narrative fiction and print journalism. Anderson's study is salutary among other things for its refusal to dismiss nationalism as simply a pathology of contemporary political life. It aligns the nation with questions of religion, faith, kinship, and emotional allegiance; unlike others, it seeks to understand the *affect* of the nation through its splits, repressions, and ambivalences. It refuses to assume a true-false judgmentality and positivism in understanding the nation; the concept of imagination, of nation as representation, is at the heart of this analysis. The nation is never automatically there, even as a geographical, physical entity; as a place of mobility, migrancy, movement, it has to be literalized through pilgrimages and the travels of the indigenized bureaucracy of the colonial state. Nations must be *seen* as well as read as novels or newspapers.[37] In several ways, however, Anderson reproduces the affect he seeks to analyze and duplicates the homogenizing tendency of nationalisms in his conception of a "homogeneous empty time" of the nation that produces the normative citizen.

The essays in *Nation and Narration* offer implicit and explicit critiques of this, pointing to the internal contradictions of the nation, to its dialectical logic, to its status as a differential principle, and to the repressions that are necessary to produce the people as one. Geoff Bennington points to the ways in which the nation must necessarily be constructed from the outside in:

> It is tempting to try to approach the question of nation directly, by aiming for its centre or its origin. . . . [But] such access is in general illusory: the approach to the nation implies borders, policing, suspicion, and crossing (or refusal of entry)—try to enter a country at the centre (by flying in, say), and the border is still there to be crossed, the frontier shifted from periphery to centre. . . . The frontier does not merely close the nation in on itself, but also, immediately, opens it to an outside, to other nations.[38]

While Renan had insisted on the nation's resolution or transcendence of its contradictions, tensions, and fissiparous tendencies through a gigantic act of collective will, Bennington argues that it is these very differences that make the idea of the nation fragmentary, contentious, and discontinuous. A nation therefore has to be narrated in order to exist; it requires a foundational fiction—which is always necessarily a fiction—to mark its legitimation and continuity.[39]

The instance of *Kim* provides a most productive illustration of and commentary upon the construction of nationness and nationness as construct. Though the action of the novel is set in the 1880s (Kim encounters the old Rissaldar after the Golden Jubilee of Victoria's coronation in 1887) it was conceived in Vermont in the mid-1890s and finished in Sussex about six years later.[40] Kipling, as we might know, was born in India (in 1865) and spent his first six years there, years that were, in his recall, idyllic to a degree. Raised by Indian servants, he claims to have been familiar with the bazaars and temples and Indian neighborhoods of Bombay and to have thought in Hindustani. When he was sent to school in England at the age of six, he was apparently traumatized in ways he never forgot. This was a common enough experience for Anglo-Indian children as young inhabitants of an "invaded colony" rather than a "settler colony."[41] Angus Wilson points to the numerous reasons that made such a separation of the English child from India seem necessary:

> Ostensibly the reason that parents sent their children at an early age back to England was the care of their health, the avoidance of the Indian climate which, particularly given the limitations of nineteenth-century medicine, was perilous, especially in the hot seasons. . . . The children of English people in the lower echelons of the Anglo-Indian hierarchy stayed there and went to boarding schools like Kim's at Lucknow or up in the hill stations, . . . Those children who went there, however, would share their lives with boys of "dubious" social origin and with those Portuguese names that so sprinkle Kipling's stories of half-caste life. To health, then, were added social and racial reasons. Anyone who was anyone would send his children home. Children speaking an Indian tongue more easily than English, or recounting Hindu fables, or mouthing the names of outlandish gods and goddesses, were charming up to, at the most, six years. . . . Ayahs, native servants of all kinds were "wonderful with children", but they spoiled them. . . . Then the standards of all natives were not ours—in matters of truth-telling, of hard work, of hygiene, and . . . in sexual life where, as the terrible child marriages showed, they were notoriously precocious.[42]

Kipling returned to India when he was sixteen, to resume residence with his parents in Lahore, and he served on the staff of the *Pioneer* and the *Civil and Military Gazette* for a few years. This was also the period when he established his fame (more fully perhaps in England than in Anglo-India) as the writer of *Plain Tales from the Hills* as well as other fictions of Anglo-Indian life. In his midtwenties he left for an extended tour of the world that took him to England (which, once again, he hated) and then to the United States, to the home of his new bride, Carrie. Kipling was then writing his great novel about India after his permanent departure from the country of his birth and early childhood (he was to return only once, for a brief visit); he was writing it from the outside, as an exile (exiled at one point from both India and England). It is precisely this placement, I will argue, that allows him to conceive of a national horizon for the geographical space designated doubly as "India" and as "colony." It is this distance, too, and the sense of India as a totality that this distance enables, that gives the novel its distinctly monumental, if not epic, flavor.

If liminality is central to the construction of the nation, then Kipling's India is certainly produced and reproduced at its borders. Who, after all, are the primary Indian characters of the nation that names itself India? The central Indian character is of course the Buddhist lama from Tibet; indeed, Kipling has been sometimes criticized (by patriotic Indian critics) for making Buddhism, which was exported out of India in the third and fourth centuries B.C. and which in any event has been a minor presence in the country for centuries, representative of Indian spirituality.[43]

The Pathan Mahbub Ali, who is at home in Kabul and border towns like Peshawar, is another player on the Indian scene, and he too is exorbitant to colonial space and to Indian national space. In the 1840s and once again in the 1880s, the colonial government in India had fought two bloody and humiliating wars over the control of Afghanistan, which marked the point at which British and Russian colonialisms encountered each other. Despite the energetic execution of a British "Forward Policy," Afghanistan remained unassimilable into the British Empire, and the North-West Frontier Province (from which Mahbub Ali apparently hails) remained in a stormy and contested relationship with the government in Delhi.[44] The third Indian, Hurree Babu, evokes not geographical but—as we have seen—political and ideological liminality (as well as centrality) in colonial discourse. He is thus a character in whom very specific cultural meanings are vested. He himself is well aware of them, and even as he *is* the typical Bengali, verbose, cowardly, superstitious, he also knows how to *play* the boastful Bengali babu or the malcontent babu to perfection.

If India in this novel is represented best by liminal figures, much of its action also occurs in the margins of the nation. Its narrative takes place not in central or southern India, though Kim travels widely, as far south as Bombay, and so apparently does the lama. Much of what happens happens in northern India, in Lahore, Ambala, and the hills that mark the point of contact between India and its northern neighbors—and other imperial powers. This of course was the India most familiar and beloved to Kipling. He spent most of his adult years in India in Lahore and Allahabad; he saw southern India only through the window of a train, and he seems to have had little physical contact with the country's eastern reaches, despite "The City of Dreadful Night" (1888) which is one of the most famous literary indictments of Calcutta.[45] English officials in his stories ("William the Conqueror" is but one example) pride themselves on being "Punjabis."[46] But, more importantly, for India to be invoked as a totality, as a nation, it must be constructed at its borders; a boundary has to be invoked in order to construct a center. As Bhabha points out in "DissemiNation," liminality is at the very heart of the national idea.[47]

In a very real sense, the nation in the novel is also created quite literally out of the very fact of travel. Benedict Anderson speaks of the ways in which travel by administrators literalized the imagined community, as did the travel undertaken by ordinary people on the new railway systems.[48] In late-nineteenth-century India the civil service, which had been partially indigenized, may also have produced the nation as an effect of travels, territorial-

izations, and contextualizations. The trope of pilgrimage in *Kim*, pilgrimage
without a specific local object—the River of the Arrow is, like the idea of the
nation, mythical and internal and therefore necessitates travel to all places—
serves to concretize and make visible the form of the nation. What this
evokes is the spectacle of Gandhi's endless peregrinations (in Richard
Attenborough's film), both on foot and by train, through a geographical
space that assumes the lineaments of a nation through this very process. (To
this end Indian political leaders practice *padayatras* [an elevated term for
"traveling on foot" that does not translate easily—*yatra* for instance is not
simply travel, it is also pilgrimage] for political ends. In the last decade the
Bharatiya Janata Party has undertaken numerous *yatras* in a bid to assert
"national unity," a fairly transparent code for the expression of anti-Muslim
sentiment.

If the nation has always to be coaxed into existence, if the idea of the
nation is not native, is always imported, then who or what constitutes the national subject? This is a critical question for *Kim*. It is in its engagement with
this question that we see Kipling's implicit dialectic with the idea of (Indian)
nationalism. If nationalism's project is to locate and name a native self and
an alien self, then Kipling too must make such discriminations. It has been
said by John McClure that the project of this novel is to naturalize the Englishman in India, or at least to naturalize British control of India.[49] How is
rule presented as something else? How does one belong and not belong?
I would argue that this emphasis is quite literally relocated in *Kim*; it is
far more ambitious in its reach than other novels about India. The Anglo-
Indian for Kipling becomes the site of the dissolution and reconfiguration
of the native-alien opposition. *Kim* distinguishes between Indian Englishness and English Englishness; it incorporates and co-opts the anticolonial
argument about foreign rule by making the Anglo-Indian (almost) an unhyphenated Indian. Kipling knew very well that the best defense of colonialism was to argue its self-reflexive and self-monitoring capacity, as well as
its faculty for internal reform, and it is his privileging of the Anglo-Indian
as the true insider that allows him both to criticize British India and to ensure its permanence. Thus the Sahiba can say, of Strickland and his ilk:
"'These be the sort to oversee justice. They know the land and the customs
of the land. The others, all new from Europe, suckled by white women and
learning our tongues from books, are worse than the pestilence. They do
harm to Kings'" (*Kim*, 124). Kim, too, gives his assent to the Anglo-Indian
boys who are his compatriots at St. Xavier's:

> The mere story of their adventures, which to them were no adventures, on
> their road to and from school would have crisped a western boy's hair. . . . And
> every tale was told in the even, passionless voice of the native-born, mixed
> with quaint reflections, borrowed unconsciously from native foster-mothers,

and turns of speech that showed they had been that instant translated from the vernacular. Kim watched, listened, and approved. This was not the insipid, single-word talk of drummer-boys. (*Kim*, 172)

Kipling must have been well aware that his target audience for such a philosophy was not just the Indian (who might require persuasion of the Anglo-Indian's indigeneity) but also Anglo-Indians themselves. As Angus Wilson puts it,

> The English remained, throughout their rule in India, as transient in their final image of themselves, despite all the home-making of the memsahibs, as they had been in the East India Company days of "make your lakhs of rupees and come home". It was to be Kipling's chief difficulty, when he later dreamed of an Anglo-Saxon Empire, of fitting India, his beloved, into the sisterhood of Canada, Australia, New Zealand and South Africa. However miserable, however made impotent by retirement to Bognor or Torquay or Eastbourne, "home" was not just a name for the mother country for Anglo-Indians, as it continued to be for Australians or New Zealanders or English South Africans until the Second War; England was their real home. . . . The English as a whole were dug into India to stay as long as the mind could imagine, and yet individual English men and women, although their families might have served India for generations, were there not to settle but to serve their time.[50]

It is Kipling's task, then, to make the Anglo-Indian perform as first citizen of a country named India. The Strickland of the stories may have been caught up in trying to solve the problem of how one can be inside and outside at the same time. The issues are not extraneous to *Kim*, but what this novel takes on is the figuring of the colony as nation. If Anderson had spoken of the nation as an imagined community, Kipling speaks of the colony in the same terms. He in fact collapses the oppositions between colony and nation. In such an arrangement, it is not the "Indian" Indian who features as the primary national subject but the Anglo-Indian, who is carefully distinguished from the Englishman and who in a sense may be said to "choose" India in a manner not available to the native.[51] B. J. Moore-Gilbert, however uncritically he might read Anglo-India's representation of itself, nonetheless usefully reminds us that "the growing community of foreigners in India was to produce its own quite distinctive contributions to . . . [Orientalist] discourse. . . . It would be a mistake to assume that Anglo-Indians were simply the British abroad."[52] He points to a distinctively Anglo-Indian literary and journalistic tradition going as far back as the 1830s, a tradition that generates and reflects the community's sense of its specific audience and its unique locational and experiential identity.[53] Anglo-Indians like Kim and Strickland and presumably Creighton and Lurgan (and, of course, Kipling himself), who have been born and raised in India and who have what is certainly represented as a native's access to indigenous language and culture, are an entirely different breed from the despised and alien English, whose awkwardness, intolerance, and ignorance justifies Kim's contempt for them. These Anglo-Indians are also different, and better educated in citizenship and nationness, than are the teeming but transparent masses that populate the pages of the novel, the masses that have no capacity to transcend their differences in order to imagine the nation. They are superior above all to the Eurasians, those disturbingly visible rem(a)inders of the illegitimate, because (hetero)sexual traffic across the racial divide, a traffic that can only produce hyphenated Indians. Kipling is particularly revulsed by the "half-caste," the Eurasian (known in postcolonial India as Anglo-Indian!) who is neither flesh nor fowl. The Anglo-Indian (that is, the India-raised white man), because he is an (almost) unhyphenated Indian, becomes the native of the Indian nation.

And yet Kim's own whiteness is never something that can be taken as given; it must also be learned, demonstrated, and defended. His whiteness is never a fully secure inheritance; his racial identity is always interstitial and contested. He is, after all, Irish, an ethnic-national category often conflated with the Indian and in many instances affiliated with Indian nationalism;[54] it is surely of some interest to remember Kipling's own Scottish, Irish, and Welsh ancestry on his mother's side.[55] He is, besides, the son of an alcoholic and degraded private, and is "a poor white of the very poorest" (*Kim*, 49). He is only tenuously connected with the whiteness of Colonel Creighton and Lurgan Sahib, and the novel oscillates between defining sahibness as a property that is biological and as something that must be carefully culti-vated. Gyan Prakash is surely right to point to the doubleness that marks the production of Kim's whiteness (and he also notes that it may be possible to see Kim's mother as ethnically unmarked):

> Obvious and easy though it is to see how *Kim* asserts racial polarities, it is equally significant to observe that these oppositions are rendered profoundly enigmatic in the process of their formulation. Thus Kim's whiteness does not stand separate from his blackness but is bleached from his "burned as black" skin. So immersed is the formation of Kim's racial identity and authority in difference—whiteness formed on the borderlines of black and white, fact and fable, English and the vernacular—that liminality marks the emergence of a powerful colonizer-colonized hierarchy.[56]

When "discovered" by Father Victor and the Reverend Arthur Bennett, he speaks very much in the accents of the Eurasian from whom he is careful, later, to distinguish himself in caste terms: "Their eyes are blued and their nails are blackened with low-caste blood, many of them. Sons of *mehtera-nees*—brothers-in-law to the *bhungi* [sweeper]" (*Kim*, 192). When Kim con-templates his racial identity, it is often, significantly, in terms of what must be learned—"I must needs go to a *madrissah* [school] and be turned into a

Sahib" (*Kim*, 138)—and what must be remembered: "One must never forget that one is a Sahib, and that some day, when examinations are passed, one will command natives" (*Kim*, 173).

The (Anglo-Indian) nation thus conceived also has its other citizens, and certainly Mahbub Ali and Hurree Babu are among them by virtue of their training for and participation in the Great Game. Indeed, the Great Game, which employs the most liminal subjects, which conceives of India as a unified field upon which actions, travels, and exchanges must occur ceaselessly, becomes the institution that tropes the nation. And if Anglo-Indians are the founding fathers and representative citizens of the Indian nation, how do they guarantee, consolidate, and reproduce this Indianness? What ensures that their Indianness will be persuasive and uncontested? How do the "Indian" Indians signify national identity? What are the rituals of nationness that the national institution of the Great Game demands?

Mimicry and exchange are key to the Great Game: the exchange of messages and information, the exchange of clothing, and the mimicry of "Indian" identities (and "English"/"Anglo-Indian" ones). These exchanges must be continually performed; paradoxically, this continual movement between identities is necessary to fix identity/Indianness. Hence the extraordinary gratuitousness that often seems to attend the rituals of impersonation and nationness. There is no point at which Kim's identity becomes stabilized; making him Indian, and keeping him Indian, is an ongoing process. The signs of national life must always kept visible through miming the various modalities of national identity. What can or must be represented is not the insurgent subject, who is always outside the circuits of exchange mandated by the Great Game. Instead the players must mimic themselves and each other as "Indians"; what results in this continuous representation of the nation is a mirroring dynamic in which all players are implicated in a circuit of (reciprocally constitutive) desire.

Note that the various encounters between the members of the Game are organized around a semiotic of dressing and undressing. It is not surprising that perhaps the proudest moment for Kim in the novel is when he transforms the Maratha agent into a sadhu: "Kim had been trained by Lurgan Sahib; E23, by virtue of his business, was no bad actor. In place of the tremulous, shrinking trader there lolled against the corner an all but naked, ash-smeared, ochre-barred, dusty-haired Saddhu, his swollen eyes . . . luminous with insolence and bestial lust" (*Kim*, 252). This is Kim's masterpiece, a performance/production that produces two mimic subjects in the same process: himself as *chela* with magical powers, E23 as half-naked sadhu. This process of ceaseless mimicry is obviously not without its (homo)erotic charge. What Kim receives as a gift from Mahbub Ali at the end of his apprenticeship is, first, a gift of clothing which not only (re)produces Kim as Indian but quite specifically names him as an eroticized body ("Oh, the hearts to be broken! Oh, the eyes under the eyelashes, looking sideways!" [*Kim*, 219]). What this chain of impersonations does is (re)produce the bond that exists within the members of the fraternity. The national polity, as numerous scholars have noted, is typically constituted through the marginalization of women as symbolic figures; it is troped as a passionate brotherhood or as, in Jonathan Goldberg's words, an "ideal of union between men."[57] Citizenship and nationness are generated and consolidated in this endless circuit of exchange and impersonation between Anglo-Indian and other Indian men.

Does the nation have a gender? Does the national subject? The motherland model of nationness is familiar from Indian and other nationalisms: woman becomes that which represents the nation, the culture, and her purity, integrity, and seclusion are the concepts that are foregrounded in the struggle for possession. Many nationalist movements have bought into this masculinism and have conceived of themselves in virilized terms, a situation that of course requires enactment at the expense of women. The ideology of cultural restoration assumes the guise of radical nationalism; women are the revered objects of the collective act of national deliverance and the role model for the new nationalist collective which was analogous to the patriarchal family. Women as the carriers of culture have represented the nation, which must be saved and restored; at the same time they have existed in an oppositional relation to the nation, because in order to conceive of itself as one, the nation has to suppress internal difference.

If citizenship is only available for and between men, then what is the relation of woman to men in these personifications of the nation? The marginalization of women in *Kim* has been noted by more than one reader. Edward Said says of it:

> It is an overwhelmingly male novel. . . . The women in the novel are remarkably few in number by comparison, and all are somehow debased or unsuitable for male attention: . . . to be always pestered by women, Kim believes, is to be hindered in playing the Great Game, which is best played by men alone. So not only are we in a masculine world dominated by travel, trade, adventure and intrigue, we are in a celibate world, in which the common romance of fiction and the enduring institution of marriage have been circumvented, avoided, all but ignored.[58]

In this novel, women seem precluded even from a symbolic role in the (re)production of the nation. In the various nationalist discourses that circulated in nineteenth- and twentieth-century India, the nation had to be imagined as the great mother—Mother India—as a prelude to any conceptualization of the national subject.[59] This (re)production of the (male) citizen by the symbolic mother is marvelously literalized in a novel like Salman Rushdie's *Midnight's Children* (1981); though this Mother India is (misogynistically) transformed into a monstrous figure by the end of the novel, becoming the widow Indira Gandhi (about whom the sycophantic slogan—"India is Indira and Indira is India"—is generated), who devours her children.

Some of this sense of the monstrosity of the mother—or of the female—is certainly anticipated in *Kim*, which seeks rather desperately to erase the motherland model of nationness. Kim himself betrays no interest either in his dead mother or in the Eurasian woman who apparently stands in loco parentis to him until his adolescence; the latter represents the repulsive fact of interracial sexual relations that Kim must scrupulously forego and, further, may in fact be held (partially) responsible for the death of the Father. He spends his energies attaching himself to actual and symbolic fathers throughout the novel: the lama, Mahbub Ali, Creighton, Lurgan, Hurree Babu, all of whom compete rather jealously for his time and loyalty. Is Mother India then abolished from the Anglo-Indian national imaginary? I would argue that the maternal model is displaced in a number of ways. If there is a positive maternal figure at all in the novel, and one who may be said to provide a partial representation of a good Mother India, it is the lama.[60] In interesting ways he anticipates the epicene figure of Gandhi, who also occupied a space of ambivalent gendering, especially in relation to the discourse of nationalism.[61]

Though *Kim* attempts to excise women from the performance of nationness, it is at the same time curiously dependent upon women—often prostitutes—for innumerable services, particularly the mechanics of the impersonation that induces nationness. It is through prostitutes like the Flower of Delight that the enemies of the colonial state attempt to obtain information from Mahbub Ali; it is a generous prostitute from Amritsar who pays for Kim's and the lama's train tickets; and it is to the courtesans of Lucknow that Kim goes when he wishes to convert from whiteness to Indianness for his travels through India. When Kim is finally initiated into the Great Game by Mahbub Ali, the initiation involves a visit to the prostitute Huneefa, who produces spiritual protection and a disguise for Kim simultaneously. Significantly, his visit to a prostitute upon reaching symbolic manhood does not involve any form of (hetero)sexual initiation. Kim is of course a figure of significant sexual attractiveness to women, and his sexual attentions are continually solicited by women through the novel. These must repeatedly be disavowed: "How can a man follow the Way or the Great Game when he is so-always pestered by women?" thinks Kim. "There was that girl at Akrola of the Ford; and there was the scullion's wife behind the dovecot—not counting the others. . . . When I was a child it was well enough, but now I am a man and they will not regard me as a man" (*Kim*, 306). This disavowal is most explicit in the instance of the Woman of Shamlegh, where Kipling will not permit a cross-racial heterosexual union despite the ethical claim the Woman is said to have on Kim's sexual regard.

The prostitute is, obviously, the most literal figure of exchange in a sexual economy which is also intimately linked to an economy of disguise and mimicry. She becomes one of the primary counters in the circulation of information, identity, and homosocial power. It is her presence—that of the carnal and completely embodied female figure—that facilitates the overt disavowal of all femininity in national space, including the maternal model of femininity and nationness (the mother, of course, signifying a disembodied but nonetheless gendered subject). Thus, through the prostitute, the domain of heterosexuality is also invoked and repudiated.

It is, of course, noteworthy that no Anglo-Indian or English women—whether as mothers, prostitutes or (potential) citizens—feature in this performative model of the nation; in fact, they find no place in the narrative at all.[62] What novel inflections are accumulated in this new definition of nationness? Women (including mothers) are, as we have seen, both necessary and superfluous to the staging of citizenship; they are the source of a certain unease in the novel's conception of an alternative national polity. The reproductive paradigm of nationness, which is embodied in the maternal model, is (dis)embodied in *Kim* through the mimicry of identities—rather than the duplication of bodies—the mimicry that (re)produces the nation. In the absence of Mother India, the men who would be Indian must always keep performing.

FOUR

As the Master Saw Her

Western Women and Hindu Nationalism

The title of this chapter repeats with a difference the title of a book Margaret Noble wrote in 1910, *The Master as I Saw Him.* Noble, who came to be known as Sister Nivedita, went to India in the last decade of the nineteenth century in order to serve as a disciple of the Hindu monk and religious leader Swami Vivekananda and to serve, at his behest, as a model and guide for downtrodden Hindu women. In this chapter I use the figure of Nivedita as a point of entry into questions of colonialism, nationness, and gendering, especially as they are mediated through religious discipleship in late-nineteenth-century India. I examine the ways in which a certain position (here discipleship) within religion (here Hinduism, of both the "high," or Vedantic, variety and the less-elevated forms) figures as the ground upon which traffic around gender identification and national identity can circulate. In particular I contemplate the western woman as "native"; I also scrutinize the ways in which she is solicited as central to the project of imagining India/ Hinduness[1] and imagining Hindu masculinity and yet simultaneously constructed as a blank space, as the receptacle of the displacements of various religious, sexual, and nationalist imperatives. But if the western woman, here called Nivedita, is the name of a set of displacements, we cannot begin with her. In order to speak of her at all, we have to speak of a number of intersubjective relays, involving her, Ramakrishna, and Vivekananda. So we have to begin elsewhere; we have to begin with Ramakrishna.

THE GURU

Ramakrishna Paramhansa was the guru of Vivekananda (the latter translated the word *guru* as *Master*, a translation Nivedita retained), who in turn was Nivedita's guru.[2] Ramakrishna features as an important figure in nineteenth-century Bengali culture, and he continues to function as an iconic figure even in the present, largely, I believe, because of the appeal of his dynamic and well-known disciple Swami Vivekananda. Ramakrishna continues to be significant for middle-class Bengali Hindus though, as Partha Chatterjee points out, not all are uncomplicatedly reverential: "In the public postures of the Bengali intelligentsia to this day, its relationship to Ramakrishna has been both uneasy and shamefaced."[3]

Ramakrishna was born in 1836 in Kamarpukur in rural Bengal and grew up barely literate in an orthodox Brahman family. In his teens he went to Calcutta to officiate as a priest (a fairly lowly position) at the temple of the goddess Kali at Dakshineshwar, where he lived for the rest of his life. It was here that he is said to have practiced a variety of taxing spiritual disciplines for more than a decade. Through all this he was supported and sheltered, first by his wealthy patroness, Rani Rashmoni, and later by her son-in-law, both of whom were convinced of his sanctity despite the widespread belief that he was delusional, if not mad. By the 1870s his reputation was in the ascendant. He had established a character as a mystic and had attracted a large number of devotees, almost all of whom were male. By the time of his death in 1886, many of his disciples had begun to think of him as an avatar, an incarnation of God; this was a belief that eventually gained a fair amount of currency among Bengali Hindus.

Interestingly enough, for an unlettered and somewhat eccentric sadhu, a considerable number of Ramakrishna's unmarried and householder disciples came from the *bhadralok* (emergent urban Bengali bourgeoisie) class. As Tapan Raychaudhuri notes

> The social origins of the young men led by Vivekananda, who became disciples of the mystic, Ramakrishna Paramhamsa, and were later duly ordained as *sanyasis* [monks—though often without the institutional affiliations of Catholic or Buddhist monks], were in no way different from those of other well-known protagonists of the new enlightenment [the liberal, reformist movements of the nineteenth century]. . . . It is their decision to abandon the comfortable occupations of their forebears in quest of the ultimate spiritual experience in the older religious tradition that marks them out from their predecessors and contemporaries.[4]

Most of these disciples were bourgeois in occupation and English-educated, well versed in the Utilitarian and Positivist thought of the nineteenth century, and inclined to rationalism and skepticism in religious questions, though few—according to the testimony of the *Ramakrishna Kathamrita* and the accounts of other disciples and biographers—were as openly disbelieving of the guru's powers and visions as Vivekananda initially was. The significance of these class and intellectual origins was not lost on the disciples themselves. Ramakrishna's disciple and biographer Saradananda avowed that the purpose of his guru's life was "to bring the western-educated Indians who had strayed into the blind alley of rationalist scepticism and materialist aspirations back into the Hindu spiritual-religious fold."[5]

Despite his professed indifference to and ignorance of social reform movements and political questions, Ramakrishna nonetheless was personally acquainted with several of the leading figures of nineteenth-century Bengal. He met (on occasion upon his own initiative) with Vidyasagar, Pandit Shashadhar Tarakachudamani, Shibnath Shastri, Bankim Chandra Chatterjee, Debendranath Tagore, "National" Nabagopal Mitra, Michael Madhushudan Dutta, and apparently even Dayanand Saraswati of the Arya Samaj. With Keshab Chandra Sen of the Brahmo Samaj of India he had a more than casual acquaintance, meeting him frequently at his residence and at the gatherings of the Navavidhan Sabha. It was through Keshab's generous report on the sage of Dakshineshwar that Ramakrishna became known to the general populace of Calcutta;[6] this may account at least in part for the overwhelmingly *bhadralok* and English-educated makeup of his following. In fact, after his death and during the ascendancy of Vivekananda, followers of Keshab and Ramakrishna quarreled quite bitterly about which of the two men had had the greater influence on the other.

Ramakrishna was well known as an idiosyncratic figure who claimed to have tested, through a ritualized and highly literal process of psychic identification, the truth of the varied sects that are subsumed in the nineteenth century under the label Hindu, as well as of other religions like Buddhism, Islam, and Christianity. He was inducted, at different points in his early manhood, into Tantric and Vaishnava spiritual disciplines, as well into the philosophy of Vedantic nondualism. He also practiced, though without the aid of a preceptor, the form of religious devotion known as *bhakti*, by assuming the form of Hanuman, the monkey devotee of Rama. In this form he subsisted on roots and fruits, jumped about instead of walking, and apparently experienced spinal developments resembling a tail. During this devotion to Rama he had a vision of Rama's consort Sita, which culminated with the merging of Sita's body into his own. At another point, when he visited Nadia, the birthplace of the fifteenth-century Hindu mystic Chaitanya (the founder of Vaishnavism in Bengal), "he had a vision of two boys [identified as Chaitanya and his companion Nityananda], 'bright as molten gold', who rushed to meet him, smiling, and were merged into his own body."[7]

Toward the end of 1866, Ramakrishna was initiated into Islam by an unorthodox Muslim "guru," a Hindu practitioner of Sufism called Govinda Roy. Ramakrishna described his possession by the spirit of Islam in the following terms: "I devoutly repeated the name of Allah, wore a cloth like the Arab Moslems, said their prayers five times daily and felt disinclined even to see images of the Hindu gods and goddesses, much less worship them—

for the Hindu way of thinking had disappeared altogether from my mind. I spent three days in that mood, and I had the full realization of the *sadhana* [spiritual practice] of their faith."[8] In one version of the story (admittedly one that is not often repeated) he even consumed beef, though he had to assume the form of a dog feeding on the carcass of a cow in order to do so.[9] As a result the prophet Muhammad appeared to him in a vision and literally merged into his body. Several years later, in his "Christian" phase, brought on by the contemplation of the Madonna and the Christ-child at the home of a Hindu devotee, the experience was repeated, though with greater intensity, when he achieved a comparable union with the body of an adult Christ.

It has been suggested that some of this religious eclecticism—though not these modes of religious experience—may have been Keshab's gift to him, though Sumit Sarkar persuasively argues (in his incomparable essays on Ramakrishna) that the catholicism of Kamarpukur's religious culture may well have contributed to it as well.[10] Unlike Keshab, though, he made no intellectual investigation of these faiths, and there is no evidence that his understanding of religious matters was in any way challenged or transformed by his encounters with Islam or Christianity. In fact, through all his life Ramakrishna demonstrated a marked anti-intellectualism, always proclaiming the superiority of "experience," especially the experience of possession or impersonation that was peculiarly his.

Analogous to this kind of mobility between varieties of religious identification was another, and more obviously if differently gendered, transaction. Ramakrishna located in (what we will very conditionally call) heterosexual masculinity[11] and in the greed of material possessions (a configuration he conflated and designated *kaminikanchan*, woman-as-seductive-figure and gold) the greatest obstacle to religious truth. For Ramakrishna, attachment to wealth or to woman in this sense constituted the two most potent forms of enslavement to which the (heterosexual) male was subject. Of the two, *kamini*—for Ramakrishna, almost always a powerful, sexually voracious, and irresistible figure—was the more dangerous and therefore to be guarded against by vulnerable and exploited males. Partha Chatterjee has convincingly elucidated the appeal of such a philosophy to the nineteenth-century Bengali bourgeois male. For this subject, the figure of *kaminikanchan* in the *Kathamrita* had a resonance that went beyond the fairly orthodox Brahmanical exhortations to cultivate chastity and poverty (both forms of nonattachment) and spoke quite directly to the dilemmas and anxieties engendered by colonialism:

> In the specific context of the *Kathamrta* in relation to middle-class culture, the figure of woman-and-gold could acquire the status of a much more specific sign: the sign of the economic and political subordination of the respectable male householder in colonial Calcutta. . . . The figure of woman-and-gold also

signified the enemy within: that part of one's own self which was susceptible to the temptations of an ever unreliable worldly success. From this stemmed a strategy of survival, of the stoical defence of the autonomy of the weak.[12]

At the same time, Chatterjee tells us, the "gospel" of Ramakrishna was appropriated for what might be termed a bourgeois nationalist project of the mediation of popular culture in the pursuit of hegemony. Hence the attempts of "M" (Mahendranath Gupta), the author of the *Ramakrishna Kathamrita*, to elevate and classicize that text with English phrases and quotations from European thinkers as well as citations from the Sanskrit texts of Brahmanical Hinduism. (A similar process of anglicization and Semiticization may be said to be at work in *The Gospel of Sri Ramakrishna* [emphasis mine], the English translation of the work by Swami Nikhilananda.) Ramakrishna knew neither English nor Sanskrit; his own Bengali, as Sumit Sarkar points out, was colloquial, rustic, and "pre-colonial."[13] Chatterjee points to the use of these European and classical Indian languages and idioms as symptomatic: "For both [the bourgeois nationalist] narrator and reader of the *Kathamrta* [the Bengali text], the terrain of European thought is familiar ground—familiar, yet foreign—from which they set out to discover, or perhaps, rediscover, the terrain of the indigenous and popular, a home from which they have been forcibly wrenched."[14]

What I wish to examine, however, is not the *Kathamrita* as text or the questions of class mediation raised by the encounter of Ramakrishna and colonialism; some of that ground in any event has been most ably covered by Sarkar as well as by Chatterjee. My interest in the figure of *kaminikanchan* is more directly concerned with the questions of identification and sexuality that are raised in a colonial-nationalist context by the concept of guruship and discipleship. We have seen that of the two impulses, *kamini* and *kanchan*, the first was, according to Ramakrishna, infinitely the more powerful and dangerous.[15] He was thus very severe on his householder (married) disciples for their persistent attachment to woman (as seductive figure), synecdochically described as "blood, flesh, fat, gut, worms, urine, shit"; he continually admonished them to practice celibacy after the birth of one or two children. Unmarried male disciples were exhorted to avoid not simply sexual contact with women but contact of any kind with women. He himself was careful to avoid the company of women, except when he could identify them in a relatively uncomplicated manner as maternal figures (his wife apparently was one such figure) or when he himself "became woman." All encounters with women (even those not characterized as *kamini*) were dangerously suffused with (hetero)sexuality: "It is not good for a sannyasi to sit in the company of a woman devotee, or even to talk to her. . . . There are eight kinds [of sexual intercourse]. To listen to a woman and enjoy her conversation is one kind; to speak about a woman is another kind; to whisper to her privately is a third kind; to keep something belonging to a woman and enjoy it is a fourth kind; to touch her is a fifth."[16]

Sexual desire could not however be kept in check by mere abstinence; it could only be transcended by becoming this troubling object of desire. The only way to shun woman (as seductive figure) was to become woman (of another kind). I hardly need add that this feminine identification was quite compatible with a marked gynophobia.[17] This "transvestic" discipline was enjoined in a general way upon the unmarried male disciples, though, interestingly, it was not enjoined upon Narendranth Dutta (later Swami Vivekananda), whom Ramakrishna identified at several points as fixed firmly in a masculine identification. (I will return to this point later.) He identified several of his (male) followers as feminine and was pleased to note their partiality to "the womanly attitude" (*Gospel*, 458–59). In an address to the disciples, he stated that: "A man can change his nature by imitating another's character. By transposing on to yourself the attributes of woman, you gradually destroy lust and the other sensual drives. You begin to behave like women. I have noticed that men who play female parts in the theatre speak like women or brush their teeth like women while bathing" (*Gospel*, 176). At several points in his life, therefore, he literalized his transcendence of the body by assuming all the outward and inward signs of female identity, including menstruation; Saradananda's biography claimed that he had periods when he was a woman.[18] He had from his early youth shown a marked talent for mimicry, and as a boy in the village of Kamarpukur had been involved in directing and acting in village theatricals. He was particularly adept at mimicking women's voices and behaviors; in his teens he had posed as a woman and gained access to the zenana of a neighbor's house, and in adulthood he sometimes lived, as a woman, with the women of his patron's household in Calcutta. As a practitioner of the *madhura bhava* [the attitude of the mistress] of Vaishnava discipline in Dakshineshwar, he assumed women's clothing and jewelry, as well as the feminine speech and behavior of the female devotee Radha. This discipline apparently reached its apex when Krishna revealed himself to him and merged in his body.[19]

This assumption by Ramakrishna of corporeal and psychic femininity was crucial for the transcendence of (what we are here calling) heterosexuality. It is worthy of note, however, that in "becoming woman," he became neither *kamini* nor mother but the "handmaid of God."[20] And the meaning of mimicry itself was translated into the experience of *possession*. Thus the transcendence of the (heterosexual) body made the body itself its vehicle and was made manifest in a continuum of corporeal, gendered signs: "I spent many days as the handmaid of God. I dressed myself in women's clothes, put on ornaments, and covered the upper part of my body with a scarf, just like a woman. . . . Otherwise, how could I have kept my wife with me for eight months? Both of us behaved as if we were the handmaids of the Divine Mother. I cannot speak of myself as a man" (*Gospel*, 603).What the general response to this impersonation might have been is difficult to establish. Christopher Isherwood tersely states that "Ramakrishna's latest *sadhana* caused a whole series of scandalous rumours," but he does not elaborate upon them.[21] At different points in his life, Ramakrishna was identified with a variety of feminine figures and icons, though he himself claimed to have functioned as woman for a short period. To some disciples he was a maternal figure; others among his circle identified him with Radha and eventually even with Kali herself. Hinduism of course does provide paradigms for shifting gender identifications or what may very provisionally be designated "transvestic"[22] display or androgyny for men.[23] Ashis Nandy claims that "'bisexuality' [a term that for him has everything to do with identification and nothing at all with object choice] in India has always been considered an indicator of saintliness and yogic accomplishments."[24] Only males are allowed to be "bisexual"/"transvestic"/androgynous; for women, masculine identification is, generally speaking, taboo. Thus Chaitanya dressed as a woman and regarded himself as an avatar of Radha; other Vaishnavas were likewise urged to identify with Radha, not with Krishna. Wendy Doniger provides further clarification by identifying the multiple valences of the androgyne (who is often conflated with the eunuch, the transvestite, the male homosexual, and/or the impotent male) in Vedic, Puranic, Tantric, and popular forms of Hinduism. The hermaphrodite god/dess Ardhanarishwara (literally, "the god who is half woman") may perhaps be said to provide one (decidedly patriarchal) paradigm, as might Tantric disciplines that prescribe the satiation and internalization of sexual desire as the means of transcending it.[25] Doniger summarizes the meaning of androgyny in Hindu thought in the following terms, which have important implications for our examination of Ramakrishna and his disciples: "A man can be a woman, but a woman cannot be a man. . . . A man can be a woman, but this makes it difficult, if not impossible, for him to be *with* a woman."[26]

Ramakrishna's practice, then, was not entirely eccentric within the norms provided by certain strains of Hinduism, and this obviously is not what I wish to assert. What I *would* like to argue is that becoming woman, is, for Ramakrishna, an entry into guruness, into mastery; my interest is in the gendering of guruness and discipleness. In most varieties of Hinduism that subscribe to the guru-*shishya* (guru-disciple) institution, the guru is almost always male, and his disciples almost always male as well.[27] The guru-disciple relationship is situated within a nonmoney economy, an economy moreover that functions outside relations of reciprocity; that is to say, the guru makes a gift of his knowledge to the disciple, who compensates the former in the currency of service, which can never, of course, be adequate to the gift.[28] In this respect the relationship between men in discipleship is notably different from the relationship of men with women; as Ramakrishna saw it, the relationship with women was always mediated by money.

Through most of his later life, following the conclusion of his spiritual disciplines and his conquest of desire through becoming woman, Ramakrishna sought out young, unmarried, male devotees. The longing for disciples and spiritual companionship was expressed with a singular though characteristic intensity:

> There was no limit to the yearning I had then. During the daytime I managed somehow to control it. The secular talk of the worldly-minded was galling to me, and I would look forward wistfully to the day that my beloved companions would come. . . . When the day came to a close, I could not curb my feelings. . . . When during the evening service the temple rang with the sound of bells and conch-shells, I would climb to the roof of the building in the garden, and writhing in anguish of heart cry at the top of my voice, "Come, my boys! Oh, where are you? I cannot bear to live without you!" A mother never longs so intensely for the sight of her child, nor a friend for his companion, nor a lover for his sweetheart, as I did for them! Oh, it was indescribable.[29]

When the young boy disciples began to arrive (probably in response to the recommendations of Keshab and the Brahmos), around 1879, Ramakrishna welcomed them with great eagerness. Many of his disciples were to speak of his tenderness and solicitude for them. Visitors commented on his "boyishness" (he played leap-frog with his boy disciples and displayed a decidedly nonadult hankering for sweets and other delicacies) and "on his childlike" freedom from bodily shame (in states of *samadhi* [religious trance] his clothes sometimes fell off his body). Some of the disciples in turn were willing to participate in this drama of prepubescent identifications and satisfactions; one of them, Rakhal, actually assumed the mannerisms of a little boy, jumping onto Ramakrishna's lap and shoulders and manifesting jealousy of other young disciples.

These young male disciples had to demonstrate the highest degree of spiritual and sexual purity, which had to be manifest in tangible ways. With his characteristic literalism, Ramakrishna would inspect their physiognomies and their bodies to ascertain their fitness for discipleship. Naren, of all the young men who visited the sage of Dakshineshwar, not only evinced the most promising corporeal signs but was also commended repeatedly on his masculine nature. Ramakrishna's relationship with his disciples was affective and highly physical in nature—a marked contrast to his phobic response to female bodies. In addition to examining their bodies for positive marks of spiritual fitness, Ramakrishna often fed his disciples with his own hands, sat on their laps or shoulders, stroked their bodies, leaned upon them, and placed his foot on their bodies either during or preparatory to entering a state of *samadhi*. He was also remarkable for inducing religious ecstasy through touch, even in a young man as skeptical as Naren. Naren's first ecstasy, in his late teens—or, rather, his memory of it—was a remarkable experience:

> Sri Ramakrishna drew near him in an ecstatic mood, muttered some words, fixed his eyes on him, and placed his right foot on Naren's body. At this touch Naren saw, with eyes open, the walls, the room, the temple garden—nay, the whole world—vanishing, and even himself disappearing into a void. He felt sure he was facing death. He cried in consternation: "What are you doing to me? I have my parents, brothers, and sisters at home."
>
> The Master laughed and stroked Naren's chest, restoring him to his normal mood. He said, "All right, everything will happen in due time."[30]

This mystical experience (as Naren recalls it), involving the dissolution or at least the reconfiguration of the boundaries of the ego, is very much in a Brahmanical Hindu tradition. What seems to me remarkable about this experience, however, is the interplay of two quite distinct registers—the mystical and the familial/social—that are introduced into the narrative by Naren's panicked and perhaps somewhat unexpected invocation of his natal family. One can only speculate that his own seduction into the realm of mystical dissolution may have been homologous for Naren to the guru's traffic in a variety of (troublingly gendered) identities. His defensive reaction against this is, significantly, the memory of the social and more specifically the normative reproductive sexuality of the familial unit.

The guru, however, was more than the divine lover. It is interesting to note that in the hagiographies and the posthumous testimonies of disciples he was also simultaneously constructed as the object of corporeal contemplation; the relationship with the disciples was charted as a drama of mutual attraction and solicitation.[31] The biographies as well as the accounts of disciples speak often enough of an attractiveness that was apparently both bodily and spiritual. They speak of the lightness of his complexion (an index of attractiveness in much of India; Brahmo accounts, on the other hand, speak of him as a small, dark man, not engaging in appearance) and of the grace and "golden" radiance of his body in *samadhi*.[32] Ramakrishna himself claimed to have been transformed into a luminous spectacle during the period of his severest spiritual disciplines, so much so that he had to keep his upper body, normally bare, covered with a shawl.[33] It is said that during this period he visited his ancestral village of Kamarpukur. As he was leaving in a palanquin (normally used to transport women) a crowd collected around him. "Dressed in scarlet silk cloth, with a gold amulet on his arm, his lips crimson from betel, he was a picture of exquisite grace. A crowd had gathered to see him off. . . . Said Hriday [his nephew and attendant], 'You are going away, and they won't see you for some days. . . . The thing is, you look so handsome in this dress, and they have come to see you.'"[34] The guru himself became the object and recipient of (spiritual) desire.

The favorite disciple, Naren was, however, slow to respond to Rama-krishna's fascination, even though he was loved by the guru with a special intensity. Ramakrishna routinely spoke of him as a spiritually perfect soul, one marked out for great things. At their first meeting he hailed the youth as Narayan (Vishnu) and fed him sweets (somewhat to Naren's discomfi-ture) with his own hands, an act of special intimacy. The young man, how-ever, was skeptical, if flattered, and responded with embarrassment and even revulsion to the guru's solicitations. Everyone noted Ramakrishna's special attachment to Naren; he would occasionally pass into *samadhi* stam-mering his name and, when the young man stayed away, would be heart-broken and tearful. On occasion he even sought Naren out at his home or at the meetings of the Sadharan Brahmo Samaj, episodes that left the dis-ciple (who had not yet chosen discipleship) mortified. He often identified himself and the young man in terms of antithetical gender identifications: "He has a manly nature and I have the nature of a woman" (*Gospel*, 693).

I might point out that the intensity of this bond did not pass without notice, even among the most devout. That this conspicuous attachment was perplexing and even embarrassing for some of his devotees is evidenced by the phobic remarks of some of the older male (and married) devotees: "Put your mind in God [*sic*]. There is no reason to think about those boys."[35] One of them even accused him of being partial to handsome and well-to-do lads (*Gospel*, 812).[36] There was as well the discomfort voiced by the fa-vorite young disciple himself, who more than once castigated his guru for his "infatuated" pursuit of him. (This intensity of attachment was to be re-peated, years later, with Vivekananda's own eastern and western disciples; both as guru and as disciple, he was the object of adoration.) Ramakrishna himself had his doubts about his attachment to his boy disciples: "Oh Mother [Kali], what is this you have brought me to? All my heart is centred in these lads!"[37] But he soon had a revelation that vindicated his attach-ment as an aspect of religious adoration: "Mother said to me: 'You love him [Naren] so much because you regard him as Narayana himself. If the day ever comes when you don't see Narayana in him, then you won't spare him a single glance!'"[38] Even so, he is noted on one occasion to have expressed relief about the infrequency of Naren's visits, saying, "I am overwhelmed by his presence" (*Gospel*, 279).

THE SWAMI

Despite this early "recognition" by Ramakrishna as the chosen one, Naren did not actually accept Ramakrishna's status as his guru until a few months before the latter's death in 1886. His discipleship was profoundly marked—as that of his fellow disciples seems not to have been—by skepticism, conflict, and rejection on his part contending with the inexplicable appeal of the unlettered holy man.[39]

This history of conflict requires some consideration of Naren's social and intellectual milieu during his youth and early adulthood. He was born in 1863 into an upper-middle-class Bengali household in Calcutta and was western educated, as indeed were many others among the disciples. He was a rationalist, and he seems to have been challenged in obvious ways by colonialism, by Christianity, and by the Enlightenment intellectual heritage in its colonial and specifically South Asian inflection. I do not wish of course to assert that Ramakrishna was *not* hailed by colonialism. In fact, Chatterjee has persuasively described Ramakrishna's teachings and life as offering an ideal of weakness, detachment, and nonstriving that was particularly attractive to a male Bengali bourgeoisie assaulted by colonialism's mandate to accumulate and to assert an aggressive masculine heterosexuality.[40] (Even Protap Chandra Majumdar, a member of the New Dispensation, a devotee of Christ, and a self-confessed rationalist [and later Vivekananda's antagonist], recorded with some bewilderment and candor the "mysterious" fascination of Ramakrishna's temperament.)[41] Ramakrishna even demonstrated at various points a fairly lucid understanding of the scope of British political and military power in India, and he was cognizant, too, of the hegemonic power of western values and western education; he would occasionally urge Naren and other disciples, usually "M" (who was a schoolteacher) to conduct debates on philosophical subjects in English. It is even possible that Naren's attraction for him had something to do with the young man's putative embodiment of the rationalist masculinity of colonialism.[42] One early-twentieth-century scholar has even asserted (as did Saradananda in his biography of Ramakrishna; see above) that Ramakrishna's message represented "a 'Counter-Reformation' against not only the foreign religions, Islam and Christianity, but also the reforming movements of India."[43] This seems to me, however, a partial truth at best; it required a Vivekananda to effect such a reaction, and this in turn required many significant departures from the "gospel" of his guru. What I would suggest, instead, is that Ramakrishna probably was hailed by colonialism-and-nationalism (I speak of this here as a single category)[44] in a way distinct from the ways in which his best-known disciple was hailed. At this point I will simply say that this category occupies a recessive space in the *Ramakrishna Kathamrita* and in the saint's life. This is the gap Vivekananda seeks to address (and redress) in his own capacity as guru.

A child of the Bengal Renaissance and of colonial reason, Naren was a skeptic and a reformist in his impulses in his youth and early adulthood. As a teenager he had joined the Sadharan Brahmo Samaj, which had broken not only with the traditional polytheistic, caste-bound, image-worshipping Hinduism of nineteenth-century Bengal but also with the relatively conservative Adi Brahmo Samaj led by Debendranath Tagore and the Brahmo Samaj of India (later the Navavidhan Sabha) of Keshab. Like many members of the Brahmo Samaj he read Ramakrishna's withdrawal into *samadhi* (an event that occurred several times a day) as a hallucination or a fit.[45] He was embarrassed by these raptures, as he was by the way Ramakrishna openly doted on him. Unlike the other disciples, who shared both his class position and his intellectual predilections and who delighted in Ramakrishna precisely because he seemed to offer an alternative to the hegemony of post-Enlightenment and colonial reason, Naren was unable or unwilling to abandon reason altogether, even after he had accepted the guruship of Ramakrishna.

Initially, believing Ramakrishna to be a hypnotist in addition to being an illiterate and a madman, he took great pains to maintain his self-possession and his distance, though he was unable to abandon the sage of Dakshineshwar altogether. For several years he remained skeptical of his guru's powers, dismissing *samadhi* as a trick of a disordered brain, deriding the saint's devotion to the unsavory goddess Kali, and waxing sarcastic about the philosophy of Vedantic nondualism. He may have been persuaded, or at least must have been flattered, by Ramakrishna's predictions about his own future greatness—through most of his life he seemed to assume authority with an easy sense of his own fitness for it—though he sometimes attributed these predictions to the older man's immoderate and indecorously expressed love. For his part, Ramakrishna permitted him to voice his skepticism in a manner that seems not to have been accorded the other young men, and he exempted him in addition from the regulations, restrictions, and acts of menial service to the guru that were imposed upon others.

The guru would brook no criticism of this indulged disciple. What others saw as arrogance or stubbornness in the young man he attributed to his rational mind and a commanding and admirable masculinity. When, after his father's death, Naren stayed away from Dakshineshwar and it was rumored that he had given himself over to sexual and other dissipations, Ramakrishna angrily dismissed all such reports.

Naren's long-delayed formal acceptance of Ramakrishna as his guru and his concomitant renunciation of worldly life may not have been precipitated by a family crisis, but it certainly was coincident with it. His father's death transformed his life of easy affluence; as the oldest son, he was expected to provide for his mother and his younger siblings, as well as to liquidate the entirely unanticipated debts the dead man had left behind him. One can speculate that Naren was drawn at this point to his guru both out of the anxieties generated by his family's financial crisis and his own lack of success at procuring employment and by the cultural tensions he shared with other western-educated bourgeois males of his time. Characteristically, however, he remained a skeptic in some things, refusing for instance to join the other disciples in proclaiming the avatarhood of his guru.[46] (In later life, and under rather different circumstances, he conceded Ramakrishna's divinity.) During Ramakrishna's bout with cancer he, unlike many of the other disciples, refused to see the disease as deriving from any but natural causes and rebuked the others for their sentimentality in imagining that the guru could will the cancer away. Following the guru's death, his skepticism and restlessness were renewed, and he alternated between a deeply impassioned religious longing and a rationalist demand for proof of the existence of God. In fact, a few years later he almost accepted another religious teacher as guru, before being overcome by guilt at his meditated disloyalty.[47]

Soon after Ramakrishna's demise, a small group of his unmarried young male disciples, including Naren, who considered themselves initiated into monkhood, began living a quasi-monastic existence in a house in the Calcutta suburbs. But Naren was not to be there long. He left the monastery for a protracted bout of travel as a wandering monk through northern India in 1887–1888. In 1890 he left once again, unaccompanied this time, and spent the next three years traveling throughout India, apparently attracting distinguished admirers and disciples along the way.[48] In 1893 he went to Chicago to attend the World Parliament of Religions (which was being held in conjunction with the Columbian Exposition). He went there as Swami Vivekananda, a name suggested to him by his supporter the Maharajah Ajit Singh of Khetri (who also provided him with a first-class ticket and a gorgeous wardrobe of silk robes and turbans). There his eloquence, his exotic looks and attire, his anticolonial fervor, and his message of Hindu religious tolerance helped to make him an instant and phenomenal success. The *New York Herald* raved: "Vivekananda is undoubtedly the greatest figure in the Parliament of Religions. After hearing him, we feel, how foolish it is to send Missionaries to this learned nation."[49] He spent the next few years touring and lecturing in the United States and England, gathering around himself a band of disciples, mostly British and American women. He had by this time acquired a considerable Indian reputation (from a distance, of course),[50] and when he returned to India in 1897, he was given a delirious welcome by Hindu crowds all over the country. There he proceeded to organize his brother disciples into the Ramakrishna Order of monks, an order which was relatively unorthodox in its dedication to the spiritual life as well as social service. (Some of the other disciples complained that the emphasis on organization and service was inspired by Vivekananda's long sojourn in the west.) The few years before his death in 1902 were divided among India, Europe, and the United States, lecturing, training disciples like Nivedita, and disseminating the message of Hinduism ascendant.

What were the filiations, if any, between the doctrine and personality of the triumphant Swami Vivekananda and those of his deceased guru? What was the nature of Vivekananda's investment in the religious and gender traffic articulated by Ramakrishna, especially when it was traversed, as it certainly was for him, by colonial and nationalist concerns? It has often been noted that in almost every conceivable way this favorite disciple seemed to set himself against the example set by Ramakrishna after the latter's death. Rakhal Nath asserts with some degree of validity that "Ramakrishna's contribution to the religious scene of 19th century Bengal . . . was essentially in the nature of a personal influence rather than of ideas that were of any great historical importance."[51] He states that on Vivekananda, likewise, Ramakrishna's influence was "personal rather than intellectual."[52] This is not incorrect, but it is certainly open to some dispute. While Vivekananda remained always ambivalent about his guru (in a way that was, interestingly, analogous to the saint's own ambivalence about the rural, nonbourgeois, and often unorthodox spiritual practices of his own past) and abandoned many of his most cherished doctrines, he was nonetheless unable and unwilling to shake him off completely, even in the comparative psychic security of his later life. As with the other disciples, Ramakrishna had become his mode of access to popular spirituality;[53] furthermore, the guru had demonstrated the incapacity of liberal reform movements in Hinduism to provide the full range of psychic satisfactions demanded by the bourgeois Hindu nationalist male in the moment of (colonial) modernity.

Even so, in his travels through India in 1890–1893 and in the west, Vivekananda almost never spoke of Ramakrishna at all, and he was to preach a doctrine of "masculine" activism and rationality in many ways so alien to the teachings of Ramakrishna that several of his fellow disciples were to accuse him of promoting himself rather than the Master. Many acquaintances and disciples were to comment besides on his eminently *secular* talents, as an orator, "warrior," "patriot," and "leader." "Neither by temperament nor by constitution," writes one historian about him, "was he cut out to be a mystic."[54]

Vivekananda himself seemed quite aware of the warring energies in his psyche. He was fond of allegorizing the conflict as a dream in which he was offered two options: wealth and power in worldly life, or the destiny of a wandering ascetic. He may additionally have comprehended this dream as a schematic representation of the contrary pulls of "east" and "west," in which the former exemplified the contemplative life, and the latter the life of activity, material success, and fame; certainly in his conscious state he was given to distinguishing east from west according to this binary logic. In his dream, which was an obsessive and recurrent one, he always chose the second of the two alternatives; but the conflict had to be undergone and the choice affirmed on a daily basis. In his waking life, the options were more decisively yoked together, even if not reconciled.

Perhaps unsurprisingly, what Vivekananda continued to emphasize throughout his career as both disciple and guru was a reciprocally advantageous commerce between contemplation and action, between India and the west.[55] Under his tutelage following Ramakrishna's death, his brother monks read Plato and Aristotle, Kant and Hegel, Carlyle's *French Revolution*, histories of Joan of Arc and the Rani of Jhansi (the Indian warrior queen notable for her resistance to the British in the Mutiny of 1857), and Thomas à Kempis in addition to religious texts in Sanskrit.

Apart from his departures from the teachings of Ramakrishna, Vivekananda's reticence about his guru was striking. He almost never mentioned him in his early travels through India; there is a single recorded talk in the west entitled "My Master," and the references to the guru in his western discourses are scarce. He attributed this reserve to feelings of humility as well as to the reluctance to seem to be preaching a sectarian version of Hinduism rather than a perfect, comprehensive, and undivided Vedantic Hinduism.[56] It is said that on one occasion, when he was to have addressed an audience in Boston on the subject of his guru, he was so enraged by the contemplation of his listeners' wealth and worldly success that he attacked them bitterly for their materialism. (He is said to have understood from this outburst his unfitness to speak of his guru and to have resolved not to discuss him in public or in print again.)[57] It is not too fanciful, I think, to read these responses not simply as a calculated move to avoid repelling western audiences but also as an index of Vivekananda's continuing ambivalence about the Master and the inability to come to terms with the ecstatic, nonrational, unrefined, and occasionally very orthodox religiosity of Ramakrishna.

His relations with his brother disciples were similarly marked by decidedly equivocal feelings. When he left for his travels through India in 1890, he angrily dismissed those of them who wished to accompany him. He was not to reopen communication with them for years, not, in fact, for several months after his triumph at Chicago. (They were to learn from other sources that the monk who had electrified audiences at Chicago was none other than their Naren.) Ever after, he was a severe taskmaster to them, castigating them frequently for their lack of initiative and "manliness."

For him Ramakrishna's unlettered, intuitive, otherworldly ecstasy was not merely not reproducible, it was not a fit model to emulate. I find it difficult to concur with Raychaudhuri's claim that Vivekananda was "more than anything else a mystic in question of the Ultimate Reality within a specific Indian tradition."[58] His own brand of Hinduness had—for the most part—a distinctly activist, nationalist, martial, worldly, and westward-looking cast to it. Using his authority as Ramakrishna's favorite disciple and the heir to his spiritual crown, he peremptorily put aside his guru's indictments of aggressive (heterosexual) masculinity as well as his condemnation of social activism (both associated, as Partha Chatterjee points out, with the regime of modernity and colonial reason[59]). In its place he "made the search for a mystical communion with God no longer a matter of sundry spiritual practices gone through in seclusion . . . but a prototype of all human adventures."[60] In this mission he seems to have been indebted not simply to a purportedly western ideal but also, perhaps, to the works of a popular contemporary like Bankim Chandra Chatterjee, especially a novel like *Anandamath* (1882), which showcased a band of militant Hindu monks fighting to liberate the motherland from foreign domination. (It hardly needs repeating that the novel functioned as a seminal text for anticolonial revolutionaries of the early twentieth century, including Aurobindo Ghosh; Vivekananda likewise was an inspiration to them, as well as to the participants in the Swadeshi movement.)[61]

Also in distinction to Ramakrishna, Vivekananda insisted on a stabilization of personal and national identity (and identification) in gender terms. In light of the gendered representation of the colonial encounter, such a response is hardly unexpected. As Partha Chatterjee says, drawing upon Ashis Nandy's argument, "The 'hyper-masculinity' of imperialist ideology made the figure of the weak, irresolute, effeminate babu a special target of contempt and ridicule."[62] Vivekananda's call for Hinduism and nationalism, like that of many of his western-educated and nationalist contemporaries like Bankim, was therefore a call to Indian men to reclaim a lost or forgotten masculinity and to repudiate femininity. His Hindu woman, it should be noted, was a markedly docile and self-effacing creature, distinctly different from the monstrous and appetitive female figures of Ramakrishna's credo. This call to virilization must also be seen, therefore, as a phobic response to Ramakrishna's unseemly demands; that is to say, it is a phobic response not just to femininity but to its disturbing location in masculinity. Unlike his guru, Vivekananda could neither become woman himself nor exhort Indian/Hindu men to become woman in the interest of transcending (hetero)sexuality, since the problem with Indian men was that they were Indian women. So for him Hindu men were not, as they were for Ramakrishna, too manly for their own (spiritual) good, they were too womanly for their own (nationalist) good.

Vivekananda's message to his own (feminized) countrymen was to inculcate manliness: "The older I grow, the more everything seems to me to lie in manliness. This is my new gospel. Do even evil like a man! Be wicked, if you must, on a grand scale."[63] This, as we have seen, was profoundly different from the inwardness and seclusion mandated by his guru and indeed by much of Hindu religious tradition. It was also, as we have also seen, typical of nineteenth-century Hindu nationalism in its implicit response to the colonial critique of the effeminate babu.[64] It is not surprising, therefore, that, if Vivekananda in his address to the east was emphatic about "man-making," in his address to the west he assumed the posture of a "Napoleon of religion."[65] His identification with and promotion of "manliness" was thus a twofold project. It implied not only a repudiation of the feminine identification urged by Ramakrishna but also a paradoxical embrace of colonial masculinism that could then be deployed against colonizing males. He therefore characterized his mission to the west quite explicitly as a pugnacious and anti-imperialist one. Despite the gospel of the oneness and viability of all faiths that made him famous at the Parliament of Religions, he insisted at the same time and with greater vehemence on the vast superiority of Hinduism over other faiths—a superiority that, paradoxically, was guaranteed by its nonjudgmental acceptance of all creeds. Like almost all bourgeois and Hindu nationalist responses to the challenges of colonialism and Christianity,[66] Vivekananda's gospel sought to rein in multiple and often discrepant impulses. Part of Vivekananda's mission was to insist on the equality if not the superiority of the Hindu to the westerner on the latter's own terms. To this end he not only asserted the Aryan brotherhood of Indians, Europeans, and Americans but suggested the Hindu and Buddhist inspirations of Christianity and castigated Christians for their failure to practice the religion of Christ. At the same time he also insisted on the *difference* of Hindu civilization, a difference that made for preeminence in the spiritual realm and that was marked by a laudable indifference to material prosperity and military conquest. He insisted, therefore, on an "aggressive Hinduism" which could traffic freely and on equal terms with an affluent and powerful west. His posture was that of an aggressive defensiveness on behalf of an India and a Hinduism assaulted by colonialism and Christianity. The extraordinary popular acclaim that greeted the swami on his return home in 1897 was proof that, among his countrymen at least, he had struck a responsive chord. Several Indian newspapers were wildly enthusiastic about the prospect of "evangel[izing] the civilised world, according to the tenets of the Hindu spiritual ethics"[67] and accepted Vivekananda's claims about the imminent conversion to Hinduism of the western nations.

To all his followers, but especially to the western ones, his message was that of Hinduism and India triumphant. To his admirer Josephine Mac-Leod, who asked what she might do to serve him, he replied simply, "Love India." Even the devoted Nivedita has provided accounts of his passionate, often cantankerous, partisanship on the national issue: "sometimes unpleasant, but always superbly *manly*." A good part of her discipleship and that of the other English and American followers of the swami consisted in traveling through India with Vivekananda and receiving instruction in the glories of Indian history. The spiritual mastery over the west was a reversal of the long conquest inaugurated by colonialism, and, on home ground at least, the swami insisted on complete deference from his western disciples. The reversal implied a revolution in the colony, in that very space where Europeans had established hegemony: "If European men or women are to work in India, it *must* be under the black man!"[68] Contemptuous of dietary and caste restrictions himself, he was insistent that the same freedom could not and should not be available to a western woman in India. "You must give up all visiting, and live in strict seclusion. . . . You have to set yourself to Hinduise your thoughts, your needs, your conceptions, and your habits. Your life, internal and external, has to become all that an orthodox Hindu Brahman Brahmacharini's ought to be. . . . *You have to forget your own past, and to cause it to be forgotten. You have to lose even its memory!*" he told Nivedita.[69] She, for her part, observed caste and dietary restrictions strictly and maintained purdah rules in the school she established in Calcutta. Christine Greenstidel, an American devotee who was to join Nivedita later in Calcutta, had similar instructions to "Hinduize" herself. (There is no evidence of Vivekananda's having made similar demands on western males.)

To most observers Vivekananda himself appeared the personification of the manliness that was so central to his message, and his manliness was not simply intellectual but also corporeal. The various contemporary (and present-day) accounts of Vivekananda speak almost obsessively of his "powerful" body and his "commanding" good looks, which distinguished him from his fellow monks and devotees; his impact abroad is almost invariably represented in biographies and newspaper reports (primarily American, but also Indian) of the time in terms not just of his message or his personality but also of his appearance, including details of his clothing. Descriptions such as the following were common in the United States and England:

> When I met him he was twenty-seven years old [?]. I thought him as handsome as a god of classic sculpture. He was dark of skin, of course, and had large eyes which gave one the impression of "midnight blue." He seemed larger than most of his race. . . . He had a head heaped with short black curls. . . . He wore on that occasion his orange cassock, a cincture of deep rose-red silk, and his turban of white shot with threads of gold. . . . I was twenty-four, fair, tall, and slender, with golden hair and grey-blue eyes.[70]

On one occasion he was especially enjoined by those arranging his lecture to wear his "rajah's costume." Though he is said to have been incensed by this request, he himself had decided early on to reserve western garb for everyday use and to keep his robe and turban for lecturing.[71] Many commentators remarked on the appeal of his clothes and his appearance, especially his eyes, for the women in audience. His disciples, too, were to speak with mingled pride and embarrassment about the "promiscuous admiration" of "gushing and impressionable young women."[72]

Some of his detractors, particularly Christian missionaries in India whom he had attacked with marked fervor, attributed his great popularity to his looks and attire alone,[73] and there was gossip on more than one occasion about his relationship with his female followers. Whether or not these rumors were true does not concern me here. What should be noted, though, is the fact of erotic spectacle, an eroticism that could coexist with, and indeed was dependent upon, sexual abstinence. The fact is that Vivekananda's detractors were reasonably shrewd about the kind of appeal that both his person and his message was likely, perhaps calculated, to produce upon sympathetic, heterosexual women.

It may be instructive to consider briefly the representation of the swami's body in photographs, especially in contrast to that of the other religious figure, Ramakrishna. Ramakrishna (in the most famous, "worshipped" portrait) wears the scanty clothing of the lower-class Hindu male, not necessarily the clothing of the religious ascetic. He claimed to have been in a state of *samadhi* when the photograph was taken, a state that implies heedlessness of one's surroundings or of the effects of one's appearance, speech, or actions; apparently he could not bear to be photographed in a state of full self-consciousness.[74] Vivekananda on the other hand is almost always photographed standing upright and fully clothed in a mixture—usually—of Indian and western clothing. He is by Bengali standards a strongly built man; and his poses seem calculatedly "masculine" and grave. I do not of course wish to imply that Ramakrishna was unself-conscious about being photographed (in fact, he was quite fascinated by the process of photography) or that there is a greater degree of premeditation or self-reflexiveness in Vivekananda's photographic representations. My assertion, rather, is that Vivekananda's photographs, as indeed the descriptions of his "personality" (a fairly transparent and habitual code for his body), undoubtedly had the effect of masculinizing and eroticizing him, first to a western audience and then to an Indian one.

The body of Vivekananda is thus made available—particularly after his return from the United States and Europe—as (erotic) spectacle through travels and addresses and photographs. One of the modes of Vivekananda's visibility was the *darshan*, which he appropriated—as other political figures and film stars were to do later—for a nationalist idiom. Within Hinduism, *darshan* is a particular form of staging the body in the public domain which Gayatri Spivak explains thus: "In Hindu polytheism the god or goddess, as indeed mutatis mutandis the revered person, is . . . an object of the gaze, "from below."[75] Hindu nationalism in South Asia—and perhaps other nationalisms as well—in fact could be read as the dual activity of peregrination and staging the spectacle of the male body for adoration.

For Vivekananda, gender as a foundational category of identity was fixed; gender identity, moreover, implied a very specific object choice. To be (properly) masculine was to be heterosexual. The young monk, whose

Figure 1. Ramakrishna Paramhansa.

"manly" body had been erotically solicited for discipleship by Ramakrishna, seeks, as guru, to sublimate and relocate that eroticism at least partially within a heterosexual imaginary. This is a simple enough explanation of his turn to heterosexual female disciples. His audience of admirers and disciples, however, is quite heterogeneously constructed, in ways that complicate his insistence on masculine heterosexuality. I shall explain this shortly.

If, as the previous chapter asserts, the concept-metaphor of the nation cannot be imagined except in relation to an outside, then Vivekananda can

Figure 2. Swami Vivekananda at the World Parliament of Religions, Chicago.

Figure 3. Swami Vivekananda in the United States.

only be what he is through a process of disavowal and recognition *from without*. That is to say, Vivekananda discovers himself as the swami, as Vivekananda, as Indian, as Hindu, and as male, an implicitly heterosexual male, in the west, outside the Indian nation-space. It is his placement in the United States and in England that allows Vivekananda to conceive of a national horizon for the geographical and moral space designated "India"; he discovers India in Chicago. This is why for him Hinduism and nationalism both become very specifically an address to the west. Besides, in order to identify as a masculine and heterosexual Hindu subject, he has to interpellate a fit female audience, but a female audience less intimate and less powerful than and, paradoxically, more mobile than Indian/ Hindu womanhood. The nationalist dialectic of his mission—which demands a recognition of the colonized male as (heterosexual) male by the (male) colonizer—also makes Indian women incapable of supplying the swami with the satisfactions of guruness. The fittest audience, then, is western woman; most of his western disciples, among whom Nivedita was only the most prominent, were women. Thus, through his travels in the west, Vivekananda the disciple becomes Vivekananda the guru, the guru of Margaret Noble in London in the 1890s as well as of other western women. Margaret Noble/Nivedita becomes crucial to Vivekananda's gendered conceptualization of Hindu psychic and national identifications; Vivekananda, in other words, is made possible by Nivedita.[76] Mary Ann Doane says in her discussion of the place of white women in a racist economy that "whiteness becomes most visible, takes form, in relation to the figure of the white woman."[77] Vivekananda's solicitation of Nivedita and others like her is an understandable but also complicated response to such a psychic schema. Crudely put, he functions as the erotic object for female worship, specifically for western (white) female worship.

So while Ramakrishna mimed woman, Vivekananda had to mime masculinity and heterosexuality (though his miming has, of course, to be understood differently from that of Ramakrishna's experience of possession). It is interesting to note that while Ramakrishna transcended (hetero)sexual desire by becoming (one kind of) woman, Vivekananda transcended it through sublimation; he claimed to have acquired his force of personality through a concentrated masculinity, in other words through a strict avoidance of both (hetero)sexual acts and (hetero)sexual thoughts.[78] Sudhir Kakar, in his reading of the lingam (the phallic symbol that is an emblem of Shiva), advances an explanation of the competing valences of the symbol that may be apposite for an understanding of Vivekananda's sexuality:

> Shiva, the renunciator and arch-ascetic, claims the erect phallus with all its erotic connotations as his particular symbol. . . . [Some] texts have advanced the somewhat tortuous argument that the erect phallus is a symbol of chastity since the semen has not yet been shed and the linga thus symbolizes concen-

trated sexual vitality, which, in the Hindu tradition, it is incumbent upon yogis to transform into mental power. . . . In other words, the linga is not a symbol of object libido but of narcissistic libido, of sexual investment in the self. Thus, although sexuality is the essence of the symbol, the linga is both "chaste" and "erotic" at the same time.[79]

Likewise, Vivekananda propounds the theory of *ojas*, a form of concentrated and carefully husbanded sexual power that translates directly into spiritual and intellectual prowess.[80] Celibacy for him functions as something that must be other and more than a negative attribute, a feature that detracts from full heterosexual masculinity; he actively endeavors to transform that celibacy into the cause of his virility and attractiveness (to female disciples, but, as we shall see, not to them alone).

So much for the centrality of the western female disciple. What about other audiences, which were not female and not necessarily constructed in discipleship? Vivekananda remains, for instance, an important figure for Indian males (far less so for western males); this audience poses a number of interesting questions. How does he hail them? How do they hail him? Steve Neale's reading of the problems of spectatorship and the spectacle of masculinity, albeit grounded in the codes of Hollywood cinema, affords nonetheless a fruitful point of theoretical entry into our colonial Indian situation.[81] Neale outlines and distinguishes among the three psychic functions and processes—identification, voyeurism, and fetishism—that come into play in a consideration of the male as object of the look, arguing that all of these work to conceal or deflect homoeroticism.[82] Now, as we know, Vivekananda gendered Indian men as a "nation of women,"[83] who were unattractive (to whom?) precisely because of this feminization. His own exorbitant masculinity was, though, in this context, not without its own intellectual and libidinal complications. He had to construct himself as masculine and therefore heterosexual in response both to the emasculizing process of colonialism and to the erotic solicitations of Ramakrishna. But though woman as concept-metaphor, in setting off his masculinity and heterosexuality, assumed a value for him that she had not for his guru, he could not sanction the presence of femininity in the male. Hence he was overtly contemptuous of Indian males who, like his guru, were "feminine" in their psychic identification and who conceivably directed their erotic attention to other, more "masculine" males. But it was clearly his masculinity that had attracted the guru; so, in consolidating this feature of his appeal, he could conceivably be making himself an even more attractive erotic object for men like Ramakrishna. In his hyperbolized masculinity, Vivekananda is available obviously as an identificatory figure, as an ego ideal. But obviously, and especially in the light of his relations with his guru and other Indian males, one cannot rule out the solicitation of a fetishistic and masochistic contemplation from this audience. Certainly he functioned toward his audience of

Indian males as a figure of severe and even punitive authority, even as he was adored for his imperious Hindu nationalism and his "majestic" appearance. His first disciple, Sadananda, frankly confessed that he had taken on the swami as a guru not for spiritual reasons but because of "a pair of devilish black eyes."[84]

How does this conceptualization of Indianness and Hinduness conceive of Ramakrishna's unruly *kamini*? For Vivekananda, this Indian/Hindu masculinity can only be realized through a localization and circumscription of the feminine and its ultimate relocation outside a libidinal economy, in a place where Hindu/Indian woman will be neither subject nor object of desire. He deals with Hindu femininity—which Ramakrishna had almost invariably characterized as powerful, active, indeed predatory—by rewriting Hindu womanhood in specifically bourgeois nationalist terms. The (Hindu/Indian) woman question for Vivekananda becomes abstracted, regulated, and desexualized in a suffering and idealized Mother India (quite a different figure from the powerful Mother Kali).[85] It is a familiar pattern. Hence his remapping and elaboration of the contiguous and overlapping terrains of sexuality/matrimony and the religious life. For Ramakrishna, any (hetero)sexual contact with the uncontrollable and sexually demanding figure of woman was antithetical to male religious experience. For the bourgeois as well as the Hindu nationalists, on the other hand, woman represented that "spiritual domain [in which] the East was superior to the West."[86] For Ramakrishna's disciple (and his disciple in turn), woman in a heterosexual alliance was likewise a much more pliable and reassuring figure than was Ramakrishna's virago; this wife was a figure who assumed the posture of a devotee toward her husband-master. It should be noted that Vivekananda, like his guru, believed in strict celibacy for both monks and nuns. Yet his ideal of the devotee-disciple was not so much the celibate Hindu nun but the Hindu widow, whose life of enforced quasi-religious fidelity to a deceased husband he greatly admired. It is this model, in fact, of erotic feminine energy sublated as worship of the husband/male, in a nonreciprocal union, that he seems to have replicated in his model of the guru-*shishya* relationship. Nivedita, who appears to have reproduced faithfully in her writings Vivekananda's notion of Hindu femininity, provides the following description of the wife as devotee:

> [T]he Indian bride comes to her husband much as the Western woman might enter a church. . . . For the woman supreme love is . . . a duty. Only to the man his mother must always stand first. In some sense, therefore, the relation is not mutual. And this is in full accordance with the national sentiment, which stigmatises affection that asks for equal return as "shopkeeping." . . . As a disciple might, she prostrates herself before him, touching his feet with her head before receiving his blessing. It is not equality. No. But who talks of a vulgar

equality, asks the Hindu wife, when she may have instead the unspeakable
blessedness of offering worship?[87]

Here the articulation between spiritual and the libidinal is almost seamless.

What is worth considering in this reconceptualization of Hindu masculinity (and femininity) under colonialism-and-nationalism is the question
of the Hindu male's relationship to certain symbolic forms of femininity. An
extended scrutiny of the Hindu male reformer's or the Hindu male nationalist's construction of Hindu womanhood is outside the scope of this paper
and, in any event, has been fairly well documented.[88] But what does call for
investigation in relation to Vivekananda's masculinization of his personality
and message is the place of the goddess Kali in his conceptual apparatus
as well as Ramakrishna's. Kali was most commonly represented as a nude,
black-skinned woman, garlanded with skulls or severed heads and carrying
a bloodstained weapon in one hand and a severed head in another; her foot
was placed on the body of a prostrate man, commonly believed to be her
husband, Shiva. The goddess was universally regarded by the English—and,
generally speaking, by the overwhelming majority of Anglo-European Orientalists, not excluding Max Mueller (who admired Ramakrishna)—as representing the worst impulses in popular Hinduism. Of Shaktism, to which
Kali-worship is central, Monier Williams said that it was "Hinduism arrived
at its worst and most corrupt stage of development."[89] The evidence of
chapter 2 makes clear that Kali was widely considered to be a bloodthirsty
goddess who demanded human sacrifices of the kind offered by the thugs
in the nineteenth century and the bomb-throwing revolutionaries of Bengal in the next. Shaktism was, in addition, notorious for its putative endorsement of a variety of erotic rituals as acts of homage to the goddess.
While some of the Bengali *bhadralok* were trying to transform the tribal goddess into a more decorous figure,[90] most of them distanced themselves from
Kali with as much horror as did any Christian missionary.

Ramakrishna was especially devoted to the goddess, though he claimed
to have performed her worship without the customary sexual assistance of
a female partner. He refused, however, to condemn the sexual disciplines
of the Vamachari ("left-hand") Tantriks, or Kali-worshippers, even though
for him the goddess was manifest as the mother of the universe. It was in this
spirit of (desexualized) mother worship that he worshipped his own wife as
mother.[91] He also exhorted his disciples on occasion to approach all women
as the "blissful mother," even though he also believed women to be voracious, predatory, and sexually threatening.

At first Naren, like most bourgeois, reformist Bengali males, was openly
disapproving of his guru's object of worship. Even though he came eventually to accept the divinity of Kali ("Kali-worship is my special *fad*," he told a
western disciple), he was notably reticent about her, as he was about his

guru, outside India. Kali, Vivekananda is said to have felt, was uniquely Indian and Hindu, a figure who would not survive the passage to the west without repelling western audiences. As in the case of his guru, Vivekananda's relationship with the Hindu feminine principle as represented by the goddess was marked by profound complications and ambivalences. On the one hand, Ramakrishna's notion of the motherhood of God became for him displaced onto an abstract and idealized body, that of Mother India, a conception that was gaining popularity in the late nineteenth century. This figure, unlike that of Kali, called for a protective veneration against the onslaughts on western culture and Christianity rather than the childlike awe of his guru. Of his devotion to the mother goddess/motherland, Nivedita was to say, "He was born a lover, and the queen of his adoration was his Motherland."[92] On the other land, he inveighed fiercely against Tantric sexual practices, describing them as "devilish" to Nivedita on one occasion and forbidding the other monks of the Ramakrishna Order to have anything to do with them. Ramakrishna's demanding and dominant woman returns in Vivekananda both as powerful Mother Kali (who must be worshipped but must also be distanced through the cult of manliness) and as victimized and helpless Hindu woman.

Gayatri Spivak usefully reminds us that such a split, if indeed it is a split, is nothing new and does little to destabilize patriarchal notions of gender. The "goddess-infested reverse sexism of the Hindu majority," she writes, is completely capable of reconciling the worship of a powerful and punishing goddess with the most horrific forms of gender oppression.[93] In light of this, Vivekananda's views on gender are fairly predictable, though it should be noted that he is unable to withhold his allegiance from either the goddess or the project of reason. What is noteworthy also is his belief that Kali cannot "translate." While an investigation of the place of Kali and indeed of other symbolic forms of Hindu femininity in Vivekananda's conceptual apparatus (as well as Ramakrishna's) is outside the scope of this paper, I would speculate that his reticence about Kali in the west might be of a piece with his silence about his guru; both appear to be associated in his mind with the most unseemly kinds of gender identification and sexuality.

It is interesting to note, too, in this context, Vivekananda's characteristic response to inquiries (from western disciples) about his private religious experiences: "A hot flush and a delicate *hauteur* were his immediate response, even to such merely theoretical questions as appeared to him to demand too intimate a revelation of the personal experience."[94] As Raychaudhuri notes, he was not a modest man in most things,[95] nor can it really be said to be conventional in Hindu religious practice to be secretive about mystical experience; Ramakrishna, for one, spoke freely about his many austerities and about the rather extraordinary events that made up his religious life. What then might account for Vivekananda's taciturnity, indeed his uneasiness about the issue? I can only guess, from the language of intimacy, shame, and exposure that tropes his response, that for him private mystical experience formed part of a continuum that embraced his guru's mortifying candor about his own religious and erotic experience as well as the compelling but untransposable figure of Kali.

THE DISCIPLE

In this last section I examine the western woman, a consideration of whose identifications and position has been deferred from the very beginning. What was her relationship to the swami? What indeed did the swami think of the western women who welcomed him so enthusiastically and who formed so large a proportion of his discipleship? What was the nature of the western woman disciple's kinship, if any, to the Hindu woman? From all accounts the swami's initial response took the form of a profound (though uneven) admiration for the independence and self-assurance of American women; in this respect, as in so many others, he shared, though equivocally, the perspective of the nineteenth-century social reformers rather than that of the bourgeois nationalists or the Hindu orthodoxy. About a year after the Parliament of Religions at Chicago, he wrote to his brother disciples in Bengal:

> They [American men] look with veneration upon women, who play a promi-
> nent part in their lives. Here this form of worship has attained its perfec-
> tion. . . . Well, I am almost at my wit's end to see the women of this country!
> They take me to the shops and everywhere, as if I were a child. They do all
> sorts of work—I cannot do even a sixteenth part of what they do. They are like
> Lakshmi (the Goddess of Fortune) in beauty, and like Sarasvati (the Goddess
> of Learning) in virtues—they are the Divine Mother incarnate, and worship-
> ping them, one verily attains perfection in everything. Great God! Are we
> to be counted among men? If I can raise a thousand such Madonnas, In-
> carnations of the Divine Mother, in our country, before I die, I shall die in
> peace. . . . Most wonderful women, these! They are about to corner the men,
> who are nearly worsted in the competition.[96]

Later, however, his views became more pronouncedly ambivalent. With the passage of time in the west, he became increasingly an apologist for Hindu orthodoxy's views on women's status. He upheld the ideal of the voluntary sati and extolled the worship of maternality (as opposed to companionate conjugality) in India. He antagonized among others the members of the Ramabai Circles in the United States by his denial of the ill-treatment of widows in Hindu society and by his glorification of the Hindu widow's life of (enforced) renunciation.[97] This conservatism is easily explicable as a nationalist reaction to occasionally racist questions from his American audiences about the sufferings of Indian women; he was notably thin-skinned about any criticisms of India. Yet in India, the rationalist and social reformer which had never quite become subsumed in the Hindu nationalist often manifested itself in radical critiques of casteism, class privilege, child marriage, hypocritical religiosity, and women's lack of access to education and opportunity. He was ruthlessly critical of Hindu social conventions in ways that few reformers dared to be. He has in fact routinely been accused of inconsistencies in his pronouncements on India and on Hinduism and on subjects such as caste, modernity, and Indian womanhood. He has been arraigned as being neither a reformer nor a conservative—the two positions of enunciation available in late-nineteenth-century India. The conflicted and shifting responses of a journal like *The Indian Social Reformer*, which lauded him for his "robust manliness of thought and utterance" and for his opposition to a number of Hindu social customs while also demonstrating a certain unease about his romanticized vision of Hinduism and his opposition to the temper of reformers, best demonstrate the difficulty his contemporaries had in coming to terms with him.[98] But what is manifest as contradiction is, I think, explicable in terms not simply of the swami's psychic and social tensions but also of a strategic politics of location. The swami had varied audiences; in Britain and the United States, he preached Hinduism triumphant and brooked no criticism of Hindu social ills, however egregious, while he was more willing to play the reformer at "home."[99] But this anomalous combination of reform-plus-orthodoxy was also undoubtedly a way of distinguishing himself both from the orthodox position and, more importantly, from reformist bodies like the Brahmo Samaj and the Ramabai Circles, which were already familiar to the west. It was profoundly important to him to establish that he was the first of his kind, the first "real Hindu" to present Hinduism to the west, and hence he was strongly, even immoderately, critical of both the Brahmo Samaj and the Theosophical Society, both of which had sent their representatives to Chicago.

Despite these discrepant, shifting, and imperfectly articulated postures on the position of women, woman as concept-metaphor remained central to his religious-nationalist schema. He never failed to declare to Nivedita and others that he was committed to the cause of "Woman and the People," whose oppression was the cause of Indian degradation. Nivedita in fact was recruited precisely for the purpose of uplifting Indian women. How this uplift was to be achieved, however, was never fully worked out. Besides, Vivekananda insisted, though Nivedita was to be the direct agent of uplift, that she conform in the strictest possible way to orthodox Hindu codes. She did open a girls' school in her north Calcutta neighborhood of Bosepara Lane, though the swami left the organization and management almost entirely up to her and eventually lost interest in the scheme altogether.

What is striking in this is that Vivekananda, in his capacity as exemplar of the "Modern Transition,"[100] was continually riven by the contradictions of his own position. Like the nationalists of whom Partha Chatterjee writes, he believed in a characteristically Victorian doctrine of "separate spheres"; he felt that "not only was it not desirable to imitate the West in anything other than the material aspects of life, it was not even necessary to do so" in the psychosocial sphere because of Indian spiritual superiority over the west.[101] Yet he was significantly dependent upon the west, especially upon western women, for validation as nationalist, masculine, heterosexual. He needed, then, to make a place for them in the Hindu polity. In what capacity, though? As saviors of Hindu women (who were in need of saving, *and* not in need of saving, according to his testimony)? Or as Hinduized, assimilated western women? This is the point at which Vivekananda's program of the reconfiguration of Hindu masculinity through the figure of the western woman reaches a point of impasse and finds itself unable to proceed. Vivekananda himself was unable to work through this impasse except to gesture—obviously inadequately and contradictorily, given the contingencies of the historical context—at the already available but unsatisfactory (because associated most obviously with both colonialism and indigenous but English-inspired social reform movements) model of western women as teacher (though not guru). His foremost disciple, Nivedita, lost little time after his death in downplaying the cause of female education.

The life of Nivedita itself illustrates, though with inevitable and interesting differences, some of the tensions of the swami's position. Born into an Irish nationalist family, she was distinguished in early adulthood for her disquiet with traditional Christianity and her interest in women's issues.[102] She was powerfully drawn to the swami's personality when she encountered him in London in 1897, and it was this, rather than any admiration for the originality of his thought, that led her to call him "Master" within a month of their first meeting. He on his part recognized in her the ideal disciple, who could also serve as a power in her own right: "I am now convinced that you have a great future in the work for India. What was wanted was not a man but a woman; a real lioness, to work for the Indians, women especially. India cannot yet produce great women, she must borrow them from other nations."[103]

An appeal of this kind was not new. In a highly successful visit to England in 1870, during which he was feted by several notables, including Queen Victoria, Keshab had issued the following call to British women: "At the present a thousand Hindu houses are open to receive and welcome English governesses—well-trained, accomplished English ladies, capable of doing good to their Indian sisters, both by instruction and personal example. . . . I speak to you not for one, not for fifty, but for millions of Indian sisters, whose lamentations and wails penetrate the skies and seem to come over to England to stir up the hearts of their English sisters."[104] The parallels between Keshab's reception in England and Vivekananda's in the United

States are quite striking, though, of course, Keshab did not—as far as I know—function as an erotic figure, nor did he carry the message of Hinduism militant. Keshab did stress the importance of female education and of the instrumentality of the Hindu widow as an agent for educating other Hindu women; these were favorite themes with Vivekananda a quarter-century later. Keshab did manage to persuade one Englishwoman, Annette Akroyd, to come to India to serve Indian women, though (since Keshab was at this point a liberal, procolonial reformer) she did not come as his disciple or protégée; in fact, their differences soon led to a parting of the ways. Nivedita's recruitment by Vivekananda, like that of other British women by other reformist Hindu men, as the most proper teacher of Hindu/Indian women, followed in some respects an already available trajectory. It is notable that the necessity for the western woman disciple meant that Vivekananda had to remember to forget Indian women except as symbolic figures or as figures for rescue. He spoke of Indian (primarily Hindu) women as bereft of Indian female leadership and, further, as incapable at the present moment of generating such figures; he was able to insist on this, moreover, despite his personal encounters with the associates of Pandita Ramabai, despite his acquaintance with Sharada Devi,[105] and despite the abundant evidence of female education, professional activity, and feminist organization in several parts of India, including Bengal.[106]

What made this trajectory different in Nivedita's case from the one offered by Keshab was that it was necessary for western woman to become Hindu woman in order to educate Hindu women. Of Indian males, Indian females, and western females, it was only the last that could take up Ramakrishna's call to be Indian woman. Several of Vivekananda's western female disciples, but most especially Nivedita, were asked to submit to a complete makeover in India. Nivedita changed more than her name, which she would have had to do under monastic rules anyway. Despite being unable to assume any of the assigned subject positions of mother, wife, or widow assigned to Hindu women—she settled finally for the position of Vivekananda's "daughter," perhaps the only position in the Hindu family romance she could assume—she lived a fairly orthodox life with regard to diet, worship, and the observance of caste taboos. Though she did not maintain purdah herself, and in fact traveled, lectured, and wrote copiously, she spoke and wrote with considerable ardor in favor of Hindu ideals of femininity.

It must be obvious that such a position of enunciation is impossible to reduce to the "transgressive" *or* the "imperialist." Nivedita obviously must function only as partial substitute (not quite/not white, or is it not quite not quite/not white?) for Indian woman, since it is her very (racial) difference that guarantees Vivekananda's, and paradigmatically, the Indian male's, Indianness and masculinity. But more importantly, Nivedita, like the figure of the western woman in general, functions for dominant Hindu males like

Vivekananda as a sign of subjective insubstantiality or as the repository of their psychic displacements; she acquiesces paradoxically to being the object onto which or whom meanings are (dis)located. The white woman functions here as the gendered site or the medium of important religious and nationalist transactions. Of all the figures in the colonial scene—western man, Indian man, western woman, and Indian woman—it seems that it is only the western woman whose identity is available—for the Indian man—as relatively open, mobile, malleable. She is distinct from the Indian woman, whose identity has to be in the nationalist context, fixed quite as much as the Indian male's is.[107] What we have here is the familiar process of (colonial) mimicry performed in reverse, and for the Indian nationalist male; (Hindu) nationalism demands at this point its mimic woman. Ramakrishna's demand for ambulatory identifications in discipleship finds, for Vivekananda and the Hindu nationalist movement, its best prototype in the western woman.

This identification, however, was not achieved without conflict, and Nivedita's account of her discipleship, *The Master as I Saw Him,* was notably different from the usual biographies of the swami in touching upon the agonistic, conflictual nature of the guru-disciple relationship. The conflicts were not simply ideological—though Vivekananda took her to task for her loyalty to Britain and the empire and her views on gender—but also affective and libidinal. Commentators hint as much when they speak, typically, of her "passionate adoration" of the guru; Romain Rolland is only the most candid among them when he says, "Although Nivedita's feelings for him were always absolutely pure, he perhaps saw their danger."[108] Nivedita herself was to speak of this in a fairly circumspect way. The emphasis in her narrative is on Vivekananda's demand for complete submission in his disciple, a demand quite different, by the way, from anything that his own guru had made of himself. Living with the shock of "constant rebuke and attack" upon all her existing ideas, she came at this stage to see the experience of discipleship as emotionally harrowing: "Suffering is often illogical, and I cannot attempt to justify by reason the degree of unhappiness which I experienced at this time, as I saw the dream of a friendly and beloved leader falling away from me. . . . I was made to realise, as the days went by, that in this there would be no personal sweetness."[109] Earlier Vivekananda had warned her about the absence of reciprocity in their relationship: "I see persons giving me almost the whole of their love. But I must not give anyone the whole of mine in return, for that day the work would be ruined. Yet there are some who will look for such a return, not having the breadth of the impersonal view. It is absolutely necessary to the work that I should have the enthusiastic love of as many as possible, while I myself remain entirely impersonal. . . . A leader must be impersonal."[110] This nonreciprocity, then, was to be the keynote of their relationship. She was necessary for the consolidation of his nationalism, his guruness, his masculinity, his heterosexuality. She was to adore him fully and exclusively, but without demanding a return (as she initially had); when, on a trip to Europe, she became the temporary intellectual helpmate of the sociologist Patrick Geddes, Vivekananda construed her act as infidelity and was conspicuously cold to her. He was to remain forever a guru, with whom she could never aspire to intellectual, emotional, or spiritual equality. One might speculate that Nivedita's fervent defense of Hindu gender orthodoxy is also a meditation on her own discipleship, as well as a reparation for the "failures" of that discipleship.

If Nivedita was to be Hindu woman in her worship of the Master, what precise form was her discipleship to take and what was its relation to Hindu women? The first form it took was the establishment of a school for girls in north Calcutta. This school, catering to young, unmarried girls and child widows, was situated in Nivedita's own home in Bosepara Lane, for reasons of economy, no doubt, but also undoubtedly to ensure as little separation as possible between the "home" and the "world." Nivedita was careful to keep the education religious (that is, Hindu) and domestic in tone and free from "denationalizing" influences. The school was supported by Nivedita's own savings as well as by contributors in the west (which necessitated fundraising trips to the United States and to England). The swami's role in the school was quite limited and generally restricted to approving Nivedita's plans, promising moral support, and introducing her occasionally to potential contributors. In fact, his interest in the project appeared at one time so small that Nivedita wondered whether he had forgotten to what ends he had recruited her and invited her to India. His indifference to the pedagogical project may have ensured the school's early closure. It was revived again after Vivekananda's death, this time with the assistance of an American woman disciple, Sister Christine (Christine Greenstidel), as well as of an Indian teacher, Sister Sudhira. Nivedita, however, became less and less involved in the running of the school, having involved herself in a variety of nationalist projects; when her assistants abandoned the institution for the Brahmo Girls' School in 1911, she was unable, perhaps unwilling, to keep it going.

In this she was doing no more than emulating the Master and was, quite possibly, seeking some mastery herself. From all accounts, Nivedita's training in discipleship was a fundamentally nationalist rather than a spiritual one. Most of her apprenticeship consisted in accompanying Vivekananda in his travels to northern India, where he schooled her in the glories of Indian civilization and hammered away at her English partisanship. The lesson was so well learned that even before Vivekananda's death Nivedita began to betray some impatience with the "limited" project of women's education. In a letter she wrote about the proliferating and discrepant allegiances that were present before her:

I am afraid . . . I shall want my Mother [Kali] to stand between me and my Father's [Vivekananda's] wrath. . . . To my great horror, freedom has meant something to me, for my life has come to include many elements that Swami would probably not have put there. They are all for him, however, I trust, in the end—and he will not hold me less his child than before. . . . And I belong to Hinduism more than ever I did, but I see the *political* need [that of independence from colonial rule] so clearly, too! [111]

It is not entirely clear how Vivekananda himself responded to his disciple's nationalist politics. In the years before his death, he was known to assert that spirituality rather than politics was India's greatest strength, and the Ramakrishna Order that he established after his return from the west in 1897 was explicitly nonpolitical in nature.[112] This may, of course, have been a way of both forestalling the unwelcome attention of a colonial government and placing himself above party politics. He remained, however, a nationalist, though unevenly so, and more actively so in relation to western disciples than Indian ones. Nivedita's own involvement in Indian nationalist politics, however, proved a somewhat complex matter. Some biographies of her maintain that the swami was too weary and close to death to elucidate a position about her (new) politics. Other accounts (dependent upon the testimony of Sister Christine, whom one may reasonably suspect of having her differences with Nivedita) claim that the swami told her to choose between religion and politics.[113] In any event, what is noteworthy about the matter is Vivekananda's failure to endorse fully his disciple's new commitment to nationalist politics, given that his mission had been to Indianize her (that is, to make an Indian/Hindu nationalist of her). This failure, or this hesitancy, seems to me explicable in terms of his conception of the gendering of nationalism and political agency. The struggle was to be carried out in the name of woman and in a manner that allowed (western) woman to serve as a counter in the nationalist game. Nivedita's assumption of orthodox Hindu femininity and Hindu nationalism would have represented, to her guru, the triumph of Hindu nationalist masculinity. For her to become actor (and an implicitly masculinized one), however, rather than symbol or counter, fit very uneasily with his notion of a Mother India served by nationalist sons—who were adored by western women.

If he had been ambivalent about Nivedita's actively nationalist politics, his brother monks were not. Immediately after his death, they compelled her to choose between religion and politics, a somewhat difficult choice in an era antedating the hegemony of the bourgeois (and putatively secular) nationalist politics of the Congress Party. She chose politics, detaching herself thereby from any formal association with the Ramakrishna Order. At this time she wrote to Josephine MacLeod: "We talk of 'woman-making', but the great stream of Oriental woman's life flows on. Who am I that I should seek in any way to change it? Suppose even I could add my impress to ten or twelve girls, would it be so much gain?. . . . I think my task is to wake the nation, not to influence a few women."[114] Thereafter she was to associate primarily with Indian male political leaders like Gokhale and Aurobindo Ghosh, though she also continued her association with Sharada Devi and her companions. She had little to do with Bengali women's organizations, whose members were primarily women of the Brahmo Samaj;[115] nor did she associate except very briefly with Annie Besant, another Irish supporter of Hinduism and an ambivalent advocate of Indian nationalism who was, moreover, active in Congress Party politics. Nationalism and gender concerns intersected only occasionally and unsystematically for her, as when during the Swadeshi movement of 1905–1911 she took her students to patriotic lectures and included the song "Bande Mataram" (banned by the colonial government) in the daily prayers of the school as part of a specifically feminine training.[116]

In other words, the dynamic of the masquerade shifted decisively after the guru's death. While she had exoticized him in order to eroticize her own submission, it is possible that she saw India as a sphere where she could assume a more commanding role (than in England or Ireland, say) because of her whiteness, which could serve as a counterpoint to the disadvantage of her femininity. And if he had seen her as a figure of mobility, who could be recast and redeployed for the ends of Hindu masculinity, she became rather more mobile than he had expected or desired, remaking herself as a (partial) figure of mastery and thus interrogating and remaking the guru. She became after his death more emphatically a supporter of causes political and "public," rather than primarily religious, women-centered, and "private," though, like Vivekananda, her message was one of "manliness." She was often impatient with the Congress Party's demand for constitutional reforms and probably came to believe that armed resistance to colonial rule was both inevitable and necessary.[117] As a consequence, she became something of a minor irritant to the Raj, and her correspondence was routinely scanned by colonial authorities in India. Indeed, she played the role of the militant nationalist so well that a vast popular mythology about her mentorship of the Bengal anticolonial terrorists through figures like Aurobindo and Bhupendranath Dutta (the swami's younger brother) began to take shape during her lifetime.[118] It is of some interest to speculate in what relation, if any, her Irishness coexisted with her early imperialism and the strong anti-imperialism of her last decades. Vivekananda had, in the early stages of his acquaintance with her, attributed her fitness for her mission to her "Celtic blood." She herself says almost nothing about her Irish ethnicity, but for her Indian admirers (who were not a few, especially in the years following the swami's death), her status as an Irish rather than an English anti-imperialist was self-evident. One cannot rule out, of course, Nivedita's achievement of greater visibility and power on the Indian nationalist scene than might have been possible on an Irish or an English stage.[119]

The relay of discipleship (though not the process of displacement) came to an end with Nivedita. As a foreign-born woman, one who had never formally converted (even the process of *shuddhi* [literally, purification] would have been unavailable to her, since that presupposed a once and future Hinduness) to Hinduism at that, it is doubtful that she could herself have been acknowledged as guru by Hindu subjects in India (or even by western subjects), despite her eager Hindu doctrinal orthodoxy and nationalism. Many Indians, however, were within the ambit of her informal guidance and encouragement. To the end of her life, Nivedita remained an authoritative and active personality, publishing, lecturing, and advising about topics as diverse as education, national art, and the "woman question." Her biographers (particularly those associated directly or indirectly with the Ramakrishna Mission) speak rather uneasily of her political involvements, as they do of her allegedly uncompromising and decisive personality, and of her sustained attempts at mastery over her friends and acquaintances.[120] To them, it is almost as if she had violated the implicit taboo against assuming the role of the guru—albeit in a secular-nationalist sphere—instead of being the perpetual disciple she had been chosen to be.

It is evident that Nivedita herself felt some guilt about this deviation from proper (female) discipleship. The subject position that the swami had envisaged for her was occupied instead by another (western) female disciple, Sister Christine, who was performing the reclusive, religious, female-oriented service for which she had been earmarked. "All the things Swami dreamt for me, *she* is fulfilling," Nivedita wrote to Josephine MacLeod,[121] yet this realization did not keep her from her activities or from expounding and miming the manliness of her own guru. How Sister Christine conceived of and played Hindu womanhood, the performance of which had been displaced on to her, is unknown (though she is known to have been somewhat disapproving of the better-known disciple's unwomanly activities). The position of Hindu woman in this early nationalist moment could not, it turns out, be filled by those who would most commonly be recognized as Hindu women; for all other subjects, it either was or became an ideologically untenable position. The production of the mimic (wo)man, envisaged variously and distinctly by Ramakrishna, Vivekananda, and Nivedita, was to remain a continually deferred and displaced, yet continually urgent, project.

FIVE

Becoming Women
The Genders of Nationalism

The last chapter showed us, in part, the process of self-legitimation that (a masculine, heterosexual) Hindu nationalism deployed at a crucial moment in its imagining of itself; this chapter takes up that figure who had to be evacuated out of Vivekananda's conception of Indian womanhood in order for the white woman to function as the proper interlocutor for the male nationalist. The swami had insisted in paradoxical fashion on the concurrent hopelessness and happiness of Hindu women, as well as on their inability to ameliorate their own melancholy condition; only a western woman-turned-Hindu could serve as a (partial) proxy for them, pending their deliverance. Nivedita, on the other hand, was more disposed to emulate the virile nationalism of the guru; unable to be a guru in her own right, she sought a route to mastery in the "public" sphere of the nation, a public sphere whose separation from the "women's sphere" in this moment has been elaborated by Partha Chatterjee. By the turn of the century, however, these putatively discrete spheres had entered into a substantial commerce with each other, facilitating Indian women's participation in nationalism in the late nineteenth and early twentieth centuries; elite Indian women (Hindu, Muslim, and other) were summoned in unprecedented numbers to a range of nationalist causes in this period. This much is well known. This chapter foregrounds one among such figures; moreover, it features the Indian mimic *woman*, a figure undreamed of by Macaulay or Vivekananda, or for that matter Fanon.[1] It maps—through a scrutiny of the case of Sarojini Naidu, a well-known poet, read and published in both India and England, and a prominent nationalist figure of the Gandhian period—her emergence in colonial, imperial, and bourgeois nationalist contexts and seeks to tease out the ambivalent seductions of a figure excessively and unsatisfactorily English and simultaneously never properly Indian (woman).

It is now a truism of the scholarship on nationalism's gendering that Indian women, in addition to bourgeois males (like Vivekananda) and white women (like Nivedita), had to be remade under nationalism. Sumanta Banerjee has pointed to the ways in which the new *bhadramahila* (bourgeois woman or, more fittingly, proper lady) of the nineteenth and twentieth centuries had to be carefully marked out as such, and her production as a traditional Bengali Hindu woman had to be orchestrated in terms of her separation not only from the immodest and individualistic English memsahib in India but also from the company and mores of lower-class women like Vaishnav singers, prostitutes, and other such unsavory characters.[2] The fashioning of the *bhadramahila* (a subject that an indigenous patriarchy designated as singularly and inviolably Indian, sequestered from the corrupting though obligatory westernization attending the domain marked out as public) was, however, curiously analogous to the making of a Victorian angel in the house; this is evident from Partha Chatterjee's description (though he never articulates the connection in these terms) of the ideology of *ghar* (home) and *bahir* (the world) that, according to him, allowed nationalist patriarchies to "resolve" the woman question.[3]

In a splendid recent essay, Mrinalini Sinha has argued that elite women in nationalism were not entirely content to be remade and that they themselves participated (albeit in terms at least partially set by others) in "the shaping of gendered national subjectivities around the nationalist construct of Indian womanhood" in their struggles for authority and influence.[4] It is salutary to keep this in mind, even as we note that the nationalist movement had to deal with the woman question on many fronts, and it had to do so with a certain degree of flexibility and liberalism if it was to compel some kind of consensus from those subjects it sought to remake. Chatterjee points to the ways in which bourgeois nationalism's ideology of the separate spheres functioned with a remarkable degree of metaphoricity, allowing women to function in what came to be recognized as the public domain and even to hold positions of visibility and power without compromising the notion of their gendered essence,[5] or reconfiguring gender relationships within the patriarchal family.

The question, however, of what constitutes an appropriate and self-evident Indian womanhood, and who can be hailed as an Indian woman in the nationalist movement, especially in its later phases, is a vexed one. How does nationalism distinguish the "real thing" (Indianness, femininity) from its simulacra or its inadequate substitutes, such as white women, feminists, or otherwise improper Indian women? What is the relationship between the female nationalist struggling to signify Indian femininity (and learning to become woman) and a (male) nationalism seeking to feminize itself? How is the nationalist encounter between the (Indian) mimic woman and the (Indian) mimic man staged? And why, finally, is the career of a prominent female poet and nationalist so persistently troped in terms of spectacle, extravagance, and lack? I rehearse these questions through the case of one of the best-known female figures of the Indian nationalist movement, Sarojini Naidu. Sarojini's case is a particular one, and yet, as I will show, it is also perhaps a test case, illuminating for the insights it proffers about bourgeois nationalism's struggles to establish a model of Indian femininity in the register of authenticity, depth, and iconicity.

Beginning her career as a lyric poet nurtured by Edmund Gosse, Arthur Symons, and members of the Rhymers' Club in 1890s London, Sarojini became, by her mid-thirties, an avowed disciple of Gandhi, a dedicated Congress Party worker, and an advocate of women's causes. She came to be called the Nightingale of India in acknowledgment both of her poetic achievements and of her mellifluous oratory. Her successful poetic impersonation, first of an English identity, then of a traditionally feminine Indian one, made her a compelling figure for Indian nationalism. And yet, as we shall see, Sarojini personifies for nationalists something of the pathos of the mimic figure, who is a creature of surfaces but never quite a proper woman. Sarojini's career as poet-politician raises certain compelling questions for our understanding of authenticity, miming, and display in a nationalist theater. In seeking to tease out the implications of these questions, the chapter takes up three interlocked trajectories. The first examines Sarojini's production as mimic woman, as she is scripted first as the poet of Englishness and then as the poet of Indianness. I read this through the optic of what Spivak has characterized as the "enabling violation," that which nourishes as much as it damages and which, once known, cannot be disavowed.[6] The second explores the feminist, literary critical, and nationalist responses to the poetic corpus and to the political oratory (commonly read as an extension of the poetic gift) of the Nightingale as an uncanny reiteration of the idioms of authenticity and fakery that governed its imperial reception. The third is a meditation on style and the truth of detail for questions of identity; it ponders the existential and ethical charge of Sarojini's and Gandhi's femininity in order to ask: How does the nationalist moment stage the discovery of "real" femininity? What forms of femininity must be exorcised even as the (male or female) nationalist "becomes woman"?

BECOMING ENGLISH, BECOMING INDIAN

The woman who was to be christened the "Nightingale of India" by Gandhi and who was to be one of the most prominent personages in Congress (and especially Gandhian) nationalist politics in the decades leading up to independence was born in 1879 in a place that was, strictly speaking, outside British India even if not outside the ambit of British paramountcy in the subcontinent. She was born into a Brahmo family, headed by Dr. Aghore-

nath Chattopadhyay, in the princely state of Hyderabad; and it was Hyderabad that she was to look to in later years, as a model of Hindu-Muslim unity
and civilizational harmony, for the Indian nation. The state of Hyderabad
had an English Resident who was the de facto authority in the kingdom, but
there were far fewer of the obvious reminders of colonial rule than would
have been visible to Sarojini had she grown up in, say, the colonial capital
of Calcutta. This is not of course to assert that colonialism, or its not-quite-
Other, nationalism, were foreign to Hyderabad, though, as Karen Leonard
usefully reminds us, the princely states, which for the most part were governed by a modern *Indian* (not British) administrative elite drawn from outside the states, experienced tensions that were not necessarily congruent
with the anti-British character of bourgeois Congress nationalism in British
India.[7]

Though Bengali, the Chattopadhyays' cultural and linguistic affiliations
were eclectic; at home, the parents spoke Bengali to each other but Hindustani to the children and—according to some accounts—Telugu to the servants. Sarojini appears to have been in some important ways the prototype
of a nationalism shifting decisively away from Bengali dominance. Of the
future poet's acquaintance with English, the story is told that, upon refusing to learn the language at the age of eight, she was locked up by her father in a room for a day as punishment for her recalcitrance. She apparently
emerged from the room speaking English, which was to be her language of
preference from then on: "I came out of it a full-blown linguist. I have never
spoken any other language to him or to my mother, who always speaks to
me in Hindustani."[8] Curiously, this coercion into linguistic facility seems to
have aroused little overt resentment either of the language or of the pedagogue—at least in her memory of it—though, as Meena Alexander perceptively points out,

> It would seem crucial that the language of colonisation, English, was ac-
> quired by the young girl via the closed room, the forerunner of the countless
> rooms in prison she was forced to inhabit as an activist in the National move-
> ment. Nor was it merely an accident that she chose that very language to
> speak to both parents in, both mother and father severed from her through
> the deliberate choice of English—the language both of punishment and
> accomplishment.[9]

There is a curious sense of predestination that seems to mark Sarojini's account of her encounter with the unspeakable in that locked room. English
seems to have functioned for the nascent poet as it did for Assia Djebar in
Algeria many years later; it was the father's gift of a colonial language that
liberated her even as it wrenched her from the mother tongue.[10] It is no
surprise that the adoption of English by Sarojini had asymmetrical conse-
quences for her father and her mother, aligning the daughter with the for-

mer, especially as the latter's facility in the language appears to have been less pronounced than her husband's.[11] However, the new language proved to be of some use when, a few years later, Sarojini was able to reject partially an identity as her father's daughter (and to invoke her mother's poetic accomplishments) by repudiating the scientific career that Aghorenath had originally pursued and which he wished his oldest daughter to embrace: "My training under my father's eye was of a sternly scientific character. He was determined that I should be a great mathematician or a scientist, but the poetic instinct, which I inherited from him and also from my mother (who wrote some lovely Bengali lyrics in her youth) proved stronger."[12]

Sarojini, who had a brilliant academic career, matriculating in the University of Madras at the age of twelve and taking first place in the Presidency, was an autodidact; she read copiously and enthusiastically in the English Romantic and Victorian poets, speedily acquiring a modicum of fame in the Nizam of Hyderabad's court as an extraordinarily gifted young girl. At the age of sixteen she was sent to England (accompanied by Annie Besant), where she was to remain for three years (1895 to 1898), studying first at King's College of the University of London and then at Girton, though without taking a degree. This period proved a crucial turning point in Sarojini's career (for she already had one), for it was here, under the tutelage of English poets and intellectuals, that she learned how to be an Indian poet and, almost certainly, how to be a female poet as well. By her own account, she had been writing poetry for several years; at least some of it, according to her, was pastiche, being modeled faithfully upon the work of Scott, Barrett Browning, and other nineteenth-century poets. But the first public revelation of her persona as an English-language poet seems to have occurred during her English sojourn. The tale of her transformation into an Indian poet under the guidance of Edmund Gosse is well known. The critic who had earlier been responsible for introducing that other precocious Bengali poetess, Toru Dutt,[13] to the west was (at least retrospectively) taken with Sarojini's peculiarly "eastern" maturity and learning: "She was a child of sixteen years, but as unlike the usual English maiden of that age as a lotus or a cactus is unlike a lily of the valley. She was already marvellous in mental maturity, amazingly well-read, and far beyond a Western child in all her acquaintance with the world."[14] But he was disappointed at the lack of fit between the enchanting eastern life and the English poetry that she gave him to read, finding in the latter a counterfeit westernness so uninspired as to be indistinguishable from caricature:

> The verses which Sarojini had entrusted to me were skilful in form, correct in grammar and blameless in sentiment, but they had the disadvantage of being totally without individuality. They were Western in feeling and in imagery, they were founded in reminiscences of Tennyson and Shelley; I am not sure

that they did not even breathe an atmosphere of Christian resignation. I laid them down in despair; this was but the note of the mocking bird with a vengeance.[15]

Gosse advised her against this masquerade of a banal Englishness, at which she had shown herself to be so disturbingly proficient, and sought to bring the work into conformity with a life that he saw as unequivocally and magnificently "authentic." The phenomenon of the mimic woman was not edifying; or was it the fact of her being a mimic *woman* rather than a mimic man? In any event, he counseled her instead to embrace another identification, that of the (Indian) national poet writing in English, articulating quite explicitly what he (as the representative figure of the English critic and reader) expected of an Indian poetess: "What we wished to receive was, not a rechauffé of Anglo-Saxon sentiment in an Anglo-Saxon setting, but some revelation of the heart of India, some sincere penetrating analysis of native passion of the principles of antique religion and of such mysterious intimations as stirred the soul of the East long before the West had begun to dream that it had a soul."[16] As in the instance of the first turn to English, Sarojini submitted to her male pedagogue with "the docility and rapid appreciation of genius," becoming Indian with as much facility as she had become English. This moment of interpellation was decisive. Thereafter she made herself into the quintessential (female) Indian poet and was admiringly received as such by the Rhymers' Club and a host of notable literary figures, including Oscar Wilde and Arthur Symons.

Sarojini was to publish, after her return to India, three volumes of poetry, *The Golden Threshold* (1905), *The Bird of Time* (1912), and *The Broken Wing* (1917), which were critically well received in addition to being bestsellers in England. The first contained a lengthy introduction by Symons and the second, one by Gosse, each detailing the impact of her personality on the English literary scene in London and describing the process by which she came to be hailed as an Indian poetess. Gosse insisted that she was "the most brilliant, the most original, as well as the most correct, of all the natives of Hindustan who have written in English";[17] he was entirely persuaded— even as he remembered proudly his own mentorship of her—that she was "in all things and to the fullest extent autochthonous. She springs from the very soil of India; her spirit, although it employs the English language as its vehicle, has no other tie with the West."[18] For several years after her return to India, Sarojini corresponded with Gosse as with a mentor, but with the greater confidence of the native informant describing her milieu.[19] Once again, she had proved an apt pupil.

It is on the one hand an all too familiar and racially marked tale of the making of a gendered Indianness through the patronizing election of the masculinist Orientalist guru. Yet we might also do well to recognize and remember the *instrumentality* for Sarojini of mentors like Gosse and Symons, whose mentoring of her—as the "Indian poet," one who was especially authoritative because she had been "English" first—made possible her considerable fame and influence. Her skillful negotiation of an Indianness-for-England was to translate into considerable cultural capital with not only an English audience but also an Indian nationalist one. And since this identity as Indian poet was to prove her passport into the arena of Indian nationalism (which is not to say that she could not have entered it otherwise), we might also wish to ponder the paradox of identity as the gift of, and for, the Other. We would do well to remember the way in which Spivak, for instance, metaphorizes English in India (an instance for her of the enabling violation) as the "child of rape," a thing that cannot be demonized or refused and that has, moreover—through whatever forms of coercion—become (uneasily) one's own.[20]

During her lifetime, any serious consideration (whether laudatory or critical) of Sarojini's poetic accomplishment was, for the most part, disallowed by her status as the Nightingale, the premier female poet of the new India.[21] In more recent times, the response to her poetry by Indian poets and critics, feminist and otherwise, has been markedly irresolute and contradictory; most of them have oscillated uneasily between echoing the fulsome and patronizing adulation of Gosse and Symons and dismissing the work as lightweight and maudlin. The poetry has been described by as antimodernist and retrogressive in both form and content and invested in the representation of a Kiplingesque India;[22] Nissim Ezekiel's dismissal of an embarrassing poetic foremother is only the best known of these counterblasts to the early admiration of her work: "It was Sarojini's ill-luck that she wrote at a time when English poetry had touched the rock bottom of sentimentality and technical poverty. By the time it recovered its health she had entered politics, abandoning the possibility of poetic development and maturity."[23]

The work has also been remarked by feminist readers for its celebration of an ethos very contrary to Sarojini's self-staging as public figure. It is a critique remarkably similar in some ways to that of the Gosse, who perceived a significant hiatus between "life" and "work"; while Gosse was disappointed at the poet's too-facile mimicry of a colonial model of expressiveness, feminists are dissatisfied about the same thing, though they differ from Gosse in their sense of what constitutes the colonial model. Interestingly, the same questions (why do the life and the work not echo each other? why does one fail to be the other's mirror?) are posed by the Orientalist as well as by the (anticolonial) feminist, though the resolution is strikingly different for each. Both critiques are about the failure of a certain experiential model to "take," or to reproduce itself in the poetry. Meena Alexander, in a superb essay on Sarojini the poet, proves to be the exception. She seeks to explain

what commonly appears as a "radical cleft between the intense, if impris-
oning passions of her poetry and the political life she espoused,"[24] cannily
reading the poetry as staging the gendered constraints of Indian culture as
a prelude to attacking the constraints of colonialism.

What has commonly been described as the (irreconcilable) tension between the "life" and the "work" can be seen to mirror the constitutive contradictions of gendered citizenship in the nation, in its nationalist and its
postcolonial formations. Partha Chatterjee usefully reminds us that "[the]
new subjectivity that was constructed here [by nationalism] was premised
not on a conception of universal humanity, but rather on particularity and
difference: the identity of the 'national' community against other communities."[25] It is precisely this *different* idea or deployment of national identity
and national modernity that possibly bridges what appear to be the contradictions between Sarojini's poetic and political personae. Thus, writes Chatterjee, while the nationalists divided the domain of culture into *ghar* and
bahir, the first associated with femininity and the latter with masculinity,
they were also ingenious enough to accommodate a metaphoric understanding of these seemingly opposed spaces:

> It is this latter criterion [femininity], now invested with a characteristically na-
> tionalist content, that made possible the displacement of the boundaries of
> the home from the physical confines earlier defined by the rules of purdah to
> a more flexible, but nonetheless culturally determinate, domain set by the
> *differences* between socially approved male and female conduct. Once the es-
> sential femininity of women was fixed in terms of certain culturally visible
> qualities, they could go to schools, travel in public conveyances, watch public
> entertainment programs, and in time even take up employment outside the
> home. But the "spiritual" signs of her femininity were clearly marked—in her
> dress, her eating habits, her social demeanor, her religiosity.[26]

This, furthermore, must not be construed to mean that women were admitted into the public sphere only in lowly or marginal positions, though a
benevolent tokenism remained an integral part of this new patriarchy's
practice; what this doctrine of "essential femininity" ensured was that women
could engage in many of the same professions and activities as men without
posing a threat to "essential masculinity." Chatterjee's explanation goes a
long way toward explaining the seemingly anomalous position of a figure
like Sarojini, as well as of other (elite) Indian women who were solicited to
join the nationalist movement. Nonetheless, what merits additional consideration—and this is what I am primarily concerned with—is the deeply
troubled and ambivalent responses to women in powerful or visible positions. Sarojini's public life, and the responses it evoked, are an instructive
instance of such ambivalence, as we shall see.

Viewed in the light of Chatterjee's argument, can Sarojini's poetry (and
some of her nationalist rhetoric) be seen to function as a hostage given over

to a nationalist patriarchy as the price of political admission? (The fact of
one volume having been published before her entry into political life is beside the point; what matters, for the purposes of this chapter, is its status as
symbolic tender in the enterprise of bourgeois nationalism.) Her poetry is,
as most of her critics, including some of her contemporaries and most of
our own, have recognized, distinguished by a striking and consistent archaism, not just in its choice of form—a form that was already outmoded by the
time she published her third volume of poetry, *The Broken Wing*—but also
in its celebration of an India always hyperbolically traditional. It was for this
of course that Gosse praised her as "completely autochthonous" and which
many Indian readers of her time (including Tagore) found compelling and
attractive; nationalism as part of the project of modernity requires, as its
condition of possibility, the trace of the archaic. One must not discount either the (equivocal) attractiveness of an archaism quite visibly stamped as
"Made in England" in its idioms and in its language of expression, particularly as manifested in the corpus of a female poet whose own political (and
personal) life seemed arranged according to an entirely different script.

It is precisely this fraught nexus of the poetic and the political that I wish
to revisit, though not in order to establish one as more or less "real" than
the other. An examination of Sarojini's public status as poet poses a number of interesting questions for the gendering of bourgeois nationalism in
the twentieth century. What forms of violence and what intimacies link the
poet writing in English with the female nationalist? Why is the poet's career
one that must be both renounced and remembered in that moment which
is defined as the political? I am interested in the way in which the poetry
serves as collateral in the sphere denominated the political and defines her
place in it; I am interested as well as in the deeply equivocal pattern of responses to her as the figure of the nationalist and national poet (which
seems proleptic of the decidedly equivocal responses of latter-day literary
critics). What I argue in this chapter is that the seeming breach between the
poetic persona and the public one should not lead us—as Alexander reminds us—to overlook the profound articulations between the two spheres.
I also argue that it is precisely the celebratory archaism of Sarojini's poetry,
including its parade of submissive and sacrificial women, as well as its stance
against modernity (a modernity of telos as well as of poetic form), rather
than the implicit critique of such an India, that permits Sarojini a point of
entry into the nationalist movement. The sacrificial women of the poetry
are, I believe, most productively read as emblems of a monumentalized and
longed-for yet only partially emulable past. It is precisely the dialectic between the heroic submission of these mythical women and the (Indian)
modernity of the contemporary woman that nationalism seeks to maintain
rather than repress. The former must claim the latter as her own (progeny);
neither can be abandoned. At the same time the poetry functions, I believe,

as a kind of an alibi, embodying an idealized Indian femininity that partially exonerates the poet's imperfect emulation of those gendered models.

In reading the Nightingale thus as a figure of convergence and tension between seemingly discrete impulses, I have found Anne McClintock's recent essay on gender and nationalism particularly helpful. McClintock, remarking on the "Janus-faced" quality of the nation first noted by Tom Nairn, describes the nation's simultaneous and paradoxical adherence to a primeval past and its turn to the future. This "temporal anomaly within nationalism" brings together in a mutually uncomfortable but necessary alliance the elements of nostalgia and social and cultural atavism with the notions of modernity and "progress." The incommensurability of these two sets of terms is resolved "by figuring the contradiction as a 'natural' division of *gender*." Women are "the atavistic and authentic 'body' of national traditions"; they signify nationalism's link to a deep past, its conservative principle. Men on the other hand stand in for the modernity of nationalism, which is dynamic, aggressive, and revolutionary.[27] We know, besides, that peasants, tribals, and other subalterns are also figured in this way, in their "failure" to be modern. Women, along these other traditionally marginalized groups, function as "the living archive of the national archaic."[28]

For the most part Sarojini's verse, especially in the early part of her career, eschewed "public" and "modern" events and comprised lyrics about what had come to be coded quite decisively as the timeless and the private (which in the imaginary of Indian nationalism was also the zone of tradition and of inviolable Indianness). Not surprisingly, in light of the carefully chosen archaism that characterized her corpus, many of the best-known lyrics were quite explicitly derived from "folk" sources ("Palanquin-Bearers," "Indian Weavers," "Suttee," "In the Bazaars of Hyderabad," and "Bangle-Sellers," among others) and from classical Persian and Urdu ones ("The Song of Princess Zeb-un-nissa," "Humayun to Zobeida," and "The Queen's Rival," all in *The Golden Threshold*). Alexander directs our attention to the Tennysonian and late Romantic heritage of this poetry in its romanticization of the folk and its fascination with women in conditions of deathly passivity: "The young Sarojini would seem to have learnt her lesson all too well, embracing for herself the world-weary sensations, the stasis, the unmistakable agony of women who have nowhere in the world to go. The irony is of course that she should learn from Symons or Dowson, carrying back their diction to India, making up in her poetry images of exhausted women, hermetically sealed, a double colonisation that the interchange of cultures drew her to."[29]

The echoes that Alexander describes are unmistakable, but it is possible that part of the Indian poet's inspiration may have derived as well from indigenous sources—for instance from the highly self-conscious and conspicuously gendered invention of tradition, particularly in late-nineteenth-

and early-twentieth-century Bengal.[30] Thus the sequestered woman in "The Purdah Nashin" (and we cannot forget that the campaign to bring women out of purdah was a very important plank of the reform movements of the nineteenth century) is celebrated, though not entirely unequivocally, as "guarded and secure / Behind her carven lattices, / Like jewels in a turbaned crest, / Like secrets in a lover's breast."[31] Likewise, sati is represented (in "Suttee") not in the familiar reformist registers of women's oppression or of social melioration but in that of feminine secondariness, which is also coded as love: "Life of my life, Death's bitter sword / Hath severed us like a broken word, / Rent us in twain who are but one . . . / Shall the flesh survive when the soul is gone?"[32] It is not so much that sati is *chosen* by the grieving widow; life itself is inconceivable, indeed preposterous, for her in the absence of a husband. In her avatar as political figure, Sarojini's approach to the reproducibility of a history celebrated as glorious was considerably more guarded and canny; sati as a practice in the current time was unwarranted because contemporary Indian men did not "deserve" sati.[33] The burden of memory—and of memorialization—had to be borne while leading a life that was the opposite of what was remembered and celebrated.

For a figure so prominently associated with the nationalist movement, Sarojini wrote relatively few poems that could be construed as overtly public or modern (both terms being locatable within a single associative continuum). In the volumes following *The Golden Threshold* her poetry expanded in scope from love songs and songs commemorating a folk everyday to include poems with a more specifically "national" and historic orientation, as witnessed by "The Broken Wing," "The Imam Bara," "Imperial Delhi," "Gokhale," "The Lotus" (addressed to Gandhi), "The Prayer of Islam," "Kali the Mother," and "Awake!" (addressed to her friend Jinnah)—all of which appeared in *The Broken Wing*. These either memorialized the glories of a bygone era (now marked more subtly as *historic* rather than timelessly Indian), celebrated Hindu-Muslim unity, or worked as exhortations to the soul of India, often invoking the (by now) familiar and evocative maternal model of Indian nationness.[34]

In speaking of the incongruousness between poetry and biography, we have already noted the fact that for Sarojini poetry functions as the register in which a woman's dues are paid. It is her most conspicuous offering or sacrifice to the nationalist cause; it is one of the emblematic ironies of the gendered colonial situation that the same tribute is equally acceptable to Orientalists and nationalists. The poetry serves for Sarojini as a token of her good faith as an Indian woman. It does not simply constitute an account of willing feminine sacrifice; the poet herself must enact the renunciation she describes, if not by reproducing the submission of her meek heroines, then by abjuring the poetry that has made her famous. The poetry is an offering to the cause of (a masculinist) nationalism; the renunciation of the poetry is no less so. As we shall see in the next section, however, the figure of the female poet/renouncer is attended by fascination as well as unease; her creative power must be harnessed or kept at bay even as it is deployed. When manifest in the prose of political rhetoric or in the arena of public life, the bardic gift establishes Sarojini as too hypnotically enthralling for comfort, even as a figure of seduction, even as she can be dismissed as a mere talker, whose bombast and the scandal of whose life alike point to a damning lack of substance. Both as poet and as politician, Sarojini serves as the vacant or even counterfeit figure of the mimic woman, always at a certain remove from the genuine article.

THE UNBECOMING WOMAN

Historical scholarship as well as popular opinion on bourgeois Indian (Congress) nationalism in the twentieth century have established that the movement created (as the Algerian revolution was to do later in the century)[35] a new subject position for women—women as nationalists, activists, and public figures. Gandhi in particular among the (male) nationalists is believed to have played a crucial role in the "feminization" of nationalist activity. A nationalist for whom the purification and reform of Indianness rather than the transfer of political power from English to Indian hands constituted true *Swaraj* (independence),[36] he is commonly understood to have feminized himself through satyagraha (literally, persisting in the truth—a one-word code for his nonviolent moral opposition to British rule in India). He is credited, too, with having made a significant departure from "the attitude of many of the leaders of the reform movements of the late nineteenth century, who tended to see women as passive recipients of more humane treatment through the initiative of enlightened male effort."[37] It must, however, be remembered, as Radha Kumar points out, that women had already entered the public domain on a number of fronts, and Gandhi's most important function was perhaps to legitimize this move as well as to expand existing definitions of "women's work."[38] Gandhi did this partially in the manner described by Chatterjee, not so much by making women's rights a question of modernity and its ethical claims but by a deployment of the rhetoric of (Indian) female exceptionalism and purity. Thus he invoked traditional Hindu heroines like Sita and Draupadi as exemplars of moral courage and self-sacrifice. Women were, according to this scheme, peculiarly and intuitively suited for the exigencies of satyagraha and nonviolent struggle; the qualities of mind required for such enterprises had, on the other hand, to be learned by men. While this insistence on the autonomy and dignity of women—as well as the transformation of spinning on the *charkha* (spinning wheel) into a profoundly political act—undoubtedly had the effect of broadening women's possibilities for action, they also, as Madhu

Kishwar reminds us, "helped ensure the entry of women into public life without their having to assume a competitive posture *vis-à-vis* men."[39]

Sarojini's entry into the arena of the political as such cannot be construed outside this framework, and in a fundamental way it was not incongruous with the nature of her poetic corpus or indeed with the trajectory of her poetic career. In a vital sense, her entry into politics (or at least the role she came to play in the nationalist struggle) would have been far less easy without her first having been the kind of poet that she was. This we have seen. Female nationalists had to be feminized just as much as male nationalists did. In Sarojini's case (as in that of Nivedita, to some degree, in an earlier period) it was possible be a public figure because the writing had provided a guarantee of her unimpeachable femininity. And in many important ways she showed herself to be the proper woman politician, who could be a true woman despite her great consequence and fearlessness in the public sphere and despite her considerable contributions to women's issues as an orator and activist. Her life as a champion of women's rights thus can exist in a productive (because generally subordinate) counterpoint to her life as a nationalist. In 1917 and 1918 she led the delegation to press for women's suffrage before the Montagu commission and the Southborough Franchise Commission, and in the latter year she helped pass a resolution in support of women's franchise at the Congress session. In 1919 she went to England as a member of the Home Rule League to press these claims before a Joint Parliamentary Committee. In 1931 she attended the second Round Table Conference in London as the representative of Indian women, though she, in common with the vast majority of bourgeois women nationalists, was to contend that women needed no special favors or separate representation.[40] She was careful to insist on the complete congruity of these two aspects (the gendered and the nationalist) of her struggle; like many other Indian women, she insisted that the Indian women's movement was distinct from those in the west in not being "feminist,"[41] the latter presumably marked with its attendant band of repugnant associations, being committed to sameness and equality rather than complementarity and difference, existing in an adversarial relationship with men rather than a supportive and amicable one, insisting on rights rather than duties, and operating outside a situation of colonial dominance. As Joanna Liddle and Rama Joshi point out, the participants in the women's movement "attributed their oppression not to men as a group, but to custom. . . . They argued that women's issues could not be separated from the question of foreign domination, and this analysis had the effect of defusing male opposition and winning support for the women's cause within India."[42]

Despite this wariness about claiming the label of feminism (a wariness that has persisted over the decades[43]), Sarojini was rarely content to be silent on women's issues. She was willing, for instance, to castigate Indian men for not responding seriously to the criticisms of Katherine Mayo's *Mother India* (1927), even as she challenged Mayo's right to speak for Indian women.[44] For her, women's uplift could only strengthen male nationalist demands, rather than be counterposed against them. Thus one of Sarojini's earliest public speeches (the one that brought her to the attention of the first of her nationalist gurus, Gokhale), which was in support of a resolution for women's education at the Indian Social Conference in Calcutta in 1906, situated feminist issues firmly within the domain of nation building: "When the Indian races are seeking for the ultimate unity of a common national ideal, it is well for us to remember that the success of the whole movement lies centred in what is known as the woman question."[45] Not only did the deprivation of women constitute a minus in the calculus of the national good, it might even have been the condition of possibility for colonial domination:

> Does one man dare to deprive another of his birthright to God's pure air which nourishes his body? How, then, shall a man dare to deprive a human soul of its immemorial inheritance of liberty and life? And yet, my friends, man has so dared in the case of Indian women. That is why you men of India are to-day what you are: because your fathers, in depriving your mothers of that immemorial birthright, have robbed you, their sons, of your just inheritance.[46]

Freedom is a patrimony that is passed, curiously, through the female line; and if woman is to be the conduit (rather than the recipient or the giver) of such an inheritance, she cannot be allowed to be the weak link that prevents the sons from coming into their own.

This privileging of woman in her maternal aspect—and, moreover, as the mother of sons—was to be the keynote of Sarojini's approach to the woman question. Thus, addressing the 1916 session of the Congress (under the presidency of Annie Besant that year), she made her appeal on the Arms Act not as a representative citizen of an imagined community but, once again, and somewhat paradoxically, in the accents of a mother demanding rights for a son intent upon winning or preserving his manhood: "It is suitable that I who represent the other sex, that is, the mothers of the men whom we wish to make men and not emasculated machines, should raise a voice on behalf of the future mothers of India to demand that the birthright of their sons should be given back to them."[47] Sarojini certainly made the appeal in the conventional and self-effacing accents of the maternal, which had come to trope woman's identity as nation(alist). Within this frame of reference, woman cannot expect to be citizen on her own account but only for something larger than herself; her citizenship is a moving away from the claims that constitute normal (that is, normatively male) citizenship. But there was at the same time a certain paradox in her arroga-

tion of the authority to make the appeal, since only the disinterested peti-
tion by the decisively not-male on behalf of the once-male or the to-be-male
(or the would-be-male) could guarantee the latter's (slippery) manhood.

In a complex and fraught relationship with this attempted (but never
fully successful) embodiment of a maternal Indian polity was Sarojini's
apparent willingness to take on the role of disciple to a succession of prominent men; first her father, then Gosse, then Gokhale, and then finally
Gandhi was her guru.[48] If Gosse was the first to discipline her efforts and to
claim her for India, Gokhale was to do the same nearly two decades later,
when she was already an established poet; her relationship with him re-
hearses some though not all of the difficulties of a nationalist patriarchy
with the figure of the westernized nationalist woman as public persona.
Having heard her move the resolution on women's education in the Calcutta meeting of the All-India Social Conference in 1906, he wrote to ex-
press his admiration: "Your speech was *more than an intellectual treat* of the
highest order. . . . We all felt for the moment *to be lifted to a higher plane.*"[49]
The praise is extremely warm; but it should not escape notice, either, that
what is also being invoked is, in the words of the feminist and nationalist
Margaret Cousins, "Ruskin's idea of woman being the inspirer and guide
rather than the dominator or leader."[50] The modality of this response was
to repeat itself through Sarojini's political career (though often inflected
more disparagingly), as the effects of her oratory and poetry were written in
the register of sensibility and sensation rather than the register of intellectual suasion. All her life she functioned as a figure (often an empty one) of
inspiration, rather than as a thinker or even a doer.

From the moment of that initial solicitation she became, albeit infor-
mally, a disciple of the great nationalist. Despite his praise for her elocu-
tionary power, Gokhale was apparently rather suspicious of her fame as a
poet, nervous about the effect on her of immoderate adulation, and appre-
hensive about the affect she was capable of producing. And yet (in her telling of it), when he claimed her for the nation he could only do so—in the
most florid arabesques, no less—by hailing her as a poet: "Stand here with
me, with the stars and hills for witness and in their presence consecrate your
life and your talent, your song and your speech, your thought and your
dream to the motherland. O poet, see visions from the hill-tops and spread
abroad the message of hope to the toilers in the valleys."[51] Poetry had to be
renounced as an indulgence (a feminine one, undoubtedly) in the face of
the nation's need, and it would be precisely this capacity for sacrifice and
self-abnegation that would mark her as a woman-for-the-nation. Yet it was
her status as a poet that made her worthy to be called to the nation's service
in the first place.

Discipleship to Gokhale was followed by a more lasting yet more complex
and troubled tie with Gandhi. His disciple she undoubtedly was, both in her

own telling of their relationship and in the accounts provided by other observers. But unlike the guru, she was anything but ascetic; in marked contrast to him, she loved English civilization even as she fought against British colonialism in India. Also unlike the vast majority of Gandhi's female disciples, and some of the male ones, Sarojini had a profound distaste for the austerities of the satyagrahi (practitioner of satyagraha), including those of the guru, and her discipleship was characterized by a refusal to emulate the guru in his spartan, indeed self-flagellating, ways. No doubt she went to prison (as did her nationalist compatriots) several times, but she had little use for his regime of austerity and self-denial as an everyday and intimate practice,[52] and she dismissed his diet as "grass and goat's milk." She appears more than anything else to have found his self-enforced poverty rather comical (if not a shade self-aggrandizing), remarking on one occasion that it required a millionaire to keep the great leader in poverty;[53] the reference was to the wealthy industrialist G. D. Birla, with whom Gandhi often stayed. She also resolutely refused to spin or to regard the *charkha* with any piety, despite the fact that the spinning of *khaddar* (coarse handspun cloth) was central to Gandhian satyagraha and was considered a peculiarly feminine activity. Nor would she, despite her long association with the mahatma, be subject to the substantial rigors of Sabarmati Ashram. She did wear *khaddar* for two years, in the initial stages of the Non-Cooperation movement, upon Gandhi's urging, but reverted to her silk saris and elaborate jewelry before very long. She was always regarded in some ways as an anomaly in the mahatma's camp, a figure who was never completely invested with high seriousness. She was instead "the licensed jester of the Mahatma's court,"[54] the one disciple privileged to speak of him openly as "Mickey Mouse" and to comment on his general ugliness and perversity.

Besides, Sarojini's own life as a nationalist Indian woman was by no means exemplary. Despite her repeated paeans to the meek and self-sacrificing female figures from the Hindu epics, her repeated invocation of the sati as a model for the satyagrahi, and her showcasing of her own status as mother (all of which were coupled with her frequently disparaging remarks about her own femininity), she was in her personal life quite markedly different from the ideals she conjured up. Her relationships with some of her family members were notably strained. She distanced herself publicly from the activities in Europe of her revolutionary communist brother Virendranath, an act which estranged her from her father.[55] We know little of her relationships with her mother or her other siblings; her youngest brother, the poet Harindranath, hardly mentions her in his autobiography, despite her substantial reputation as a poet.[56] Moreover, much of her life after 1914 was spent away from her husband and children, who lived in Hyderabad. She did travel in India and abroad with her daughters Padmaja and Lilamoni, especially the former, but her husband remains a shadowy figure in her biographies and seems not to have appeared even at her funeral. In a recent biography, there is a brief mention of the resentment on the part of her own family at her absences and the criticism she faced about spending relatively little time with her husband.[57] This was of course one of the central paradoxes of nationalism's engagement with the woman question. Woman was hailed as (wife and) mother; these markers of femininity were internalized so that she could be woman even in the public sphere. But how could the figure who *literalized* the familial imaginary of the nation dedicate herself as Sarojini did to both nation (and its spiritual patriarch) and her own family without failing the latter? Gandhi tried to resolve this by politicizing the domestic, through the act of spinning, and it was by far his preferred model of nationalist struggle for women. Yet there were those who wished for a fuller involvement in the nationalist struggle; Gandhi's response was to ask the unmarried ones among them to seek a vocation higher than wifehood, that of celibate singleness and service to the nation. This was the route followed by—among others—Mirabehn and Sushila Nayyar. But it obviously made the position of Sarojini and other married women like herself quite anomalous.

Nor was Sarojini's love of magnificent clothing and fine furnishings easily recuperable into a nationalist schema of taste and consumption; in this she was distinct from her sister-in-law Kamaladevi Chattopadhyay (or from the Pupul Jayakars of a later period), whose keen interest in handlooms and folk arts of various kinds was not seen to be marked in the same way by mere womanly vanity or weakness.[58] In fact, all the accounts of Sarojini emphasize this important difference from the ideal practiced by Gandhi; they all point repeatedly to her love of comfort and good living, including good food and clothing and comfortable accommodations. She is described all too often in the register of the private and of "taste." Her most prominent biographer, Padmini Sengupta, begins her work with a chapter entitled "Sapphire and Gold," which is an extended description of her "intense love for colour," most notably manifest in her love of rich and flamboyant clothing.[59]

These were to be the terms in which Sarojini was most often invoked, by many observers, Indian and European, some sympathetic to Indian nationalism and some hostile. To many of them she seemed like a society grande dame of the best kind (which to many satyagrahis was the worst kind). Margaret Cousins, attentive to the details of Sarojini's toilette and diction, was reminded, in Sarojini's home, of the atmosphere of a French salon.[60] To the liberal young English Member of Parliament Robert Bernays she was like the socialite Patricia Campbell, and moreover the only Indian woman who managed to make *khaddar* look attractive.[61] Even the vitriolic Beverly Nichols, who found little to love in India, was bowled over by a figure he described, not unadmiringly, as "so very Mayfair":

Among these figures [major Indian politicians] Mrs. Naidu stands out, and always stood out, in high relief. 64 years old, she has lived—to put it mildly—a full life. She was the first Indian woman to be elected President of Congress; wherever the fight has been thickest, she was to be found, fluttering a gaily-bordered saree, with feminine defiance, in the face of the British Raj. She had been swept into *lathi* [baton] charges, had held Gandhi's hand at some of the most crucial moments of his career, and . . . while finding time to produce a considerable family, had written a great deal of enchanting poetry. . . . The fact remains that she still gives the impression of being a young woman. She has allure, and she knows it.[62]

This allure (a highly complex affect, in Sarojini's case) was, for other nationalists a source of some discomfort. It is important to remember this even as one recalls that she served as an eminent ally of Gandhi's in many important missions. She was sent by the mahatma on a grand tour of the United States following the publication of Katherine Mayo's searing (if undeniably racist) critique of the sexual pathologies of Indians and of the victimization of Hindu women by Hindu men (especially nationalists) who claimed to revere motherhood. Though she said almost nothing in public about *Mother India*, Sarojini's lectures and her social appearances appear to have been clearly designed to serve as a rebuke to the allegations of that infamous book; and her "love letters" to Gandhi from the United States, detailing her triumphs, were regularly reproduced in the pages of his journal *Young India*. (For once, she carried off what was for a nationalist patriarchy a convincing imitation of a genuine and appropriately modern Indian femininity.) She served in other ambassadorial capacities: she was an emissary to conferences on the status of expatriate Indians in South Africa and East Africa, and she was to accompany Gandhi as a delegate to the Second Round Table Conference in London in 1932. She was also to be the first Indian woman president of the Congress, and one of only two or three until Indira Gandhi's nomination in 1959.

But a more than casual reading of the details of her career makes it obvious how precarious her position in nationalist politics was, despite her high profile and her long association with the mahatma. She was famous for her oratory, moving persons as unlike each other as Gokhale, Lado Rani Zutshi, Jawaharlal Nehru, and Margaret Cousins. It was her oratory as much as her poetry that kept alive in the public mind her status as poet, as the Nightingale of India. Yet there was also a profound suspicion of the affect produced by her speeches, of the very rhetorical brilliance that could lull the reason into a kind of stupefaction. Motilal Nehru is known to have commented caustically after Sarojini's presidential address to the Congress in 1925—an address that is reputed to have moved most of the audience to tears—"But what did she say?"[63] The younger Nehru, too, no mean orator himself and a friend of Sarojini's (and given, like her, to extempore speech-making) wrote at a later date in his diary: "Sarojini's poetical fervours made her say fine nothings."[64] His praise in his autobiography of her eloquence is less conspicuously damning, though it is distinctly ambivalent about his one-time callow admiration of her fluency: "I remember being moved also, in those days after the Lucknow Congress, by a number of eloquent speeches delivered by Sarojini Naidu in Allahabad. It was all nationalism and patriotism and I was a pure nationalist, my vague socialist ideas of college days having sunk into the background."[65] Her impact is written almost as a seduction against which vigilance must be vigorously exercised. Is it any surprise that Nehru was to have a long-standing romantic relationship with her daughter Padmaja (who was, like her mother, flamboyant and charismatic though politically far less visible)?[66]

Even Gandhi seems to have regarded her with a certain wariness. In reply to G. D. Birla's objections (what these were is not known) to Gandhi's having nominated her for the presidency of the Congress session in 1925, the latter provided this rather equivocal support:

> You are unnecessarily worried about Sarojini. She has served India well, and is still doing so. While I have done nothing in particular just now for her presidentship, I am convinced that if others who have so far accepted that position, were fit for it, she too is fit. Everybody is enamoured of her enthusiasm. I myself bear witness to her courage. I have noticed nothing wrong about her.
>
> But from all this you need not infer that I approve of all that she or anybody else does.
>
> > God has inhabited this our world with objects
> > Living and inanimate, good, bad, indifferent;
> > The wise are concerned only with the good
> > Just as the swan sucks milk, leaving water alone.[67]

Among the factors that seemed to make Sarojini central to Indian nationalism, while ensuring her distance from it, was the apparent linguistic anomaly of a being a national poet writing in English; the mimic (wo)man is despised as much as she is solicited. On the one hand the choice was logical: she was born to Bengali parents, brought up in the Urdu-speaking environment of princely Hyderabad, compelled to learn English at an early age, educated partially in England, and married to an Andhra man. The choice of English would seem logical, if not inevitable, in her case. It would also seem to be what allowed her to be hailed as the Nightingale of India, and to function as such. In what language could the poet of "unity in diversity" write and speak if not in English? As in the case of Vivekananda, what could account for her stature in India if not her reception in England? Yet this also ensured her partial alienation from a nationalist project, especially a Gandhian one that insisted on the un-Indianness of English and the centrality of Hindi to any conception of national culture.[68] (When Sarojini did speak in an Indian language—which was not often—it was the Urdu of her native Hyderabad, and Urdu poetry that she deployed, rather than the Hindi preferred by a Congress now firmly dominated by North Indian Hindus.)

Despite her status as the laureate of nationalism and her presidency of the Indian National Congress, Sarojini was in many fundamental ways a marginal figure in the decision making of that nationalist body. This is not to deny that she may have been symbolically central. In this her role was not significantly different from that played by other women participants in the nationalism; "the participation of women in the freedom movement," says Kishwar, "was limited, both quantitatively and qualitatively."[69] No women, for instance, were invited by Gandhi to form part of his band of seventy-odd satyagrahis who were to march to the sea at Dandi to break the Salt Laws, in the single most dramatic instance of confrontation with the tyranny of colonial law. Several nationalist women protested and compelled Gandhi and the Congress Committee to withdraw their opposition to women's participation in the salt satyagraha, though not in the march itself.[70] Large numbers of women, acting individually and as members of women's organizations, joined the salt satyagraha. Sarojini was at the beach at Dandi to hail Gandhi as the "Deliverer." When he was arrested, and his successor Abbas Tyabji after him, she led the raid upon the Dharasana Salt Works in what was to be one of the most brutal episodes of the nationalist period, as the police systematically beat the nonviolent activists into "bloody pulp."[71] She was the first woman to be arrested in this campaign.

Given the distinctly secondary and supportive role Sarojini (and other women) had been assigned in the civil disobedience movement, it is no surprise to find her not invited to run for election in 1936 (though a few women did contest seats).[72] Nehru is known to have been very unwilling to have her serve on the Working Committee of the Congress party in 1936 (despite the convention of always having a woman in the Cabinet).[73] We also have it on M. O. Mathai's (admittedly dubious) authority that Gandhi persuaded Nehru to leave her out of the Working Committee in 1946 for fear of her "talk[ing] loosely and leak[ing] out secrets"; this was a decision that apparently enraged Sarojini.[74] After independence in 1947, there seemed no obvious place for her, a fact that biographers have noted. She did become governor (or governess, as she caustically put it) of the United Provinces, the largest state in independent India, but only after Bidhan Chandra Ray, to whom Nehru had first offered the position, declined the offer. It was a largely ceremonial position, and supposedly well suited to Sarojini's great powers as a bon vivant and hostess. It is perhaps quite consistent with the other details that while she was invited to many university convocations as governor, at Shantiniketan, at Lucknow University, at Benares Hindu

University, and in that capacity conferred honorary doctorates upon many intellectuals and prominent nationalists including Nehru, Homi Bhabha, and Govind Vallabh Pant, she received no such honors herself.

BECOMING WOMAN

In what ways could Sarojini be considered a representative figure of the elite Hindu woman in Indian nationalism? An extended comparison of Sarojini's standing in the nationalist movement with that of other prominent women nationalists, such as Vijaylakshmi Pandit, Rajkumari Amrit Kaur, and Kamaladevi Chattopadhyay,[75] is not possible here, but my contention is that the case of Sarojini may raise some productive questions of a generalizable nature,[76] even though the specific details of her life or the trajectory of her career may not have corresponded with those of the other figures. (For instance, her status as a poet is a complicating factor of some magnitude.) Partha Chatterjee's useful point about Indian nationalism's capacity to absorb women in powerful positions needs to be fleshed out, and perhaps even troubled, at this point, by some of the questions that the case of Sarojini raises. Rather than comparing her case with that of other women nationalists of the Congress, it may in fact be more illuminating to compare Sarojini and Gandhi, certainly one of the most feminine actors in the nationalist movement. The parallels are fascinating and instructive.

In important respects the personae of Sarojini and her mentor Gandhi display a striking specularity. As Kishwar points out, Gandhi "more than any other leader tried to live his personal life as publicly as possible, . . . [and] many of his experiments which most people consider eccentricities and obsessions are inextricably linked to his vision of new types of relationships between men and women."[77] Hence the emphasis, both in Gandhi's own accounts of his life and practices and in the responses of people to him, on the staging of such everyday questions as clothing, diet, sexual activity, and personal hygiene.[78] His autobiography is full of details regarded as mundane and also intimate, too intimate and unsublimated sometimes even for bourgeois autobiography (which after all is dedicated to the transcendentalization of the banal).[79] Such a showcasing and politicization of the everyday was, as Kishwar also reminds us, vital to Gandhi's reconfiguration of women's domestic and routine activities (like cooking or spinning) as revolutionary.

> Gandhi's relentless propaganda in favor of *charkha* spinning and wearing of khadi [*khaddar*] was designed to bring the spirit of nationalism and freedom into every home, even in the remotest village. In this way, abstract political ideas, such as struggle against colonial rule, assumed concrete form for ordinary people. This was a very remarkable way of reaching out to women and bridging the gap between their private lives and the economic-political life of the country. The decision of what to wear or not to wear is one of the deci-

sions likely to be more in the control of a woman, and Gandhi was able to im-
bue this seemingly mundane sphere of life with a new political and moral
significance. The choice of spin [sic] and wear khadi was at once the simplest,
least dramatic of choices, calling for no obvious heroism. At the same time, it
symbolised each individual's conscious choice of a philosophy, a way of life. To
wear khadi came to mean many things—opposition to colonial rule, identification with the poor and the exploited, and an assertion of the spirit of self-
reliance, of freedom.[80]

In foregrounding these mundane, "womanly" activities, Gandhi did more
than invite large numbers of (not always privileged) women into the domain of nationalist politics. The strategy transformed him in many respects
into a "woman" himself. To cite one obvious instance of this feminization: to
his grandniece Manu Gandhi he comported himself as a mother, hence the
seeming incongruity in the title of her book on the mahatma: *Bapu* [Father,
the name by which Gandhi was often known], *My Mother.*[81] On another occasion, he said to one of his women disciples, "I trust you have not missed
the woman in me";[82] he made such assertions on several occasions.

Oddly enough, Sarojini's everyday life seems to have received almost as
much attention as Gandhi's. The accounts of her life focus on her clothing,
her preferences in food, her shopping, her taste in decor, on everything
routinely considered the domain of the everyday, the unremarkable, the
feminine, the outside-the-political. While Gandhi's life has been received as
his message, so in a perverse way has Sarojini's. It is remarkable that these
figures, who are considered as unlike as two figures can be, are remembered
in the same register of the everyday, which by the way is also that of exhibitionism and of theatricality. However—and this is the important distinction—Gandhi's femininity was not seen (either in his lifetime or in historical remembrance) as analogous to Sarojini's. She, too, was seen and
represented in the register of quotidian habits of consumption and behavior; she was seen in a real sense as fundamentally feminine in the least elevated ways in her love of clothing and food and good living. Yet none of this
was translatable, as Gandhi's actions were, into another and higher register,
into the story of her experiments with truth. These actions were, in other
words, not signs pointing to something other than themselves. It should be
noted that I speak here more of the effects produced respectively by Sarojini and Gandhi and less of their status as intending agents. Gandhi's autobiography, as well as his copious writings in *Harijan* and *Young India* and the
evidence of numerous interviews and other encounters in which public
reflection about the politics of everyday practice is made manifest, may be
said to facilitate such a reading. Besides, as Lloyd and Susanne Rudolph
note, such details contributed to his aura of saintliness that in the popular
Indian context translated into considerable political capital.[83] In Sarojini's
case, on the other hand, there is a notable taciturnity in the letters about

"private life," despite the obvious delight in gossip about mutual acquaintances and talk about visits and daily routines. (One can only imagine, and I use this word in the most nonrestrictive sense, what her investment might have been in nationalism, in discipleship, in the women's movement, and in the politics of daily practice.) She wrote no autobiography, unlike Gandhi; nor did she edit any journals. The question here is one of the reception of these two figures, given that there was in some respects such a striking overlap in the practices of the everyday and despite their both featuring as figures of the feminine. Gandhi is seen to have an existential substance that is not available in Sarojini. And this, paradoxically, is because she is too phenomenal a creature to have any philosophical core; she is seen as a creature entirely of surfaces, entirely of the moment, with no depth whatsoever. She is characterized entirely by ephemera, and as such is not available for abstraction. She is precisely that figure whose activities cannot be recorded or monumentalized. She cannot be a historical figure; she can only be a subject-effect, can only provide the impression of being an agent. What we have in her case is a series of actions that cannot be transcendentalized and that disclose no existential depth. Her femininity, then, is set against the femininity of a Gandhi, who is seen to embody far more fully and profoundly the lineaments of an essential Indian femininity, often represented as Mother India—self-sacrifice, nurturance, nonviolence, and a commitment to everyday heroism. Sarojini on the other hand is the figure not so much of this philosophically thick Mother India as of another femininity, talkative, sparkling, vain, the essence of which is that it has no essence. If anything, she corresponds analogically to the figure of the seductive woman whose lack of sobriety and austerity threatens to destabilize the endeavors of spirituality and politics. Of the two, Gandhi is the better woman. I would like to emphasize that I do not wish to describe Gandhi's femininity as unreal or as a "theft" that robs Sarojini of her "real" femininity;[84] I wish, rather, to draw attention to the kinds of femininity that are accommodable by bourgeois nationalism and to those that must be kept at arm's length or rendered trifling even as their allure cannot be disavowed.

This may be why, in speaking of Sarojini the political figure, other political figures were rendered speechless (as Nehru was in his eulogy of her) and could only speak of her in terms of the ineffable. Many political figures as well as literary critics insisted that she was not quite a politician, that she was to be understood above all as a poet,[85] which was the coded way of asserting that her essence was style (a word with a double valence, meaning both personal and poetic style) and that her achievements were unquantifiable. Language seems to fail to describe the figure seen as the quintessence of poetry.

Faced with the task of coming to terms with her political contributions, biographers and nationalists alike seem to have been hard put to point to something solid, quantifiable, or decisive. Thus one of her biographers (a sympathetic one) says, "There was . . . considerable material of historical interest available in the National Archives, but as I had anticipated, great gaps existed in this information because *it was probably physically impossible to record the brilliant outpouring of both profound thought, human concern and the light-hearted banter that was the hallmark of Sarojini Naidu's personality.*"[86] This may, of course, be an unusually frank and thoughtful admission of the absolute Otherness of the biographical subject, but it also entirely consonant with the general difficulty for nationalists of defining Sarojini's substance or contributions (though the biographer was in this case a woman). Thus Nehru, upon her death, was unable to define the essence of Sarojini (despite her many decades of highly visible nationalist activity and work in women's organizations, quite apart from her career as a poet) except in terms of a lack, or in terms of an affect rather than something relatively more tangible: "So we think of her as a brightness, as a certain vitality and vividness, as poetry infused into life and activity, as something tremendously important and rich and yet something which in terms of the material world is rather insubstantial, difficult to grasp and difficult to describe, as something which you can only feel, as you can feel beauty, as you can feel the other higher things in life."[87]

Nehru's eulogy enacts some of the difficulties involved in "fixing" Sarojini, who functions—as we have seen—as all things to all people, and yet never as quite the right thing. She is on the one hand—especially in relation to the saintly mahatma—too corporeal and too trivially worldly to be allegorized as a figure of Mother India. Yet she is also, at the same time, a figure who carries a peculiarly numinous charge. She is unrepresentable and imponderable, and she can be praised but not particularized or understood; such a (lack of) definition is what usually distinguishes the sacred. Is this an apotheosis that is the characteristic modality of the nation's memory of its great women? Or is it the stutter caused by a female figure whose (biographical) femininity exemplifies not sacrifice and self-effacement but their opposite? Is her aura a function of her status as a (female) poet, or as a (particular kind of) woman, or both? In any event, Sarojini functions as the name for a certain kind of (female) trouble for nationalism, a trouble that will not go away.

SIX

Figuring Mother India

The Case of Nargis

PROLOGUE

In India, the 1970s, 1980s, and 1990s have witnessed an extraordinary increase in the (one-way) traffic between the domain of the popular cinema and the domain of national and state-level elective politics. The first celluloid star to translate his star quality into political capital was M. G. Ramachandran (MGR), the hero of more than two hundred and fifty films, mostly in Tamil, and the leader of his own party, the All-India Anna Dravida Munnetra Kazhagam (AIADMK), which he founded in 1972. Having carefully cultivated an image of himself as a subaltern revolutionary and savior through his films (an image that was to transcend the limitations of his histrionic abilities, which according to most film critics were meager), he became, with the aid of fan clubs that "instantly became his grass-roots political set-up,"[1] the wildly popular chief minister of Tamil Nadu in 1977. M. S. S. Pandian has compellingly chronicled the ways in which MGR's calculated deployment of widely resonant folk idioms served to produce him as a figure who was more a god than an elected official and therefore outside the reach of common kinds of political accountability; this accounts for the fact that he was rarely, in his decade-long tenure as chief minister, blamed by his rural and working-class voters for the repressive and failed policies of his administration.[2] When he died in 1987, thirty-one of his grieving followers committed suicide, and several shrines appeared in which he was worshipped as a deity.[3]

In the adjoining state of Andhra Pradesh, the film star N. T. Rama Rao (NTR), who had achieved a dominance in the Telugu cinema comparable to MGR's in Tamil, was renowned for his portrayals of divine and semidivine characters in the genre of the mythological. (MGR had eschewed playing gods or mythological figures because of the atheist and anti-Brahman ideological plank of the Dravida Munnetra Kazhagam [DMK], with which he was originally affiliated.) [4] When he entered state politics in 1982 in quest of the chief ministry, he made his campaign travels in a modern-day chariot that freely evoked his godlike roles on screen. He won the election handily in 1983 under the aegis of his newly formed Telugu Desam party. His ambitions soon assumed a national scale when he called a meeting of all opposition parties in his home state; for some the meeting "pointed to the possibility of a national alternative to Indira Gandhi." [5] But, unlike MGR's tenure in Tamil Nadu, NTR's was plagued with scandals and discontent, much of it arising from his impulsive, high-handed, and eccentric behavior. He lost his office in the late 1980s but was returned to power for a brief period in 1994–1995. [6]

Stars in the Bombay cinema have nurtured and acted upon similar political desires and ambitions. The elections of 1984 saw three of them—Sunil Dutt, Vijayantimala Bali, and Amitabh Bachchan, the "angry young man" superstar of the 1970s and 1980s—elected to the Lok Sabha. [7] More recently, Rajesh Khanna (the leading man of the 1970s), Shatrughan Sinha (best known for his compelling portrayals of the villain, rather than the hero), and Raj Babbar have contested seats on behalf of the Congress, the Bharatiya Janata Party, and the Samajwadi Party, respectively. None of these figures has enjoyed the astonishing success of an MGR, proving (if proof was needed) that for the Indian electorate, the moral dramas of the film world were (in Farrukh Dhondy's words) "a public vow, something to live up to," [8] rather than a literal rendition of the "truth" of the star character. In fact, Amitabh's unparalleled filmic popularity (which transcended in important ways the divisions of region and language) could not save him from the ignominy of the Bofors arms deal, in which he was widely believed to be implicated, along with Rajiv Gandhi, his friend and the prime minister; he soon abandoned politics for the relatively more predictable world of Bombay films. Nonetheless, the fact remains that these stars accumulate a kind of cultural capital in the cinema which seems eminently amenable to that other form of public life that is elective politics. What connects the publicness of the film star with the publicness of politics, elective or otherwise? And what happens to the rendezvous of national politics, broadly defined, and national cinema when its actors are gendered differently, and/or when their religious identities are differently produced?

This chapter can only multiply some of these questions, especially as it seeks to examine a more subterranean, fugitive, and speculative version of the filmic icon than the instances mentioned above. It examines the publicness of the actress Nargis, who was a highly regarded star of the 1940s and 1950s and who, though fascinated by politics and by political figures, never sought elective office herself. In her case, then, there is a caesura between the publicness of the actress and the publicness of the politician; yet the caesura, as one knows, connects as much as it separates. This chapter mimes the operations of the caesura, proceeding through a set of indirections, deferrals, and displacements. It examines the transformation of Nargis into a national icon (signifying Indian womanhood), especially in the context of her highly acclaimed role in Mehboob Khan's *Mother India* (1957), and the way in which this fixes and monumentalizes a notoriously unstable star text.[9] Indeed, a recent biography of this "First Lady of Indian Cinema" finds no gap between the role she had famously played in *Mother India* and her real-life persona:

> The best actors and actresses are . . . the embodiment of the characteristics of their own people. In that sense Nargis epitomised the Indian woman in both her strengths and weaknesses, her aspirations, her inherent dignity and her capacity for uncomplaining suffering. Inasmuch as these were deathless virtues, her constituency transcended the frontiers of her time. . . . What she had achieved in sum was a walk into history. In every way she was Indian womanhood itself. In many ways she was Indian cinema. In some ways she was India.[10]

In every succeeding sentence, as T. J. S. George stumbles for ways to metaphorize the actress, her representativeness becomes more and more all-encompassing. This chapter ponders the way in which she *literalizes* the figure of the nation, to such a degree that acting itself becomes impossible after the making of that film.[11] In taking up this question of the iconicity of the actress, it also takes up perforce the question of Nargis's elusive but inescapable Muslimness; how does the Other become the icon that represents nationness? A tentative answer takes the form of a story about a phantom; and the story of Nargis, as I see it, is the story of a haunting, a story of the undead Muslimness that is neither present nor absent, not quite there but not quite convincingly buried, either. My story therefore is as much about Nargis dead as it is about Nargis alive and about her afterlife in the current conjuncture of Hindu fundamentalist ascendancy. In taking up the question of who or what bears the burden of Nargis's Muslimness, this story finds itself to be as much about the son of Mother India as it is about the mother herself. This chapter, then, functions as a brief, speculative analysis of the functions of iconicity and surrogacy in the registers of (Bombay) cinema and politics and of the discursive displacements from one to the other in the figures of Nargis and Sanjay Dutt. It is, if you will, a reading of the reciprocal and uneasy substitutability of two figures who carry considerable symbolic weight in ongoing struggles and anxieties regarding filmic and political representation, and "real" and "simulated" Indianness.

Any analysis of the parallel and sometimes intersecting production of the star biography and the filmic text must take into account the work of Rosie

Thomas, who has brilliantly traced the contours of Nargis's star status, especially in relation to questions of her chastity in her personal life and in her filmic/mythical life as Radha in *Mother India*.[12] Pandian's fine study of MGR the cinematic and political star has likewise helped us understand the commerce between the two domains (cinema and politics). My concern here is with the female star, who raises different questions and occupies a different place from the male star in the symbolic economy of the cinema, and with the star whose connection with politics is metaphorically and discontinuously established even as her enactment of Indian womanhood is literally and almost infallibly realized. Moreover, my concern is with the politics of the nation-state, to which the Bombay cinema bears a special and privileged relation, unlike the Tamil cinema, despite the latter's numerically larger output.[13] Finally, and most importantly, I am interested in the ways the gendered star text might be interwoven with another form of identity—the religiopolitical one.

The instance of Nargis's variable success at being persuasively Indian underscores how persistently questions of religiopolitical identity in postcolonial India continue to be coded through the tropes of originality and impersonation, ownership and expropriation, depths and surfaces. This is particularly the case when questions of Muslim Indian identity are at stake. It is a commonplace that in the Hindu imaginary of the Indian nation, the Muslim carries a double and conflicting valence in relation to questions of indigeneity and authenticity. He (and this figure is usually though not invariably imagined as male) is the alien invader, destructive of properly Indian (read "Hindu") institutions, religious monuments, and ways of life; his loyalties are directed elsewhere, and he aggressively insists on his separateness from—but nonetheless within—an Indian and Hindu imagined community. Even when he appears to have renounced a Muslim identity politics and to have embraced the (Hindu) ethic of assimilation, he is not entirely to be trusted, his essential Muslimness being irreducible and apt to surface at any point. At the same time, though, that his religious Otherness is seen as essential, his profession of an authentic difference is spurious, since his Muslimness is the result of a (sometime) conversion. He is thus really a Hindu, albeit a lapsed, treacherous, or unwilling one, and he can be compelled by the Hinduness from which he has been forcibly wrenched. Hence, modern Hindu endeavors at conversion of Muslim or Christian Indians is named not as conversion but as purification, *shuddhi;* it is a purging and a return to what one always was but had momentarily forgotten.

In their suturing of origin and legitimacy, both accounts—which reinforce rather than undo each other—stage Muslim Indian identity not only as a problem but also as a problem of (an always dubious) impersonation. It is upon this uncertain ground that one must locate the life and afterlife of the assimilated Muslim actress. What makes her the obvious choice for the ideologically freighted figure of (a Hindu) Mother India? In what ways is her filmic and personal exemplification of good Hinduness/good Indianness/ good femininity both exceptional and counterfeit? How are we to read the process by which Sanjay Dutt becomes Nargis, and becomes Muslim, in the current moment? These are some of the questions to which this chapter on Muslim impersonation will address itself.

NARGIS: THE LIFE

At the time of the release in 1957 of *Mother India*, which was the film with which she was conclusively associated from then on, Nargis was among the most prominent figures of the Indian cinema; the facts of her biography are now legend, but they do need to be rehearsed briefly. Nargis's mother, Jaddanbai, was by birth a *kothewali* (professional singer and performer/ courtesan), well known in Allahabad and Calcutta as a specialist in the musical form known as *thumri*. She had, according to her daughter's biographer,[14] married at seventeen and become the mother of two sons; nothing is known of this first partner or indeed of how formalized such a domestic arrangement might have been. In any event, when in 1928 a wealthy young medical student named Mohanbabu proposed to convert to Islam (thus becoming Abdul Rashid) to marry her, she consented. Nargis was born the following year. (It may be of interest to note the demand that the respectable and wealthy medical student convert for the sake of the [already married] courtesan, a demand that Nargis, at the height of her career, was unable or unwilling to make of Raj Kapoor or Sunil Dutt.) Jaddanbai moved to Bombay in the mid-1930s, having by this time established herself as a film producer, music director, and actress (this being the era predating the ascendancy of the playback singer, an era in which roles were assigned according to vocal talent). She was soon to become a Bombay institution, attracting many of the leading figures of the film world to her home and to the studio where she worked. Though Nargis appeared as a child actress in *Talash-e-Haq* (1935), she was carefully educated, and her access to the world of films was strictly controlled. She was a student at St. Mary's, an elite girls' school in Bombay, and was to entertain hopes of training as a doctor, an ambition that her own father, Mohanbabu, had abandoned in order to marry Jaddanbai. She was with difficulty persuaded by her mother and her mother's friend, the director Mehboob Khan, to perform her first "adult" role at fourteen in the latter's *Taqdeer* (1943). All such scruples were set aside after the success of *Taqdeer*, though the young Nargis is said to have faced some degree of social ostracism from the families of her more respectable, non-*filmi* classmates.[15] While Nargis's rapid change of heart is all too easily attributable to her great youth, coupled with the glamour of the industry in which she found herself, the sense of isolation and degradation that accompanies the glamour and responsibility is not without interest. Certainly Nargis's feeling that the decision to be an actress was one from which there was no going back ("Quite rapidly she realised that life would never be the same again for her or her family. Nothing more was heard about Mehboob's promise to leave her to her studies or indeed about the planned studies") [16] is coded in terms analogous to those attendant upon a narrative of the loss of sexual innocence. Rosie Thomas's report of the Nargis mythology conforms more unambiguously to such a trajectory: "Once she reached adolescence, however, Nargis's mother not only tricked her into (most unwillingly) starring in a film for her friend Mehboob Khan but also allegedly put her daughter's *nath* (virginity) on the market and allowed a wealthy Muslim prince to pay handsomely for her. This episode is sometimes denied, or recounted as her first affair. Its purpose seems to be to construct as already tarnished before meeting Raj Kapoor." [17] Nargis never quite lost the sense of being less than fully respectable that such an ancestry and such a career implied, and she always cherished as a utopian possibility the dream of becoming a doctor. She appeared in several more films in the 1940s, achieving star status by the time she was approached by a then comparatively unknown Raj Kapoor, to play opposite him in his first production, *Aag* (1948). After a number of hits, which featured her opposite some of the best-known leading men of the day, especially Raj Kapoor and Dilip Kumar, she became one of the most important luminaries of the newly emerging star system in Bombay cinema; she was routinely billed above her male leads, and, for some years in the 1950s, she commanded higher fees than any of them did. The international success of some of the films (*Awaara*, 1951; *Shri 420*, 1954) that she had made with her lover, Raj Kapoor—which were runaway hits in the Soviet Union, West Asia, and North Africa—added another kind of nuance to her star image, as she became, in these post-Independence years, the ambassador of "Indian culture" on a world stage.

Nargis achieved a significant measure of star power in the years between the late 1940s and mid-1950s, not only because of her histrionic virtuosity (which was considerable) but also because of her very public romance with the rising male star Raj Kapoor. While it is true that Nargis was, as a review of a book on Raj Kapoor's films unequivocally states, central to the making of Raj Kapoor himself as an actor and a director and of RK Studios [18] (she worked at minimal wages for the studio and, in a partial throwback to the early days of the studio system, acted in non-RK films only at the pleasure of her lover), it was also true that her association with Raj helped invest her fully with star status. He had begun to pursue her very early in their association, and by the time they acted together in *Andaaz* and *Barsaat* (both 1949), they were already an item. Raj Kapoor was married and a father, in addition to being a Hindu. Their love affair was conducted without any particular subterfuge; and since they were young, glamorous, and successful, and from all accounts passionately in love with each other, they were envied as well as reproached. As her biographer admits, "It was her appearance with Raj Kapoor that thrilled audiences. Their romance had an appeal that nothing else could rival."[19] The love scenes in *Barsaat* in particular were marked by an intensity hitherto unseen in the Bombay cinema. Critics have pointed to the unorthodox camera work and sound effects in the love scenes, with their lingering close-ups and a low-decibel pitch that intimates intimacy.[20]

The star biography took another significant turn in the mid-1950s, when Nargis realized that Raj Kapoor would not marry her, that is, he would not make her his second wife; he began instead to demonstrate a marked romantic interest in other actresses. Besides, it was becoming clear to her that her that her near-exclusive association with RK Studios was keeping her from important roles (such as that of Anarkali in K. Asif's *Mughal-e-Azam*, for which she had been chosen); some of her most highly regarded performances (though not necessarily the ones that brought her stardom)—in *Andaaz, Anhonee, Jogan,* and *Mother India*—were performed outside RK Studios, which had a fairly limited vision of the female lead's role in a film.[21] She had once complained to screenwriter K. A. Abbas about the triviality of her role in the wildly successful *Awaara*, insisting that he create for her a more substantial role in *Anhonee*, produced under the Naya Sansar banner.[22] Accordingly, she let Mehboob (who had "discovered" her and who had always begrudged Raj Kapoor his powerful claims on her) know that she was available for *Mother India*. A remake of Mehboob's 1940 classic, *Aurat* (Woman), *Mother India* was more self-consciously epic and nationalist. It was designed (among other things) to function as an implicit rebuttal of Katherine Mayo's notorious book of 1927 that had detailed the pathological sexual practices of Hindu males.[23]

The film was three years in the making, involving enormous resources and the paid and unpaid labor of thousands of people. When it was released in 1957, it was successful on a scale unprecedented in Bombay cinema. It ran for fifty weeks in Bombay, breaking all box-office records, and was granted tax-exempt status in the Bombay province; it was the first Indian film to be nominated for an Oscar (in the foreign-film category), and it won Nargis the Filmfare Award for 1957 as well as the Best Actress award at the Karlovy Vary film festival.[24] The role of Radha in *Mother India* was the one that irrevocably defined Nargis for the Indian cinema-going public as well as for the history of Indian film, not simply because of its epic scope and her own brilliance in it, but also because it effectively marked her departure— at the height of her career—from Bombay cinema. Several other films, on which she had been working concurrently with *Mother India*, were released in 1957–1958, though she bowed out of her acting career once Mehboob Khan's epic was completed. She was to appear in the movies only once after this, in *Raat aur Din* [Night and Day, 1967], in order to help her producer brothers out of a severe financial crisis.[25]

The fascination of the film was augmented by a behind-the-scenes story of its making, a story that was to constitute an epic narrative in itself. It is said that during the famous fire scene in the film, Nargis was trapped behind some burning haystacks and was rescued at considerable personal risk by the relatively unknown young actor Sunil Dutt, who played her wayward son Birjoo in the film. This is one of the stories most often repeated about Nargis, satisfying every expectation about life imitating art. "Mother" and "son" fell in love and were married quietly in March 1958, at which point Nargis retired from her acting career. Marriage is said to have been her salvation; said one of her costars, K. N. Singh, "With marriage it was like she had reached home. She thought God had come to earth in the form of Sunil Dutt. So much did she worship him."[26] She became an exemplary wife and the devoted mother of three children, especially of her son Sanjay. She also dedicated herself to a number of charitable causes, including that of spastic children. She led an active life, working for her husband's film-production company, participating in government-sponsored delegations to foreign countries, and serving briefly as a member of the Rajya Sabha, to which she was nominated by her friend Indira Gandhi. During these years she was made unhappy by the delinquency and drug addiction of her much-pampered son and by her husband's criticism of her overindulgence of Sanjay. In 1980 a diagnosis of pancreatic cancer took her to New York for treatment; she died in Bombay in 1981, a month before her fifty-second birthday.

Before we read the intertextuality of the epic film and the epic life, we need to speak briefly of the film itself. *Mother India*, which is said to have played continually in one part or another of the country since its release, is one of the great classics of the Bombay cinema. It is the story of the trials of the peasant woman Radha, who spends her life battling the malign forces of nature and humanity and who assumes the mythic stature of the matriarch by the film's end. A devoted wife and the mother of four boys, she toils heroically at home and in the fields, enduring poverty and the rapacious extortions of the village moneylender, Sukhilala. Her husband loses his arms in an accident and forsakes his home, unable to bear the shame of his dependence on her. After floods have killed two of her sons and devastated her home and her harvest, the moneylender proposes to feed her children in exchange for making her his mistress. Sorely tempted though she is, she prizes her *laaj* (chastity) above all else and manages to rebuild her life. She raises her sons on her own and becomes "the mother of the whole village," keeping the villagers from fleeing their home after the floods. As she sings to them, in the name of Mother Earth, a map of pre-Partition India forms on the screen. In the second part of the film, Radha is older, her sons grown. Her older son, Ramu, is domestic and law abiding; her younger and rebellious son, Birjoo, is passionately devoted to her, a devotion that is intimately bound up in his keen sense of the wrongs done to her and to the village by Sukhilala. Becoming a bandit, he kills Sukhilala and attempts to abduct the moneylender's daughter in an attempt to counter the insult offered earlier to his mother's honor; but his mother, who regards the chastity of the village women as her own, kills him rather than letting him bring disgrace to the village.

In retrospect, Nargis's decision to play the role of the heroine in *Mother India* seems to be charged with extraordinary symbolic import. Not only did it signal her break with her erstwhile lover, it also meant a markedly differently role from the ones that she had been used to playing. She typically played the glamorous Indian woman whose modernity coexisted with her rhapsodic submission to a whole ensemble of "Indian" values.[27] This gendered drama of the overthrow of western cultural values through an elaborately reinflected Indian tradition was (and is) a staple of the Bombay cinema, allowing for a staging of the differential seductions of both modernity and tradition. The role of Radha, on the other hand, was entirely without any such obvious glamour, requiring her to play a poor peasant woman (an extraordinary demand for a glamorous star, especially before the advent of the so-called parallel cinema) and to age more than twenty years in the course of the film.

Tales of Nargis's professionalism and her strong identification with the role are legendary. She (at least in her recall of it) saw this as a dream role, in which she could play the paragon, the identificatory ideal of the Indian woman. P. K. Nair recalled with what relish she deglamourized herself for the role and the way she "completely transformed herself into the 'Kali' image of the 'Mother.'"[28] Even the notoriously acerbic film critic Baburao Patel was moved to exclaim: "Remove Nargis and there is no *Mother India*. Nargis is both the body and soul of the picture. . . . *Nargis lives the role better than Radha could have lived it*."[29] It is instructive to read her description of her experience of the film, especially the horrific scene of the burning haystacks, which she chose to do herself instead of entrusting it, as was expected, to a double:

> Preparations were being made for the fire sequence in *Mother India*. Nargis, made up to look like an old woman, was talking . . . of death and saying how much her hands, with the make-up on them, resembled her mother's hands. . . . . She ran in, to embrace the flames. The flames responded willingly. They embraced her and planted burning kisses on her weary but determined brow.
>
> It was soon over. Nargis was rescued. She had sustained burns. But, in the flames, she had at last found the Truth she had been searching for, the Truth which freed her. The old Nargis died in those flames.[30]

The filming, and especially the trial by fire which was fortuitously authenticated by real-life occurrences, is explicitly coded as transformative of the "life" and as the repository of a certain truth. What is perhaps more curious for me is the monumentalizing and distancing effect of the use of the third person. Nargis seems quite aware of herself as legend, larger than life; but in a moment of simultaneous subjective splitting and incorporation, she is also curiously positioned as the obituarist of an older, legendary self. She dies to the old forms of existence, in order to achieve a certain transcendence and entry into a new legendary status; and death alone provides the condition of possibility for such transcendence.

Part of the fascination of the film for Indian audiences is of course the iconicity of various constitutive moments: the trial by fire and the rescue, the prestige of motherhood, and the attainment of mythic status. This was to prove, for Nargis, literally the role to end all roles. Given the mythic quality of the role, and given the mythic status she had herself attained because of its publicity and its wide circulation and popularity, it seemed that she had effectively made herself unfit for ordinary roles. Only marriage and motherhood in "real life" could provide a script that matched the epic quality of the film. And while it is true that the female star's renunciation of films for marriage is the norm rather than the exception in the popular Hindi cinema and is routinely attended by the inflated rhetoric of the felicities of matrimony and motherhood, there is a way in which Nargis's preparation for that last, most exalted role had been distinctively, indeed uniquely heralded, by her own professional trajectory. It is precisely her renunciation—which seemed so great and so apposite at the same time—that allowed someone like K. N. Singh to rate her wifehood as the culmination of a brilliant acting career: "I think her greatest achievement was getting a husband like Sunil. Twenty-two years of married life were her happiest years."[31]

NARGIS: THE STAR

Nargis was to remain a legend long after her exit from the screen, and any analysis of her enduring image must come to terms with the status of the star in Bombay cinema, which is, generally speaking, greater than anything that obtains in Hollywood. As Behroze Gandhy and Rosie Thomas point out in their essay on stardom in Hindi cinema, "The parallels between Indian stars and the gods of the Hindu pantheon are frequently remarked upon: both are colourfully larger than life, their lives and loves, including moral lapses, the subject of voyeuristic fascination and extraordinary tolerance, and stars accept, on the whole graciously, an adoration close to veneration."[32] Furthermore, "it [is] firmly believed that stars are a crucial ingredient in the success of any mainstream Indian film."[33] This is in large part, and in the current conjuncture, more true of male stars than of female ones, who have (since the 1960s) come to have increasingly subordinate roles in relation to the male lead.

The star system in Bombay cinema is not, of course, an indigenous phenomenon, and it cannot be understood outside the context of Hollywood cinema, which was immensely popular in the subcontinent for the first four decades of the century, until the "talkies" had effectively displaced the silent film. Erik Barnouw and S. Krishnaswamy tell that us that in 1926–1927 "15 percent of the features released in India were Indian, 85 percent were foreign. Most of these were American."[34] (It is said that it was the advent of the talkies that effectively "nationalized" Indian cinema.)[35] Douglas Fairbanks, Eddie Polo, and Charlie Chaplin (the last of whom Raj Kapoor was to imitate in the 1950s with considerable aplomb) enjoyed considerable popularity among Indian audiences,[36] and Indian stars of the silent screen and the talkies such as Master Vithal, Fearless Nadia, Devika Rani, and Prithviraj Kapoor had considerable drawing power. But in the 1920s and 1930s production was organized for the most part around studios which operated much like extended families, with their own laboratories, recreational facilities, and canteens, the "star" being "an employee . . . not the pivot of planning and . . . not in control."[37] The modern-day star system, which was the product of freelancing, began to emerge only in the 1940s, when independent producers, made wealthy by war profiteering and illegal arms trafficking, drew stars away from studios by bidding up their price. This was to lead eventually to the recasting of mainstream commercial cinema as "the cinema of the star rather than the cinema of the director, or the studio";[38] stars were signed up even before decisions about script or direction were made.

The star system has been almost from the first overwhelmingly male dominated, female stars usually commanding (as in Hollywood) smaller fees and enjoying relatively brief careers as romantic leads. This is easily explicable in light of the industry's rampant sexism, which can only imagine a short shelf life for the female lead. But it is also due in part to the fact that the female star's marriage has traditionally been considered incompatible with the pursuit of an acting career; it is fairly safe to generalize that, with a few notable exceptions (mainly actresses associated with the New Wave cinema), the female star's career is automatically extinguished upon marriage. That this is still taken as a given, even among film figures generally considered "progressive" (the director Gulzar, for example)[39] speaks to the fraught history of the actress in the Indian film industry. In the early years of the industry, few respectable women from the Hindu or Muslim communities were willing to risk the loss of modesty that association with the performing arts, including cinema, implied. Even prostitutes, it is said, spurned the offers of filmmakers;[40] *Rajah Harishchandra* (1913), one of the first Indian feature films, featured a young man in the female lead, as did several other films of that decade. The early female stars, such as Sulochana (Ruby Myers), Sita Devi (Renee Smith), and Patience Cooper, were Anglo-Indian (Eurasian) women, whose liminal status allowed them relatively easy entry into the disreputable world of the cinema. Some of the early actresses of the Indian screen also had associations with the world of the *tawa'if* (courtesan, usually Muslim), especially because of their training in vocal music and dance. Since the Indian talkie distinguished itself from the start with its exclusive reliance on songs and dance (*Alam Ara* [1931], the first of these, was to advertise itself as an "all-talking, all-singing, all-dancing" feature), and since playback singers did not make their advent until the 1940s, the industry found itself drawing upon a class of women trained in performance practices which had traditionally formed a continuum with sexual services.[41] Over the years the industry did manage to attract women of higher social standing (the Maharashtrian Brahman Durga Khote being one of the earliest of them), but the female star's status has continued to be a morally ambiguous one, not only because she has functioned as a sex symbol but also because she has simultaneously had to carry an elevated moral charge. Actors and actresses are perhaps the only public figures whose erotic lives are the object of intense, widespread, and institutionalized curiosity (there is no inquisitiveness of corresponding scale about the sex lives of female or male politicians, though the real and alleged romantic involvements of Nehru, Indira Gandhi, and Feroze Gandhi have certainly been much discussed). The industry of course shares fully this public ambivalence about its own sexual (mis)deeds, especially as it pertains to women. Nargis herself is said to have worked strenuously to keep her nieces and nephews out of the orbit of Bombay cinema. In the case of her own son Sanjay, she was eager to see him become a doctor but became reconciled to his strong desire to be an actor. In the case of her daughters, she believed that the era of the serious actress had passed: "I feel there is no future for an actress except to make a lot of money for a certain number of years,"[42] though she also confessed to envying contemporary actresses some of the interesting roles they had played. Raj Kapoor, whose family was easily the first family of the Bombay cinema (his father, brothers, and sons have all been affiliated with the industry in one capacity or another), was less ambiguous, and he is said to have forbidden the involvement of any of the "Kapoor women" in the dirty business. In this context, his infamous comment about wives and actresses is certainly apropos: "My wife is not to be my actress and my actress is not to be my wife."[43]

Where male actors have (unlike Raj Kapoor), actually married actresses, it has almost invariably been with the stipulation that the wedding coincide with professional retirement. It speaks to the profoundly liminal status of the female star that she has so often occupied (or wished to occupy) the (distinctly secondary and officially illegal) position of the "second wife"; this includes some of the best-known actresses of the dominant and the paral-

lel cinemas. It may speak to why these actresses are anxious to erect a cor-
don sanitaire between their status as lawfully wedded wives and their status as (mere) actresses. Nargis, for one, was anxious about the possibility of
a respectable marriage, asking (in the context of a possible marriage with
Sunil Dutt) only half-playfully, "Who will marry the daughter of a singing
woman?"[44] His offer of marriage may help in part to explain (what was commonly regarded as) her devotion and her gratitude to her relatively obscure
and far less talented actor-husband.

NARGIS: THE SEQUEL

The Bombay film industry has been, and continues to be, intertwined uneasily but closely with the gendered and religiously inflected discourse of
nationalism and the nation-state; it is continually anxious to establish its legitimacy in the eyes of a state that looks upon it with suspicion as "both pal-
try and powerful."[45] Nargis was thus doubly liminal as an actress and as a
Muslim subject; both identities involved complex negotiations not only
within the postcolonial state but also within an industry whose inaugural
moment was ineluctably tied to an emergent idiom of cultural nationalism.[46] We might remember that Dadasaheb Phalke's inspiration for *Rajah
Harishchandra* was famously prompted by the desire for a mimesis that involved a specifically Indian address:

> In 1910 I happened to see the film *The Life of Christ* in the America-India Pic-
> ture Palace in Bombay. . . . That day also marked the foundation in India of
> an industry which occupied the fifth place in the myriads of big and small pro-
> fessions that exist. . . . While the life of Christ was rolling fast before my phys-
> ical eyes I was mentally visualising the Gods, Shri Krishna, Shri Ramchandra,
> their Gokul and Ayodhya. I was gripped by a strange spell. I bought another
> ticket and saw the film again. This time I felt my imagination taking shape on
> the screen. Could this really happen? Could we, the sons of India, ever be able
> to see Indian images on the screen? . . . There was no doubt whatsoever about
> the utility of the profession and its importance as an industry. . . . This was the
> period of the Swadeshi movement and there was profuse talking and lectur-
> ing on the subject. For me personally, this led to the resignation of my com-
> fortable government job and taking to an independent profession.[47]

As Somnath Zutshi points out, the mapping of an upper-caste (and northern Indian) Hindu masculine identity onto the space designated the national happens as a matter of course; in this context, Phalke's association
with Tilak and with his (Hindu) nationalist magazine *Kesari* comes as no surprise.[48] But what is also worthy of note is the way in which the terrain of the
cinema was claimed from the first as the ground upon which the struggle
for an Indian nation would be waged: "A whole technology, to say nothing
of a major culture industry, could now designate itself as Swadeshi [indige-

nously Indian]."[49] The pre-Independence history of the Bombay cinema is replete with instances of films provoking the wrath of British censors because of their incorporation of (Congress) nationalist icons like spinning wheels, Indian flags, and portraits of leaders such as Gandhi or Nehru, or their rendition of scenes of mutiny, or songs or "dialogues" that could be construed as anticolonial. (Theodore Baskaran has persuasively demonstrated the extent to which South Indian, primarily Tamil, cinema was also invested in nationalist topoi and affiliated with prominent nationalists like Rajaji in the decades preceding Independence.)[50] In fact, the Bombay industry would claim on more than one occasion to have functioned as a de facto arm of state in generating through affect and consent a national unity in diversity that the postcolonial state had been markedly unsuccessful at achieving through its own institutions.

However, Congress nationalism of the 1930s and 1940s and, indeed, of the post-Independence decades could not but be haunted by the specter of its other, Muslim nationalism and, by sympathetic identification, the figure of the Muslim herself/himself as the sign of that intimate enemy. Faisal Devji's analysis of the Muslim in the symbolic economy of the Indian nation-state, while implicitly invoking a male subject, obviously has its resonances for pre-Independence Congress nationalism as well as for the Bombay cinema that is locked in an embrace with it: "In the history that the Indian state obsessively re-enacts, the Muslim separatist is nothing more than the original sign of its failure. The Muslim, in other words, represents a fundamental anxiety of nationalism itself: of the nation as something unachieved."[51] This anxiety is most obviously managed in the cinema through a structure of prohibitions and repressions; the industry functioned then (as it still does) under the constraints of censorship protocols which proscribed the representation of subjects that might tend to inflame "communal passions," a proscription that ensured that "communal passions" or Muslim religio-political identities except of an oppressively benevolent variety remained unnamed and unexaminable. (We might remember that M. S. Sathyu's *Garm Hawa* [1973] was banned before it went on to win a special award for promoting national integration.) At the same time, as the source of profound psychic anxiety for the (new) nation, Muslimness also had to be exorcised again and again. One common vehicle for the enactment of such exorcisms was the historical film; Sumita Chakravarty is surely right in underscoring the ways in which the Bombay cinema has "not so much addressed the Hindu-Muslim relationship as sublimated it by displacing it onto the canvas of history. . . . The historical film has been the privileged site of elaboration of the Muslim sensibility."[52] But that this sublimation was only a partial one is evidenced by the ideology of religious identity that informs such "Muslim historicals" (many of which were made by Muslim directors) as Mehboob's *Humayun* (1945, starring Nargis, Veena, Ashok Kumar, and Chandramohan) and K. Asif's *Mughal-e-Azam* (1960, starring Dilip Kumar, Madhubala, and Prithviraj Kapoor). *Humayun* represents Babar, the founder of the Mughal dynasty in India, as fervently devoted to the mutual love of his Hindu and Muslim subjects and as a king who accepts a Rajput Hindu princess as his adopted daughter. Given the potency of the myth of the sexually aggressive Muslim male and the violated Hindu woman, it is not surprising that Mehboob cast the Hindu woman as a daughter (rather than a wife), and a spirited one at that; there is, however, a considerable if unspoken erotic charge that binds the princess, the prince Humayun (her adopted brother), and her Hindu lover.[53] The film, despite its high production values and fine performances by many of its stars, was panned by a range of critics for its historical "inaccuracies" and for its alleged soft-pedaling of Muslim "tyranny" over Hindus. Mehboob was never to make a like film again. K. Asif's *Mughal-e-Azam* was safer in its choice of Akbar, the Mughal ruler most assimilated to a Hindu nationalist sensibility, but it, too, was careful to represent him as religiously eclectic, celebrating Hindu festivals, and utterly dedicated to a polity always already marked as Indian and literalized by the map of a pre-Partition India at the beginning of the film.

If this is what the films give us, what kinds of evidence might be adduced by what we will call the "life"? There, one looks almost in vain for those places where Nargis's Muslimness might be manifest. If there is one thing that characterizes such a figure, it is what might be deemed her "cosmopolitanism," a cosmopolitanism that overwrites the possibility of a Muslim difference and is aligned not only with that of the emerging Indian nation-state and its commitment to a secular modernity so-called but also with a specifically filmic variety of religious marking and unmarking. Unlike a figure like Mehboob, who was famous for the regularity of his prayers and who might be said to have simultaneously showcased his Muslim difference and made repeated and hysterical efforts to establish his good Indianness, she was not overtly religious. Her background in fact marked her out as the interstitial figure representative of a new Indian modernity. Though her mother was a Muslim and her father had officially converted in order to marry her, his conversion is usually treated both as a matter of form and a sign of his magnanimity, as meaningless in one register but meaningful in another.

Nargis entered acting and adulthood at a time when religious identities were being monumentally and violently reconstellated. It is likely that she suffered the impact of this, as did most other Muslims in pre- and post-Partition India. Partition also had its special set of implications for popular Hindi cinema. While it undoubtedly was solidly anchored in Bombay, it had always maintained a commerce with the Punjab (especially Lahore) and Bengal, both of which were torn asunder by the new national configurations. Several people, Muslim, Hindu, and Sikh, crossed new and impermeable borders in 1947; stars like Noorjehan and Khurshid left for Pakistan, while Hindu and Sikh counterparts went to India. K. A. Abbas's autobiography provides an account of the traumas of those Muslims who never left India; Nargis's biographer says more tersely: "Leading Muslim personalities in Bombay were momentarily alarmed and were looked upon by some with suspicion."[54] An advertisement was to appear in the *Times of India* in late 1946 under her name, at the time of particularly vicious anti-Muslim riots, pleading for peace: "Nargis awaits the return of peace—with the rest of the city."[55] This understatement seems to be the mode in which an identity never overtly acknowledged as religious can be articulated.

As an actress, Nargis was noted for having moved away, after the commencement of her involvement with Raj Kapoor, from "the Muslim crowd" (including Mehboob), though she made several films with Raj Kapoor's rival, Dilip Kumar. When involved with Raj Kapoor (and hopeful of being his second wife), she routinely wore the *sindoor* of the Hindu wife, and it is possible that the relationship may have helped detach her from the signifiers of Muslim identity. When she married the Hindu Sunil Dutt, it was in an Arya Samaj (reformist/revivalist Hindu) ceremony; their children were given Hindu names.

What is one to make of such unmarking, which while voluntary is rarely neutral? I do not wish of course to assert that Muslim identity is something conceived or experienced in the same way by all subjects designated as Muslim nor to accuse Nargis of having abandoned an authentic Muslim identity; but I do wish to speak of this identity (especially the identity of the "good Muslim Indian") as a persistent, insuperable, and continually negotiated problem. Paola Bacchetta has cogently described the varying place of the Muslim woman in Rashtriya Swayamsevak Sangh (RSS) fantasies about its own masculine heterosexuality; what is particularly fascinating is her account of the way the Muslim woman often figures as the subject of a (usually unreciprocated) desire for the Hindu nationalist male.[56] Nargis's devotion can fruitfully be read through such a lens, which may serve as a grid even for those who are not overtly Hindu nationalists, for Hindu nationalist thought, rather than necessarily contradicting the commonsense of the modern Hindu subject, represents it in radical form. Her legendary status is secured and her transcendence of her Muslimness confirmed through her desire for and devotion to a Hindu male savior. She can atone both for her Muslimness and for her enticement of a married Hindu male by living the *Mother India* allegory, which not only scripts her as heroically chaste but also—in the extraordinary scene showing an undivided continent reforming in response to her summons to the villagers to return—as a renouncer of Muslim separatism. Rosie Thomas has brilliantly described the appeal of *Mother India* to Indian audiences in terms of the gossip attaching to the sexual histories of its stars. I wonder whether part of the appeal is not also due to the very fact of Nargis's Muslimness, this Muslimness functioning as an asset rather than a blot upon her status as ideal Indian woman, precisely because it can be shown to be erasing or overwriting itself in the assumption of the Radha role. If *Mother India* is, at least partially, an allegory of the repudiation of Muslim difference and of a becoming Hindu, then only a Muslim can assume the iconic position of that maternal figure.

What interests me here is precisely this recessive, displaced quality of the Muslimness in the star persona and, indeed, in the filmography itself: Nargis—unlike her female Muslim compatriots Madhubala and Meena Kumari, for instance—did not appear in any major "Muslim" role.[57] I am interested in the (absent, ephemeral, discreet) Muslimness of the actress and in the ways in which this barely articulated religious identity might provide a point of entry into questions of Muslim femininity and Indian nationalism. How is Muslim woman represented in the (filmic) space of the nation? Where can one find it, if it is not only or most satisfactorily locatable in Muslim characters and stereotypes or in directors, songwriters, and producers? (The Bombay film industry is well known for the considerable Muslim talent it has attracted.) As Mukul Kesavan confirms, such cataloguing is inadequate to "[encompass] the singular relationship between Hindi films and Muslim-ness. . . . When I speak of Muslim-ness . . . and the Hindi cinema, the reference is not only or even mainly to its Muslim personnel nor to its repertoire of ghetto stereotypes, but to a cultural influence that has determined the very nature of this cinema."[58] Kesavan discerningly goes on to locate Muslimness in a nonpersonalized and nontaxonomizing sphere; he locates it in the very grammar (an Urdu, usually demotic but sometimes high-flown, and distinct from the Sanskritized, *shuddh* [pure] Hindi of All-India Radio) of Bombay cinema. I am, however, more interested in the traffic between star text and religious identity, in the repressions and displacements of Muslimness to the limits of the biography; I am interested, too, in the displacements that are necessitated by Bombay cinema's exhibition of its own "cosmopolitanism," a cosmopolitanism that is made deeply anxious by that sense of the abjected, the supplementary, that is Muslimness in Indian identity.

As we have seen, Nargis's Muslimness seems not to emerge in any obvious way from the legend of her life, which seems to involve if anything a disidentification from the Muslim, *tawa'if* world of her mother. Her own publicly stated loyalties were powerfully, even hysterically, (Congress) nationalist and statist. At the first Film Seminar organized in 1955 by the Sangeet Natak Akademi, she insisted, far more vehemently than did any of the other participants from the film industry, on the role of cinema as the handmaiden of nation building: "In the new pattern of socialistic society laid down for our country, the emphasis will naturally be on rapid industrial progress, and India will need hundreds of thousands of working heroes and heroines to achieve the goal. The film artistes are duty-bound to portray them on the screen. Today, the film artistes are called upon to play more dynamic roles reflecting the spirit of 'new' India."[59] At a later date, and more notoriously, she became embroiled in controversy when, in her opening remarks as a newly appointed member of the Rajya Sabha, she attacked the films of Satyajit Ray as catering to a western taste for Indian poverty: "Why do you think films like *Pather Panchali* become so popular abroad? . . . People there want to see India in an abject condition. That is the image they have of our country and a film that confirms that image seems to them authentic. . . . His [Ray's] films are not commercially successful. They only win awards. . . . What I want is that if Mr. Ray projects Indian poverty abroad, he should also show 'Modern India.'"[60] If she sought an identification with any political figure, it was with Indira Gandhi (a personal friend, as her father Nehru had been, though to a less intense degree), whose representation as Durga or as Bharat Mata resonated powerfully with her most important role and her own sense of moral authority. (Several people—most notably Rajeswari Sunder Rajan—have in fact noted the parallels across the lives of Indira and Nargis and the reverberations of both in the script of *Mother India*—the mythic status, the imperiousness, and the devotion to an ungovernable son.) [61]

Where Nargis's Muslimness becomes most visible is in what persists as an afterlife and what refuses to stay buried. One important instance of this is the controversy that erupted immediately after her death, as if the mortality of the legend was what permitted a release of the disavowals that the fetishization of *Mother India* had reined in. Newspaper headlines marked her death as the passing of a legend: "Nargis: So Ends the Legend," "Last Journey of a Queen," "End of an Era." And yet there was something else, an appendage, an excess that seems always to haunt the figure of the "good Indian Muslim." According to Sunil Dutt, when she died he decided, for sentimental reasons (having to do with her remembrance of her parents in the last months of her life), to give her a Muslim burial rather than a Hindu cremation. There was free public speculation about this; given that Nargis had demonstrated her transcendence of her Muslimness through her films and the example of her life, her return to Islam, even in death, was deeply disturbing, raising questions about the genuineness of her (simulation of) non-Muslimness. If I may borrow a term from queer theory and queer activism, I would describe this as analogous to the outing of public figures at the time of their death; one is reminded inescapably of the trauma to heterosexual identity by the revelation of Rock Hudson's gayness when he was dying from AIDS.[62] In the case of Nargis, some reports claimed that she had left instructions to be buried as a Muslim, others that her brother (with the aid of aggressive Muslim mullahs) had insisted on Muslim rites in defiance of the widower's wishes.[63] As it was, the incident enhanced Sunil Dutt's stature as a renouncer (he had married an older woman, he had not insisted on his wife's renunciation of her religious identity, he had nursed her devotedly in her illness, and he had permitted a Muslim burial); but it also had the interesting effect of Islamicizing him, and of marking him out as the weak Hindu male, the most treacherous of the enemies within.

Sunil Dutt would come in time to be known, especially by the Hindu right, as a Muslim sympathizer. In 1993, when he was involved in providing relief to the victims of Bombay's vicious anti-Muslim riots (in which the police participated), he was accused by the Shiv Sena (a Hindu rightist group based in western India and powerful in Bombay) of undue partiality to Muslims. There were, according to Dilip Kumar, two attempts on his life, and the family received death threats. Later that year, in April 1993, and then again four months later, his son Sanjay, who was one of the highest-paid leading men in the industry, was arrested and jailed for possession of a smuggled AK–46 and ammunition in the aftermath of bombings in Bombay which are now widely believed to implicate Muslim underworld figures with ties to Pakistan and Dubai. He was believed to have obtained these from a Muslim film-production duo, Hanif-Samir, who were arrested for gun running in the Bombay blast case. He was imprisoned briefly, then released on temporary bail, allowing him to wrap up work on a film, *Khalnayak* (directed by Subhash Ghai, 1993), which went on to become a great success; by a curious coincidence, he played the role of a notorious terrorist and political assassin in that film. As in the case of his mother with *Mother India*, he began to be identified in fairly literal ways with (what was retrospectively recognized as) an important role; newspapers and magazines began to describe the new breed of violent Hindi films as inseparable from the violence of their (criminal, Muslim) backers. Hindu rightist groups campaigned against his films and those of his father. Sanjay was rearrested under the notorious Terrorist and Disruptive Activities (Prevention) Act (TADA) and charged with conspiracy and sedition in the Bombay blast case, instead of being charged under the milder Arms Act. In October 1994 he was denied bail, on the grounds that (under TADA) the very possession of prohibited weapons constituted proof of terrorist intent.[64]

The Hindu right saw in Sanjay the lineaments of his Muslim mother (and his "Muslim-loving" father). Nargis's Muslimness, then, was never fully exorcised from the star legend; but the subtext that was more or less curbed in her lifetime was to take the form of an interesting displacement. She continues in some registers to be revered as a legend, with Doordarshan recently holding a retrospective of her films, but she also figures at the same time as a species of monstrous mother, as her husband and her son come to occupy the place of her Otherness. The fact that Sanjay was a spoiled and recklessly self-indulgent young man, who had been his mother's darling, has given for some people a certain credence to the substitution. The fact, moreover, of his visibility and popularity—he was the second only to Amitabh among male stars in Bombay—is fully congruous with the sense of the Muslim as the *familiar* enemy; thus the Muslim is not one of us, and the Muslim is, terrifyingly, one of us.

The scenario of the overfond mother whose indulgence (temporarily) spoils the son is a common one in the Bombay cinema, and in the eyes of many it seems to have been played out with uncanny literalism in the Nargis-Sanjay Dutt story. She is known to have been passionately fond of him, indulging him and lying for him in defiance of her husband's call for stricter discipline, and she is believed by many to have facilitated his addiction to a variety of drugs, including heroin. I should point out that even outside the context of the charges he currently faces, Sanjay is conspicuous as his mother's son. His audiences, it is said, see him as carrying an aura of tragedy and vulnerability because of his mother's early death, an aura that belies the macho violence of his roles.[65] But the very prematurity of her death is also the sign of a refusal to die; she features as a contagion from beyond the grave, an unquiet specter inhabiting both the renegade Hindu husband and the violent, weak minded, and affectionate son. In this context, Sanjay's long and very public history of addiction makes him available as an easily pathologizable figure. The fact of his describing himself as always vulnerable to temptation ("It's a sickness that can't be cured") provides a rationalization for the stigmatization.[66] His addiction functions as an analog to, and perhaps the support for, the taint of his Muslimness.

It must be noted that, apart from the prosecutors and the Hindu right, he is believed to be innocent of the conspiracy charges, though he is believed to have had mob connections. An article in the respected fortnightly *India Today* also links the acquisition of the weapon to questions of religious identity. It conjectures that the frantic calls for help the Dutts received from besieged Muslims during the riots may have led Sanjay to this step, especially as the Hanif-Samir team began to frequent his home at this juncture.[67] He has become, unwittingly, a representative figure, not only of the enemy within but also of an entire industry's alleged subservience to Muslim mafiosi based in Dubai. The very word *Dubai* resonates powerfully in the Indian context, given the numbers of Muslim Indians who have gone there (and to other countries in the Persian Gulf) in recent decades as guest workers and returned to India comparatively wealthy and occasionally with a sharpened sense of religious affiliation. This is articulated in ways both subtle and obvious with the growing sense of Bollywood's thralldom to organized crime, especially Muslim organized crime; the trips made by famous major and minor stars to Dubai, and their reputed liaisons with alleged underworld figures, are seen as evidence of their subjection to these illicit, antinational influences.[68] Sanjay's apprehension led to considerable nervousness in the industry, nervousness that sometimes took the form of appeasing Bal Thackeray, the head of the Shiv Sena. It also became the occasion for the imposition of a number of demands by the Hindu rightist Bharatiya Janata Party in Bombay on the Film Makers' Combine: these included suspending producers and actors accused of antinational activities from trade bodies and new films and respecting "the Hindu way of life, culture and values."[69]

And while his arrest has been instrumental in increasing criticism of TADA, I would argue that the very fact of his arrest and imprisonment without bail (along with hundreds of alleged coconspirators), despite his being the son of a Congress (I) member of Parliament, at a time when the party was in power at the state and at the federal level, is something of a testimony to the fact that suspicions of his Muslimness do not emanate solely from the Hindu right. TADA is in fact notorious for having been applied with extreme rigor to religious minorities, especially Muslims and Sikhs, and has been vociferously criticized by religious minorities and the Human Rights Commission. TADA does not clarify the nature of terrorist activity, encompassing acts violent and nonviolent, private and public, and places upon the accused the burden of proving their innocence;[70] in this regard it functions in ways that are already familiar to religious minorities, casting them as the abjected who must compulsively yet unsuccessfully keep enacting their good citizenship. At the moment Sanjay is out on bail and has resumed his acting career, thanks to the intervention of Thackeray. This is not testimony to the waning of Hindu fundamentalist zeal. Rather, it speaks to the power of the RSS chief, who can manifest his potency perhaps even more persuasively by withholding punishment than by inflicting it.

This is a sequel, not yet completed, to the life of Nargis. Even after death, she remains, as good Muslimness remains in the Indian polity and in Indian/Hindu public culture, as a phantasm, a ghost that lives and moves uncannily in our midst, not quite tangible and never fully exorcisable. Her career—in life and after it—illustrates in fascinating ways how disturbing and enigmatic a figure of (gendered) trouble the good Muslim is for Indianness. (The "bad Muslim," as a figure who insists on forms of religiously based separatism and retains the obvious signifiers of Muslim identity, is a far easier entity to respond to or manage.) As we have seen, the industry itself has showcased Muslim talent—in acting, direction, writing, and music—in a very substantial way; many Muslim actors and actresses have entered the imaginary of a movie-going public in the most spectacular ways. The good Muslim, then, is not simply a phobic object, to be responded to with punitive laws and pogroms and other forms of bigotry; s/he is also, and at the same time, the object of love and identification. Above all, s/he is a figure of unhappy intimacy who, despite manifold repressions and conversions, returns repeatedly and inauspiciously to haunt the wholeness of an Indian (Hindu) psyche/polity. (Post)colonial Hindu/Indian identity must simultaneously disavow and be consumed with the intimate enemies that it can scarcely distinguish from itself.

Epilogue

The mechanism of colonial mimicry so brilliantly and persuasively elaborated by Homi Bhabha and Frantz Fanon has, as the foregoing chapters might suggest, a remarkable degree of versatility and usefulness for a critical understanding not only of the colonial situation but also of the postcolonial aftermath that looks simultaneously backward and forward. Post/ colonial mimicry is not only the scene of agonistic racial encounter but, importantly and sometimes unexpectedly, a locus of traffic marked by the multiple mediations of gender, ethnicity, sexuality, religion, class, and competing nationalisms. Acting on this hypothesis, this work has attempted to trouble the somewhat circumscribed and sometimes too-hopeful character of the work on colonial subjugation and global encounter. Setting the powerfully suggestive notion of colonial mimicry to work in new—that is, non-European—contexts (while also resituating it within familiar ones) shows us the ways in which indigenous models of identity formation (whether it be religious discipleship, gendered nationalism, or the modalities of movie stardom) are often traversed by it, but in ways that might be functional to the interests of Indian nationalisms. This is by no means to claim that anticolonial resistance or nationalism (which are not the same thing) and colonial discourse are governed by identical protocols. The discourses of anticolonial mobilization and colonial domination cannot simply be read off each other; the evidence of the reorientation of imperial tropes on colonial and national ground serves as a salutary warning against the reduction and thoughtless commingling of categories. Yet the evidence of Indian nationalism in its varied forms also suggests (and this is something toward which both Partha Chatterjee's notion of nationalism as a derivative discourse and Sara Suleri's work on "English India" gesture, albeit in terms distinct from each other and from my own) that colonial tropes and colonial processes of subjectification have a powerful explanatory force and a tenacious afterlife, though often in unfamiliar forms, in the discourses of the opposition. If this work can be said to perform the task of dislodging and rendering uncanny relationships between a colonizing west and a colonized rest, it does so by detailing the ways in which the production of the tropes and stereotypes of colonialism was never entirely, or entirely securely, a British project. What a revisioning of Indian nationalism through the mimetic trope also opens up is the considerable and productive libidinal charge that informs and vexes the encounter of the historical actor and sociopolitical formations. The practice of mimicry forms the ground, as it were, upon which a dizzying array of gendered and erotically charged desires and identifications are enunciated and enacted. Detached from its originary home in the figure of the elite, Anglicized male, the trope thus permits a reexamination of the operations of gender in colonialism and nationalism, enabling us, for instance, to note the structural significance of the mimic *woman* (whether western or Indian, Hindu or Muslim) for these projects.

The field of colonial and postcolonial studies has turned its attention in recent years not so much to the mapping of distinct politicojuridical, economic, cultural, and psychic domains designated as colonial or as metropolitan but to the intertwined, indeed mutually constitutive, character of nation and colony and of nation formation and empire building. Thus it is that the reconfiguration of the mimic wo/man within the discourses of the imperial, the national, and the transnational can cue us into the multiple and sometimes unexpected global dislocations, contestations, and transformations of the gendered colonial (and national) encounter. Resituated and remade in a variety of contexts, and standing in in many ways for the constitutive predicament of the postcolonial critic (who is wracked by a keen and characteristically postcolonial anxiety of influence), s/he haunts both colonialism and postcoloniality as the figure of lack and the emblem of desire who will not go quietly into the colonial grave.

NOTES

INTRODUCTION

1. Thomas B. Macaulay, "Minute on Indian Education," in *Selected Prose*, ed. John Clive (Chicago: University of Chicago Press, 1972), 241.

2. Frantz Fanon, *Black Skin, White Masks*, trans. Charles Lam Markmann (New York: Grove Weidenfeld, 1952), 10.

3. Diana Fuss, "Interior Colonies: Frantz Fanon and the Politics of Identification," *diacritics* 24 (Summer-Fall 1994): 21.

4. Homi K. Bhabha, "Of Mimicry and Man: The Ambivalence of Colonial Discourse," in *The Location of Culture* (London and New York: Routledge, 1993). Bhabha's response to Fanon's theoretical/political work is the fascinatingly conflictual one of the disciple to the teacher; see his "Interrogating Identity: Frantz Fanon and the Postcolonial Prerogative," in *The Location of Culture*, 40–65. Henry Louis Gates Jr. faults Bhabha for attempting to recast the Antillean psychoanalyst and revolutionary as a latter-day poststructuralist ("Critical Fanonism," *Critical Inquiry* 17 [Spring 1991]: 457–70). Even if one concedes (as I do not) that there is a more historically persuasive Fanon that exists apart from the one Bhabha gives us, it seems to me that critical work can proceed only through such violent "translations"; what fascinates me more is something that Gates notes, albeit censoriously: Bhabha's obvious anguish and impatience with Fanon's "failures" to sustain "his most radical theoretical insights."

5. Robert Young, *White Mythologies: Writing History and the West* (London and New York: Routledge, 1990), 147.

6. The histories of these often contiguous, overlapping, yet not-identical theorizations of identity formation are both too long and too well known to need an elaborate recapitulation here. The following is a very provisional list of some of the key statements on these questions: Simone de Beauvoir, *The Second Sex*, trans. H. M. Parshley (New York: Vintage Books, 1952); Joan Riviere, "Womanliness as a Masquerade," in *Formations of Fantasy*, ed. Victor Burgin, James Donald, and Cora Kaplan

(London: Methuen, 1986); Luce Irigaray, *This Sex Which Is Not One*, trans. Catherine Porter (Ithaca, N.Y.: Cornell University Press, 1985); Mary Ann Doane, "Film and the Masquerade: Theorising the Female Spectator," in *Femmes Fatales: Feminism, Film Theory, Psychoanalysis* (New York and London: Routledge, 1991), 17–32; Judith Butler, *Gender Trouble: Feminism and the Subversion of Identity* (New York: Routledge, 1990), and *Bodies That Matter* (New York and London: Routledge, 1993); Adrian Piper, "Passing for White, Passing for Black," *Transition* 58 (1995): 4–32; Nella Larsen, *Passing* (New York and London: Knopf, 1929), and *Quicksand* (New York and London: Knopf, 1928); James Weldon Johnson, *The Autobiography of an Ex-Colored Man* (New York: Sherman, French, 1912); Deborah McDowell, "'That Nameless . . . Shameful Impulse': Sexuality in Nella Larsen's *Quicksand* and *Passing*," in *Studies in Black American Literature III: Black Feminist Criticism and Critical Theory*, ed. Joe Weixlmann and Houston A. Baker Jr. (Greenwood, Fla.: Penkevill Publishing, 1988); Valerie Smith, "Reading the Intersection of Race and Gender in Narratives of Passing," *diacritics* 24 (Summer-Fall 1994): 43–57; Sue-Ellen Case, "Toward a Butch-Femme Aesthetic," In *Making a Spectacle*, ed. Lynda Hart (Ann Arbor: University of Michigan Press, 1989); Morris Meyer, ed. *The Politics and Poetics of Camp* (New York and London: Routledge, 1993); Vito Russo, "Camp," *Gay Men: The Sociology of Male Homosexuality*, ed. Martin Levine (New York: Harper & Row, 1979); Jenny Livingston, dir. *Paris Is Burning*, 1991; Kobena Mercer, *Welcome to the Jungle: New Positions in Black Cultural Studies* (New York and London: Routledge, 1994); Eric Lott, *Love and Theft: Blackface Minstrelsy and the American Working Class* (New York: Oxford University Press, 1993); Marjorie Garber, *Vested Interests: Cross-Dressing and Cultural Anxiety* (New York: Routledge, 1992); Carole-Anne Tyler, "Boys Will Be Girls: The Politics of Gay Drag," in *Inside/Out: Lesbian Theories, Gay Theories*, ed, Diana Fuss (New York: Routledge, 1990).

7. Ranajit Guha, "On Some Aspects of the Historiography of Colonial India," in *Subaltern Studies I: Writings on South Asian History and Society*, ed. Ranajit Guha (Delhi: Oxford University Press, 1982; reprinted in *Selected Subaltern Studies*, ed. Ranajit Guha and Gayatri C. Spivak [New York: Oxford University Press, 1988]), 43.

8. Benedict Anderson, *Imagined Communities: Reflections on the Origin and Spread of Nationalism* (London: Verso, 1991 [1983]).

9. Partha Chatterjee, *Nationalist Thought and the Colonial World: A Derivative Discourse* (Minneapolis: University of Minnesota Press, 1993), 22.

10. For a compelling account of the transformation of a purportedly modular notion/genre (in this case the realist novel) on Indian terrain, see Meenakshi Mukherjee, *Realism and Reality: The Novel and Society in India* (Delhi: Oxford University Press, 1994 [1985]).

11. Partha Chatterjee, *The Nation and Its Fragments: Colonial and Postcolonial Histories* (Princeton, N.J.: Princeton University Press, 1993). This book will be discussed more fully in chapter 5. I am in substantial agreement with Chatterjee's arguments, but it should be noted on Anderson's behalf that what he emphasizes is the modularity of the *idea* of nationness; he does not insist that nation-states or other national formations everywhere will be identical. Hence his important rejection—one which marks him out from earlier theorists of the nation—of any distinction between "true" and "false" forms of nationhood. For some of the key statements on the na-

tion and on nationalism, see John Hutchinson and Anthony D. Smith, eds., *Nationalism* (Oxford and New York: Oxford University Press, 1994).

12. Some instances of an engagement with this problematic are provided by the following works: Dipesh Chakrabarty, "Open Space/Public Space: Garbage, Modernity and India," *South Asia* 14, no. 1 (1991): 15–31; and "Postcoloniality and the Artifice of History: Who Speaks for 'Indian' Pasts?" *Representations* 37 (Winter 1992): 1–26; Gyan Prakash, "Science 'Gone Native' in Colonial India," *Representations* 40 (Fall 1992): 1–26; and R. Radhakrishnan, "Postcoloniality and the Boundaries of Identity," *Callaloo* 16, no. 4 (1993): 750–71. If it appears that terms like "originality" and "authenticity" are being used interchangeably, it is because I see them as part of the same associative continuum for the debates in question.

13. Chakrabarty, "Postcoloniality and the Artifice of History," 3.

14. See, for instance, Bette London, "Of Mimicry and English Men: E. M. Forster and the Performance of Masculinity," in *A Passage to India*, ed. Tony Davies and Nigel Wood, Theory in Practice Series (Buckingham, England: Open University Press, 1994). Also see Young, "Ambivalence of Bhabha," in *White Mythologies*.

15. Jenny Sharpe, "Figures of Colonial Resistance," *Modern Fiction Studies* 35 (Spring 1989): 138 (emphasis mine). Sharpe notes that the nature of colonial discourse actively encourages the cloaking of subalternity and class identity, its aim being "to substitute metonymically the educated colonial for the native as such" (p. 139). The Benita Parry essay in question is the widely read metacritical statement, "Problems in Current Theories of Colonial Discourse," *Oxford Literary Review* 9, no. 1–2 (1987): 27–58.

16. I use the term *catachresis* in Spivak's sense: "a metaphor without an adequate literal referent, in the last instance a model for all metaphors, all names." See Gayatri Chakravorty Spivak, "The New Historicism: Political Commitment and the Postmodern Critic," in *The Post-Colonial Critic: Interviews, Strategies, Dialogues*, ed. Sarah Harasym (New York: Routledge, 1990), 154.

17. I would like to reinvoke the notion of ambivalence that attends Bhabha's initial theorization of this question.

18. This is not to deny that Kim's Irishness, and his poor-white status, make him distinct from more privileged whites.

19. Gayatri Chakravorty Spivak, "The Political Economy of Women as Seen by a Literary Critic," in *Coming to Terms: Feminism, Theory, Politics*, ed. Elizabeth Weed (London: Routledge, 1989), 227. Rey Chow, *Woman and Chinese Modernity: The Politics of Reading Between East and West* (Minneapolis: University of Minnesota Press, 1991), which contests the academic representation of a nonwest that is evacuated of "fantasy, desires, and contradictory emotions" (p. xiii) is of interest here (though it is by no means completely congruent with the trajectory of Spivak's demand for other "psycho-biographies").

20. Carole-Anne Tyler, "Passing: Narcissism, Identity, and Difference," *differences* 6 (Summer-Fall 1994): 212–48. Also see Peggy Phelan, *Unmarked: The Politics of Performance* (London and New York: Routledge, 1993).

21. One of my models for such an enterprise (though his project is very different from my own) is Arjun Appadurai's brilliant (and now classic) essay, "Disjuncture and Difference in the Global Cultural Economy," *Public Culture* 2 (Spring 1990): 1–23.

22. Gayatri Chakravorty Spivak, "Poststructuralism, Marginality, Postcoloniality and Value," in *Literary Theory Today*, ed. Peter Collier and Helga Geyer-Ryan (Ithaca, N.Y.: Cornell University Press, 1990), 223.

23. Paul Gilroy has provocatively described the triangulations, traffic, and mutual transformations of Africa, the Americas, and Europe in the moment of modernity (*The Black Atlantic: Modernity and Double Consciousness* [Cambridge, Mass.: Harvard University Press, 1993]). A puzzling feature of this otherwise pivotal work is its elision of any consideration in *The Black Atlantic* of the Asian diaspora in England, Africa, and the Caribbean.

24. Among the best contemporary accounts of the western woman's occasional (sometimes willed) subordination in nationalist or postcolonial contexts is Sara Suleri, *Meatless Days* (Chicago: University of Chicago Press, 1989). In this novel Suleri movingly describes the unceasing yet unavailing effort of her Welsh mother to become Pakistani (pp. 163–64):

> Did she really think that she could assume the burden of empire, that if she let my father colonize her body and her name she would perform some slight reparation for the race from which she came? Could she not see that his desire for her was quickened with empire's ghosts, that his need to possess was a clear index of how he was still possessed? . . . What could that world [Pakistan] do with a woman who called herself a Pakistani but who looked suspiciously like the past it sought to forget? Then my mother learned the ironies of nationhood—of what can and cannot be willed—when she had to walk through her new context in the shape of a memory erased. . . . She let commitment and belonging become my father's domain, learning instead the way of walking with tact on other people's land.

25. Chandra Talpade Mohanty's landmark essay, "Under Western Eyes: Feminist Scholarship and Colonial Discourses" (in *Third World Women and the Politics of Feminism*, ed. Chandra Mohanty, Ann Russo, and Lourdes Torres [Bloomington: Indiana University Press, 1991]), forcefully demonstrates the imbrication of much (though not all) western feminist scholarship on the "Third World" with the assumptions of colonial discourse. The burden of Mohanty's argument is substantiated in the analysis by (among others) Antoinette Burton of "imperial feminism" in *Burdens of History: British Feminists, Indian Women, and Imperial Culture, 1865–1915* (Chapel Hill and London: University of North Carolina Press, 1994). Also of interest are Nupur Chaudhuri and Margaret Strobel, eds., *Western Women and Imperialism: Complicity and Resistance* (Bloomington: Indiana University Press, 1992); Deirdre David, *Rule Britannia: Women, Empire, and Victorian Writing* (Ithaca, N.Y., and London: Cornell University Press, 1995); and Laura E. Donaldson, *Decolonizing Feminisms: Race, Gender, and Empire-Building* (Chapel Hill: University of North Carolina Press, 1992). See, too, Sandhya Shetty, "(Dis)Locating Gender Space and Medical Discourse in Colonial India," *Genders* 20 (1994): 188–230, for a splendid account of the instrumentality of colonial rule and reason for white women seeking membership in a hitherto closed medical fraternity. Kumari Jayawardena, *The White Woman's Other Burden: Western Women and South Asia during British Rule* (New York and London: Routledge, 1995) provides a rather different but significant point of entry into this vexed question, pointing up as it does the significant commitment of some western women to a variety of causes not necessarily congruent with colonialism or an Eurocentric feminism. For further details, see chapter 4.

26. Rosalind O'Hanlon and David Washbrook, "After Orientalism: Culture, Criticism, and Politics in the Third World," *Comparative Studies in Society and History* 34 (January 1992): 141–67; Arif Dirlik, "The Postcolonial Aura," *Critical Inquiry* (1993): 328–56; and Aijaz Ahmad, *In Theory: Classes, Nations, Literatures* (London: Verso, 1992). (Ahmad is not a historian but a literary scholar by training; nonetheless, his archaeology of certain theoretical developments is similar enough to those of the historians listed here that the association is not unwarranted.) For responses to Ahmad's influential book, see *Public Culture* 6 (Fall 1993), especially the essays by Vivek Dhareshwar ("Marxism, Location Politics, and the Possibility of Critique," 41–54) and Nivedita Menon ("Orientalism and After," 65–76). See also Kalpana Seshadri-Crooks, "At the Margins of Postcolonial Studies," *Ariel* 26, no. 3 (1995): 47–71; and Caren Kaplan and Inderpal Grewal, "Transnational Feminist Cultural Studies: Beyond the Marxism/Poststructuralism/Feminism Divides," *positions* 2, no. 2 (1994): 430–45.

27. Gyan Prakash, "Writing Post-Orientalist Histories of the Third World: Perspectives from Indian Historiography," *Comparative Studies in Society and History* 32, no. 2 (1990): 383–408.

28. Gyan Prakash, "Can the 'Subaltern' Ride? A Reply to O'Hanlon and Washbrook," *Comparative Studies in Society and History* 34 (January 1992): 168.

29. Conversation with Kalpana Seshadri-Crooks, Toronto, December 1993.

30. Anne McClintock, "The Angel of Progress: Pitfalls of the Term 'Post-Colonialism,'" *Social Text* 31/32, 10, nos. 2–3 (1992): 84–98; and Ella Shohat, "Notes on the 'Post-Colonial,'" *Social Text* 31/32, 10, nos. 2–3 (1992): 99–113. It seems to me somewhat unfair to make Bill Ashcroft, Gareth Griffiths, and Helen Tiffin, eds., *The Empire Writes Back: Theory and Practice in Post-Colonial Literatures* (London: Routledge, 1989), serve a representative function; both essays accord it that kind of centrality. R. Radhakrishnan points to the ways in which "the spatiality of the 'post' has to be simultaneously critiqued and endorsed" ("Postcoloniality," 752).

31. Stuart Hall, "When Was the 'Post-Colonial?' Thinking at the Limit," in *The Post-Colonial Question: Common Skies, Divided Horizons*, ed. Iain Chambers and Lidia Curti (London and New York: Routledge, 1996), 254. See, too, Gyan Prakash's witty description of postcoloniality's deviation from a cumulative temporality: "Containing a link to the experience of colonialism but not contained by it, postcoloniality can be thought of as a form of realignment that emerges in *media res*, critically undoing and redrawing colonialism's contingent boundaries" ("Who's Afraid of Postcoloniality?" *Social Text* 49, 14, no. 4 [1996]: 188–89).

32. I use the essays by McClintock and Shohat only as representative instances here, as the proper name for the discontent generated by the term in a number of scholars. See, for instance, Tejumola Olaniyan, "On 'Post-Colonial Discourse': An Introduction," *Callaloo* 16, no. 4 (1993): 743–48; Graham Huggan, "Postcolonialism and Its Discontents," *Transition* 62 (1993): 130–35; Linda Hutcheon, "Introduction. Colonialism and the Postcolonial Condition: Complexities Abounding," *PMLA* 110, no. 1 (1995): 7–16; Lata Mani and Ruth Frankenberg, "Crosscurrents, Crosstalk: Race, 'Postcoloniality' and the Politics of Location," *Cultural Studies* 7 (May 1993): 292–310; and Michael Sprinker, "Introduction," in *Late Imperial Culture*, ed. Roman de la Campa, E. Ann Kaplan, and Michael Sprinker (London and New York: Verso, 1995).

33. Spivak, "Political Economy of Women," 221.

34. Ellen Rooney, "What Is to Be Done?" in *Coming to Terms: Feminism, Theory, Politics*, ed. Elizabeth Weed (New York: Routledge, 1989), 235.

35. Gayatri Chakravorty Spivak, "A Literary Representation of the Subaltern," in *In Other Worlds: Essays in Cultural Politics* (New York and London: Routledge, 1987), 254.

36. Gayatri Chakravorty Spivak, "Criticism, Feminism, and the Institution, *Post-Colonial Critic*, 15.

37. Stuart Hall, "Cultural Studies and Its Theoretical Legacies," in *Cultural Studies*, ed. Lawrence Grossberg, Cary Nelson, and Paula A. Treichler (New York: Routledge, 1992), 284.

1. ORIENTAL EXHIBITS

1. Sir Arthur Conan Doyle, "The Adventure of the Empty House," in *The Complete Sherlock Holmes*, preface by Christopher Morley (New York: Doubleday, 1930), 488.

2. Homi K. Bhabha, *The Location of Culture* (London and New York: Routledge, 1993), 85–92.

3. Quoted in Isabel Burton, *The Life of Captain Sir Richard F. Burton, K.C.M.G., F.R.G.S., by His Wife* (London: Chapman and Hall, 1893), 1: 154.

4. Edward Rice, *Captain Sir Richard Francis Burton: The Secret Agent Who Made the Pilgrimage to Mecca, Discovered the Kama Sutra, and Brought the Arabian Nights to the West* (New York: HarperCollins, 1990), 72, 86.

5. Isabel Burton states: "During those first seven years in India, Richard passed in Hindostani, Guzaratee, Persian, Maharattee, Sindhee, Punjaubee, Arabic, Telugu, Pushtu (Afghan tongue), with Turkish and Armenian" (*Life of Sir Richard F. Burton*, 159).

6. Ibid., 135.

7. Ibid.

8. Ibid., 109.

9. Ibid., 135–36.

10. Ibid., 109.

11. H. T. Lambrick, "Editor's Introduction," in *Sindh, and the Races That Inhabit the Valley of the Indus*, by Richard Burton (Karachi: Oxford University Press, 1973), vi–xiii. Also see I. Burton, *Life of Sir Richard F. Burton*.

12. Quoted in Rice, *Sir Richard Francis Burton*, 164.

13. Richard F. Burton, *Personal Narrative of a Pilgrimage to Al-Madinah and Meccah* (New York: Dover Publications, 1964), 1: xxii–xxiii. All subsequent citations will be incorporated parenthetically into the text.

14. Lambrick, "Editor's Introduction," xiii.

15. Georgiana M. Stisted, *The True Life of Captain Sir Richard F. Burton, K.C.M.G., F.R.G.S., etc., Written by His Niece, with the Authority and Approval of the Burton Family* (New York: D. Appleton; London: H. S. Nichols, 1897), 43.

16. Quoted in Rice, *Sir Richard Francis Burton*, 160.

17. Ibid., 191–92.

18. Lambrick, "Editor's Introduction," xv. I should add—in case it is not already abundantly clear—that I am interested not in the veracity of Burton's recall or account of his experiences but in the fantasies of cross-cultural exchange that inform his work.

19. Richard F. Burton, *Goa, and the Blue Mountains; or, Six Months of Sick Leave,* edited with an introduction by Dane Kennedy (Berkeley: University of California Press, 1991 [1851]).

20. Richard F. Burton, *Scinde; or, The Unhappy Valley* (London: Richard Bentley, 1851), 2: 7.

21. Quoted in Rice, *Sir Richard Francis Burton,* 164.

22. Richard F. Burton, "Terminal Essay," in *The Book of the Thousand Nights and a Night,* vol. 10 (London: Kama-shastra Society, 1885).

23. Fawn M. Brodie, *The Devil Drives: A Life of Sir Richard Burton* (New York: W. W. Norton, 1967), 347.

24. Rice, *Sir Richard Francis Burton,* 128–30. See also James Casada, *Sir Richard Francis Burton: A Bibliographical Study* (Boston: G. K. Hall, 1989), 12.

25. R. F. Burton, *Goa,* 97.

26. Gail Ching-Liang Low, "White Skins/Black Masks: The Pleasures and Politics of Imperialism," *New Formations* 9, no. 24 (1989): 96.

27. R. F. Burton, *Goa,* 160.

28. Burton was to continue in the employ of the Indian Army (of the British East India Company) for several more years.

29. Joseph Conrad, *Heart of Darkness,* ed. Robert Kimbrough (New York: Norton, 1971), 8. Also see Joseph Conrad, "Geography and Some Explorers," in *Last Essays* (New York: Doubleday, 1926).

30. Thomas Assad, *Three Victorian Travellers: Burton, Blunt, Doughty* (London: Routledge and Kegan Paul, 1964), 19.

31. Thomas Richards, "Archive and Utopia," *Representations* 37 (Winter 1992): 110.

32. Rice, *Sir Richard Francis Burton,* 180, 168, 280, and passim.

33. Bhabha, "Of Mimicry and Man."

34. Ibid., 86.

35. This does not mean that the mimic man necessarily intends any menace; Bhabha locates the disturbance of mimicry in the process itself, rather than circumscribing it in an intending subject. The mimic man signifies a defamiliarization, rather than intending it.

36. Homi K. Bhabha, "Sly Civility," in *The Location of Culture,* 93–101.

37. Satya P. Mohanty, "Drawing the Color Line: Kipling and the Culture of Colonial Rule," in *The Bounds of Race: Perspectives on Hegemony and Resistance,* ed. Dominick LaCapra (Ithaca, N.Y.: Cornell University Press, 1991), 315.

38. Kaja Silverman, "White Skin, Brown Masks: The Double Mimesis, or With Lawrence in Arabia," *differences* 1 (Fall 1989): 3–54.

39. Ibid., 19.

40. Edward W. Said, *Orientalism* (New York: Random House, 1978), 195.

41. I am grateful to Sandhya Shetty for bringing this to my attention.

42. George W. Stocking, *Victorian Anthropology* (New York: Free Press, 1987), 253.

43. Silverman, "White Skin, Brown Masks," 26.

44. Patrick Brantlinger, *Rule of Darkness: British Literature and Imperialism, 1830–1914* (Ithaca, N.Y.: Cornell University Press, 1988), 160.

45. Homi K. Bhabha, "The Other Question: Stereotype, Discrimination and the Discourse of Colonialism," in *The Location of Culture*, 70–71.

46. Quoted in Brodie, *Devil Drives*, 89.

47. I am grateful to the anonymous readers of *boundary* 2 for bringing this point to my attention.

48. Richard F. Burton, *First Footsteps in East Africa*, ed. Gordon Waterfield (New York and Washington, D.C.: Frederick A. Praeger, 1966).

49. Many adopted Indian clothing, languages, cuisine, and living arrangements; some of them were known to have married Indian women and to have participated in local forms of worship.

50. Mary Louise Pratt, *Imperial Eyes: Travel Writing and Transculturation* (London and New York: Routledge, 1992), 78.

51. Said, *Orientalism*, 92–93.

52. See Mary Louise Pratt, "Conventions of Representation: Where Discourse and Ideology Meet," in *Georgetown University Round Table on Languages and Linguistics 1982* (Washington, D.C.: Georgetown University Press, 1982), for an analysis of the "master-of-all-I-survey" trope that distinguishes much nineteenth- and twentieth-century travel writing. See, too, James Clifford's description of Marcel Griaule's adoption of the "panoptic viewpoint [of the airplane] as a habit and a tactic" in ethnographic observation (*The Predicament of Culture: Twentieth-Century Ethnography, Literature, and Art* [Cambridge, Mass., and London: Harvard University Press, 1988], 69).

53. Brantlinger, *Rule of Darkness*, 162–63.

54. Gayatri Chakravorty Spivak, "Three Women's Texts and a Critique of Imperialism," in *"Race," Writing, and Difference*, ed. Henry Louis Gates Jr. (Chicago and London: University of Chicago Press, 1986).

55. Chakrabarty, "Postcoloniality and the Artifice of History," 18. Chakrabarty notes the utilization and success of these devices in some distinctly "modern" institutions and projects (like nationalism).

2. DISCOVERING INDIA, IMAGINING *THUGGEE*

1. Radhika Singha, "'Providential' Circumstances: The Thuggee Campaign of the 1830s and Legal Innovation," *Modern Asian Studies* 27 (February 1993): 83.

2. Guha, "Historiography of Colonial India."

3. Ranajit Guha, "The Prose of Counter-Insurgency," in *Subaltern Studies II: Writings on South Asian History and Society*, ed. Ranajit Guha (New Delhi: Oxford University Press, 1983). Also see Ranajit Guha, *Elementary Aspects of Peasant Insurgency in Colonial India* (Delhi: Oxford University Press, 1983).

4. Gayatri Chakravorty Spivak, "Deconstructing Historiography," in *In Other Worlds: Essays in Cultural Politics* (New York and London: Routledge, 1987), 204.

5. This is not to suggest that Bhabha forecloses on any of these other possibilities.

6. James Hutton, *A Popular Account of the Thugs and Dacoits, the Hereditary Garroters and Gang-Robbers of India* (London: W. H. Allen, 1857), 90–91.

7. Reproduced in George Bruce, *The Stranglers: The Cult of Thuggee and Its Overthrow in British India* (New York: Harcourt, Brace & World, 1968), 13–26.

8. Philip Meadows Taylor, "Introduction," in *Confessions of a Thug* (London: Richard Bentley, 1858 [1839]), 5.

9. A. J. Wightman, *No Friend for Travellers* (London: Robert Hale, 1959), 15.

10. See Francis C. Tuker, *The Yellow Scarf: The Story of the Life of Thuggee Sleeman* (London: J. M. Dent & Sons, 1961), 197–98.

11. Geoff Bennington, "Postal Politics and the Institution of the Nation," in *Nation and Narration*, ed. Homi K. Bhabha (London and New York: Routledge, 1990).

12. Sandria Freitag argues that thugs were—in contrast to members of criminal castes and tribes—regarded as "admirable and awesome opponents." See her "Crime in the Social Order of Colonial North India," *Modern Asian Studies* 25, no. 2 (1991): 227–61. While some of this horrified admiration does inform Wightman and Meadows Taylor's representations, such admiration is more usually carefully repressed; there is, in fact, an interesting tension between the awe-inspiring (if damnable) thug of these texts and the contemptible figure that the other texts strenuously accentuate.

13. James Sleeman, *Thug, or A Million Murders* (London: Sampson Low, Marston, 1933 [1920]), 5.

14. Sir George MacMunn, *The Religions and Hidden Cults of India* (London: Sampson Low, Marston, 1931), 172–73. See, too, Meadows Taylor, "Introduction," i:

> At the present time it [the novel] may deserve a more attentive study; recent events will have too well prepared the Reader's mind for implicit belief in all the systematic atrocities narrated. . . . It will scarcely fail to be remarked, with what consummate art such numerous bodies of men were organized, and for a long time kept absolutely unknown, while committing acts of cruelty and rapine hardly conceivable; . . . Captain Taylor's Introduction . . . may . . . furnish some clue to the successful concealment of a rebellion, in the existence of which many of our oldest and most experienced officers, and men high in authority, absolutely withheld belief, till too late and too cruelly convinced of their fatal error.

15. Katherine Mayo, *Mother India* (New York: Harcourt, Brace, 1927).

16. Hiralal Gupta, "A Critical Study of the *Thugs* and Their Activities," *Journal of Indian History*, 37, part 2 (August 1959), serial no. 110: 169–77.

17. Sandria B. Freitag, "Collective Crime and Authority in North India," in *Crime and Criminality in British India*, ed. Anand Yang (Tucson: University of Arizona Press, 1985), 158–61.

18. Stewart N. Gordon, "Scarf and Sword: Thugs, Marauders, and State-Formation in 18th Century Malwa," *Indian Economic and Social History Review* 6 (December 1969): 403–29. It should be noted that Gordon does not ascribe the activities of the marauding groups to "Oriental anarchy" or oppose "marauders" to "states," arguing that both entities had the same ends in view and were using the same methods of legitimation, though with differing degrees of success.

19. J. Sleeman, *Thug*, 108.

20. David Arnold, *Police Power and Colonial Rule: Madras 1859–1947* (Delhi: Oxford University Press, 1986), 3. He notes the transformation of the Thuggee and Dacoity Department into the Central Intelligence Department in 1904; this body shifted its initial focus on wandering gangs and criminals to "the collation of politi-

cal intelligence, relaying information about political leaders and organizations to the various provinces concerned" (p. 187).

21. Freitag, "Collective Crime and Authority," 142.

22. Freitag, "Crime in the Social Order," 230.

23. Ibid., 234.

24. Fanny Parks, *Wanderings of a Pilgrim in Search of the Picturesque* (Karachi and London: Oxford University Press, 1975 [1850]), 1: 153.

25. Kali became a figure of increasing respectability in the nineteenth century; before this she was a deity adored (in Bengal at least) largely though not exclusively by tribal and other subaltern subjects, including thugs and dacoits. It is not clear if Kali was identical with other female deities addressed as Devi or Bhawani.

26. See, for instance, Nicholas B. Dirks, "Castes of Mind," *Representations* 37 (Winter 1992): 59: "It is increasingly clear that colonialism in India produced new forms of society that have been taken to be traditional, and that caste itself as we now know it is not a residual survival of ancient India but a specifically colonial form of civil society. As such it both justifies and maintains the colonial vision of an India where religion transcends politics, society resists change, and the state awaits its virgin birth in the postcolonial era."

27. This had not, of course, been entirely true for Burton, perhaps because of his sojourn in Sind or his early studies in Arabic. As might be expected, the particular discourse being engaged would determine the Hinduness, or otherwise, of the territory designated "India."

28. Lata Mani, "Contentious Traditions," in *The Nature and Context of Minority Discourse*, ed. Abdul JanMohamed and David Lloyd (New York: Oxford University Press, 1990).

29. John Masters, *The Deceivers* (New York: Carroll and Graf, 1952), 240. All further references to this novel will be incorporated parenthetically into the text.

30. Charles Hervey, *Some Records of Crime (Being the Diary of a Year, Official and Particular, of an Officer of the Thuggee and Dacoitie Police)* (London: Sampson Low, Marston, 1892), 1: 50–51.

31. Ranjit Sen, *Social Banditry in Bengal: A Study in Primary Resistance, 1757–1793* (Calcutta: Ratna Prakashan, 1988), 2–3.

32. Sanjay Nigam, "Disciplining and Policing the 'Criminals by Birth,'" *Indian Economic and Social History Review* 27, no. 2 (1990): 131–64; 27, no. 3 (1990): 259–87.

33. Michel Foucault, *The History of Sexuality*, trans. Robert Hurley (New York: Vintage Books, 1978), 1: 43.

34. Radhika Singha argues that "the introduction of laws dealing with ill-defined 'criminal communities' introduced certain fissures into the ideology of the equal, abstract and universal legal subject" ("'Providential' Circumstances," 86, n. 10).

35. Edward Thornton, *Illustrations of the History and Practices of the Thugs* (London: W. H. Allen, 1837), 145–46. This frankness is relatively rare in the writings on *thuggee;* the issue of the genuineness of the confessions, though, is an issue in all, judging from the unfailing vehemence with which the method of conviction through approvers' testimony is defended as just, if not unexceptionable.

36. Ibid., 374.

37. J. Sleeman, *Thug*, 120.

38. William H. Sleeman, *Ramaseeana, or a Vocabulary of the Peculiar Language Used by the Thugs* (Calcutta: G. H. Huttmann, Military Orphan Press, 1836), 32–33.

39. Thornton, *Illustrations*, 70, 11.

40. Wightman, *No Friend for Travellers*, 112.

41. J. Sleeman, *Thug*, 106.

42. William H. Sleeman, *Report on Budhuk Alias Bagree Dacoits and Other Gang Robbers by Hereditary Profession* (Calcutta: J. C. Sherriff, Bengal Military Orphan Press, 1849), 2–3.

43. Foucault, *History of Sexuality*, 1: 35.

44. Homi Bhabha, "Sly Civility" and "Of Mimicry and Man," in *The Location of Culture*.

45. See Mala Sen, *India's Bandit Queen: The True Story of Phoolan Devi* (New Delhi: Indus/HarperCollins, 1991) for an example of the way in which the colonial discourse of *thuggee* (in this instance, Tukar's *Yellow Scarf*) continues, in contemporary India, to frame the way in which certain forms of collective violence are understood by the law-and-order machinery of the state.

46. Tuker, *Yellow Scarf*, 38.

47. William H. Sleeman, *Rambles and Recollections of an Indian Official*, ed. Vincent A. Smith (London: Humphrey Milford, Oxford University Press, 1915), 555.

48. Taylor, *Confessions of a Thug*, 330.

49. W. H. Sleeman, *Ramaseeana*, 3.

50. Freitag, "Collective Crime and Authority," 146.

51. Singha, "'Providential' Circumstances," 84.

52. W. H. Sleeman, *Report on Budhuk*, 173. The *thuggee act* had the following provisions:

> 1. Whoever shall be proved to have belonged, either before or after the passing of this Act, to any gang of Thugs, either within or without the Territories of the East India Company, shall be punished with imprisonment for life, with hard labour.
>
> 2. And . . . every person accused of the offence . . . may be tried by any court, which would have been competent to try him, if his offence had been committed within the Zillah where that Court sits, any thing to the contrary, in any Regulation contained, notwithstanding.
>
> 3. And . . . no Court shall, on a trial of any person accused of the offence . . . require any Futwa from any Law Officer.

53. Singha, "'Providential' Circumstances," 136–37.

54. J. Sleeman, *Thug*, 117.

55. Michel Foucault, *Discipline and Punish*, trans. Alan Sheridan (New York: Vintage Books, 1979), 38.

56. Shahid Amin, "Approver's Testimony, Judicial Discourse: The Case of Chauri Chaura," in *Subaltern Studies V: Writings on South Asian History and Society*, ed. Ranajit Guha (Delhi: Oxford University Press, 1987).

57. William H. Sleeman, *Report on the Depredations Committed by the Thug Gangs of Upper and Central India* (Calcutta: G. H. Huttmann, Bengal Military Orphan Press, 1840).

58. Bruce, *Stranglers*, 154.

59. W. H. Sleeman, *Report on Budhuk*, 303–5.

60. Freitag, "Crime in the Social Order," 236. It is said that thugs had routinely existed in a symbiotic relationship with landlords, providing military protection and supplying booty from expeditions in return for land and respectability.

61. W. H. Sleeman, *Ramaseeana*, 186–87.

62. I should add here that the phrase *going native* is vested in my paper with a multiplicity of valences; for instance, it encompasses both the colonialist desire to "pass for" the native and the condition that signifies racial regression.

63. R. Radhakrishnan, "Ethnicity in an Age of Diaspora," *Transition* 54 (1991): 106.

64. David Arnold, "European Orphans and Vagrants in India in the Nineteenth Century," *Journal of Imperial and Commonwealth History* 7, no. 2 (1979): 104–27.

65. Homi K. Bhabha, "DissemiNation: Time, Narrative, and the Margins of the Modern Nations," in *Nation and Narration*, 299.

66. Spivak, "Can the Subaltern Speak?" See Michel Foucault, "Intellectuals and Power: A Conversation between Michel Foucault and Gilles Deleuze," in *Language, Counter-Memory, Practice: Selected Essays and Interviews*, by Michel Foucault, trans. Donald F. Bouchard and Sherry Simon (Ithaca, N.Y.: Cornell University Press, 1977), 205–17.

67. Gayatri Chakravorty Spivak, "Translator's Foreword to 'Draupadi,' by Mahasweta Devi," in *In Other Worlds: Essays in Cultural Politics* (New York and London: Routledge, 1987), 180.

3. ANGLO/INDIANS AND OTHERS

1. Rudyard Kipling, "Miss Youghal's *Sais*," in *Plain Tales from the Hills*, ed. H. R. Woudhuysen, with an introduction and notes by David Trotter (Harmondsworth: Penguin Books, 1987), 51. All subsequent references will be incorporated parenthetically into the text as *PTH*.

2. See, for instance, Rudyard Kipling, *Letters of Marque* (New York and Boston: H. M. Caldwell, 1899).

3. Stephen Arata describes Kipling's penchant for the "unglossed allusion, the unapologetic gesture towards structures of feeling and experience which had no counterpart outside the enclosed world of Anglo-India" ("A Universal Foreignness: Kipling in the Fin-de-Siècle," *English Literature in Transition* 36, no. 1 [1993]: 12).

4. Gail Ching-Liang Low, *White Skins/Black Masks: Representation and Colonialism* (London and New York: Routledge, 1996), 191.

5. Rudyard Kipling, *Life's Handicap, Being Stories of My Own People*, ed. P. N. Furbank (Harmondsworth: Penguin Books, 1987). All further references will be incorporated parenthetically into the text as *LH*.

6. Quoted in Zohreh T. Sullivan, *Narratives of Empire: The Fictions of Rudyard Kipling* (Cambridge, England: Cambridge University Press, 1993), 93.

7. Ibid., 112. The story does affirm the mutual love of Jellaludin and his wife, but it is, of course, impossible to separate the fact of his marriage from the scenario of his (damnable but glorious) degradation.

8. Charles Carrington, *Rudyard Kipling: His Life and Work* (Harmondsworth: Penguin Books, 1970 [1959]), 103.

9. Benita Parry asserts that "[if] 'To be Filed for Reference' both intimates and averts a challenge to British knowledge, then *Kim* (1901) confidently reaffirms its validity" ("The Content and Discontents of Kipling's Imperialism," *New Formations*, no. 6 [Winter 1988]: 54).

10. Irving Howe, "The Pleasures of *Kim*," in *Rudyard Kipling: Modern Critical Views*, ed. Harold Bloom (New York: Chelsea House, 1987), 35.

11. Mark Kinkead-Weekes, "Vision in Kipling's Novels," in *Kipling's Mind and Art: Selected Critical Essays*, ed. Andrew Rutherford (Stanford, Calif.: Stanford University Press, 1964), 232.

12. J. M. S. Tompkins, *The Art of Rudyard Kipling* (London: Methuen, 1959), 21–22.

13. Rudyard Kipling, *Something of Myself and Other Autobiographical Writings*, ed. Thomas Pinney (Cambridge, England: Cambridge University Press, 1990), 3.

14. For instances of Kipling's representation of the uncomplicated love between Anglo-Indian children and their adult Indian caretakers and companions, see his "Tod's Amendment," in *Plain Tales from the Hills*; and "Wee Willie Winkie" and "His Majesty the King," in *Wee Willie Winkie*, ed. Hugh Haughton (London: Penguin Books, 1988). See, too, "Simla Notes," *Civil and Military Gazette*, 29 July 1885 (reprinted in *Kipling's India: Uncollected Sketches 1884–88*, ed. Thomas Pinney [Basingstoke and London: Macmillan, 1986], 112–18).

15. James Harrison, *Rudyard Kipling* (Boston: Twayne Publishers, 1982), 2.

16. It is precisely this lack of a tragic dimension that Edmund Wilson, "The Kipling That Nobody Read," *Atlantic Monthly* 167 (1941): 201–14 [reprinted in *Kipling's Mind and Art: Selected Critical Essays*, ed. Andrew Rutherford (Stanford, Calif.: Stanford University Press, 1964), 30–31] has famously seen as the novel's most damning flaw:

> Now what the reader tends to expect is that Kim will come eventually to realize that he is delivering into bondage to the British invaders those whom he has considered his own people, and that a struggle between allegiances will result. . . . But . . . the alternating attractions felt by Kim never give rise to a genuine struggle. . . . Nor does Kipling allow himself to doubt that his hero has chosen the better part. Kim must now exploit his knowledge of native life for the purpose of preventing and putting down any native resistance to the British; but it never seems to occur to his creator that this constitutes a betrayal of the lama. A sympathy with the weaker party in a relationship based on force has again given way without a qualm to the glorification of the stronger.

17. Bhabha, "DissemiNation," 310.

18. Thomas Richards ("Archive and Utopia," 119–20) describes the ethos of Creighton's world thus: "Though everything in the novel takes place 'under the sign of War' (p. 128), it is the sign of war that is not yet war, the sign of a permanent state of emergency, the sign of a state apparatus maintaining political equilibrium, the sign of what Virilio has called 'the passage from wartime to the war of peacetime.'"

19. Rudyard Kipling, "The Phantom Rickshaw," in *The Man Who Would Be King and Other Stories*, ed. Louis Cornell (Oxford and New York: Oxford University Press, 1987), 26.

20. I am indebted in a general way to Ronald Inden's *Imagining India* (Oxford, England, and Cambridge, Mass.: Basil Blackwell, 1990), which does for Indological studies (with its fixation on caste) what Said has done for knowledge about the Arab

world in *Orientalism*. Louis Dumont's *Homo Hierarchus: The Caste System and Its Implications*, trans. Mark Sainsbury and others (Chicago: University of Chicago Press, 1980 [1966]) is of course the principal twentieth-century Orientalist text in the figuration of caste as the key to knowing India.

21. Rudyard Kipling, *Kim*, ed. Edward Said (Harmondsworth: Penguin Books, 1987), 50. All subsequent references to the novel will be incorporated parenthetically into the text.

22. See Joseph Bristow's statement that "India remains, so to speak, a realm of *difference without difference*" (*Empire Boys: Adventures in a Man's World* [London: HarperCollins Academic, 1991], 202). For more on the classifying imagination of British colonialism, see Bernard S. Cohn, "The Census, Social Structure and Objectification in South Asia," in *An Anthropologist among the Historians and Other Essays* (Delhi: Oxford University Press, 1990), 224–54; and Arjun Appadurai, "Number in the Colonial Imagination," in *Orientalism and the Postcolonial Predicament: Perspectives on South Asia*, ed. Carol A. Breckenridge and Peter van der Veer (Philadelphia: University of Pennsylvania Press, 1993), 314–39.

23. Patrick Williams, "*Kim* and Orientalism," in *Kipling Reconsidered*, ed. Phillip Mallett (London: Macmillan, 1989).

24. Spivak, "Questions of Multi-culturalism," in *Post-Colonial Critic*, 66.

25. Gauri Viswanathan, *Masks of Conquest: Literary Study and British Rule in India* (New York: Columbia University Press, 1989).

26. Gayatri Chakravorty Spivak, "The Burden of English Studies," *The Lie of the Land: English Literary Studies in India*, ed. Rajeswari Sunder Rajan (Delhi: Oxford University Press, 1992), 276.

27. Edward W. Said, "Introduction," in *Kim*, 27.

28. Philip E. Wegner notes briefly that "Kipling does not deny the existence of an anti-imperial presence, but rather engages in a careful *negation* of it" ("'Life as He Would Have It': The Invention of India in Kipling's *Kim*," *Cultural Critique* 26 [Winter 1993–1994]: 140).

29. Brantlinger, *Rule of Darkness*, 199. On the Mutiny and its aftereffects, see Thomas R. Metcalf, *The Aftermath of Revolt: India 1857–1870* (Princeton, N.J.: Princeton University Press, 1964); Eric Stokes, *The Peasant Armed* (Delhi: Oxford University Press, 1986); Gautam Bhadra, "Four Rebels of Eighteen-Fifty-Seven," in *Subaltern Studies IV: Writings on South Asian History and Society*, ed. Ranajit Guha (Delhi: Oxford University Press, 1985), 229–75.

30. Jenny Sharpe, *Allegories of Empire: The Figure of Woman in the Colonial Text* (Minneapolis and London: University of Minnesota Press, 1993), 85. Sharpe provides an excellent account of the ways in which the narrative of the Mutiny directed its attention to the institution of the "English Lady."

31. The Subaltern Studies group has of course been pivotal for a reconsideration of colonial and bourgeois nationalist historiography, but the work of scholars not a part of this collective—scholars like Anand Yang, Bernard Cohn, Barbara Metcalf, Faisal Devji, Kamala Visveswaran, and Terence Ranger—has also been important in this endeavor.

32. For a nuanced and thorough account of the imperial theater in which Bengali masculinity was produced, see Mrinalini Sinha, *Colonial Masculinity: The "Manly*

Englishman" and the "Effeminate Bengali" in the Late Nineteenth Century (Manchester and New York: Manchester University Press, 1995). John Rosselli notes that "the Bengali elite . . . seems peculiar in its markedly physical sense of collective degradation. In the work of Iqbal and . . . other Indian writers . . . , the collective grievance was subjection, decline from a high estate, enslavement to western culture: though Iqbal was prepared to deride the brainy but physically flabby graduate there was no hint that entire Indian groups (Tamils, say, or Muslims) were constitutionally weak. . . . The one group that had to wrestle with a notion of its own constitutional weakness was the Bengali elite" ("The Self-Image of Effeteness: Physical Education and Nationalism in Nineteenth-Century Bengal," *Past and Present* 86 [February 1980]: 133–34). In this essay, he also provides a useful and succinct definition of the Bengali Hindu elite: "the land- and service-based groups which by the 1850s and 1860s were benefiting from English education and moving in increasing numbers into administrative and clerical posts, chiefly in government service, and into the legal profession" (p.121). On the Bengali Hindu elite (also known as *bhadralok*, respectable people) as a sociopolitical group, see John McGuire, *The Making of a Colonial Mind: A Quantitative Study of the Bhadralok in Calcutta, 1857–1885* (Canberra: Australian National University, 1983).

33. See MacMunn, *Religions and Hidden Cults of India*, for a fairly representative reading of terrorist activity as a product of combined religious and sexual pathologies.

34. Rudyard Kipling, "The Head of the District," in *Life's Handicap*, 120.

35. Ernest Renan, "What Is a Nation?" in *Nation and Narration*, 13.

36. Anderson's characterization of the nation as imagined community needs to be supplemented by Arjun Appadurai's caution in his "Patriotism and Its Futures," *Public Culture* 5 (Spring 1993): 414: "The modern nation-state, in this view, grows less out of natural facts—such as language, blood, soil, and race—but is a quintessential cultural product, a product of the collective imagination. . . . In many of these theories of the nation as imagined, there is always a suggestion that blood, kinship, race, and soil are somehow less imagined, more natural than the imagination of collective interest or solidarity."

37. Anderson, *Imagined Communities*, passim.

38. Bennington, "Postal Politics," 121.

39. For a useful elaboration of this idea, see Doris Sommer, *Foundational Fictions: The National Romances of Latin America* (Berkeley: University of California Press, 1991).

40. Tompkins, *Art of Rudyard Kipling*, 21.

41. The terms to mark this distinction—a common enough one—are borrowed from Ashcroft, Griffiths, and Tiffin, *Empire Writes Back*.

42. Angus Wilson, *The Strange Ride of Rudyard Kipling* (Harmondsworth: Penguin Books, 1979), 20–21.

43. Cited in ibid., 132.

44. R. C. Majumdar, H. C. Raychaudhuri, and Kalikinkar Dutta, *An Advanced History of India* (London and Delhi: Macmillan, 1967), 2: 823–32. We might recall that in the Sherlock Holmes stories, Dr. Watson's wound (acquired at the battle of Miani) is always painfully present.

45. Rudyard Kipling, "The City of Dreadful Night," in *From Sea to Sea: Letters of Travel* (New York: Charles Scribner's Sons, 1906 [1899]), 2: 287–363.

46. See Lewis Wurgraft, *The Imperial Imagination: Magic and Myth in Kipling's India* (Middletown, Conn.: Wesleyan University Press, 1983), for British psychic investment in the frontier and in the myth of the "Punjabi" as the architect of British greatness in India.

47. Bhabha, "DissemiNation," 305.

48. Anderson, *Imagined Communities*, 55–56.

49. This is the thrust of John McClure's argument in *Kipling and Conrad: The Colonial Fiction* (Cambridge, Mass.: Harvard University Press, 1981). I am indebted to this insight, though the trajectory of my argument is obviously different from McClure's.

50. A. Wilson, *Strange Ride*, 22. Ali Behdad uses the term *self-exoticization* to describe the situation of the Anglo-Indian: "The British colonizers spent long periods, sometimes their entire lives, in India, and so they often felt alienated from 'home' (and in that sense inclined to identify themselves as 'Indians') while simultaneously remaining alienated (as 'English') with respect to the Indians as 'natives'" (*Belated Travelers: Orientalism in the Age of Colonial Dissolution* [Durham, N.C., and London: Duke University Press, 1994], 77–78).

51. Sara Suleri astutely remarks about Kim's putative freedom that "[despite] his ostensible mobility and cultural dexterity, . . . Kim is an imperial casualty of more tragic proportions than he is usually granted. It is not as though Kim stands outside the colonial system called the Great Game and—as Edmund Wilson implies—has the luxury of choosing whether or not to play it: instead, Kim *is* the game, and finally is unable to separate it from the parameters of his own history. Kim's collaboration is therefore emblematic of not so much an absence of conflict as the terrifying absence of choice in the operations of colonialism" (*The Rhetoric of English India* [Chicago and London: University of Chicago Press, 1992], 116). Thomas Richards describes the use of the Great Game's agents in similar terms: "the state constitutes a kind of infra-individual implant detached from the active consciousness of its subjects yet, at the same time, an activating part of them" ("Archive and Utopia," 113).

52. B. J. Moore-Gilbert, *Kipling and "Orientalism"* (London and Sydney: Croom Helm, 1986), 5–6.

53. It is difficult, however, to sympathize with his fetishization of residence in India in "Introduction: Writing India, Reorienting Colonial Discourse Analysis," in *Writing India, 1757–1990: The Literature of British India*, ed. Bart Moore-Gilbert (Manchester and New York: Manchester University Press, 1996), 1–29; in this essay he insists that the fact of Indian residence placed Anglo-Indian writers outside the circuit of Orientalist racism.

54. It is striking to observe how many of the non-Indian figures most sympathetic to India and to Indian nationalist demands have been Irish. Radha Kumar mentions the Freedom for India and Ireland group in the United States in the early twentieth century, in *The History of Doing: An Illustrated Account of Movements for Women's Rights and Feminism in India, 1800–1990* (New Delhi: Kali for Women; London and New York: Verso, 1993), 66. See also V. G. Kiernan, *The Lords of Humankind* (London: Century Hutchinson, 1969). Abdul JanMohamed describes quite persua-

sively Kim's *"personal* and *emotional* allegiance to the Indians . . . and, on the other, his *impersonal* and *rational* relation to the Englishmen" ("The Economy of Manichean Allegory: The Function of Racial Difference in Colonialist Literature," in *"Race," Writing, and Difference*, ed. Henry Louis Gates [Chicago and London: University of Chicago Press, 1986], 99). I am not in disagreement with this reading of Kim's alignments, though I will point to the ways in which the emotional charge of the "Indian" relationships is not outside the calculus of the Great Game, which uses everything that is at hand.

55. Carrington, *Rudyard Kipling*, 34.

56. Prakash, "Science 'Gone Native,'" 154. Joseph Bristow also remarks that the "slippage between his 'Englishness' and 'Irishness' indicates how Kim variously represents white superiority *and* white subordination" (*Empire Boys*, 198). Finally, see Christopher Lane: "If the meaning of race is disputable in *Kim*, the text also designates a split between racial identity and political identification that leads it into potential crisis even as it insists that each is finally commensurate" (*The Ruling Passion: British Colonial Allegory and the Paradox of Homosexual Desire* [Durham, N.C., and London: Duke University Press, 1995], 42).

57. Jonathan Goldberg, "Bradford's 'Ancient Members' and 'A Case of Buggery . . . amongst Them,'" in *Nationalisms & Sexualities*, ed. Andrew Parker et al. (New York and London: Routledge, 1992), 63.

58. Said, "Introduction," 12.

59. Ashis Nandy speaks of "the mythography of India as a powerful mother" in *The Intimate Enemy: Loss and Recovery of Self under Colonialism* (Delhi: Oxford University Press, 1983), 92. For more on this subject, see chapters 4–6.

60. Many readers have seen him, not surprisingly, as a "feminized" figure.

61. My thanks to Sandhya Shetty for suggesting this to me.

62. Williams ("*Kim* and Orientalism," 45–49) speaks of their absence as

function[ing] as a potential escape clause by allowing, within the terms of the text, the unspoken displacement of the condemnation of women from women in general to Indian women in particular, since the latter are the only ones we see. . . . Racial superiority was, by the end of the century, one of the few remaining justifications for British rule, and the perceived threat from uncontrolled female sexuality (here rendered as uncontrolled *Indian* female sexuality, the truth [of white women's desire for Indian males] being literally unspeakable), was a grave one indeed."

4. AS THE MASTER SAW HER

1. If it seems at several times in my paper that Indianness and Hinduness are being conflated, this is because they usually functioned as a single term for Vivekananda, Nivedita, and other Hindu revivalists of this period. At the present time, the Hindu revivalist Bharatiya Janata Party continually inscribes national geography as sacred geography. For an astute and historically rigorous critique of Hindutva's production of an ancient, singular and recognizable Hinduism, see Romila Thapar, "Imagined Religious Communities? Ancient History and the Modern Search for a Hindu Identity," *Modern Asian Studies* 23, no. 2 (1989): 209–31. I do not, of course, wish to assert the sameness of Vivekananda's Hindu revivalism and the anti-Muslim

bigotry of today's Hindu fundamentalists. Vivekananda's address was not so much to a South Asian Islam as it was to a "west"; in this he was markedly unlike figures such as the nineteenth-century Bengali novelist Bankim, who frequently invoked the Muslim as the enemy. And while his speeches and writings do contain some conventionally anti-Muslim material (when he speaks of Islam or of Muslims at all), they also, sometimes simultaneously, conceive of Muslim Indians as contributing something worthwhile (physical strength, for one thing) to an imagined community. I am therefore in partial agreement with the assertion of Tapan Basu, Pradip Datta, Sumit Sarkar, Tanika Sarkar, and Sambuddha Sen that the swami is not as easily appropriable for contemporary Hindu fundamentalism as the proponents of Hindutva would like to believe, though I also believe that he inaugurates the terms of a discourse that has persisted (with transformations) into the present day. It does seem to me that their claim that the swami would never (unlike contemporary religious rightists) have defended retrograde practices in the name of Hindu nationalism is altogether too generous. See Tapan Basu et al., *Khaki Shorts and Saffron Flags: A Critique of the Hindu Right* (New Delhi: Orient Longman, 1993), 6–8.

2. "M's" (Mahendranath Gupta's) *Sri Ramakrishna Kathamrita*, published in several volumes at the turn of the century, is a highly unusual diary of one disciple's encounters with his guru and with other disciples over the last four years (1882–1886) of Ramakrishna's life. In this text, which is written in Bengali, Ramakrishna is referred to as *thakur*, which is both a common way of designating a Brahman as well as a word meaning god; "M," who was a schoolteacher, is called "master" in this work. In the English translation of 1942 by Swami Nikhilananda, *The Gospel of Sri Ramakrishna* (New York: Ramakrishna-Vivekananda Center, 1973 [1942]), "the Master" is the standard appellation for Ramakrishna; this usage may have been popularized by Vivekananda.

3. Partha Chatterjee, "A Religion of Urban Domesticity: Sri Ramakrishna and the Calcutta Middle Class," *Subaltern Studies VII: Writings on South Asian History and Society*, ed. Partha Chatterjee and Gyanendra Pandey (Delhi: Oxford University Press, 1992), 65.

4. Tapan Raychaudhuri, *Europe Reconsidered: Perceptions of the West in Nineteenth Century Bengal* (Delhi: Oxford University Press, 1988), 219.

5. Quoted in ibid., 231. For further details, see Swami Saradananda, *Sri Ramakrishna: The Great Master*, trans. Swami Jagadananda, 2 vols. (Madras: Sri Ramakrishna Math, 1978 [1952]).

6. There were many references to the Paramhansa in Keshab's journal, the *New Dispensation*, and in the late 1870s Keshab published *Paramhanser Ukti*, a ten-page Bengali booklet of Ramakrishna's sayings.

7. Christopher Isherwood, *Ramakrishna and His Disciples* (London: Methuen, 1965), 141.

8. Quoted in ibid., 124.

9. Cited in Brian K. Smith, "How Not to Be a Hindu: The Case of the Ramakrishna Mission," in *Religion and Law in Independent India*, ed. Robert P. Baird (New Delhi: Manohar, 1993), 343–44.

10. Sumit Sarkar, "The Kathamrita as Text: Towards an Understanding of Ramakrishna Paramhamsa," Occasional Paper 22 (New Delhi: Nehru Memorial Museum and Library, 1985), 21 and passim. Also, see Sumit Sarkar, "'Kaliyuga,' 'Chakri' and

'Bhakti': Ramakrishna and His Times," *Economic and Political Weekly*, 18 July 1992, 1543–66. Ramakrishna's disciples claimed that he had gone through his "Muslim" and "Christian" phases before he met Keshab; please note that all the dates in Ramakrishna's life are culled from accounts by devotees and admirers.

11. The term *heterosexuality* is here used catachrestically, since Ramakrishna seems to be obviously outside the formations within which we would situate "modern" Indian subjects, including Vivekananda. The very terms *homosexuality/ heterosexuality* (and, indeed, *transsexuality*, which may also be said to resonate for Ramakrishna) are too western and modern to be completely adequate to the task of analysis. I use them very provisionally, in the absence of another vocabulary and epistemology that might enable me to understand premodern, Indian/Hindu conceptualizations of sexuality. In this context, I am reminded of Diana Fuss's generous and sensitive reading of Fanon's claim (in *Black Skin, White Masks*) that there is no (male) homosexuality in the Antilles ("Interior Colonies," 33):

> Fanon's insistence that there is no homosexuality in the Antilles may convey a more trenchant meaning than the one he in fact intended: if by 'homosexuality' one understands the culturally specific social formations of same-sex desire as they are articulated in the West, then they are indeed foreign to the Antilles. . . . Can one generalize from the particular forms sexuality takes under Western capitalism to sexuality *as such?* What kinds of colonizations do such discursive translations perform on 'other' traditions of sexual differences?

Such a caution must be borne in mind, even as one cannot but deploy, however hesitantly, the idioms of modern western sexualities. See Jeffrey Kripal, *Kali's Child: The Mystical and the Erotic in the Life and Teachings of Ramakrishna* (Chicago and London: University of Chicago Press, 1995) for a careful and fascinating reading of the relationship of Ramakrishna's "homosexuality" to his mysticism. I regret that I have not been able to make fuller use of the Kripal text, which was published after this chapter was written.

12. Chatterjee, "Religion of Urban Domesticity, 60–61.

13. S. Sarkar, "Kathamrita as Text," 50–71.

14. Chatterjee, "Religion of Urban Domesticity, 45. Sumit Sarkar claims, moreover, that the period of Ramakrishna's popularity coincided with a "kind of hiatus in bhadralok history," when dreams of social reform had been frustrated, official racism was marked, and liberation through the overthrow of British rule not really conceivable ("'Kaliyuga,' 'Chakri' and 'Bhakti,'" 1547).

15. It is interesting to note that the disciples of Ramakrishna, notably Vivekananda, preferred the term *kamkanchan*, "lust-and-gold," over the Master's *kaminikanchan* and went to great lengths to explain that the sage's "symbolic" use of the term did not imply any misogyny.

16. Nikhilananda, *Gospel of Sri Ramakrishna*, 701. All subsequent references will be incorporated parenthetically into the text.

17. This insight derives in a general way from Carole-Anne Tyler's reading of the ambivalent politics of gay drag ("Boys Will Be Girls: The Politics of Gay Drag," in *Inside/Out: Lesbian Theories, Gay Theories*, ed. Diana Fuss [New York: Routledge, 1990]) as well from Kaja Silverman's account of the mastery permitted by T. E. Lawrence's reflexive masochism ("White Skin, Brown Masks"). In *The Inner World: A Psychoanalytic Study of Childhood and Society in India* (Delhi: Oxford University Press,

1978), 103, Sudhir Kakar characterizes Hindu transvestism thus: "Rituals such as these represent not only the boy's attempt to identify with his mother but also the man's effort to free himself from her domination. By trying to be like women—wearing their clothes, acquiring their organs, giving birth—these men are also saying that they do not need women (mothers) any longer." For a sympathetic psychoanalytic reading of Ramakrishna's assumption of femininity, see Kakar, "Ramakrishna and the Mystical Experience," in *The Analyst and the Mystic: Psychoanalytic Reflections on Religion and Mysticism* (New Delhi: Viking, 1991), 1–40.

18. Cited in S. Sarkar, "Kathamrita as Text," 9.

19. D. S. Sarma, *Studies in the Renaissance of Hinduism in the Nineteenth and Twentieth Centuries* (Benares: Benares Hindu University, 1944), 237.

20. I am grateful to Gayatri Spivak for pointing out to me the numerous, and *discontinuous*, ways in which the English term *woman* translates into Bengali (and/or Sanskrit). Even so, it is interesting to note how often other forms of femininity threaten for Ramakrishna to collapse into the figure of the *kamini*. Hence his warning to one of his young male disciples to beware of women who claim to be actuated by maternal feelings towards him.

21. Isherwood, *Ramakrishna and His Disciples*, 113.

22. I put this term in quotation marks to indicate that is placed under erasure. One cannot assume that transvestism was inflected in the same way for a nineteenth-century (straight?) Hindu male as it might be for, say, a contemporary straight North American male. One has to concede that his masculinity might have been constituted differently, and in a different relationship to femininity, than might be the case for our hypothetical North American male.

23. I am thinking here of N. T. Rama Rao's assumption of feminine attire, makeup, and jewelry, on one-half of his body in the days of his chief ministership of Andhra Pradesh, apparently in a bid to consolidate his political/spiritual power. Philip Spratt also provides detailed anthropological evidence of religious transvestic ceremonies all over India (*Hindu Culture and Personality* [Bombay: Manaktalas, 1966]). See, too, Kathryn Hansen's splendid essay, "Making Women Visible: Female Impersonators and Actresses on the Parsi Stage and in Silent Cinema" (unpublished manuscript).

24. Ashis Nandy, *At the Edge of Psychology: Essays in Politics and Culture* (Delhi: Oxford University Press, 1990), 38.

25. Wendy Doniger, *Women, Androgynes, and Other Mythical Beasts* (Chicago and London: University of Chicago Press, 1980), 319.

26. Ibid., 331.

27. Women could, on occasion, function as gurus; the Bhairavi Brahmani, for instance, was Ramakrishna's first guru. Other historical and contemporary figures like Andal, Mahadeviakka, Mirabai, and Anandamoyi Ma come to mind as well. Sharada Devi (Ramakrishna's wife) herself had several (female and male) disciples. I do not think, however, that this militates against my understanding of the guru-disciple relationship as functioning for the most part for and among males nor against my reading of its gendered significance in early nationalism.

28. I am obliged to Sandhya Shetty for pointing this out to me. The *gurudakshina* (the gift to the guru) is situated outside (economic) exchange and functions in a

symbolic capacity only. The instance of Drona the archer and his low-caste disciple Eklavya, who had to sacrifice his thumb to ensure the superiority of the guru's favorite pupil Arjuna, only demonstrates that in the guru-*shishya* configuration what is offered by the disciple is incommensurable with what is given by the guru.

29. *Life of Sri Ramakrishna, Compiled from Various Authentic Sources* (Calcutta: Advaita Ashrama, 1964), 296.

30. Swami Vivekananda. *Vivekananda: The Yogas and Other Works*, ed. Swami Nikhilananda (New York: Ramakrishna-Vivekananda Center, 1953), 13.

31. There is no "secular," critical biography of Ramakrishna except that by Max Mueller, *Ramakrishna: His Life and Sayings* (New York: Charles Scribner's Sons, 1899). While this inveighs against the miraculizing tendencies of Ramakrishna's disciples, not excepting Vivekananda, and refuses to take Ramakrishna's avatarhood seriously, it is nonetheless entirely reverential about the man himself.

32. *Life of Sri Ramakrishna*, 117.

33. Ibid., 144–45.

34. Ibid., 294.

35. Swami Chetanananda, ed. *Ramakrishna as We Saw Him* (St. Louis, Mo.: Vedanta Society of St. Louis, 1990), 110.

36. Sumit Sarkar notes: "Girish Ghosh confessed that seeing Ramakrishna 'playing' with a young disciple made him recall a 'terrible canard' that he had once heard about the saint" ("Kathamrita as Text," 103).

37. Sister Nivedita [Margaret E. Noble], *The Master as I Saw Him* (Calcutta: Udbodhan Office, 1910), 64.

38. Isherwood, *Ramakrishna and His Disciples*, 204.

39. This is not, of course, to assert that the conflicts were unique to Naren; as we have seen, in terms of class position and intellectual training he appears to have been no different from the majority of the disciples. The others, however, appear to have been less outspoken in their skepticism than he was. I hardly need add that the memory and the narrative of these conflicts is overdetermined; if Naren had not become Vivekananda, we would probably have heard far less of his interactions with his guru. As it is, in *The Gospel of Sri Ramakrishna* his iconoclasticism is not as evident as that of, say, Bankim or Dr. Mahendralal Sarkar (neither of whom was a disciple). Nonetheless, he does seem to have been the unequivocal favorite of Ramakrishna. And it also seems clear that he was accorded a degree of freedom of speech and behavior not permitted most of the other disciples. (Girish Ghosh, who was notorious for his drinking, patronage of prostitutes, and occasional foul-mouthed invectives against the guru, was one of the very few others who was granted such a license.)

40. Chatterjee, "Religion of Urban Domesticity." Sumit Sarkar emphasizes the saint's determined pursuit of *bhadralok* disciples as well as his reticence about religious practices (of the Baul, Kartabhaja, and *vamachari* Tantric varieties) that might have offended their sensibilities ("The Kathamrita as Text," 36).

41. Chetanananda, *Ramakrishna as We Saw Him*, 385–90.

42. My thanks to Inderpal Grewal for suggesting this possibility to me.

43. Hervey De Witt Griswold, *Insights into Modern Hinduism* (New York: Henry Holt, 1934), 58.

44. Nationalism's dependence on colonialism has been extensively documented,

to some degree by Nandy, *Intimate Enemy*, but most notably by Chatterjee, *Nationalist Thought*. Certainly nationalism-and-colonialism seems to function as one category for Vivekananda.

45. Not all Brahmos were as skeptical as Shibnath Shastri, who, much though he admired Ramakrishna, believed that the saint's austerities at the beginning of his spiritual career had had deleterious effects on his mental state; Keshab for one seems to have been less incredulous of the spiritual nature of the saint's trances. Sumit Sarkar points out, interestingly, that while Ramakrishna's family and neighbors in Kamarpukur and Dakshineshwar attributed the trances to madness or "possession," his *bhadralok* disciples and admirers described them as the *samadhi* state extolled by high Hindu doctrine.

46. Ramakrishna himself made conflicting assertions about his own avatarhood; at points he dismissed the possibility derisively, while at other times he claimed to be an avatar of Krishna, Chaitanya, and/or Kali.

47. Swami Nikhilananda, *Vivekananda: A Biography* (New York: Ramakrishna-Vivekananda Center, 1953), 42.

48. It is not possible to establish whether any of the swami's supporters were simply admirers or actually disciples. It is not inconceivable that they may have become disciples retroactively, following Vivekananda's success in the west.

49. Sankari Prasad Basu and Sunil Bihari Ghosh, eds., *Vivekananda in Indian Newspapers 1893–1902* (Calcutta: Dineshchandra Basu Bhattacharya, 1969), 9.

50. It should be noted that the swami's Indian reputation was—to some degree, at least—induced by himself, as a defensive measure no doubt against the criticisms he encountered not only from Christian ministers in the United States but also from members of the Brahmo Samaj and perhaps the Theosophical Society as well. His early letters to his disciples in Madras were full of exhortations to them to hold a meeting in his honor and to proclaim him to the west as a true spokesperson of Hinduism. He was also careful to keep them informed about favorable reviews in the U.S. press.

51. Rakhal Chandra Nath, *The New Hindu Movement 1886–1911* (Calcutta: Minerva, 1982), 126.

52. Ibid., 129.

53. Chatterjee, "Religion of Urban Domesticity."

54. Nath, *New Hindu Movement*, 115.

55. Vivekananda was rarely consistent in this view; this was typical of him. At times he deployed the rhetoric of free trade to imply mutual and equal advantage to east and west; at other times he insisted that Indians were superior to the west in their indifference to material things and that in fact the west called out for spiritual conquest by an "aggressive Hinduism." In this vacillation Vivekananda was not untypical of the bourgeois neo-Hindu nationalists of his time.

56. He also enjoined his brother monks in India not to insist on the acceptance of Ramakrishna's avatarhood in would-be devotees and disciples of the new order.

57. Harold W. French, *The Swan's Wide Waters: Ramakrishna and Western Culture* (Port Washington, N.Y.: Kennikat Press, 1974), 58.

58. Raychaudhuri, *Europe Reconsidered*, 230.

59. Chatterjee, "Religion of Urban Domesticity."

60. Nath, *New Hindu Movement*, 114.

61. Ibid., 17. Note that Bankim's novel was undoubtedly the product of a distinctly westward-looking nationalism. Nath describes Aurobindo's "Bhawani Mandir" as derived from *Anandmath* (and remarkably similar to Vivekananda's own cult of the warlike monk) in its emphasis on manliness and in its devotion to Kali.

62. Chatterjee, "Religion of Urban Domesticity," 61.

63. Vivekananda, *Vivekananda: The Yogas and Other Works*, 151.

64. The Rashtriya Swayamsevak Sangh's cult of physical fitness and martial arts training has a great deal in common with Vivekananda's endorsement of "beef, biceps, and Bhagavad-Gita."

65. *Reminiscences of Swami Vivekananda, by His Eastern and Western Admirers* (Calcutta: Advaita Ashrama, 1964 [1961]), 347.

66. At this point in Indian history, bourgeois and Hindu nationalisms—the first represented by "moderates" in the Congress Party calling for secular and constitutional reforms, the latter by Tilak, Bankim, and others—have assumed the status of two distinct categories, though quite often they function as one. I bear in mind also Sudipta Kaviraj's important caveat against the conflation of distinct nationalisms (his own concern is with "early" and "mature" nationalisms), which must be seen as disjunct rather than articulated phenomena in Indian history; see Sudipta Kaviraj, "The Imaginary Institution of India," in *Subaltern Studies VII: Writings on South Asian History and Society*, ed. Partha Chatterjee and Gyanendra Pandey (New Delhi: Oxford University Press, 1991).

67. Basu and Ghosh, *Vivekananda in Indian Newspapers*, 27.

68. Nivedita, *The Master as I Saw Him*, 231.

69. Ibid., 388 (emphases in the original).

70. *Reminiscences of Swami Vivekananda*, 252. The speaker in this instance was a woman, Constance Towne.

71. Marie Louise Burke, *Swami Vivekananda in America: New Discoveries* (Calcutta: Advaita Ashrama, 1958), 16.

72. *Reminiscences of Swami Vivekananda*, 14.

73. *Swami Vivekananda and His Guru* (London and Madras: Christian Literature Society for India, 1897), iv.

74. There is, to the uninstructed viewer, little if anything of the disarrangement of limbs or clothing that normally marked the sage's experience of *samadhi*.

75. Gayatri Chakravorty Spivak, "A Literary Representation of the Subaltern," in *In Other Worlds* (London and New York: Routledge, 1987), 264.

76. Nivedita functions here as a type of the western female disciple.

77. Mary Ann Doane, "Dark Continents: Epistemologies of Racial and Sexual Difference in Psychoanalysis and the Cinema," in *Femmes Fatales: Feminism, Film Theory, Psychoanalysis* (New York and London: Routledge, 1991), 244.

78. Marie Louise Burke, *Swami Vivekananda: His Second Visit to the West; New Discoveries* (Calcutta: Advaita Ashram, 1973).

79. Kakar, *Inner World*, 160.

80. See, for instance, Romila Thapar: "[The ascetic] is celibate and yet, at the same time, the most virile of men. The ascetic's demonstration of sexual prowess is not a contradiction in terms: it is in fact a demonstration of his complete control

over body functions, since ideally the emission of semen is prohibited to him" ("Renunciation: The Making of a Counter-Culture?" in *Ancient Indian Social History: Some Interpretations* [Delhi: n.p., 1978], 94). Also see Joseph Alter: "The whole purpose of *brahmacharya* [celibacy] is to build up a resilient store of semen so that the body—in a holistic, psychosomatic sense—radiates an aura of vitality and strength" ("Celibacy, Sexuality, and the Transformation of Gender into Nationalism in North India," *Journal of Asian Studies* 53, no. 1 [1994]: 51).

81. Steve Neale, "Masculinity as Spectacle," in *The Sexual Subject: A* Screen *Reader in Sexuality* (London and New York: Routledge, 1992), 277–87.

82. Ibid., 286.

83. Swami Vivekananda, "The Future of India," in *Lectures from Colombo to Almora* (Calcutta: Advaita Ashrama, 1956), 267.

84. *Reminiscences of Swami Vivekananda*, 196. Sister Christine (Christine Greenstidel) goes on to remark on the companionship of Sadananda and Vivekananda on their North Indian pilgrimage: "Both were artistic, both were poets by nature, both were attractive in appearance. Artists raved about them."

Nivedita also confesses, though far more discreetly, that she was drawn to the swami by his "personality" rather his philosophy, which she initially found unoriginal. Her "biography" of him, *The Master as I Saw Him*, is remarkable for its reticence about his corporeality.

85. That such a construction of femininity was not necessarily exclusive to Hindu reformers/revivalists is borne out by Faisal Fatehali Devji: "[Muslim] reformist literature replaces the aggressive sexual woman with the pathetic or suffering woman-as-mother" ("Gender and the Politics of Space: The Movement for Women's Reform in Muslim India, 1857–1900," *South Asia*, 14, no. 1 [1991], 151).

86. Partha Chatterjee, "The Nationalist Resolution of the Women's Question," in *Recasting Women: Essays in Indian Colonial History*, ed. Kumkum Sangari and Sudesh Vaid (New Brunswick, N.J.: Rutgers University Press, 1990), 237.

87. Sister Nivedita, *The Web of Indian Life* (London: William Heinemann, 1904), 32–45.

88. See, among others, Lata Mani, "Contentious Traditions: The Debate on *Sati* in Colonial India," in *The Nature and Context of Minority Discourse*, ed. Abdul JanMohamed and David Lloyd (Oxford and New York: Oxford University Press, 1990); Kumkum Sangari and Sudesh Vaid, eds., *Recasting Women: Essays in Indian Colonial History* (New Brunswick, N.J.: Rutgers University Press, 1990); Chatterjee, *Nation and Its Fragments;* and Madhu Kishwar, "Gandhi on Women," *Economic and Political Weekly*, 5 October 1985, 1691–1702.

89. Monier Monier-Williams, *Religious Thought and Life in India* (New Delhi: Oriental Books Reprint Corporation, 1974 [1883]), 184–85. Also see David R. Kinsley, "Kali: Blood and Death Out of Place," in *Devi: Goddesses of India*, ed. John S. Hawley and Donna M. Wulff (Berkeley and London: University of California Press, 1996); and Ajit Mookerjee, *Kali: The Feminine Force* (New York: Destiny Books, 1988).

90. Sumanta Banerjee, "Marginalization of Women's Popular Culture in Nineteenth Century Bengal," in *Recasting Women: Essays in Indian Colonial History*, ed. Kumkum Sangari and Sudesh Vaid (New Brunswick, N.J.: Rutgers University Press, 1990), 158.

91. Ramakrishna was married at the age of twenty-three to Sharadamoni Debi, a child-bride of five. According to custom, she remained in her natal home, while Ramakrishna continued his spiritual disciplines at Dakshineshwar, forgetful of her existence. At eighteen she sought him out at Dakshineshwar and acceded to his request that their marriage remain unconsummated. Over the remaining decade and a half of Ramakrishna's life, she spent extended periods at Dakshineshwar, doing his housekeeping and cooking and (usually) living in a separate building in the temple complex.

92. Nivedita, *The Master as I Saw Him*, 65.

93. Gayatri Chakravorty Spivak, "A Literary Representation of the Subaltern," in *In Other Worlds: Essays in Cultural Politics* (New York and London: Routledge, 1987), 244.

94. Nivedita, *The Master as I Saw Him*, 83.

95. Raychaudhuri, *Europe Reconsidered*, 242.

96. Swami Vivekananda, *Letters of Swami Vivekananda* (Calcutta: Advaita Ashrama, 1964), 167–68.

97. Pandita Ramabai Saraswati (1858–1922) was a notable scholar and a Hindu widow who converted to Christianity during a visit to England and dedicated her life to the uplift of young Hindu widows. Her book, *The High-Caste Hindu Woman* (London: George Bell and Sons, 1888), as well as her travels in England and the United States, gained her sympathy from feminists as well as Christian missionaries abroad and censure from Hindu conservatives at home. Her shelter for widows, the Sharda Sadan in Pune, was supported in large part by funds raised by Ramabai Circles in the United States and England. Her travels in the United States in the 1880s received extensive coverage in the U.S. press.

98. Basu and Ghosh, *Vivekananda in Indian Newspapers*, 421–68.

99. This is necessarily a simplification of Vivekananda's very complicated responses to the issues of (gender and other) reform, nationalism, and colonialism. The split was not simply between "home" (where reform had to endorsed) and abroad (where Hinduism had to be defended); even at "home" he had decidedly mixed responses to reform and (religious and social) orthodoxy.

100. The phrase is Nivedita's (*The Master as I Saw Him*, 124). In an interesting departure from the hagiographical tradition in which accounts of Ramakrishna and Vivekananda are produced (and in which tradition Nivedita's own work uneasily belongs), she emphasizes not the continuity of their respective "gospels" but their distinctness from each other. She does this, besides, in a fashion that highlights the swami's struggles and doubts: "Sri Ramakrishna had been, as the Swami himself said once of him, 'like a flower,' living apart in the garden of a temple, simple, half-naked, orthodox, the ideal of the old time in India, suddenly burst into bloom, in a world that had thought to dismiss its very memory. It was at one the greatness and the tragedy of my own Master's life that he was not of this type. His was the modern mind in its completeness. . . . His hope could not pass by unheeded, . . . the hope of men of the nineteenth century" (*The Master as I Saw Him*, 124–25).

101. Chatterjee, "Nationalist Resolution," 237–38.

102. She was not, however, recognizably a nineteenth-century British feminist—at least from the evidence of her early writings—even though much has been made

in the biographies of her feminism and other "excesses." Apparently Vivekananda himself made fun of her putative feminism.

103. Quoted in Barbara Foxe, *Long Journey Home: A Biography of Margaret Noble (Nivedita)* (London: Rider, 1975), 32–33.

104. Quoted in Vron Ware, *Beyond the Pale: White Women, Racism and History* (London and New York: Verso, 1992), 121.

105. Sharada Devi seems to have been a figure who was not unequivocally reverenced by the followers of Ramakrishna. Many devotees visited her at Jayrambati and Kamarpukur, and she initiated several people into discipleship. She was sometimes spoken of as an avatar—like her husband—and the heiress to his spiritual kingdom. But she was also often accused of being excessively worldly. Ramakrishna's most prominent disciples visited her only rarely; Swami Nikhilananda says that this was because they hesitated to "[make] a display of their spiritual fervour." See his *Holy Mother: Being the Life of Sri Sarada Devi, Wife of Sri Ramakrishna and Helpmate in His Mission* (London: George Allen & Unwin, 1962). Spivak speaks of the way in which her official biographer, Swami Gambhirananda, staged her as "a counterecho to what he perceived as the strong voice of the Western Narcissus" ("Asked to Talk about Myself . . . ," *Third Text* 19 [Summer 1992]: 17). I would argue that this could only happen retrospectively, and at a later moment from the one that Vivekananda inhabits.

106. See, for instance, Meredith Borthwick, *The Changing Role of Women in Bengal, 1849–1905* (Princeton, N.J.: Princeton University Press, 1984), esp. chaps. 8 and 9; Ghulam Murshid, *Reluctant Debutante: Response of Bengali Women to Modernization, 1849–1905* (Rajshashi, Bangladesh: Sahitya Samsad, 1983); and Kumar, *History of Doing*, esp. chaps. 2 and 3.

107. The Indian woman was, obviously, recast in the nationalist moment—as was the Indian man; but recast and *fixed*, with little room for negotiation after the recasting had been effected. For an analysis of a nationalist woman's struggles with gendered identities in nationalism, see chapter 5.

108. Romain Rolland, *The Life of Vivekananda and the Universal Gospel*, trans. E. F. Malcolm-Smith (Mayavati, India: Advaita Ashrama, 1947), 152, n. 2.

109. Nivedita, *The Master as I Saw Him*, 136–37.

110. Quoted in Pravrajika Atmaprana, *Sister Nivedita of Ramakrishna-Vivekananda* (Calcutta: Sister Nivedita Girls' School, 1961), 30.

111. Foxe, *Long Journey Home*, 128.

112. Rakhal Nath maintains that the Ramakrishna Mission was the only *nonpolitical* body to come out of the "New Hindu" or Hindu revivalist movement (Nath, *New Hindu Movement*).

113. Foxe, *Long Journey Home*, 136.

114. Ibid., 150–51.

115. Barbara N. Ramusack, "Cultural Missionaries, Maternal Imperialists, Feminist Allies: British Women Activists in India, 1865–1945," in *Western Women and Imperialism: Complicity and Resistance*, ed. Nupur Chaudhuri and Margaret Strobel (Bloomington and Indianapolis: Indiana University Press, 1992), 130.

116. S. B. Mookherjee, "Nivedita and Indian Womanhood," in *Nivedita Commemoration Volume*, ed. Amiya Kumar Majumdar (Calcutta: Dhiraj Basu, 1968), 244.

117. She met Gandhi briefly in Calcutta, in the early years of the century. Gandhi (who in so many ways would grow to resemble the figure of Ramakrishna) admired her Hindu partisanship but was unable to agree with her on nationalist politics. The Congress Party under Gandhi had a profoundly uneasy relationship with militant nationalist women like Nivedita and the Rani of Jhansi.

118. Lizelle Reymond's *The Dedicated: A Biography of Nivedita* (New York: John Day, 1953) also helped disseminate this image, though its factual claims have since been contested. Kumari Jayawardena's chapter on Nivedita ("Irish Rebellion and 'Muscular Hinduism,'" in *White Woman's Other Burden*) describes the contradictory ways in which the disciple of Vivekananda is remembered.

119. My thanks to Carole-Anne Tyler for sensitizing me to this possibility.

120. Foxe's biography, *Long Journey Home*, is particularly derisive in this regard. What had been admirable "manliness" in Vivekananda was forwardness in the female disciple.

121. Ibid., 205.

5. BECOMING WOMEN

1. In Fanon, *Black Skin, White Masks*, the black woman whitens herself through the sole medium of sexual association with a white man. A black man, on the other hand, while seeking whiteness in the sexual embrace of a white woman, is also capable of other kinds of access—primarily education and the self-culture it makes possible—to whiteness. In "Algeria Unveiled" (in *A Dying Colonialism* [New York: Grove Weidenfeld, 1961]) the Algerian woman revolutionary who puts on European garb in order to outwit the guardians of the colonial state is emphatically no mimic—not even a canny and calculating one—of European femininity but a subject who acts with complete spontaneity.

2. Banerjee, "Women's Popular Culture." See also Sumanta Banerjee, *The Parlour and the Street* (Calcutta: Seagull Press, 1985).

3. Chatterjee, "Nationalist Resolution of the Woman Question." Note, for instance, how intimately the male nationalist gendered segregation of the home and the world is articulated with Ruskin's division, in the notorious "Of Queens' Gardens" section of *Sesame and Lilies* (London: Smith, Elder, 1865) of the Victorian universe into that of "masculine activity" and "sweet ordering." Dipesh Chakrabarty's recent argument about the *bhadramahila* as an emblem of the *difference* of Indian modernity does not, despite its considerable cogency, take into account the gendered provenance of bourgeois identity at its point of origin in Europe; the European bourgeois woman was never constituted as identical to her male European counterpart. See his "The Difference-Deferral of a Colonial Modernity: Public Debates on Domesticity in British India," in *Subaltern Studies VIII: Writings on South Asian History and Society*, ed. David Arnold and David Hardiman (Delhi: Oxford University Press, 1994).

4. Mrinalini Sinha, "Reading *Mother India*: Empire, Nation, and the Female Voice," *Journal of Women's History* 6, no. 2 (1994): 34.

5. Chatterjee, *Nation and Its Fragments*, 116–57.

6. See, for instance, Gayatri Chakravorty Spivak, "Bonding in Difference [an in-

terview with Alfred Arteaga]," in *An Other Tongue: Nation and Ethnicity in the Linguistic Borderlands*, ed. Alfred Arteaga (Durham, N.C.: Duke University Press, 1994).

7. Karen Leonard, "Aspects of the Nationalist Movement in the Princely States of Hyderabad," *Quarterly Review of Historical Studies* 21, no. 2–3 (1981–1982): 3–9.

8. Arthur Symons, "Introduction," in *The Golden Threshold*, by Sarojini Naidu (London: William Heinemann, 1909), 11.

9. Meena Alexander, "Sarojini Naidu: Romanticism and Resistance," *Economic and Political Weekly*, 26 October 1985, 69.

10. Assia Djebar, *Fantasia: An Algerian Cavalcade*, trans. Dorothy Blair (London: Quartet Books, 1985).

11. We are told that she knew English well enough to correspond with English friends; see Tara Ali Baig, *Sarojini Naidu* (New Delhi: Ministry of Information and Broadcasting, 1974).

12. Symons, "Introduction," 11–12.

13. The gifted Toru Dutt, the daughter of Bengali Christian converts, was educated partially in Europe and England and produced a fairly considerable body of English verse before dying at the age of twenty-one.

14. Edmund Gosse, "Introduction," in *The Bird of Time*, by Sarojini Naidu (London: William Heinemann, 1912), 3.

15. Ibid., 4.

16. Ibid., 5.

17. Ibid., 2.

18. Ibid., 6.

19. See, for instance, one of her better-known letters to him: "I am sending for your severest criticism five little poems I wrote last week. . . . The little *Henna Song* pleases me very much—*Henna* is a national and immemorial institution and it is customary for all girls and married women to stain their palm and finger nails and feet with bright red juice of henna leaves. It symbolises gladness and festivity" (Baig, *Sarojini Naidu*, 22).

20. Spivak, "Bonding in Difference," 276. Also see her gloss on the *pharmakon* in "Reading *The Satanic Verses*," in *Outside in the Teaching Machine* (New York and London: Routledge, 1993).

21. Among the serious critical considerations of her poetry that were published in her lifetime were James H. Cousins, *The Renaissance in India* (Madras: Ganesh, 1930), in which he praised her poetry generously and perceptively but also castigated her for valorizing the submissiveness of Indian women.

22. P. E. Dustoor, *Sarojini Naidu* (Mysore: Rao and Raghavan, 1961).

23. Nissim Ezekiel, "On Sarojini Naidu," *Sunday Standard*, 11 February 1962, 12. See, too, Ezekiel's comments quoted in Sisirkumar Ghose, "Salaam for Sarojini: Towards a Revaluation," in *Perspectives on Sarojini Naidu*, ed. K. K. Sharma (Ghaziabad, India: Vimal Prakashan, 1989), 210: "Sarojini knew nothing of the literary revolution taking place in English poetry in the twenties and after."

24. Alexander, "Sarojini Naidu," 68.

25. Chatterjee, *Nation and Its Fragments*, 75.

26. Ibid.,130. It is this successful deployment of the symbolic domain that has guaranteed the longevity of nationalism. For an able analysis of the ways in which

Hindu nationalism at the current conjuncture mobilizes some of the idioms of female liberation while holding on to patriarchal privileges, see Tanika Sarkar, "Heroic Women, Mother Goddesses: Family and Organisation in Hindutva Politics," in *Women and the Hindu Right: A Collection of Essays*, ed. Tanika Sarkar and Urvashi Butalia (New Delhi: Kali for Women, 1995), 181–215.

27. Anne McClintock, "Family Feuds: Gender, Nationalism and the Family," *Feminist Review* 44 (Summer 1993): 61–80.

28. Ibid., 67.

29. Alexander, "Sarojini Naidu," 69.

30. For a fine account of the production of gendered and high-caste Hindu tradition in the aftermath of Orientalist scholarship, see Uma Chakravarti, "Whatever Happened to the Vedic *Dasi*? Orientalism, Nationalism and a Script for the Past," *Recasting Women*, 27–87.

31. Naidu, *Golden Threshold*, 87.

32. Ibid., 46.

33. Sarojini Naidu, *Speeches and Writings of Sarojini Naidu*, 2d ed. (Madras: G. A. Natesan, 1919), 112.

34. See Tanika Sarkar, "Nationalist Iconography: Image of Women in 19th Century Bengali Literature," *Economic and Political Weekly*, 21 November 1987, 2011–15; Jasodhara Bagchi, "Representing Nationalism: Ideology of Motherhood in Colonial Bengal," *Economic and Political Weekly*, 20–27 October 1990, WS 65–71; Indira Chowdhury-Sengupta, "Mother India and Mother Victoria: Motherhood and Nationalism in Nineteenth-Century Bengal," *South Asia Research*, 12, no. 1 (1992): 20–37; Samita Sen, "Motherhood and Mothercraft: Gender and Nationalism in Bengal," *Gender & History*, 5, no. 2 (1993): 231–43; and Sandhya Shetty, "(Dis)figuring the Nation," *differences*, 7, no. 3 (1995): 50–79. For a sympathetic, if less attentively feminist, account of the feminization/maternalization of the Indian landscape, see Sudipta Kaviraj's comments on the nineteenth-century Bengali writings of Bankim in *The Unhappy Consciousness: Bankimchandra Chattopadhyay and the Reformation of Nationalist Discourse in India* (Delhi: Oxford University Press, 1995), 114:

> It becomes in Bankim, probably for the first time in Bengali literature, something emphatically other than simple neutral territory, a profane space, but sacred "ground" (with all the great complexity of this metaphor) of a community. Space is invested with sacrality in a literal sense making transfer of a moral language possible. It was not something which was fit to be geologically surveyed, but to be offered a political form of worship. From a neutral space, India becomes an evocative symbol, female, maternal, infinitely bounteous, invested with the complex and convex symbolism of the feminine in the Hindu tradition—a sign simultaneously of vulnerability and invincibility.

35. See Fanon, "Algeria Unveiled," for an illustration of the production of the nationalist woman as subject. See, too, Marie-Aimée Helie-Lucas, "Women, Nationalism and Religion in the Algerian Struggle," in *Opening the Gates: A Century of Arab Feminist Writing*, ed. Miriam Cooke and Margot Badran (Bloomington: Indiana University Press, 1991).

36. M. K. Gandhi, *Hind Swaraj, or Indian Home Rule* (Ahmedabad: Navajivan Publishing House, 1939).

37. Kishwar, "Gandhi on Women," 1691.

38. Kumar, *History of Doing*, 83.

39. Kishwar, "Gandhi on Women," 1700. Also see Ketu H. Katrak, "Indian Nationalism, Gandhian 'Satyagraha,' and Representations of Female Sexuality," in *Nationalisms and Sexualities*, ed. Andrew Parker, Mary Russo, Doris Sommer, and Patricia Yaeger (New York and London: Routledge, 1992).

40. Manmohan Kaur, *Women in India's Freedom Struggle* (New Delhi: Sterling Publishers, 1985), 160–65. See, too, Aruna Asaf Ali, "Women's Suffrage in India," and Amrit Kaur, "Women under the New Constitution," *Our Cause: A Symposium by Indian Women*, ed. Shyam Kumari Nehru (Allahabad: Kitabistan, 1935).

41. Kumar, *History of Doing*, 88.

42. Joanna Liddle and Rama Joshi, "Gender and Imperialism in British India," *South Asia Research*, 5, no. 2 (1985): 156. There were limits, as we shall see, to male support of nationalist women and their demands on behalf of women. For an account of the sometimes tense relationship between the Congress Party and two of the most prominent of Indian women's organizations, the Women's India Association and the All-India Women's Conference, see Geraldine Forbes, "The Indian Women's Movement: A Struggle for Women's Rights or National Liberation?" in *The Extended Family: Women and Political Participation in India and Pakistan*, ed. Gail Minault (Columbia, Mo.: South Asia Books, 1981), 49–82.

43. See, for instance, Indira Gandhi's refusal of the term as a description of her own political commitments and Madhu Kishwar's rejection of it as too weighted with Eurocentric baggage. Sarojini's reluctance to adopt the term as a proximate self-description is understandable in light of the deeply colonialist and racist underpinnings of the feminist work of figures like Eleanor Rathbone, one of the most prominent of those interested in the uplift of Indian women.

44. Sinha, "Reading *Mother India*," 21.

45. Naidu, *Speeches and Writings*, 14.

46. Ibid., 16.

47. Ibid., 78. Note, too, her address as President of the Indian National Congress in 1925, when she assumed, as a representative mother, the voice of Mother India: "I, who have rocked the cradle—I who have sung soft lullabies—I, the emblem of Mother India, am now to kindle the flame of liberty" (Pattabhi Sitaramayya, *The History of the Congress, Volume 1 (1885–1935)* [Bombay: Padma Publications, 1946 (1935)], 130).

48. I should point out that discipleship in this chapter does not carry exactly the same spiritual and erotic charge that it does in the preceding one, though its continuities with religious discipleship can by no means be trivialized.

49. Padmini Sengupta, *Sarojini Naidu: A Biography* (Bombay: Asia Publishing House, 1966), 76–77 (emphases mine).

50. Margaret Cousins, *The Awakening of Asian Womanhood* (Madras: Ganesh, 1922), 121–22.

51. Sengupta, *Sarojini Naidu*, 81.

52. This of course is not to overlook her prison terms (though, significantly, she was always an A-class prisoner, with considerable privileges, including use of her own furniture and other personal items, relatively pleasant accommodations, and freedom to mix with other political prisoners—privileges that Mirabehn, though a

white woman, was denied) or her genuine contributions over three decades to the cause of national independence and women's rights; it is only to note that she, unlike Gandhi and most Gandhians, fully and unabashedly enjoyed material comforts.

53. Harindranath Chattopadhyaya, "Sarojini Naidu: A Sketch," in *Perspectives on Sarojini Naidu*. ed. K. K. Sharma (Ghaziabad, India: Vimal Prakashan, 1989), 2. Numerous tales are told of her relish for *kababs, biryanis, rasgullas*, and the other staples of the gourmet's table.

54. Robert Bernays, *"Naked Faquir"* (New York: Henry Holt, 1932), 202.

55. Baig, *Sarojini Naidu*. M. O. Mathai claims that it was on account of this estrangement that she was not allowed to see her father even as he was dying (*Reminiscences of the Nehru Age* [New Delhi: Vikas, 1978], 126–27).

56. Harindranath Chattopadhyay, *Life and Myself—Dawn Approaching Noon* (Bombay: Nalanda Publications, 1948). He does, however, devote considerable space and energy to an account of his meeting in Europe with his much older brother Virendranath (who appears to have left India, never to return, when Harindranath was only a child).

57. Tara Ali Baig, *Sarojini Naidu: Portrait of a Patriot* (New Delhi: Congress Centenary [1985] Celebrations Committee, 1985), 63.

58. See Kamaladevi Chattopadhyay, *Inner Recesses, Outer Spaces: Memoirs* (Delhi: Navrang, 1986).

59. Sengupta, *Sarojini Naidu*, 3–8.

60. M. Cousins, *Awakening of Asian Womanhood*, 119.

61. Bernays, *"Naked Faquir,"* 105, 106, 161.

62. Beverley Nichols, *Verdict on India* (New York: Harcourt, Brace, 1944), 149.

63. B. R. Nanda, *The Two Nehrus* (London: Allen and Unwin, 1962), 230; see also Krishna Hutheesingh, *With No Regrets: Krishna Hutheesingh's Autobiography* (Bombay: Oxford University Press, 1944).

64. Izzat Yar Khan, *Sarojini Naidu: The Poet* (New Delhi: S. Chand, 1983), 18, n. 49. See the original in K. A. Abbas, *Sarojini Naidu* (Bombay: Bharatiya Vidya Bhavan, 1980), 66.

65. Jawaharlal Nehru, *An Autobiography*, abr. ed., ed. C. D. Narasimhaiah (Delhi: Oxford University Press, 1991), 24–25.

66. These are the terms in which Nayantara Sahgal (Nehru's niece) describes Padmaja Naidu in *Prison and Chocolate Cake* (New York: Alfred A. Knopf, 1954), 142:

> [Padmaja] was a person of indefinable charm who did not belong to—and made no pretense of fitting into—an austere political atmosphere. The bright greens, golds, and purples of her saris were a startling contrast to the sober shades around us. Her bright silks rustled unashamedly amid the subdued whisper of khadi. She always wore flowers in her hair. There was something of the bird of paradise about her, confined, restless, in a glen of sparrows.
>
> [Padmaja] had been an invalid all her life, a fact belied by her gaiety, her gift for swift repartee, and a keen sense of the ridiculous inherited from her mother. Like her mother, too, she was a poet, with a poet's intensified aesthetic sense. But in addition to this she had a sharp critical faculty, and no jarring note in dress, mood, or conversation escaped her.

67. G. D. Birla, *In the Shadow of the Mahatma: A Personal Memoir* (Bombay: Vakils, Feffer and Simons, 1968), 7.

68. M. K. Gandhi, *Hindi and English in the South*, ed. M. P. Desai (Ahmedabad: Navajivan Publishing House, 1958). Gandhi severely castigated South Indian members of the Congress for their suspicion of Hindi but not of English.

69. Kishwar, "Gandhi on Women," 1698.

70. Kumar, *History of Doing*, 74.

71. Webb Miller, *I Found No Peace: The Journal of a Foreign Correspondent* (London: Victor Gollancz, 1937), chap. 16. Also see Louis Fischer, *The Life of Mahatma Gandhi* (New Delhi: Indus/HarperCollins, 1992 [1951]), chap. 16.

72. M. Kaur, *Women in India's Freedom Struggle*.

73. Jawaharlal Nehru, *A Bunch of Old Letters, Written Mostly to Jawaharlal Nehru and Some Written by Him* (Bombay: Asia Publishing House, 1958), 177–78.

74. Mathai, *Reminiscences*, 126–27.

75. The following provide some of the information for a comparative and gendered account of Indian nationalism: M. Kaur, *Women in India's Freedom Struggle;* Usha Bala, *Indian Women Freedom Fighters, 1857–1947* (New Delhi: Manohar, 1986); B. R. Nanda, ed., *Indian Women: From Purdah to Modernity* (New Delhi: Vikas, 1976); Kamaladevi Chattopadhayay, *Indian Women's Battle for Freedom* (New Delhi: Abhinav Publications, 1983); Kumar, *History of Doing;* Kumari Jayawardena, *Feminism and Nationalism in the Third World* (London: Zed Press, 1986); and Susie Tharu and K. Lalitha, eds., *Women Writing in India*, 2 vols. (New York: Feminist Press, 1993 [1991]).

76. My sense of the exemplarity of the "case" has been facilitated by a reading of the following essays: Zakia Pathak and Rajeswari Sunder Rajan, "Shahbano," *Signs* 14, no. 3 (1989): 558–82 [reprinted in *Feminists Theorize the Political*, ed. Judith Butler and Joan W. Scott (New York: Routledge, 1992)]; and Rajeswari Sunder Rajan, "Ameena: Gender, Crisis and National Identity," *Oxford Literary Review* 16, nos. 1–2 (1994): 147–76.

77. Kishwar, "Gandhi on Women," 1691.

78. My understanding of the politics of banality is informed to some degree by Michel de Certeau, *The Practice of Everyday Life* (Berkeley and London: University of California Press, 1984). Achille Mbembe, "The Banality of Power and the Aesthetics of Vulgarity in the Postcolony," *Public Culture* 4, no. 2 (1992): 1–30, has fascinating things to say about the exhibition and carnivalization of power in the (sub-Saharan) postcolony; and it is interesting to speculate what he might say about the spectacle of asceticism rather than excess as commonly understood.

79. M. K. Gandhi, *The Story of My Experiments with Truth*, trans. Mahadev Desai (New York: Dover, 1958).

80. Kishwar, "Gandhi on Women," 1695. Combined with this endorsement of *khadi* was a castigation of fine clothes and jewelry, especially those worn by women: "there is no salvation for India, unless you strip yourselves of this jewelry and silken garments such as women wear and hold it in trust for your countrymen of India" (quoted in Eleanor Morton, *The Women in Gandhi's Life* [New York: Dodd, Mead, 1953], 118).

81. Kishwar, "Gandhi on Women," 1754. Some of the parallels with Ramakrishna are too obvious to miss. In *The Intimate Enemy*, Ashis Nandy has likened the Ramakrishna-Vivekananda association to the Gandhi-Nehru alliance of the high

nationalist period. Gandhi's response to women was less consistently phobic, though also far more limited, than Ramakrishna's; he saw them as desexualized and self-sacrificing mother figures, while for the saint of Dakshineshwar the term *woman* could stand for a range of possibilities: seducer, mother, goddess, and so forth.

82. M. K. Gandhi, *Bapu's Letters to Mira* (Ahmedabad: Navajivan Publishing House, 1949), 288.

83. Lloyd I. Rudolph and Susanne Hoeber Rudolph, *The Modernity of Tradition: Political Development in India* (Chicago and London: University of Chicago Press, 1967), 157–249.

84. For an elaboration of the incalculable logic of "theft," see Lott, *Love and Theft.*

85. Yar Khan, *Sarojini Naidu.*

86. Baig, *Sarojini Naidu: Portrait of a Patriot,* 1 (emphasis mine).

87. Quoted in K. R. Ramachandran Nair, *Three Indo-Anglian Poets: Henry Derozio, Toru Dutt and Sarojini Naidu* (New Delhi: Sterling Publishers, 1987), 92.

6. FIGURING MOTHER INDIA

1. A. S. Panneerselvan, "The MGR Mystique," *Filmfare,* 1–15 February 1988, 53. The Dravida Munnetra Kazhagam (DMK), from which MGR broke away to form the AIADMK, was of course well known for its close ties with the film world and for its use of films as a vehicle for political propaganda.

2. M. S. S. Pandian, *The Image Trap: M. G. Ramachandran in Film and Politics* (New Delhi: Sage Publications, 1992) is the most sustained account that I know of concerning the reciprocal imbrications of (Tamil) cinema and politics. Shashi Tharoor's 1991 novel, *Show Business* (New York: Arcade Publishing), a thinly disguised narrative of the career of Amitabh Bachchan, attempts, though not with particular persuasiveness, to weave the cinema and politics together as mutually implicated in deception.

3. Pandian, *Image Trap,* 17, 129–39.

4. Chidananda Das Gupta, *The Painted Face: Studies in India's Popular Cinema* (New Delhi: Roli Books, 1991), 211.

5. Chidananda Das Gupta, "The Painted Face of Politics: The Actor-Politicians of South India," in *Cinema and Cultural Identity: Reflections on Films from Japan, India, and China,* ed. Wimal Dissanayake (Lanham, Md., and London: University Press of America, 1988), 135. Much of the information on NTR is derived from this essay and from Das Gupta, *Painted Face.*

6. In August 1995 NTR was forced out of his chief ministership by a rebel Telugu Desam contingent headed by his son-in-law Chandrababu Naidu. His ouster was attributed to resentment at the growing political influence of his new wife, Lakshmi Parvati. He died in 1996.

7. Mira Reym Binford, "The Two Cinemas of India," in *Film and Politics in the Third World,* ed. John J. H. Downing (New York: Praeger, 1987), 147.

8. Farrukh Dhondy, "Keeping Faith: Indian Film and Its World," *Daedalus* 114 (Fall 1985): 130.

9. For an account of the negotiations between contradictory forces in the star

texts of three "heroines," Fearless Nadia, Nargis, and Smita Patil, see Behroze Gandhy and Rosie Thomas, "Three Indian Film Stars," in *Stardom: Industry of Desire*, ed. Christine Gledhill (London and New York: Routledge, 1991).

10. T. J. S. George, *The Life and Times of Nargis* (New Delhi: Indus/HarperCollins, 1994), 201.

11. The female star of Ramanand Sagar's *Ramayana* was cautioned, after the spectacular success of that serial, to take up no other (lesser) roles, to dress in certain approved "traditional" ways, and so forth. My thanks to Robert Goldman for reminding me of this.

12. Rosie Thomas, "Sanctity and Scandal: The Mythologization of Mother India," *Quarterly Review of Film and Video* 11, no. 3 (1989): 11–30.

13. Despite his vast popularity with the electorate of Tamil Nadu, MGR never aspired to national office, and, indeed, the principle of Tamil nationalism with which he was aligned existed in a deeply combative relationship with the nationalism of Delhi.

14. George, *Life and Times of Nargis*, 26.

15. Interview with Nargis, in *Indian Cinema Superbazaar*, ed. Aruna Vasudev and Philippe Lenglet (New Delhi: Vikas Publishing House, 1983), 252.

16. George, *Life and Times of Nargis*, 45–46.

17. Thomas, "Sanctity and Scandal," 23.

18. Gautam Kaul, "Review of Wimal Dissanayake and Malti Sahai's *Raj Kapoor: Harmony of Discourses* (New Delhi: Vikas, 1988)," *India Today*, 31 May 1988, 91.

19. George, *Life and Times of Nargis*, 96. Bunny Reuben, *Raj Kapoor, the Fabulous Showman: An Intimate Biography* (New Delhi: Indus/HarperCollins, 1995) provides further details about the romance.

20. Bikram Singh, "The Dream Merchant," *Filmfare*, 16–30 June 1988, 18.

21. George, *Life and Times of Nargis*, 127.

22. Interview with K. A. Abbas, in *Indian Cinema Superbazaar*.

23. Mayo's *Mother India* was regarded in some circles as anti-Hindu and pro-Muslim (Sinha, "Reading *Mother India*").

24. B. D. Garga, "The Feel of the Good Earth," *Cinema in India* 3 (April–June 1989): 32.

25. George, *Life and Times of Nargis*, 157.

26. Ibid., 151. See also A. A. Khatib, "Nargis: The Way She Was," *Filmfare*, 1–15 June 1981, 12–15.

27. *Jogan* (Kidar Sharma, dir., 1950), in which she plays a nun whose renunciation cannot be reconciled with the demands of eroticism, is an important exception to this generalization. She played a rural belle in *Barsaat* (Raj Kapoor, dir., 1949), but became "modernized" by the film's end. Sudhir Kakar, among others, has described the ways in which the popular cinema stages, even if it does not always reconcile, the stresses of the "transitional sector," caught between "traditional roles" and "modernization"; these stresses are, according to him, superbly illustrated in the filmic persona of Amitabh Bachchan, and may account for his phenomenal popularity ("Lovers in the Dark," in *Intimate Relations: Exploring Indian Sexuality*, by Sudhir Kakar [New Delhi: Penguin Books, 1989], 25–41). Ashis Nandy makes a version of

the same argument: "Commercial cinema romanticizes and, given half a chance, vulgarizes the problems of the survival sector, but it never rejects as childish or primitive the categories or world-views of those trying to survive the processes of victimization let loose by modern institutions" (Ashis Nandy, "An Intelligent Critic's Guide to Indian Cinema," in *The Savage Freud and Other Essays on Possible and Retrievable Selves* [Princeton, N.J.: Princeton University Press, 1995], 203).

28. Bunny Reuben, *Mehboob: India's DeMille* (New Delhi: Indus/HarperCollins, 1994), 371.

29. Baburao Patel, review in *Filmindia*, December 1957, cited in ibid., 266 (emphasis mine).

30. Nargis, *Filmfare*, 7 June 1957, cited in ibid., 248.

31. Khatib, "Nargis," 14.

32. Gandhy and Thomas, "Three Indian Film Stars," 107.

33. Ibid.

34. Erik Barnouw and S. Krishnaswamy, *Indian Film*, 2d ed. (New York: Oxford University Press, 1980), 42.

35. Ibid., 69. See also Sumita S. Chakravarty, *National Identity in Indian Popular Cinema, 1947–1987* (Austin: University of Texas Press, 1993), 13.

36. Vijay Mishra, Peter Jeffery, and Brian Shoesmith, "The Actor as Parallel Text in Bombay Cinema," *Quarterly Review of Film and Video* 11, no. 3 (1989): 52.

37. Barnouw and Krishnaswamy, *Indian Film*, 118.

38. Mishra, Jeffery, and Shoesmith, "Actor as Parallel Text," 53.

39. Interview with Gulzar, in *Indian Cinema Superbazaar*, 193–204. Nargis herself was somewhat embittered about the low status of actresses, complaining at the first Film Seminar organized in 1955 by the Sangeet Natak Akademi: "every film artiste in this country, in her heart of hearts, genuinely desires to serve the country and is even prepared to make personal sacrifices towards that end. But . . . [an] artificial barrier has been created between us and the people by irresponsible criticism of responsible people. They prejudiced the public against film actresses. . . . It is agreed that we should try to understand the people. But people must also try to understand us" (R. M. Ray, ed. *Sangeet Natak Akademi Film Seminar Report 1955* [New Delhi: n.p., 1956], 174).

40. Firoze Rangoonasala, *A Pictorial History of Indian Cinema* (London: Hamlyn, 1979), 13.

41. For an analysis of the institution of the *tawa'if*, see Veena Talwar Oldenburg, "Lifestyle as Resistance," in *Contesting Power*, ed. Gyan Prakash and Douglas Haynes (Berkeley: University of California Press, 1992). See, too, Veena Talwar Oldenburg, *The Making of Colonial Lucknow, 1856–1877* (Delhi: Oxford University Press, 1989), 133–44 ("The City Must Be Clean").

42. Interview with Nargis, in *Indian Cinema Superbazaar*, 255.

43. Sushama Shelley, "Raj's Women," *Filmfare*, 16–30 June 1988, 48. See also Ritu Nanda, *Raj Kapoor: His Life and His Films* (Moscow: Iskusstvo Publishers; Bombay: R. K. Films & Studios, 1991), 51.

44. George, *Life and Times of Nargis*, 150.

45. Kishore Valicha, "Why Are Popular Films Popular?" *Cinema in India* 3 (April–June 1989): 34. When I speak of nationalism(s) here, it is of Congress and Hindu na-

tionalisms; despite the significant involvement of Muslims in the Bombay film industry, it has never supported implicitly or explicitly any form of Muslim nationalism.

46. See Pathak and Sunder Rajan, "Shahbano," for a subtle and exhaustive account of the way in which the working-class Muslim woman can function only as a "palimpsest of identities, now constituted, now erased, by discursive displacements" (p. 268).

47. Somnath Zutshi, "Women, Nation and the Outsider in Contemporary Hindi Cinema," in *Interrogating Modernity: Culture and Colonialism in India*, ed. Tejaswini Niranjana, P. Sudhir, and Vivek Dhareshwar (Calcutta: Seagull Books, 1993), 85–86, citing D. G. Phalke, in *Navyug*, November 1917.

48. Ibid., 86–88.

49. Ashish Rajadhyaksha, "The Epic Melodrama: Themes of Nationality in Indian Cinema," *Journal of Arts and Ideas* 25–26 (1993): 62. Even Satyajit Ray, that great critic of popular Bombay cinema, insisted that what cinema in India "needs above everything else is a style, an idiom, a sort of iconography of cinema, which would be uniquely and recognisably Indian" (*Our Films, Their Films* [Bombay: Orient Longman, 1976], 22). Admittedly, his notion of Indianness was fairly distinct from that of the cultural nationalists of Bollywood. Like many scholars of that much-reviled institution, he saw it as hopelessly imitative of Hollywood conventions, though he was keenly appreciative of the eclectic genius of the Bombay film song. For a useful corrective to a reading of Bombay cinema's lack of "originality" (a corrective that does not gloss over some of the substantive problems—like sexism—of the Bombay film), see Rosie Thomas, "Indian Cinema: Pleasures and Popularity," *Screen* 26 (May-August 1985): 116–31.

50. S. Theodore Baskaran, *The Message Bearers: Nationalist Politics and the Entertainment Media in South India, 1880–1945* (Madras: Cre-A, 1981). Baskaran's understanding of the term *nationalism* is very inclusive; films about "social reform," for instance, function quite unproblematically as nationalist films in his reading.

51. Faisal Fatehali Devji, "Hindu/Muslim/Indian," *Public Culture* 5 (Fall 1992): 1. See, too, Aamir R. Mufti's analysis of the way in which Islam in South Asia is narrativized in liberal nationalist discourse as "trauma to the nation" ("Secularism and Minority: Elements of a Critique," *Social Text* 45, 14, no. 4 [1995]: 88). Gyan Pandey's scrutiny of the refusal/failure of Indian historiography to represent the colossal violence of the Partition and of sectarian riots (in which Muslims have been the main victims) as anything but an "aberration" from national history is of relevance here. See his "In Defense of the Fragment: Writing about Hindu-Muslim Riots in India Today." *Representations* 37 (Winter 1992): 27–55.

52. Chakravarty, *National Identity*, 165.

53. My thanks to Aditya Behl for reminding me of the competing myths of desire, aggression, and fetishization that circulate on the field of the Hindu-Muslim encounter in India.

54. George, *Life and Times of Nargis*, 57.

55. K. N. Subramaniam and Ratnakar Tripathy, comps., *Flashback: Cinema in the Times of India* (Bombay: Times of India, 1990), 160.

56. See Paola Bacchetta, "Communal Property/Sexual Property: On Representations of Muslim Women in a Hindu Nationalist Discourse," in *Forging Identities:*

Gender, Communities and the State in India, ed. Zoya Hasan (Boulder, Colo.: Westview Press, 1994), for a fascinating account of the Hindu nationalist male fantasy of the Muslim woman's desire for him. For a full account of the RSS, see Walter K. Anderson and Shridhar D. Damle, *The Brotherhood in Saffron: The Rashtriya Swayamsevak Sangh and Hindu Revivalism* (Boulder, Colo.: Westview Press, 1987).

57. The fullest filmography of Nargis that I have found is in *The Life and Times of Nargis*, the biography by T. J. S. George, though it does not include a few films in which Nargis (who had not yet assumed her famous screen name) had appeared as a child actress. Her first "adult" Muslim role appears to have been in Mehboob's *Humayun* (1945), in which she played Humayun's lady-love Hamida Banu, but this role is distinctly smaller than those of Ashok Kumar, Veena, and Chandramohan. Her other "Muslim" role is as the bad sister Mohinibai (who is a *tawa'if*, and in this sense marked as Muslim, despite the name) in *Anhonee* (1952). She was slated to play Anarkali in K. Asif's *Mughal-e-Azam* (1960)—a role eventually played by Madhubala—but was apparently unable to fulfill this contract on account of Raj Kapoor's disapproval.

58. Mukul Kesavan, "Urdu, Awadh and the Tawaif: The Islamicate Roots of Hindi Cinema," in *Forging Identities: Gender, Communities and the State in India*, ed. Zoya Hasan (Boulder, Colo.: Westview Press, 1994), 244–45.

59. R. M. Ray, *Sangeet Natak Akademi Film Seminar Report 1955*, 173–74.

60. Andrew Robinson, *Satyajit Ray: The Inner Eye* (Berkeley: University of California Press, 1989), 327. This response to Ray does not, however, mean that she was invariably dedicated to sloganeering for the nation-state. In an interview preceding by a year or so her comments on Ray, she was more critical of the nation-state and of its failure to respond to criticism or satire with anything other than censorship: "Sometimes our Government is very harsh on us. Suppose you want to make a farce, a political situation today. Let somebody take an idea and make a farce on this, but our politicians have not learnt to laugh at themselves. . . . In this country you can't laugh at the police, you can't laugh at the armed forces, you can't laugh at politicians" (Interview with Nargis, in *Indian Cinema Superbazaar*, 256).

61. Rajeswari Sunder Rajan has brilliantly demonstrated the ways in which Indira Gandhi tapped into the idiom of feminine and maternal power (of the kind memorably illustrated in *Mother India*) in order to consolidate her hold on the Indian polity and to deflect the patriarchal anxieties induced by the spectacle of a female head of state. The image she most assiduously cultivated was that of the mother of the nation, enacting a noble renunciation on behalf of her children/subjects and invested with irrefutable moral and political authority because of that renunciation. See *Real and Imagined Women: Gender, Culture and Postcolonialism* (London: Routledge, 1993). Biographers and political commentators have commented on the uneasy blend in her of the desire for a democratic self-image and the increasing conviction that she alone could lead the country. She was in fact routinely hailed as an embodiment of the goddess Durga, mostly notably after her brilliant victory in Bangladesh over Pakistan; she did nothing to discourage such associations and, in fact, was enraged when in later years the journalist Khushwant Singh likened her estranged daughter-in-law Maneka Gandhi to the goddess. Such a casting of the female head of state as Durga assumed iconic, indeed legendary, proportions during

the Emergency of 1975–1977. The slogan "India is Indira, and Indira is India" appeared everywhere, and the well-known painter M. F. Husain painted a triptych depicting Indira as a triumphant Durga on a tiger. That she might have found the role of powerful goddess somewhat outside her control (even though it was very flattering) is evidenced in her remark to the philosopher J. Krishnamurti that the Emergency was a tiger she could not dismount. For more on the iconicity of Indira Gandhi, see the following: Inder Malhotra, *Indira Gandhi: A Personal and Political Biography* (London: Hodder & Stoughton, 1989); Ashis Nandy, "Indira Gandhi and the Culture of Indian Politics," in *At the Edge of Psychology*; Pupul Jayakar, *Indira Gandhi: An Intimate Biography* (New York: Pantheon Books, 1992 [1988]); and Raj Thapar, *All These Years: A Memoir* (New Delhi: Penguin Books, 1992).

62. See Richard Meyer, "Rock Hudson's Body," in *Inside/Out: Lesbian Theories, Gay Theories*, ed. Diana Fuss (New York: Routledge, 1991) for an account of the heterosexual responses to the news of Hudson's gayness.

63. George, *Life and Times of Nargis*, 191.

64. Manoj Mitta, "TADA: Relentless Terror," *India Today*, 15 October 1994, 111.

65. M. Rahman and Lekha Rattanani, "Sanjay Dutt: A Fatal Attraction," *India Today*, 15 May 1993, 72.

66. Ibid.

67. Ibid.

68. M. Rahman and Arun Katiyar, "Bombay Film Industry: Underworld Connections," *India Today*, 15 May 1993; and Jeet Thayil, "From Reel to Real in 'Bollywood,'" *Asiaweek* [reprinted in *World Press Review*, October 1994, 45].

69. M. Rahman, "Sanjay Dutt: It's Not Over Yet," *India Today*, 31 May 1993, 67.

70. Harinder Baweja, "TADA: An Act of Terror," *India Today*, 15 September 1994.

SELECT BIBLIOGRAPHY

Abbas, K. A. *Sarojini Naidu*. Bombay: Bharatiya Vidya Bhavan, 1980.

Ahmad, Aijaz. *In Theory: Classes, Nations, Literatures*. London: Verso, 1992.

Alexander, Meena. "Sarojini Naidu: Romanticism and Resistance." *Economic and Political Weekly*, 26 October 1985, 68–71.

Alter, Joseph. "Celibacy, Sexuality, and the Transformation of Gender into Nationalism in North India." *Journal of Asian Studies* 53, no. 1 (1994): 45–66.

Amin, Shahid. "Approver's Testimony, Judicial Discourse: The Case of Chauri Chaura." In *Subaltern Studies V: Writings on South Asian History and Society*, edited by Ranajit Guha. Delhi: Oxford University Press, 1987.

Anderson, Benedict. *Imagined Communities: Reflections on the Origin and Spread of Nationalism*. London: Verso, 1991 [1983].

Anderson, Walter K., and Shridhar D. Damle. *The Brotherhood in Saffron: The Rashtriya Swayamsevak Sangh and Hindu Revivalism*. Boulder, Colo.: Westview Press, 1987.

Appadurai, Arjun. "Disjuncture and Difference in the Global Cultural Economy." *Public Culture* 2 (Spring 1990): 1–23.

———. "Number in the Colonial Imagination." In *Orientalism and the Postcolonial Predicament: Perspectives on South Asia*, edited by Carol A. Breckenridge and Peter van der Veer. Philadelphia: University of Pennsylvania Press, 1993.

———. "Patriotism and Its Futures." *Public Culture* 5 (Spring 1993): 411–29.

Arata, Stephen. "A Universal Foreignness: Kipling in the Fin-de-Siècle." *English Literature in Transition* 36, no. 1 (1993): 7–38.

Arnold, David. "European Orphans and Vagrants in India in the Nineteenth Century." *Journal of Imperial and Commonwealth History* 7, no. 2 (1979): 104–27.

———. *Police Power and Colonial Rule: Madras 1859–1947*. Delhi: Oxford University Press, 1986.

Asaf Ali, Aruna. "Women's Suffrage in India." In *Our Cause: A Symposium by Indian Women*, edited by Shyam Kumari Nehru. Allahabad: Kitabistan, 1935.

Ashcroft, Bill, Gareth Griffiths, and Helen Tiffin, eds. *The Empire Writes Back: Theory and Practice in Post-Colonial Literatures*. London and New York: Routledge, 1989.

Assad, Thomas. *Three Victorian Travellers: Burton, Blunt, Doughty.* London: Routledge and Kegan Paul, 1964.

Atmaprana, Pravrajika. *Sister Nivedita of Ramakrishna-Vivekananda.* Calcutta: Sister Nivedita Girls' School, 1961.

Bacchetta, Paola. "Communal Property/Sexual Property: On Representations of Muslim Women in a Hindu Nationalist Discourse." In *Forging Identities: Gender, Communities and the State in India*, edited by Zoya Hasan. Boulder, Colo.: Westview Press, 1994.

Bagchi, Jasodhara. "Representing Nationalism: Ideology of Motherhood in Colonial Bengal." *Economic and Political Weekly*, 20–27 October 1990, WS 65–71.

Baig, Tara Ali. *Sarojini Naidu.* New Delhi: Ministry of Information and Broadcasting, 1974.

———. *Sarojini Naidu: Portrait of a Patriot.* New Delhi: Congress Centenary [1985] Celebrations Committee, 1985.

Bala, Usha. *Indian Women Freedom Fighters, 1857–1947.* New Delhi: Manohar, 1986.

Banerjee, Sumanta. "Marginalization of Women's Popular Culture in Nineteenth Century Bengal." In *Recasting Women: Essays in Indian Colonial History*, edited by Kumkum Sangari and Sudesh Vaid. New Brunswick, N.J.: Rutgers University Press, 1990.

———. *The Parlour and the Street.* Calcutta: Seagull Press, 1985.

Barnouw, Erik, and S. Krishnaswamy. *Indian Film.* 2d ed. New York: Oxford University Press, 1980.

Baskaran, S. Theodore. *The Message Bearers: Nationalist Politics and the Entertainment Media in South India, 1880–1945.* Madras: Cre-A, 1981.

Basu, Sankari Prasad, and Sunil Bihari Ghosh, eds. *Vivekananda in Indian Newspapers 1893–1902.* Calcutta: Dineshchandra Basu Bhattacharya, 1969.

Basu, Tapan, Pradip Datta, Sumit Sarkar, Tanika Sarkar, and Sambuddha Sen. *Khaki Shorts and Saffron Flags: A Critique of the Hindu Right.* New Delhi: Orient Longman, 1993.

Baweja, Harinder. "TADA: An Act of Terror." *India Today*, 15 September 1994.

Beauvoir, Simone de. *The Second Sex.* Translated by H. M. Parshley. New York: Vintage Books, 1952.

Behdad, Ali. *Belated Travelers: Orientalism in the Age of Colonial Dissolution.* Durham, N.C., and London: Duke University Press, 1994.

Bennington, Geoff. "Postal Politics and the Institution of the Nation." In *Nation and Narration*, edited by Homi K. Bhabha. London and New York: Routledge, 1990.

Bernays, Robert. *"Naked Faquir."* New York: Henry Holt, 1932.

Bhabha, Homi K. "DissemiNation: Time, Narrative, and the Margins of the Modern Nation." In *Nation and Narration*, ed. Homi K. Bhabha. London and New York: Routledge, 1990.

———. "Interrogating Identity: Frantz Fanon and the Postcolonial Prerogative." In *The Location of Culture.* London and New York: Routledge, 1993.

———. *The Location of Culture.* London and New York: Routledge, 1993.

———. "Of Mimicry and Man: The Ambivalence of Colonial Discourse." In *The Location of Culture.* London and New York: Routledge, 1993.

———. "The Other Question: Stereotype, Discrimination and the Discourse of Colonialism." In *The Location of Culture.* London and New York: Routledge, 1993.

————. "Sly Civility." In *The Location of Culture*. London and New York: Routledge, 1993.

————, ed. *Nation and Narration*. London and New York: Routledge, 1990.

Bhadra, Gautam. "Four Rebels of Eighteen-Fifty-Seven." In *Subaltern Studies IV: Writings on South Asian History and Society*, edited by Ranajit Guha. Delhi: Oxford University Press, 1985.

Binford, Mira Reym. "The Two Cinemas of India." In *Film and Politics in the Third World*, edited by John J. H. Downing. New York: Praeger, 1987.

Birla, G. D. *In the Shadow of the Mahatma: A Personal Memoir*. Bombay: Vakils, Feffer and Simons, 1968.

Borthwick, Meredith. *The Changing Role of Women in Bengal, 1849–1905*. Princeton, N.J.: Princeton University Press, 1984.

Brantlinger, Patrick. *Rule of Darkness: British Literature and Imperialism, 1830–1914*. Ithaca, N.Y.: Cornell University Press, 1988.

Bristow, Joseph. *Empire Boys: Adventures in a Man's World*. London: HarperCollins Academic, 1991.

Brodie, Fawn M. *The Devil Drives: A Life of Sir Richard Burton*. New York: W. W. Norton, 1967.

Bruce, George. *The Stranglers: The Cult of Thuggee and Its Overthrow in British India*. New York: Harcourt, Brace & World, 1968.

Burke, Marie Louise. *Swami Vivekananda: His Second Visit to the West; New Discoveries*. Calcutta: Advaita Ashrama, 1973.

————. *Swami Vivekananda in America: New Discoveries*. Calcutta: Advaita Ashrama, 1958.

Burton, Antoinette. *Burdens of History: British Feminists, Indian Women, and Imperial Culture, 1865–1915*. Chapel Hill and London: University of North Carolina Press, 1994.

Burton, Isabel. *The Life of Captain Sir Richard F. Burton, K.C.M.G., F.R.G.S., by His Wife*. 2 vols. London: Chapman and Hall, 1893.

Burton, Richard F. *Falconry in the Valley of the Indus*. London: John van Voorst, 1852.

————. *First Footsteps in East Africa*. Edited by Gordon Waterfield. New York and Washington, D.C.: Frederick A. Praeger, 1966.

————. *Goa, and the Blue Mountains; or, Six Months of Sick Leave*. Edited with an introduction by Dane Kennedy. Berkeley: University of California Press, 1991 [1851].

————. *The Lake Regions of Central Africa: A Picture of Exploration*. 2 vols. London: Longman, Green, Longman, and Roberts, 1860.

————. *Personal Narrative of a Pilgrimage to Al-Madinah and Meccah*. 2 vols. New York: Dover Publications, 1964 [1855].

————. *Scinde; or, The Unhappy Valley*. Vol. 2. London: Richard Bentley, 1851.

————. *Sindh, and the Races That Inhabit the Valley of the Indus*. Karachi: Oxford University Press, 1973.

————. "Terminal Essay." In *The Book of the Thousand Nights and a Night*. Vol. 10. London: Kama-shastra Society, 1885.

Butler, Judith. *Bodies That Matter*. New York and London: Routledge, 1993.

————. *Gender Trouble: Feminism and the Subversion of Identity*. New York and London: Routledge, 1990.

Carrington, Charles. *Rudyard Kipling: His Life and Work*. Harmondsworth: Penguin Books, 1970 [1959].

Casada, James. *Sir Richard Francis Burton: A Bibliographical Study*. Boston: G. K. Hall, 1989.

Case, Sue-Ellen. "Toward a Butch-Femme Aesthetic." In *Making a Spectacle*, edited by Lynda Hart. Ann Arbor: University of Michigan Press, 1989.

Certeau, Michel de. *The Practice of Everyday Life*. Berkeley and London: University of California Press, 1984.

Chakrabarty, Dipesh. "The Difference-Deferral of a Colonial Modernity: Public Debates on Domesticity in British India." In *Subaltern Studies VIII: Writings on South Asian History and Society*, edited by David Arnold and David Hardiman. Delhi: Oxford University Press, 1994.

———. "Open Space/Public Space: Garbage, Modernity and India." *South Asia* 14, no. 1 (1991): 15–31.

———. "Postcoloniality and the Artifice of History: Who Speaks for 'Indian' Pasts?" *Representations* 37 (Winter 1992): 1–26.

Chakravarti, Uma. "Whatever Happened to the Vedic *Dasi*? Orientalism, Nationalism and a Script for the Past." In *Recasting Women: Essays in Indian Colonial History*, edited by Kumkum Sangari and Sudesh Vaid. New Brunswick, N.J.: Rutgers University Press, 1990.

Chakravarty, Sumita S. *National Identity in Indian Popular Cinema, 1947–1987*. Austin: University of Texas Press, 1993.

Chatterjee, Partha. *The Nation and Its Fragments: Colonial and Postcolonial Histories*. Princeton, N.J.: Princeton University Press, 1993.

———. "The Nationalist Resolution of the Women's Question." In *Recasting Women: Essays in Indian Colonial History*, edited by Kumkum Sangari and Sudesh Vaid. New Brunswick, N.J.: Rutgers University Press, 1990.

———. *Nationalist Thought and the Colonial World: A Derivative Discourse*. Minneapolis: University of Minnesota Press, 1993 [1986].

———. "A Religion of Urban Domesticity: Sri Ramakrishna and the Calcutta Middle Class." In *Subaltern Studies VII: Writings on South Asian History and Society*, edited by Partha Chatterjee and Gyanendra Pandey. Delhi: Oxford University Press, 1992.

Chatterji, Bankim Chandra. *Anandamath*. Translated by Basanta Koomar Roy. New Delhi and Bombay: Orient Paperbacks, 1992 [1882].

Chattopadhyay, Harindranath. *Life and Myself—Dawn Approaching Noon*. Bombay: Nalanda Publications, 1948.

———. "Sarojini Naidu: A Sketch." In *Perspectives on Sarojini Naidu*, edited by K. K. Sharma. Ghaziabad, India: Vimal Prakashan, 1989.

Chattopadhyay, Kamaladevi. *Indian Women's Battle for Freedom*. New Delhi: Abhinav Publications, 1983.

———. *Inner Recesses, Outer Spaces: Memoirs*. Delhi: Navrang, 1986.

Chaudhuri, Nupur, and Margaret Strobel, eds. *Western Women and Imperialism: Complicity and Resistance*. Bloomington: Indiana University Press, 1992.

Chetanananda, Swami, ed. *Ramakrishna as We Saw Him*. St. Louis, Mo.: Vedanta Society of St. Louis, 1990.

Chow, Rey. *Woman and Chinese Modernity: The Politics of Reading between East and West*. Minneapolis: University of Minnesota Press, 1991.

Chowdhury-Sengupta, Indira. "Mother India and Mother Victoria: Motherhood and Nationalism in Nineteenth-Century Bengal." *South Asia Research* 12, no. 1 (1992): 20–37.

Clifford, James. *The Predicament of Culture: Twentieth-Century Ethnography, Literature, and Art.* Cambridge, Mass., and London: Harvard University Press, 1988.

Cohn, Bernard S. "The Census, Social Structure and Objectification in South Asia." In *An Anthropologist among the Historians and Other Essays.* Delhi: Oxford University Press, 1990.

Conrad, Joseph. "Geography and Some Explorers." In *Last Essays.* New York: Doubleday, 1926.

———. *Heart of Darkness.* Edited by Robert Kimbrough. New York: W. W. Norton, 1971.

Cousins, James H. *The Renaissance in India.* Madras: Ganesh, 1930.

Cousins, Margaret. *The Awakening of Asian Womanhood.* Madras: Ganesh, 1922.

Das Gupta, Chidananda. *The Painted Face: Studies in India's Popular Cinema.* New Delhi: Roli Books, 1991.

———. "The Painted Face of Politics: The Actor-Politicians of South India." In *Cinema and Cultural Identity: Reflections on Films from Japan, India, and China,* edited by Wimal Dissanayake. Lanham, Md., and London: University Press of America, 1988.

David, Deirdre. *Rule Britannia: Women, Empire, and Victorian Writing.* Ithaca, N.Y., and London: Cornell University Press, 1995.

Devji, Faisal Fatehali. "Gender and the Politics of Space: The Movement for Women's Reform in Muslim India, 1857–1900." *South Asia* 14, no. 1 (1991): 141–53.

———. "Hindu/Muslim/Indian." *Public Culture* 5 (Fall 1992): 1–18.

Dhareshwar, Vivek. "Marxism, Location Politics, and the Possibility of Critique." *Public Culture* 6 (Fall 1993): 41–54.

Dhondy, Farrukh. "Keeping Faith: Indian Film and Its World." *Daedalus* 114 (Fall 1985): 125–40.

Dirks, Nicholas B. "Castes of Mind." *Representations* 37 (Winter 1992): 56–78.

Dirlik, Arif. "The Postcolonial Aura: Third World Criticism in the Age of Global Capitalism." *Critical Inquiry* 20, no. 2 (1994): 328–56.

Djebar, Assia. *Fantasia: An Algerian Cavalcade.* Translated by Dorothy Blair. London: Quartet Books, 1985.

Doane, Mary Ann. "Dark Continents: Epistemologies of Racial and Sexual Difference in Psychoanalysis and the Cinema." In *Femmes Fatales: Feminism, Film Theory, Psychoanalysis.* New York and London: Routledge, 1991.

———. "Film and the Masquerade: Theorising the Female Spectator." In *Femmes Fatales: Feminism, Film Theory, Psychoanalysis.* New York and London: Routledge, 1991.

Donaldson, Laura E. *Decolonizing Feminisms: Race, Gender, and Empire-Building.* Chapel Hill: University of North Carolina Press, 1992.

Doniger, Wendy. *Women, Androgynes, and Other Mythical Beasts.* Chicago and London: University of Chicago Press, 1980.

Doyle, Sir Arthur Conan. "The Adventure of the Empty House." In *The Complete Sherlock Holmes.* Preface by Christopher Morley. New York: Doubleday, 1930.

Dumont, Louis. *Homo Hierarchus: The Caste System and Its Implications.* Rev. ed. Translated by Mark Sainsbury, Louis Dumont, and Basia Gulati. Chicago: University of Chicago Press, 1980 [1966].

Dustoor, P. E. *Sarojini Naidu*. Mysore: Rao and Raghavan, 1961.

Ezekiel, Nissim. "On Sarojini Naidu." *Sunday Standard*, 11 February 1962, 12.

Fanon, Frantz. "Algeria Unveiled." In *A Dying Colonialism*. New York: Grove Weidenfeld, 1961.

———. *Black Skin, White Masks*. Translated by Charles Lam Markmann. New York: Grove Weidenfeld, 1952.

Fischer, Louis. *The Life of Mahatma Gandhi*. New Delhi: Indus/HarperCollins, 1992 [1951].

Forbes, Geraldine. "The Indian Women's Movement: A Struggle for Women's Rights or National Liberation?" In *The Extended Family: Women and Political Participation in India and Pakistan*, edited by Gail Minault. Columbia, Mo.: South Asia Books, 1981.

Foucault, Michel. *Discipline and Punish*. Translated by Alan Sheridan. New York: Vintage Books, 1979.

———. *The History of Sexuality*. Vol. 1. Translated by Robert Hurley. New York: Vintage Books, 1978.

———. "Intellectuals and Power: A Conversation between Michel Foucault and Gilles Deleuze." In *Language, Counter-Memory, Practice: Selected Essays and Interviews*. Translated by Donald F. Bouchard and Sherry Simon. Ithaca, N.Y.: Cornell University Press, 1977.

Foxe, Barbara. *Long Journey Home: A Biography of Margaret Noble (Nivedita)*. London: Rider, 1975.

Freitag, Sandria B. "Collective Crime and Authority in North India." In *Crime and Criminality in British India*, edited by Anand Yang. Tucson: University of Arizona Press, 1985.

———. "Crime in the Social Order of Colonial North India." *Modern Asian Studies* 25, no. 2 (1991): 227–61.

French, Harold W. *The Swan's Wide Waters: Ramakrishna and Western Culture*. Port Washington, N.Y.: Kennikat Press, 1974.

Fuss, Diana. "Interior Colonies: Frantz Fanon and the Politics of Identification." *diacritics* 24 (Summer-Fall 1994): 20–42.

Gandhi, M. K. *Bapu's Letters to Mira*. Ahmedabad: Navajivan Publishing House, 1949.

———. *Hind Swaraj, or Indian Home Rule*. Ahmedabad: Navajivan Publishing House, 1939.

———. *Hindi and English in the South*. Edited by M. P. Desai. Ahmedabad: Navajivan Publishing House, 1958.

———. *The Story of My Experiments with Truth*. Translated by Mahadev Desai. New York: Dover, 1958.

Gandhy, Behroze, and Rosie Thomas. "Three Indian Film Stars." In *Stardom: Industry of Desire*, edited by Christine Gledhill. London and New York: Routledge, 1991.

Garga, B. D. "The Feel of the Good Earth." *Cinema in India* 3 (April-June 1989): 30–32.

Gates, Henry Louis, Jr. "Critical Fanonism." *Critical Inquiry* 17 (Spring 1991): 457–70.

George, T. J. S. *The Life and Times of Nargis*. New Delhi: Indus/HarperCollins, 1994.

Ghose, Sisirkumar. "Salaam for Sarojini: Towards a Revaluation." In *Perspectives on Sarojini Naidu*, edited by K. K. Sharma. Ghaziabad, India: Vimal Prakashan, 1989.

Gilroy, Paul. *The Black Atlantic: Modernity and Double Consciousness*. Cambridge, Mass.: Harvard University Press, 1993.

Goldberg, Jonathan. "Bradford's 'Ancient Members' and 'A Case of Buggery . . . amongst Them.'" In *Nationalisms & Sexualities*, edited by Andrew Parker, Mary Russo, Doris Sommer, and Patricia Yaeger. New York and London: Routledge, 1992.

Gordon, Stewart N. "Scarf and Sword: Thugs, Marauders, and State-Formation in 18th Century Malwa." *Indian Economic and Social History Review* 6 (December 1969): 403–29.

Gosse, Edmund. "Introduction." In *The Bird of Time*, by Sarojini Naidu. London: William Heinemann, 1912.

Griswold, Hervey De Witt. *Insights into Modern Hinduism*. New York: Henry Holt, 1934.

Guha, Ranajit. *Elementary Aspects of Peasant Insurgency in Colonial India*. Delhi: Oxford University Press, 1983.

———. "On Some Aspects of the Historiography of Colonial India." In *Subaltern Studies I: Writings on South Asian History and Society*, edited by Ranajit Guha. Delhi: Oxford University Press, 1982. [Reprinted in *Selected Subaltern Studies*, edited by Ranajit Guha and Gayatri C. Spivak. New York: Oxford University Press, 1988.]

———. "The Prose of Counter-Insurgency." In *Subaltern Studies II: Writings on South Asian History and Society*, edited by Ranajit Guha. Delhi: Oxford University Press, 1983.

Gupta, Hiralal. "A Critical Study of the *Thugs* and Their Activities." *Journal of Indian History* 37, part 2 (August 1959), serial no. 110: 169–77.

Hall, Stuart. "Cultural Studies and Its Theoretical Legacies." In *Cultural Studies*, edited by Lawrence Grossberg, Cary Nelson, and Paula A. Treichler. New York: Routledge, 1992.

———. "When Was the 'Post-Colonial'? Thinking at the Limit." In *The Post-Colonial Question: Common Skies, Divided Horizons*, edited by Iain Chambers and Lidia Curti. London and New York: Routledge, 1996.

Hansen, Kathryn. "Making Women Visible: Female Impersonators and Actresses on the Parsi Stage and in Silent Cinema." Unpublished manuscript.

Harrison, James. *Rudyard Kipling*. Boston: Twayne Publishers, 1982.

Helie-Lucas, Marie-Aimée. "Women, Nationalism and Religion in the Algerian Struggle." In *Opening the Gates: A Century of Arab Feminist Writing*, edited by Miriam Cooke and Margot Badran. Bloomington: Indiana University Press, 1991.

Hervey, Charles. *Some Records of Crime (Being the Diary of a Year, Official and Particular, of an Officer of the Thuggee and Dacoitie Police)*. 2 vols. London: Sampson Low, Marston, 1892.

Howe, Irving. "The Pleasures of *Kim*." In *Rudyard Kipling: Modern Critical Views*, edited by Harold Bloom. New York: Chelsea House, 1987.

Huggan, Graham. "Postcolonialism and Its Discontents." *Transition* 62 (1993): 130–35.

Hutcheon, Linda. "Introduction. Colonialism and the Postcolonial Condition: Complexities Abounding." *PMLA* 110, no. 1 (1995): 7–16.

Hutchinson, John, and Anthony D. Smith, eds. *Nationalism*. Oxford and New York: Oxford University Press, 1994.

Hutheesingh, Krishna. *With No Regrets: Krishna Hutheesingh's Autobiography*. Bombay: Oxford University Press, 1944.

Hutton, James. *A Popular Account of the Thugs and Dacoits, the Hereditary Garroters and Gang-Robbers of India*. London: W. H. Allen, 1857.

Inden, Ronald. *Imagining India*. Oxford, England, and Cambridge, Mass.: Basil Blackwell, 1990.

Irigaray, Luce. *This Sex Which Is Not One*. Translated by Catherine Porter. Ithaca, N.Y.: Cornell University Press, 1985.

Isherwood, Christopher. *Ramakrishna and His Disciples*. London: Methuen, 1965.

JanMohamed, Abdul. "The Economy of Manichean Allegory: The Function of Racial Difference in Colonialist Literature." In *"Race," Writing, and Difference*, edited by Henry Louis Gates Jr. Chicago and London: University of Chicago Press, 1986.

Jayakar, Pupul. *Indira Gandhi: An Intimate Biography*. New York: Pantheon Books, 1992 [1988].

Jayawardena, Kumari. *Feminism and Nationalism in the Third World*. London: Zed Press, 1986.

———. *The White Woman's Other Burden: Western Women and South Asia during British Rule*. New York and London: Routledge, 1995.

Johnson, James Weldon. *The Autobiography of an Ex-Colored Man*. New York: Sherman, French, 1912.

Kakar, Sudhir. *The Analyst and the Mystic: Psychoanalytic Reflections on Religion and Mysticism*. New Delhi: Viking, 1991.

———. *The Inner World: A Psychoanalytic Study of Childhood and Society in India*. Delhi: Oxford University Press, 1978.

———. *Intimate Relations: Exploring Indian Sexuality*. New Delhi: Penguin Books, 1989.

Kaplan, Caren, and Inderpal Grewal. "Transnational Feminist Cultural Studies: Beyond the Marxism/Poststructuralism/Feminism Divides." *positions* 2, no. 2 (1994): 430–45.

Katrak, Ketu H. "Indian Nationalism, Gandhian 'Satyagraha,' and Representations of Female Sexuality." In *Nationalisms and Sexualities*, edited by Andrew Parker, Mary Russo, Doris Sommer, and Patricia Yaeger. New York and London: Routledge, 1992.

Kaul, Gautam. "Review of Wimal Dissanayake and Malti Sahai's *Raj Kapoor's Films: Harmony of Discourses* (New Delhi: Vikas, 1988)." *India Today*, 31 May 1988, 91.

Kaur, Amrit. "Women under the New Constitution." In *Our Cause: A Symposium by Indian Women*, edited by Shyam Kumari Nehru. Allahabad: Kitabistan, 1935.

Kaur, Manmohan. *Women in India's Freedom Struggle*. New Delhi: Sterling Publishers, 1985.

Kaviraj, Sudipta. "The Imaginary Institution of India." In *Subaltern Studies VII: Writings on South Asian History and Society*, edited by Partha Chatterjee and Gyanendra Pandey. Delhi: Oxford University Press, 1991.

———. *The Unhappy Consciousness: Bankimchandra Chattopadhyay and the Reformation of Nationalist Discourse in India*. Delhi: Oxford University Press, 1995.

Kesavan, Mukul. "Urdu, Awadh and the Tawaif: The Islamicate Roots of Hindi Cinema." In *Forging Identities: Gender, Communities and the State in India*, edited by Zoya Hasan. Boulder, Colo.: Westview Press, 1994.

Khatib, A. A. "Nargis: The Way She Was." *Filmfare*, 1–15 June 1981, 12–15.

Kiernan, V. G. *The Lords of Humankind*. London: Century Hutchinson, 1969.

Kinkead-Weekes, Mark. "Vision in Kipling's Novels." In *Kipling's Mind and Art: Selected Critical Essays*, edited by Andrew Rutherford. Stanford, Calif.: Stanford University Press, 1964.

Kinsley, David R. "Kali: Blood and Death Out of Place." In *Devi: Goddesses of India*, edited by John S. Hawley and Donna M. Wulff. Berkeley and London: University of California Press, 1996.

Kipling, Rudyard. "The City of Dreadful Night." In *From Sea to Sea: Letters of Travel*. 2 vols. New York: Charles Scribner's Sons, 1906 [1899].

———. "The Head of the District." In *Life's Handicap, Being Stories of My Own People*. Edited by P. N. Furbank. Harmondsworth: Penguin Books, 1987.

———. "His Majesty the King." In *Wee Willie Winkie*. Edited by Hugh Haughton. London: Penguin Books, 1988.

———. *Kim*. Edited by Edward Said. Harmondsworth: Penguin Books, 1987.

———. *Letters of Marque*. New York and Boston: H. M. Caldwell, 1899.

———. *Life's Handicap, Being Stories of My Own People*. Edited by P. N. Furbank. Harmondsworth: Penguin Books, 1987.

———. "Miss Youghal's Sais." In *Plain Tales from the Hills*. Edited by H. R. Woudhuysen, with an introduction and notes by David Trotter. Harmondsworth: Penguin Books, 1987.

———. "The Phantom Rickshaw." In *The Man Who Would Be King and Other Stories*. Edited by Louis Cornell. Oxford and New York: Oxford University Press, 1987.

———. "Simla Notes." *Civil and Military Gazette*, 29 July 1885. [Reprinted in *Kipling's India: Uncollected Sketches 1884–88*. Edited by Thomas Pinney. Basingstoke and London: Macmillan, 1986.]

———. *Something of Myself and Other Autobiographical Writings*. Edited by Thomas Pinney. Cambridge, England: Cambridge University Press, 1990.

———. "Tod's Amendment." In *Plain Tales from the Hills*. Edited by H. R. Woudhuysen, with an introduction and notes by David Trotter. Harmondsworth: Penguin Books, 1987.

———. "Wee Willie Winkie." In *Wee Willie Winkie*. Edited by Hugh Haughton. London: Penguin Books, 1988.

Kishwar, Madhu. "Gandhi on Women." *Economic and Political Weekly*, 5 October 1985, 1691–1702; 12 October 1985, 1753–1758.

Kripal, Jeffrey J. *Kali's Child: The Mystical and the Erotic in the Life and Teachings of Ramakrishna*. Chicago and London: University of Chicago Press, 1995.

Kumar, Radha. *The History of Doing: An Illustrated Account of Movements for Women's Rights and Feminism in India, 1800–1990*. New Delhi: Kali for Women; London and New York: Verso, 1993.

Lambrick, H. T. "Editor's Introduction." In *Sindh, and the Races That Inhabit the Valley of the Indus*, by Richard Burton. Karachi: Oxford University Press, 1973.

Lane, Christopher. *The Ruling Passion: British Colonial Allegory and the Paradox of Homosexual Desire*. Durham, N.C., and London: Duke University Press, 1995.

Larsen, Nella. *Passing*. New York and London: Knopf, 1929.

————. *Quicksand*. New York and London: Knopf, 1928.

Leonard, Karen. "Aspects of the Nationalist Movement in the Princely States of Hyderabad." *Quarterly Review of Historical Studies* 21, no. 2–3 (1981–1982): 3–9.

Liddle, Joanna, and Rama Joshi. "Gender and Imperialism in British India." *South Asia Research* 5, no. 2 (1985): 147–63.

Life of Sri Ramakrishna, Compiled from Various Authentic Sources. Calcutta: Advaita Ashrama, 1964.

London, Bette. "Of Mimicry and English Men: E. M. Forster and the Performance of Masculinity." In *A Passage to India*, edited by Tony Davies and Nigel Wood. Theory in Practice Series. Buckingham, England: Open University Press, 1994.

Lott, Eric. *Love and Theft: Blackface Minstrelsy and the American Working Class*. New York: Oxford University Press, 1995.

Low, Gail Ching-Liang. "White Skins/Black Masks: The Pleasures and Politics of Imperialism." *New Formations* 9, no. 24 (1989): 83–103.

————. *White Skins/Black Masks: Representation and Colonialism*. London and New York: Routledge, 1996.

Macaulay, Thomas B. "Minute on Indian Education." In *Selected Prose*, edited by John Clive. Chicago: University of Chicago Press, 1972.

MacMunn, Sir George. *The Religions and Hidden Cults of India*. London: Sampson Low, Marston, 1931.

————. *The Underworld of India*. London: Hutchinson, n.d.

Majumdar, R. C., H. C. Raychaudhuri, and Kalikinkar Dutta. *An Advanced History of India*. Vol. 2. London and Delhi: Macmillan, 1967.

Malhotra, Inder. *Indira Gandhi: A Personal and Political Biography*. London: Hodder & Stoughton, 1989.

Mani, Lata. "Contentious Traditions: The Debate on *Sati* in Colonial India." In *The Nature and Context of Minority Discourse*, edited by Abdul JanMohamed and David Lloyd. Oxford and New York: Oxford University Press, 1990.

Mani, Lata, and Ruth Frankenberg. "Crosscurrents, Crosstalk: Race, 'Postcoloniality' and the Politics of Location." *Cultural Studies* 7 (May 1993): 292–310.

Masters, John. *The Deceivers*. New York: Carroll and Graf, 1952.

Mathai, M. O. *Reminiscences of the Nehru Age*. New Delhi: Vikas, 1978.

Mayo, Katherine. *Mother India*. New York: Harcourt, Brace, 1927.

Mbembe, Achille. "The Banality of Power and the Aesthetics of Vulgarity in the Postcolony." *Public Culture* 4, no. 2 (1992): 1–30.

McClintock, Anne. "The Angel of Progress: Pitfalls of the Term 'Post-Colonialism.'" *Social Text* 31/32, 10, nos. 2–3 (1992): 84–98.

————. "Family Feuds: Gender, Nationalism and the Family." *Feminist Review* 44 (Summer 1993): 61–80.

McClure, John. *Kipling and Conrad: The Colonial Fiction*. Cambridge, Mass.: Harvard University Press, 1981.

McDowell, Deborah. "'That Nameless . . . Shameful Impulse': Sexuality in Nella Larsen's *Quicksand* and *Passing*." In *Studies in Black American Literature III: Black Feminist Criticism and Critical Theory*, edited by Joe Weixlmann and Houston A. Baker Jr. Greenwood, Fla.: Penkevill Publishing, 1988.

McGuire, John. *The Making of a Colonial Mind: A Quantitative Study of the Bhadralok in Calcutta, 1857–1885*. Canberra: Australian National University, 1983.

Menon, Nivedita. "Orientalism and After." *Public Culture* 6 (Fall 1993): 65–76.

Mercer, Kobena. *Welcome to the Jungle: New Positions in Black Cultural Studies*. New York and London: Routledge, 1994.

Metcalf, Thomas R. *The Aftermath of Revolt: India 1857–1870*. Princeton, N.J.: Princeton University Press, 1964.

Meyer, Morris, ed. *The Politics and Poetics of Camp* (New York and London: Routledge, 1993).

Meyer, Richard. "Rock Hudson's Body." In *Inside/Out: Lesbian Theories, Gay Theories*, edited by Diana Fuss. New York: Routledge, 1991.

Miller, Webb. *I Found No Peace: The Journal of a Foreign Correspondent*. London: Victor Gollancz, 1937.

Mishra, Vijay, Peter Jeffery, and Brian Shoesmith. "The Actor as Parallel Text in Bombay Cinema." *Quarterly Review of Film and Video* 11, no. 3 (1989): 49–67.

Mitta, Manoj. "TADA: Relentless Terror." *India Today*, 15 October 1994.

Mohanty, Chandra Talpade. "Under Western Eyes: Feminist Scholarship and Colonial Discourses." In *Third World Women and the Politics of Feminism*, edited by Chandra Mohanty, Ann Russo, and Lourdes Torres. Bloomington: Indiana University Press, 1991.

Mohanty, Satya P. "Drawing the Color Line: Kipling and the Culture of Colonial Rule." In *The Bounds of Race: Perspectives on Hegemony and Resistance*, edited by Dominick LaCapra. Ithaca, N.Y.: Cornell University Press, 1991.

Monier-Williams, Monier. *Religious Thought and Life in India*. New Delhi: Oriental Books Reprint Corporation, 1974 [1883].

Mookerjee, Ajit. *Kali: The Feminine Force*. New York: Destiny Books, 1988.

Mookherjee, S. B. "Nivedita and Indian Womanhood." In *Nivedita Commemoration Volume*, edited by Amiya Kumar Majumdar. Calcutta: Dhiraj Basu, 1968.

Moore-Gilbert, B. J. *Kipling and "Orientalism."* London and Sydney: Croom Helm, 1986.

Moore-Gilbert, Bart. "Introduction: Writing India, Reorienting Colonial Discourse Analysis." In *Writing India, 1757–1990: The Literature of British India*, edited by Bart Moore-Gilbert. Manchester and New York: Manchester University Press, 1996.

Morton, Eleanor. *The Women in Gandhi's Life*. New York: Dodd, Mead, 1953.

Mueller, F. Max. *Ramakrishna: His Life and Sayings*. New York: Charles Scribner's Sons, 1899.

Mufti, Aamir R. "Secularism and Minority: Elements of a Critique." *Social Text* 45, 14, no. 4 (1995): 75–96.

Mukherjee, Meenakshi. *Realism and Reality: The Novel and Society in India*. Delhi: Oxford University Press, 1994 [1985].

Murshid, Ghulam. *Reluctant Debutante: Response of Bengali Women to Modernization, 1849–1905*. Rajshashi, Bangladesh: Sahitya Samsad, 1983.

Naidu, Sarojini. *The Broken Wing: Songs of Love, Death & Destiny, 1915–1916*. New York: John Lane; London: William Heinemann, 1917.

———. *Speeches and Writings of Sarojini Naidu*. 2d ed. Madras: G. A. Natesan, 1919.

Nair, K. R. Ramachandran. *Three Indo-Anglian Poets: Henry Derozio, Toru Dutt and Sarojini Naidu.* New Delhi: Sterling Publishers, 1987.

Nanda, B. R. *The Two Nehrus.* London: Allen and Unwin, 1962.

——, ed. *Indian Women: From Purdah to Modernity.* New Delhi: Vikas, 1976.

Nanda, Ritu. *Raj Kapoor: His Life and His Films.* Moscow: Iskusstvo Publishers; Bombay: R. K. Films & Studios, 1991.

Nandy, Ashis. *At the Edge of Psychology: Essays in Politics and Culture.* Delhi: Oxford University Press, 1990.

——. *The Intimate Enemy: Loss and Recovery of Self under Colonialism.* Delhi: Oxford University Press, 1983.

——. *The Savage Freud and Other Essays on Possible and Retrievable Selves.* Princeton, N.J.: Princeton University Press, 1995.

Nath, Rakhal Chandra. *The New Hindu Movement 1886–1911.* Calcutta: Minerva, 1982.

Neale, Steve. "Masculinity as Spectacle." In *The Sexual Subject: A* Screen *Reader in Sexuality.* London and New York: Routledge, 1992.

Nehru, Jawaharlal. *An Autobiography.* Abr. ed. Edited by C. D. Narasimhaiah. Delhi: Oxford University Press, 1991.

——. *A Bunch of Old Letters, Written Mostly to Jawaharlal Nehru and Some Written by Him.* Bombay: Asia Publishing House, 1958.

Nichols, Beverley. *Verdict on India.* New York: Harcourt, Brace, 1944.

Nigam, Sanjay. "Disciplining and Policing the 'Criminals by Birth.'" *Indian Economic and Social History Review* 27, no. 2 (1990): 131–64; 27, no. 3 (1990): 259–87.

Nikhilananda, Swami. *Holy Mother: Being the Life of Sri Sarada Devi, Wife of Sri Ramakrishna and Helpmate in His Mission.* London: George Allen & Unwin, 1962.

——. *Vivekananda: A Biography.* New York: Ramakrishna-Vivekananda Center, 1953.

——, trans. *The Gospel of Sri Ramakrishna.* New York: Ramakrishna-Vivekananda Center, 1973 [1942].

Nivedita, Sister [Margaret E. Noble]. *The Master as I Saw Him.* Calcutta: Udbodhan Office, 1910.

——. *The Web of Indian Life.* London: William Heinemann, 1904.

O'Hanlon, Rosalind, and David Washbrook. "After Orientalism: Culture, Criticism, and Politics in the Third World." *Comparative Studies in Society and History* 34 (January 1992): 141–67.

Olaniyan, Tejumola. "On 'Post-Colonial Discourse': An Introduction." *Callaloo* 16, no. 4 (1993): 743–48.

Oldenburg, Veena Talwar. "Lifestyle as Resistance." In *Contesting Power,* edited by Gyan Prakash and Douglas Haynes. Berkeley: University of California Press, 1992.

——. *The Making of Colonial Lucknow, 1856–1877.* Delhi: Oxford University Press, 1989.

Pandey, Gyan. "In Defense of the Fragment: Writing about Hindu-Muslim Riots in India Today." *Representations* 37 (Winter 1992): 27–55.

Pandian, M. S. S. *The Image Trap: M. G. Ramachandran in Film and Politics.* New Delhi: Sage Publications, 1992.

Panneerselvan, A. S. "The MGR Mystique." *Filmfare,* 1–15 February 1988, 53.

Parks, Fanny. *Wanderings of a Pilgrim in Search of the Picturesque.* 2 vols. Karachi and London: Oxford University Press, 1975 [1850].

Parry, Benita. "The Content and Discontents of Kipling's Imperialism." *New Formations,* no. 6 (Winter 1988): 49–63.

———. "Problems in Current Theories of Colonial Discourse." *Oxford Literary Review* 9, no. 1–2 (1987): 27–58.

Pathak, Zakia, and Rajeswari Sunder Rajan. "Shahbano." *Signs* 14, no. 3 (1989): 558–82. [Reprinted in *Feminists Theorize the Political,* edited by Judith Butler and Joan W. Scott. New York: Routledge, 1992.]

Phelan, Peggy. *Unmarked: The Politics of Performance.* London and New York: Routledge, 1993.

Piper, Adrian. "Passing for White, Passing for Black." *Transition* 58 (1995): 4–32.

Prakash, Gyan. "Can the 'Subaltern' Ride? A Reply to O'Hanlon and Washbrook." *Comparative Studies in Society and History* 34 (January 1992): 168–84.

———. "Science 'Gone Native' in Colonial India." *Representations* 40 (Fall 1992): 1–26.

———. "Who's Afraid of Postcoloniality?" *Social Text* 49, 14, no. 4 (1996): 187–203.

———. "Writing Post-Orientalist Histories of the Third World: Perspectives from Indian Historiography." *Comparative Studies in Society and History* 32, no. 2 (1990): 383–408.

Pratt, Mary Louise. "Conventions of Representation: Where Discourse and Ideology Meet." In *Georgetown University Round Table on Languages and Linguistics 1982.* Washington, D.C.: Georgetown University Press, 1982.

———. *Imperial Eyes: Travel Writing and Transculturation.* London and New York: Routledge, 1992.

Radhakrishnan, R. "Ethnicity in an Age of Diaspora." *Transition* 54 (1991): 104–15.

———. "Postcoloniality and the Boundaries of Identity." *Callaloo* 16, no. 4 (1993): 750–71.

Rahman, M. "Sanjay Dutt: It's Not Over Yet." *India Today,* 31 May 1993.

Rahman, M., and Arun Katiyar. "Bombay Film Industry: Underworld Connections." *India Today,* 15 May 1993.

Rahman, M., and Lekha Rattanani. "Sanjay Dutt: A Fatal Attraction." *India Today,* 15 May 1993.

Rajadhyaksha, Ashish. "The Epic Melodrama: Themes of Nationality in Indian Cinema." *Journal of Arts and Ideas,* 25–26 (1993): 55–70.

Ramabai Saraswati, Pandita. *The High-Caste Hindu Woman.* London: George Bell and Sons, 1888.

Ramusack, Barbara N. "Cultural Missionaries, Maternal Imperialists, Feminist Allies: British Women Activists in India, 1865–1945." In *Western Women and Imperialism: Complicity and Resistance,* edited by Nupur Chaudhuri and Margaret Strobel. Bloomington and Indianapolis: Indiana University Press, 1992.

Rangoonwala, Firoze. *A Pictorial History of Indian Cinema.* London: Hamlyn, 1979.

Ray, R. M., ed. *Sangeet Natak Akademi Film Seminar Report 1955.* New Delhi: n.p., 1956.

Ray, Satyajit. *Our Films, Their Films.* Bombay: Orient Longman, 1976.

Raychaudhuri, Tapan. *Europe Reconsidered: Perceptions of the West in Nineteenth Century Bengal.* Delhi: Oxford University Press, 1988.

Reminiscences of Swami Vivekananda, by His Eastern and Western Admirers. Calcutta: Advaita Ashrama, 1964 [1961].

Renan, Ernest. "What Is a Nation?" In *Nation and Narration,* edited by Homi K. Bhabha. London and New York: Routledge, 1990.

Reuben, Bunny. *Mehboob: India's DeMille.* New Delhi: Indus/HarperCollins, 1994.

———. *Raj Kapoor, the Fabulous Showman: An Intimate Biography.* New Delhi: Indus/HarperCollins, 1995.

Reymond, Lizelle. *The Dedicated: A Biography of Nivedita.* New York: John Day, 1953.

Rice, Edward. *Captain Sir Richard Francis Burton: The Secret Agent Who Made the Pilgrimage to Mecca, Discovered the Kama Sutra, and Brought the Arabian Nights to the West.* New York: HarperCollins, 1990.

Richards, Thomas. "Archive and Utopia." *Representations* 37 (Winter 1992): 104–35.

Riviere, Joan. "Womanliness as a Masquerade." In *Formations of Fantasy,* edited by Victor Burgin, James Donald, and Cora Kaplan. London: Methuen, 1986.

Robinson, Andrew. *Satyajit Ray: The Inner Eye.* Berkeley: University of California Press, 1989.

Rolland, Romain. *The Life of Vivekananda and the Universal Gospel.* Translated by E. F. Malcolm-Smith. Mayavati, India: Advaita Ashrama, 1947.

Rooney, Ellen. "What Is to Be Done?" In *Coming to Terms: Feminism, Theory, Politics,* edited by Elizabeth Weed. New York: Routledge, 1989.

Rosselli, John. "The Self-Image of Effeteness: Physical Education and Nationalism in Nineteenth-Century Bengal." *Past and Present* 86 (February 1980): 121–48.

Rudolph, Lloyd I., and Susanne Hoeber Rudolph. *The Modernity of Tradition: Political Development in India.* Chicago and London: University of Chicago Press, 1967.

Rushdie, Salman. *Midnight's Children.* New York: Alfred A. Knopf, 1981 [1980].

Ruskin, John. *Sesame and Lilies.* London: Smith, Elder, 1865.

Russo, Vito. "Camp." In *Gay Men: The Sociology of Male Homosexuality,* edited by Martin Levine. New York: Harper & Row, 1979.

Sahgal, Nayantara. *Prison and Chocolate Cake.* New York: Alfred A. Knopf, 1954.

Said, Edward W. "Introduction." In *Kim,* by Rudyard Kipling. Edited by Edward Said. Harmondsworth: Penguin Books, 1987.

———. *Orientalism.* New York: Random House, 1978.

Sangari, Kumkum, and Sudesh Vaid, eds. *Recasting Women: Essays in Indian Colonial History.* New Brunswick, N.J.: Rutgers University Press, 1990.

Saradananda, Swami. *Sri Ramakrishna: The Great Master.* Translated by Swami Jagadananda. 2 vols. Madras: Sri Ramakrishna Math, 1978 [1952].

Sarkar, Sumit. "'Kaliyuga,' 'Chakri' and 'Bhakti': Ramakrishna and His Times." *Economic and Political Weekly,* 18 July 1992, 1543–66.

———. "The Kathamrita as Text: Towards an Understanding of Ramakrishna Paramhamsa." Occasional Paper 22. New Delhi: Nehru Memorial Museum and Library, 1985.

Sarkar, Tanika. "Heroic Women, Mother Goddesses: Family and Organisation in Hindutva Politics." In *Women and the Hindu Right: A Collection of Essays,* edited by Tanika Sarkar and Urvashi Butalia. New Delhi: Kali for Women, 1995.

———. "Nationalist Iconography: Image of Women in 19th Century Bengali Literature." *Economic and Political Weekly,* 21 November 1987, 2011–15.

Sarma, D. S. *Studies in the Renaissance of Hinduism in the Nineteenth and Twentieth Centuries*. Benares: Benares Hindu University, 1944.

Sen, Mala. *India's Bandit Queen: The True Story of Phoolan Devi*. New Delhi: Indus/ HarperCollins, 1991.

Sen, Ranjit. *Social Banditry in Bengal: A Study in Primary Resistance, 1757–1793*. Calcutta: Ratna Prakashan, 1988.

Sen, Samita. "Motherhood and Mothercraft: Gender and Nationalism in Bengal." *Gender & History* 5, no. 2 (1993): 231–43.

Sengupta, Padmini. *Sarojini Naidu: A Biography*. Bombay: Asia Publishing House, 1966.

Seshadri-Crooks, Kalpana. "At the Margins of Postcolonial Studies." *Ariel* 26, no. 3 (1995): 47–71.

Sharpe, Jenny. *Allegories of Empire: The Figure of Woman in the Colonial Text*. Minneapolis and London: University of Minnesota Press, 1993.

———. "Figures of Colonial Resistance." *Modern Fiction Studies* 35 (Spring 1989): 137–55.

Shelley, Sushama. "Raj's Women." *Filmfare*, 16–30 June 1988, 46–49.

Shetty, Sandhya. "(Dis)figuring the Nation." *differences* 7, no. 3 (1995): 50–79.

———. "(Dis)Locating Gender Space and Medical Discourse in Colonial India." *Genders* 20 (1994): 188–230.

Shohat, Ella. "Notes on the 'Post-Colonial.'" *Social Text* 31/32, 10, nos. 2–3 (1992): 99–113.

Silverman, Kaja. "White Skin, Brown Masks: The Double Mimesis, or With Lawrence in Arabia." *differences* 1 (Fall 1989): 3–54.

Singh, Bikram. "The Dream Merchant." *Filmfare*, 16–30 June 1988, 16–19.

Singha, Radhika. "'Providential' Circumstances: The Thuggee Campaign of the 1830s and Legal Innovation." *Modern Asian Studies* 27 (February 1993): 83–146.

Sinha, Mrinalini. *Colonial Masculinity: The "Manly Englishman" and the "Effeminate Bengali" in the Late Nineteenth Century*. Manchester and New York: Manchester University Press, 1995.

———. "Reading *Mother India*: Empire, Nation, and the Female Voice." *Journal of Women's History* 6, no. 2 (1994): 6–44.

Sitaramayya, Pattabhi. *The History of the Congress, Volume 1 (1885–1935)*. Bombay: Padma Publications, 1946 [1935].

Sleeman, James. *Thug, or A Million Murders*. London: Sampson Low, Marston, 1933 [1920].

Sleeman, William H. *Ramaseeana, or a Vocabulary of the Peculiar Language Used by the Thugs*. Calcutta: G. H. Huttmann, Military Orphan Press, 1836.

———. *Rambles and Recollections of an Indian Official*. Edited by Vincent A. Smith. London: Humphrey Milford, Oxford University Press, 1915.

———. *Report on Budhuk Alias Bagree Dacoits and Other Gang Robbers by Hereditary Profession*. Calcutta: J. C. Sherriff, Bengal Military Orphan Press, 1849.

———. *Report on the Depredations Committed by the Thug Gangs of Upper and Central India*. Calcutta: G. H. Huttmann, Bengal Military Orphan Press, 1840.

Smith, Brian K. "How Not to Be a Hindu: The Case of the Ramakrishna Mission." In *Religion and Law in Independent India*, edited by Robert P. Baird. New Delhi: Manohar, 1993.

Smith, Valerie. "Reading the Intersection of Race and Gender in Narratives of Passing." *diacritics* 24 (Summer-Fall 1994): 43–57.

Sommer, Doris. *Foundational Fictions: The National Romances of Latin America*. Berkeley: University of California Press, 1991.

Spivak, Gayatri Chakravorty. "Asked to Talk about Myself . . . ." *Third Text* 19 (Summer 1992): 9–18.

———. "Bonding in Difference [an interview with Alfred Arteaga]." In *An Other Tongue: Nation and Ethnicity in the Linguistic Borderlands*, edited by Alfred Arteaga. Durham, N.C.: Duke University Press, 1994.

———. "The Burden of English Studies." In *The Lie of the Land: English Literary Studies in India*, edited by Rajeswari Sunder Rajan. Delhi: Oxford University Press, 1992.

———. "Can the Subaltern Speak?" In *Marxism and the Interpretation of Culture*, edited by Cary Nelson and Lawrence Grossberg. Urbana: University of Illinois Press, 1988.

———. "Deconstructing Historiography." In *In Other Worlds: Essays in Cultural Politics*. New York and London: Routledge, 1987.

———. "A Literary Representation of the Subaltern." In *In Other Worlds: Essays in Cultural Politics*. New York and London: Routledge, 1987.

———. "The Political Economy of Women as Seen by a Literary Critic." In *Coming to Terms: Feminism, Theory, Politics*, edited by Elizabeth Weed. London: Routledge, 1989.

———. *The Post-Colonial Critic: Interviews, Strategies, Dialogues*. Edited by Sarah Harasym. New York: Routledge, 1990.

———. "Poststructuralism, Marginality, Postcoloniality and Value." In *Literary Theory Today*, edited by Peter Collier and Helga Geyer-Ryan. Ithaca, N.Y.: Cornell University Press, 1990.

———. "Reading *The Satanic Verses*." In *Outside in the Teaching Machine*. New York and London: Routledge, 1993.

———. "Three Women's Texts and a Critique of Imperialism." In *"Race," Writing, and Difference*, edited by Henry Louis Gates Jr. Chicago and London: University of Chicago Press, 1986.

———. "Translator's Foreword to 'Draupadi,' by Mahasweta Devi." In *In Other Worlds: Essays in Cultural Politics*. New York and London: Routledge, 1987.

Spratt, Philip. *Hindu Culture and Personality*. Bombay: Manaktalas, 1966.

Sprinker, Michael. "Introduction." In *Late Imperial Culture*, edited by Roman de la Campa, E. Ann Kaplan, and Michael Sprinker. London and New York: Verso, 1995.

Stisted, Georgiana M. *The True Life of Captain Sir Richard F. Burton, K.C.M.G., F.R.G.S., etc., Written by His Niece, with the Authority and Approval of the Burton Family*. New York: D. Appleton; London: H. S. Nichols, 1897.

Stocking, George W. *Victorian Anthropology*. New York: Free Press, 1987.

Stokes, Eric. *The Peasant Armed*. Delhi: Oxford University Press, 1986.

Subramaniam, K. N., and Ratnakar Tripathy, comps. *Flashback: Cinema in the Times of India*. Bombay: Times of India, 1990.

Suleri, Sara. *Meatless Days*. Chicago: University of Chicago Press, 1989.

————. *The Rhetoric of English India*. Chicago and London: University of Chicago Press, 1992.

Sullivan, Zohreh T. *Narratives of Empire: The Fictions of Rudyard Kipling*. Cambridge, England: Cambridge University Press, 1993.

Sunder Rajan, Rajeswari. "Ameena: Gender, Crisis, and National Identity." *Oxford Literary Review* 16, nos. 1–2 (1994): 147–76.

————. *Real and Imagined Women: Gender, Culture and Postcolonialism*. London: Routledge, 1993.

Swami Vivekananda and His Guru. London and Madras: Christian Literature Society for India, 1897.

Symons, Arthur. "Introduction." In *The Golden Threshold*, by Sarojini Naidu. London: William Heinemann, 1909.

Taylor, Philip Meadows. "Introduction." In *Confessions of a Thug*. London: Richard Bentley, 1858 [1839].

Thapar, Raj. *All These Years: A Memoir*. New Delhi: Penguin Books, 1992.

Thapar, Romila. "Imagined Religious Communities? Ancient History and the Modern Search for a Hindu Identity." *Modern Asian Studies* 23, no. 2 (1989): 209–31.

————. "Renunciation: The Making of a Counter-Culture?" In *Ancient Indian Social History: Some Interpretations*. Delhi: n.p., 1978.

Tharoor, Shashi. *Show Business*. New York: Arcade Publishing, 1991.

Tharu, Susie, and K. Lalitha, eds. *Women Writing in India*. 2 vols. New York: Feminist Press, 1993 [1991].

Thayil, Jeet. "From Reel to Real in 'Bollywood.'" *Asiaweek*. [Reprinted in *World Press Review*, October 1994.]

Thomas, Rosie. "Indian Cinema: Pleasures and Popularity." *Screen* 26 (May-August 1985): 116–31.

————. "Sanctity and Scandal: The Mythologization of Mother India." *Quarterly Review of Film and Video* 11, no. 3 (1989): 11–30.

Thornton, Edward. *Illustrations of the History and Practices of the Thugs*. London: W. H. Allen, 1837.

Tompkins, J. M. S. *The Art of Rudyard Kipling*. London: Methuen, 1959.

Trevelyan, Sir George Otto. *Cawnpore*. London: Macmillan, 1865; New Delhi: Indus/HarperCollins, 1992.

Tuker, Francis C. *The Yellow Scarf: The Story of the Life of Thuggee Sleeman*. London: J. M. Dent & Sons, 1961.

Tyler, Carole-Anne. "Boys Will Be Girls: The Politics of Gay Drag." In *Inside/Out: Lesbian Theories, Gay Theories*, edited by Diana Fuss. New York: Routledge, 1990.

————. "Passing: Narcissism, Identity, and Difference." *differences* 6 (Summer-Fall 1994): 212–48.

Valicha, Kishore. "Why Are Popular Films Popular?" *Cinema in India* 3 (April-June 1989): 34–41.

Vasudev, Aruna, and Philippe Lenglet, eds. *Indian Cinema Superbazaar*. New Delhi: Vikas Publishing House, 1983.

Viswanathan, Gauri. *Masks of Conquest: Literary Study and British Rule in India*. New York: Columbia University Press, 1989.

Vivekananda, Swami. "The Future of India." In *Lectures from Colombo to Almora*. Calcutta: Advaita Ashrama, 1956.

———. *Letters of Swami Vivekananda*. Calcutta: Advaita Ashrama, 1964.

———. *Vivekananda: The Yogas and Other Works*. Edited by Swami Nikhilananda. New York: Ramakrishna-Vivekananda Center, 1953.

Ware, Vron. *Beyond the Pale: White Women, Racism and History*. London and New York: Verso, 1992.

Wegner, Philip E. "'Life as He Would Have It': The Invention of India in Kipling's *Kim*." *Cultural Critique* 26 (Winter 1993–1994): 129–59.

Wightman, A. J. *No Friend for Travellers*. London: Robert Hale, 1959.

Williams, Patrick. "*Kim* and Orientalism." In *Kipling Reconsidered*, edited by Phillip Mallett. London: Macmillan, 1989.

Wilson, Angus. *The Strange Ride of Rudyard Kipling*. Harmondsworth: Penguin Books, 1979.

Wilson, Edmund. "The Kipling That Nobody Read." *Atlantic Monthly* 167 (1941): 201–14. [Reprinted in *Kipling's Mind and Art: Selected Critical Essays*, edited by Andrew Rutherford. Stanford, Calif.: Stanford University Press, 1964.]

Wurgraft, Lewis. *The Imperial Imagination: Magic and Myth in Kipling's India*. Middletown, Conn.: Wesleyan University Press, 1983.

Yar Khan, Izzat. *Sarojini Naidu: The Poet*. New Delhi: S. Chand, 1983.

Young, Robert. *White Mythologies: Writing History and the West*. London and New York: Routledge, 1990.

Zutshi, Somnath. "Women, Nation and the Outsider in Contemporary Hindi Cinema." In *Interrogating Modernity: Culture and Colonialism in India*, edited by Tejaswini Niranjana, P. Sudhir, and Vivek Dhareshwar. Calcutta: Seagull Books, 1993.

INDEX

Ahmad, Aijaz: 11–12, 181n26. *See also* Postcolonial studies

Alexander, Meena, 131, 133–34, 137

Anderson, Benedict: *Imagined Communities,* 2–3, 81–82, 84, 86, 178n11. *See also* Nation

Androgyny, 98

Anglicization, 3, 6

Anglo-Indians: Anglo-Indian national identity, 9, 81, 85–7, 192n50; and childhood, 75, 82–3, 189n14; and Englishmen, 75, 85–6; and Kipling, 72, 86. *See also* Kipling, Rudyard

Arab identity, 27–28, 30, 37

Babu, Bengali: in Burton, 31, 36; and colonialism, 107; in Kipling, 78–79, 80–81, 84. *See also* Masculinity; Mimicry

Becoming woman: for Gandhi, 129, 148–150; for Indian males, 4, 107; for Indian women, 10, 129; for Ramakrishna, 97–98, 114; for Vivekananda, 107

Bennington, Geoff, 45, 82

Bhabha, Homi: "DissemiNation," 64, 76, 84; "Interrogating Identity," 177n4; "Of Mimicry and Man," 1–2, 4, 18, 26–27, 55, 174, 183n35; "The Other Question," 31; "Sly Civility," 27. *See also* Mimicry

Bhadralok: anxieties about colonial modernity, 95–96, 102, 105, 190–91n32; disciples of Ramakrishna, 93, 94, 102–3, 197n40, 198n45

Bhadramahila, 129, 203n3

Burton, Richard: and Englishness, 64; exhibitionism, 19–20, 29–30; *Goa, and the Blue Mountains,* 21, 22–23; *Lake Regions of Central Africa,* 35; and "native" disguise, 8, 20–21, 24–25, 29, 33, 71; *Personal Narrative,* 8, 17, 19, 24, 25, 28, 29, 33–40 *passim;* as polyglot, 18–19, 182n5; "Terminal Essay," 22

Chatterjee, Partha: *The Nation and Its Fragments,* 3, 135, 148; "The Nationalist Resolution of the Woman Question," 116, 121, 128, 129, 203n3; *Nationalist Thought and the Colonial World,* 2–3, 174; "A Religion of Urban Domesticity," 95–96, 107. *See also* Nation

Conrad, Joseph, 23

Cultural studies, 15–16

Darshan, 110

Darwaysh, 25–26, 32

Dirlik, Arif: "The Postcolonial Aura," 11, 12

Discipleship: and conflict, 101–3, 123–24, 126, 146, 177n4; gendering of, 10, 99, 101, 126–27; of the Indian woman, 142–43, 206n48; of the Irish woman, 10, 92; and sexuality, 96, 100, 116

233

5–6, 7; and uneasiness, 32–33, 36, 73; and visibility, 24, 27–28, 29–31, 33, 43. *See also* Bhabha, Homi; Fanon, Frantz

Modernity: and the archaic, 40, 136–37, 210–11n27; and women, 135, 203n3

Muslim identity: in Bombay cinema, 165–67, 168, 171–72, 211–12n45; for Burton, 26, 27–28; and Hindu nationalism, 11, 167, 168, 172, 212n51; and indigeneity, 154; and Indian national identity, 166–67, 172–73, 212n51; Muslim women, 167, 212n46; and separatism, 165, 167–68, 172

Mutiny of 1857: and British imagination, 79–80; in Burton, 34; and "English lady," 190n30; in *Kim,* 76, 79–80; and Rani of Jhansi, 106; and *thuggee,* 47, 185n14

Naidu, Sarojini: ambivalence toward, 134–35, 142–44, 150, 204n23; and asceticism, 143; and English language, 131–32, 146; as English poet, 10, 132–33; and feminism, 134, 136–39, 140–41; and Gandhi, 142–43, 146, 148–50; and Hyderabad, 130–31; as Indian poet, 10, 133–34, 137–38; and nationalist movement, 140, 147–48; as orator, 145–46; poetry and nationalism in, 136–39, 142

Nargis: as icon of Indian womanhood, 154, 161; as mother, 170–71; and *Mother India,* 154, 158–61, 167–68; and Muslimness, 11, 154, 166–69, 170–71; and Raj Kapoor, 157–58; Rosie Thomas on, 154–55, 157, 167; and the status of the actress, 156–57, 162–64, 211n39; and Sunil Dutt, 164, 169

Nation: Anglo-Indian nationalism, 85–91; and Bombay cinema, 164–65, 168–69, 211–12n45, 212n49; bourgeois nationalism, 80–81, 199n66; conceptualization of, 2–3, 81, 135; feminization of nationalism, 10, 129, 139; gendering of national identity, 10, 89–90, 120; and Indian femininity, 114, 116, 122, 128–30, 135–40 *passim,* 144, 151, 204–5n26; male nationalist elites, 3, 10, 95–96, 190–91n32; national memory and national forgetting, 81; nationalist appropriation of popular culture, 96, 105; nationalist iconography of the maternal,

89–90, 91, 118, 141, 205n34, 206n47, 213–14n61; nationalist women, 129, 144, 147, 148, 206n42, 206n43; white women and (Indian) nationalism, 10, 91, 114, 119, 121–23, 125, 180n24. *See also* Anglo-Indians

Neale, Steve, 115

Nivedita: as disciple, 92, 123–24, 126, 127; as figure of displacement, 92, 122–23; as guru, 124, 126–27, 128; on Hindu femininity, 116–17; and Irishness, 126–27; as nationalist, 124–26

O'Hanlon, Rosalind, and David Washbrook: "After Orientalism," 11–12

Postcolonial studies: and constituencies, 14–16; criticism of, 11–13; postcolonial intellectuals, 12, 175

Prakash, Gyan: "Can the 'Subaltern' Ride?" 12; "Science Gone 'Native,'" 87; "Who's Afraid of Postcoloniality?" 181n31; "Writing Post-Orientalist Histories," 11

Ramakrishna Paramhansa: and *bhadralok* disciples, 93–94; and colonial modernity, 102; as guru, 98–101, 103; and heterosexuality, 97, 195n11; and *kaminikanchan,* 95–97, 116; and religious experience, 94–95; as woman, 97–98

Renan, Ernest, 81

Said, Edward: on *Kim,* 89; *Orientalism,* 29, 36, 56

Sharpe, Jenny: *Allegories of Empire,* 80; "Figures of Colonial Resistance," 4, 179n15

Sinha, Mrinalini: *Colonial Masculinity,* 190–91n32; "Reading *Mother India,*" 129

Sleeman, W. H.: as creator of a *thuggee* archive, 57; as discoverer of *thuggee,* 42, 44, 56

Spivak, Gayatri Chakravorty: "Asked to Talk About Myself," 202n105; "Bonding in Difference," 130, 134; "The Burden of English Studies," 78; "Can the Subaltern Speak?" 65; "Criticism, Feminism, and the Institution," 14; "Deconstructing Historiography," 43; "A Literary Representation of the Subaltern," 110, 118; "The New Historicism," 179n16; "The Political Economy of Women," 7, 13–14;

Compositor:	G&S Typesetters
Text:	10/12 Baskerville
Display:	Baskerville
Printer and Binder:	Thomson-Shore, Inc.